SPACE
COMMERCE

SPACE COMMERCE

THE INSIDE STORY
BY THE PEOPLE
WHO ARE MAKING IT HAPPEN

LANGDON MORRIS

AND

KENNETH J. COX, PH.D.

EDITORS

FOREWORD BY
BRUCE McCANDLESS II
CAPTAIN, US NAVY (RET.); 24-YEAR NASA ASTRONAUT

AN AEROSPACE TECHNOLOGY WORKING GROUP BOOK

IN PARTNERSHIP WITH

THE INTERNATIONAL SPACE UNIVERSITY

AND

THE INTERNATIONAL INSTITUTE OF SPACE COMMERCE

Cover design by Langdon Morris

Photo information:

Front Cover
Starfield: Hubble Image, NASA

Front Cover Insets, Top to Bottom
Satellite: NASA
For Sale, Astronaut Dale A. Gardner, 1984: NASA
SES Headquarters, satellite dishes reflected in a window: Michael Simpson
SpaceShipTwo: Virgin Galactic
ISS Window, Astronaut Karen Nyberg, 2008: NASA
Mars Reconnaissance Orbiter: NASA/JPL

Back Cover Inset:
NASA

Typesetting: Leah Kiefer
Copy Editing: Disa Kauk

ISBN 978-0-578-06578-6

TABLE OF CONTENTS

THE AEROSPACE TECHNOLOGY WORKING GROUP

The Aerospace Technology Working Group, also known as ATWG, is an independent space policy research and innovation group led by seasoned professionals in aerospace and other fields who seek to further humanity's exploration of space while simultaneously benefiting people on Earth.

The ATWG was instituted by NASA Administrator Richard Truly in 1990 as an independent body to perform future planning for the nation's space efforts. Initially, the ATWG began identifying and seeking improvements in both existing and developing space systems through the planned application of emerging technologies and the development of new ways of doing business, including the application of distributed missions and innovative strategic concepts in operations.

Today, the ATWG is an independent entity, using semi-annual and regional Forums, technical and strategic dialogs, personal interactions, books, articles, and speeches to explore topics pertinent to developing a space faring people and prepare policy recommendations for national and global leaders.

Using the organization's substantial base of management, engineering and scientific expertise, the ATWG also provides strategic and technical advice, public speakers, and consulting teams to address specific aerospace tasks and broad conceptual and philosophical questions. The ATWG collaborates actively with other space-related national and international organizations.

In addition, the ATWG places special emphasis on promoting and stimulating education in the sciences, mathematics, the engineering disciplines, and other technical areas.

Participants in ATWG include experts from throughout NASA, aerospace contractors, systems suppliers, entrepreneurial businesses, professional societies, universities, and government agencies including the DOD, FAA, and DOE.

You can learn more about the ATWG at www.atwg.org.

THE INTERNATIONAL SPACE UNIVERSITY

The International Space University provides graduate-level training to the future leaders of the emerging global space community at its Central Campus in Strasbourg, France, and at locations around the world.

In its two-month Space Studies Program and one-year Masters program, ISU offers its students a unique core curriculum covering all disciplines related to space programs and enterprises – space science, space engineering, systems engineering, space policy and law, business and management, and space and society. Both programs also involve an intense student research team project providing international graduate students and young space professionals the opportunity to solve complex problems by working together in an intercultural environment.

In addition, the school offers an Executive MBA focusing on the space sector, a Technical Masters in Space Systems Engineering in cooperation with The Stevens Institute of Technology, several short courses including the Executive Space Course, and an innovative 5 week program focusing on space issues of particular concern to the Southern Hemisphere will begin in Adelaide, Australia in January 2011 in cooperation with the University of South Australia.

Since its founding in 1987, ISU has graduated more than 3000 students from over 100 countries. Together with hundreds of ISU faculty and lecturers from around the world, ISU alumni comprise an extremely effective network of space professionals and leaders that actively facilitates individual career growth, professional activities and international space cooperation.

You can learn more about ISU at www.isunet.edu/.

INTERNATIONAL®
SPACE UNIVERSITY

THE INTERNATIONAL INSTITUTE OF SPACE COMMERCE

The International Institute of Space Commerce, or simply 'the Institute,' has been established on the Isle of Man through a partnership between the International Space University (ISU) and the Manx Government.

The Institute's mission is to become the leading think-tank in the study of the economics of space. It is intended to be the intellectual home for the industry and space academia around the world for which it shall perform studies, evaluations and provide services to all interested parties with the ultimate aim to promote and enhance world's space commerce to the general public. The vision for the Institute is to act as a resource for all, being an international and nonpartisan think-tank, drawing upon new ideas and solutions to existing and future problems the space industry faces by drawing together experts from academia, government, the media, business, international and non-governmental organizations, most notably those from the ISU and its extended network of people and resources. The aim of the Institute is to broaden the professional perspective and personal understanding of all those involved in the study, formulation, execution, and criticism of space commerce.

The Institute is a Not for Profit Foundation and has been located at the site of the International Business School (IBS) on the Isle of Man to capitalize on the Isle of Man's growing importance and position in the world's space industry.

You can learn more about the IISC at www.iisc.im/about.asp.

FOREWORD

BRUCE MCCANDLESS II
CAPTAIN, US NAVY (RET.); 24-YEAR NASA ASTRONAUT

This third book by the Aerospace Technology Working Group (ATWG) is a broad and fascinating survey of the important topic of Space Commerce. The authors are genuine experts within their fields, and many of them have been together in the loose collaboration of the ATWG for two decades. They share a common impatience with incremental development and bureaucracy, and will lead the reader in exploring the frontier of this emerging business venue.

The English language being what it is, the phrase "Space Commerce" can be construed in several senses. Certainly direct-broadcast television from geostationary satellites, such as delivered by Echostar®/Dish Network® and Direct TV®, would qualify, as would satellite telephony – popular with mountain climbers and others venturing into disaster or remote areas. High resolution imagery of our Earth from space is generating a modest but growing revenue stream from customers as diverse as Google, Inc. and county land use monitoring/compliance departments. New endeavors, previously the stuff of unrequited dreams, are becoming part of contemporary life.

While talk of "Space Tourism" has been around for decades, the first serious contender was Henry John Deutschendorf, Jr. In the late 1980s Mr. Deutschendorf negotiated a deal with the Soviet Space Agency to fly in a SOYUZ for US$5 million, and obtained (likely unenthusiastic) approval from the U.S. State Department for his adventure. He then approached the astronaut corps in Houston seeking our blessing to wear a blue NASA flight suit. This venture ultimately came a cropper over the fact that the crass, capitalistic, communists in Russia actually wanted their $5M in hard currency, not the assignment of prospective future royalties from paeans that would be written and performed extolling the glories of the Soviet space program by none other than Deutschendorf himself, under his stage name of "John Denver!" There's an object lesson buried in there somewhere. Since that time, seven paying "tourists" on eight missions have flown (one repeat flyer) – all with the Russians – not too different from the politically motivated manned Soviet "Intercosmos" flights of the 1970s and'80s, or our own "Spaceflight Participants" of the early Shuttle Days – except that the U.S. selected its folks in conjunction with payloads, or other criteria, eschewing explicit financial considerations. The tourism flights started out priced at around US$20M each, and prices have risen steadily since then. This low-rate but apparently endless supply of paying customers illustrates that even extreme points on the price-demand plot can be valid.

The recently announced "ticket" price contracted to NASA after the year 2012 is US$55.8M per passenger; this author believes that the sale of two out of three seats per mission at that price would cover the costs of a SOYUZ flight, with perhaps a modest profit under the Russian aerospace financial accounting system – arguably transforming it into a "commercial" operation. Michael A. Blum, in Chapter 7, does more justice to this topic than I can in this Foreword.

Probably the first major prize for technological achievement arose from a British disaster. In 1707 the British fleet under the *Commander-in-Chief of the British Fleets,* Sir Cloudesley Shovell, ran aground on the Scilly Isles as a result of navigational inaccuracies with the loss of 1,400 – 2,000 personnel including the admiral himself. This stimulated the passage of The Longitude Act of 1714, establishing prizes of up to GB£20,000 (back in the days when the pound sterling was really worth something) for a practical technique for determining a ship's longitude at sea within 30 nautical miles. To put this situation into context, it is worth remembering that the celestial determination of longitude requires an accurate time reference, and that the master clocks of the era were all pendulum instruments, which made them totally worthless in the face of normal shipboard motions at sea. The solution to the British quest was the marine chronometer, a device using an oscillating balance wheel whose period is gravity-independent (unlike the pendulum).

Fast forward 300 years, and navigation systems are still dependent upon clocks – only this time they are *atomic clocks*, and they are located in satellites orbiting the Earth. The feasibility of this was first demonstrated by the U. S. Navy's TIMATION satellite, and led directly to the development and deployment of the Global Positioning System (GPS), which has become wildly popular beyond anyone's imagination. It is a Government Program, but has spawned a secondary, space-derivative "industry" in mapping, routing, surveying, and agricultural (farming) software driven by GPS signals. And, of course, the satellites themselves are built by commercial entities under Government contract, and launched on vehicles built by some of these same contractors. Your author recently purchased a commercial, hand-held GPS unit that tracks up to 12 satellites simultaneously and receives a WAAS (Wide Area Augmentation System) signal from a geostationary satellite to drive expected position error down to approximately *seven feet*! We have (grand) children seven and ten years old using satellite technology to locate "treasures" within hidden "geocaches." They're not reinventing the wheel, they're building magnificent new vehicles upon its axles!

More recently, the value of the prize offering as an instrument of motivation has been proven many times over. The (Raymond) Orteig Prize of US$ 25,000, for example, motivated Charles Augustus Lindbergh to undertake his epic non-stop New York to Paris flight in 1927, even after six earlier prize-seekers had lost their lives in the attempt. DARPA (Defense Advanced Research Projects Agency) has used its "Grand Challenges" with one and two million dollar prizes to inexpensively obtain multiple successful design solutions to the problem of autonomous land vehicle development.

This approach attracted a large number of prospective contestants, bringing their own at risk funding with them, and effectively mustered the much-touted "American ingenuity" and inter-university rivalry (esp. Stanford vs. Carnegie-Mellon). While during the Second Grand Challenge one of the entrants, an autonomous motorcycle, toppled over upon leaving the starting line, four other vehicles successfully completed the 131.2 mile long course, laid out on both improved roadways and varied Mojave Desert terrain, within the allotted ten hours. This breakthrough, paradigm-busting achievement flew in the face of years long, multi-million dollar, classically-organized predecessors such as DARPA's Autonomous Land Vehicle Program. The "Moon 2.0" chapter by William Pomerantz, who is the Senior Director of Space Prizes at the X Prize Foundation, elaborates on this topic in depth with respect to Space Commerce.

As our National programs successively mature and wind down, we find ourselves with ever more capable industrial bases, technological capabilities, and experienced personnel. The development of the Evolved Expendable Launch Vehicle(s) (EELV), albeit in response to an Air Force solicitation, was the first major launch vehicle program carried out not by "Government scientists," but by *industry* engineers, managers, and supporting personnel. The Atlas V (Lockheed Martin) and Delta IV (Boeing) have both been unqualified successes, and in fact led to the formation of a joint venture – United Launch Alliance, LLC. This innovative combination of production facilities maintains separate engineering and marketing elements in order to provide our country with assured access to space while avoiding a monopoly supplier situation.

There has been, and continues to be, a lot of discussion regarding "commercial" transportation of cargo and crew to and from the ISS. In many respects this is a "no brainer" if it is first broken down into elements. After the Shuttle winds up its operations in the immediate future, the means for resupply of the ISS will be via PROGRESS, SOYUZ, ATV (Ariane Transfer Vehicle), and HTV (H-II Transfer Vehicle) – the services of which NASA has *bartered* for. It is only a modest jump, not even a leap, to consider paying money to a provider such as Space-X (Space Exploration Technologies Corporation) for cargo delivery/takeaway via its DRAGON capsule. The primary hesitation appears to lie in technical skepticism (much reduced since the successful launch of the first FALCON 9 on June 4, 2010), the financial ability of the company to weather unexpected pitfalls, and timing to avoid gaps in ISS resupply. The advantage to all of the foregoing is the freeing up of NASA talent and resources to pursue cutting edge exploration activities instead of engaging in "reinventing the wheel" – again.

The situation with respect to crew transportation is a bit murkier. Will NASA insist on flying the vehicle with NASA astronauts, or will they be content to have them delivered by pilots and vehicles, potentially certified/licensed by another agency such as the FAA (Federal Aviation Administration)? The end objective after all is getting the passengers from "Point A" on the Earth's surface to "Point B" aboard the ISS, and back in a timely, uneventful fashion. Currently, the SOYUZ commander is Russian, and the other two non-Russians, although having received spacecraft systems training, are basically along for the ride. Perhaps it would be sensible to engage experienced former NASA astronauts as civilian pilots to temper these discussions.

Without making light of the tasks, the mission profile for crew and cargo to/from the ISS has been pretty well standardized – especially if vehicle-specific weather constraints, such as those associated with the Space Shuttle, are eliminated or greatly loosened. A similar situation existed many years ago, when military personnel travelling on orders were directed to use "Government Air, when available," even within the United States; more recently, the military directs use of the lowest cost coach/economy class fare and dispenses with all of the burdens associated with running a *sub rosa* airline.

A frequently overlooked element of the CHALLENGER tragedy is the transition from "The National Space Transportation System" – meaning the United States' only way of launching payloads into orbit and beyond – into (NASA's) "Space Shuttle Program." The latter had a much more restricted scope of operations, and, consequently, a much lower launch rate. This resulted in greatly increased costs *per mission* as a result of the smaller divisor into the fixed costs of the "standing Shuttle support army."

It is my opinion that the Reagan Administration overreacted to the loss of life in this accident, and mortally crippled the program in the process. NASA is capable of managing towering risks internally, without outside "help." I would cite the Apollo 8 mission (around the Moon on the first manned Saturn V; the second flight of the Apollo CSM (Command – Service Module)), the Apollo 13 crisis and recovery, the launch-phase damage to the SKYLAB Workshop, and numerous Shuttle missions that confronted unplanned occurrences. I do not wish to sound crass in this regard – I have "ridden the horse" myself – but I am unaware of any cutting-edge aviation programs that have not sustained some losses, generally including human lives. These losses are regrettable; we must work to avoid/minimize them, but we must persevere in spite of and learn from them. The now-operational V-22 OSPREY tilt-rotor assault transport sustained four major accidents during its development, for a casualty count of thirty human lives; the Confederate States Submarine HUNLEY destroyed the USS HOUSATONIC in 1864, but itself sank three times in the process with 21 of its crew members' lives lost. Perhaps escaping from direct Government control over Space Commerce will enable the perseverance to truly succeed in risky undertakings, even in the face of adversity and Administration hesitations.

Exports have long been a key driver of the American economic engine, especially high-tech exports. When competing on price alone, America has difficulty undercutting Asian producers, and finds itself with a massive imbalance of trade: imports far in excess of exports. High technology, however, is not like fine red wine; it does not get better with age. Like *Beaujolais Nouveau*, it is best when "fresh." Let me be clear – I am not advocating the heedless release of military technologies that could be used against America, but I am concerned that current restrictions have gutted the international market in U.S. communications satellites, and made most other space-related exports excruciatingly difficult and time consuming to complete. Succinctly, everything related to space – hardware, software, operations, technical details, training, fuels, etc. – has been placed on *The Munitions List*. Such items are prohibited from being exported by the *International Traffic in Arms Regulations (ITAR)*. Consequently, the export process requires first obtaining a *waiver* to the prohibition, and then a *license* from the State Department for each specific transaction.

Such restrictions even hamper domestic transactions since insurers or underwriters are frequently outside of the U.S. (think Lloyd's of London), and the provision of technical information on the satellites and/or launch vehicles in order to assist in setting premiums or investigating accidents is construed as an "export" subject to all of the foregoing restrictions and "red tape." As this is written, the Obama Administration is understood to be reviewing this situation with an eye towards streamlining and simplifying it.

Into this world of eager entrepreneurship, however, a few words of caution, like rain, must fall. Not every promising concept will succeed commercially. As an excellent first example, recall the case of "Zero-'g' Electrophoresis." This technology appeared so promising for separating porcine insulin from macerated pig pancreas that the apparatus flew three times on the Space Shuttle before the CHALLENGER accident. By the time Shuttle flights were resumed, however, genetic engineers had succeeded in coaxing modified *escherichia coli* bacteria and yeast cells to produce human insulin, in a mix of lower molecular weight biologicals from which it is easily separated. As a second case, despite an initial rush to geostationary communications satellites for carrying live telephone conversations, the latency introduced by the finite speed of light proved objectionable, and the balance shifted heavily towards the deployment and use of long-haul/trans-oceanic fiber-optic cables over the much shorter point-to-point terrestrial distances. Note, however, that these GEO satellites remain popular for one-way traffic (e.g., television) and in situations where the laying of physical cables is impractical or too expensive (e.g., between the islands of Indonesia, which are separated by deep ocean trenches).

Two chapters, 21 and 22, deal with education, and there is currently much agonizing over the need to interest K-12 students in the so-called STEM fields: science, technology, engineering, and mathematics. If we develop a viable, expanding, intellectually challenging, and *financially* rewarding space enterprise, both Nationally and in Space Commerce, we will not have to worry. "Build it and they will come" applies not only to baseball, but to life choices in general. Why should youths pursue athletic "scholarships" and devote all their discretionary energies to obtaining a major league contract? Our society has need of outstanding talent in a multitude of areas, and for this need to be satisfied it will be necessary to ensure that the associated rewards are commensurate with the personal investments required, and that the opportunities for participation do not have needlessly high hurdles. In-space curricula, in particular, could be both highly selective and highly attractive!

The focus of this book is upon the current largely entrepreneurial efforts to expand Space Commerce past areas of traditional Government dominance and into hitherto speculative and in some cases "fantastical" operations. The authors of the various chapters, and I do not intend any slight or disrespect by citing only a few by name, are individuals at the hearts of their respective undertakings. In addition to entrepreneurs proper they are the engineers, managers, visionaries, catalysts, educators, and customers, and they are fully engaged in pioneering developments. Such endeavors always seem to be fettered by the "chicken vs. egg" paradox;

entrepreneurs and financiers hesitate when committing to a business plan based upon poorly substantiated *market projections*, while prospective customers are looking to *proven performance* and acceptable pricing before buying. 'Twas ever thus. As these entrepreneurs persevere they intend to transform paradox into opportunity, and I hope they succeed!

But, enough of this *ménage* of history and status reporting! This book will surely inspire readers to think deeply about the future of Space Commerce, and it is also likely to open up insights, possibilities, and opportunities that they may never have considered before. It is a genuinely *forward looking* treatise – a collection of dreams, aspirations, plans and fortunes-in-the-making!

As there is more to say than possibly could fit into the 400-odd pages of this book, I am looking forward to future ATWG contributions to this important dialogue. But right here and now this book is a wonderful contribution to understanding and to potentially becoming involved in the dynamic field of Space Commerce.

Bruce McCandless II
September 1, 2010

BRUCE McCANDLESS II

Bruce McCandless II is a graduate of the U. S. Naval Academy and a Navy fighter pilot who was selected as a NASA astronaut in 1966. He served through the Apollo and SKYLAB Programs in a variety of supporting roles and flew on two Space Shuttle missions, STS 41-B and STS-31. During most of his career with NASA he was deeply involved in the development of astronaut maneuvering units, and was the first to fly the Manned Maneuvering Unit, untethered, in space, in 1984. In connection with the Hubble Space Telescope, Bruce had the Astronaut Office responsibility for insuring its on-orbit serviceability and flew on the Deployment Mission in 1990.

After retiring from the Navy he held a variety of middle management positions with Lockheed Martin Space Systems Company before transitioning to a "casual" employment status in 2005. In addition to his Annapolis education, Bruce earned an MSEE from Stanford University and an MBA from the University of Houston, Clear Lake Campus.

SPACE
COMMERCE

CHAPTER 1

INTRODUCTION
SPACE COMMERCE, 2010 - 2020

LANGDON MORRIS

AND

KENNETH J. COX, PH.D.

There are many reasons to go to space, and one of them is surely to make money.

Space commerce is already a major industry today, generating about $175B in revenue worldwide. This tidy sum comes primarily from communications satellites and the services needed to build them, get them into orbit, and keep them there.

By tomorrow, however, this figure will grow substantially, not only because the satellite market is thriving, but because other forms of space commerce are now maturing at a rapid rate.

In fact, it appears that we are at a transition point. We are shifting from a stage where space commerce is led by governments and a single type of service, satellite communications, to a stage in which entrepreneurs and large companies are taking leadership by finding ways to create and deliver value to many different kinds of customers across a wide spectrum of products and services, from pharmaceuticals and manufacturing to tourism and energy. By 2020 we anticipate that space commerce will be earning well beyond a trillion dollars each year, and it could easily be generating two or three trillion, or more.

THE SPACE COMMERCE PIONEERS

Who are the people who are building these new industries? Many of them have contributed the chapters in this book.

- They are entrepreneurs who are building new businesses.
- They are engineers who are designing the systems.
- They are managers who are dealing with the unprecedented complexities of space-based *and* Earth-based operations in industry and government.
- They are visionaries and catalysts who see what we *should* be doing in space, and they are prodding and provoking us to make it happen.
- They are, of course, customers who will buy products and services *not* made on Earth.
- They are educators who are helping prepare the next generation of industry leaders.
- They are soldiers, who will provide security to commercial operations located beyond the confines of Earth.
- Lastly, in this book you will find the passionate and perhaps eloquent voices of many of the industry's pioneers, those who have built and launched space vehicles for the last fifty years, and who are now looking into the future to share with us what they have learned about what to do, and what *not* to do.

This book tells the inside story of space commerce from all of these perspectives, in the words people who are fully engaged in making it happen.

COMPLEXITY AND RISK

Few industries combine as many elements as space commerce. It is a business, surely, where capital is put at risk every day in the hopes and expectations of a healthy return. Today, the entrepreneurs who invest anticipate very high returns because of the very high risks they are taking.

But space commerce also embodies a different type of risk than any Earth-based business. 'Launch,' in space commerce, means something more than just starting a business; it also means getting hardware and perhaps people into space, into orbit 100 miles out and beyond. And of course launch is definitely a risky undertaking, because if your launch fails then the cost can be very high both in terms of human life and financial capital.

And launch is just the beginning of the complexities. While getting energy, food, and water to an Earth-bound office building is a matter of making a few phone calls, getting them to space, along with your highly trained staff of very motivated people, means bringing along an entire, self-sustaining living environment. We are still learning just how to do that.

In spite of these complexities, though, the thrill, promise and prospect of space commerce have always attracted a few hearty souls. Some are drawn by the wealth that is waiting to be created. Some are drawn by the fascinating nature of the scientific, engineering and management problems to be solved. Some are drawn because they feel that it is humanity's destiny to venture beyond our planet, and they want to be part of that adventure. Many are drawn by the intriguing combination of all three.

And among these many adventurous ones, some wish to share their insights and experiences by writing about it. It is the purpose of this book to bring you their voices, in the hopes that you will come to understand what this human endeavor means not only to those who choose to be directly involved, but to all of us, to humans in every nation who may benefit from the results of these efforts.

We hope you enjoy reading *Space Commerce* as much as we enjoyed preparing it for you.

CHAPTER 2

MOON 2.0
PRIVATE PLANETARY EXPLORATION AND THE NEW LUNAR ECONOMY

WILLIAM POMERANTZ
SENIOR DIRECTOR OF SPACE PRIZES, THE X PRIZE FOUNDATION

During the past two centuries, with the majority of the surface of our planet already explored, civilizations around the globe have striven to expand the sphere of human economic influence upward. This trend began with the first skyscrapers of the 1880s and has continued through the birth of commercial aviation and commercial satellites, each of which drives billions of US Dollars in annual revenues while creating infrastructure vital to the modern way of life. Although some may contend that with geostationary satellites in orbit 36,000 km above sea level our economic sphere has reached its maximum range, there are compelling reasons to believe this is not the case, and that in the near future – rather than simply in dreams inspired by science fiction – we will see commercial activities expanding out into cis-lunar space and beyond.

This chapter will examine the new markets and market niches that may exist for commercial services on and near the Moon, with a focus on markets projected to develop over the course of the next 15 years.

THE TRADITIONAL PARADIGM OF DEEP SPACE EXPLORATION

The first spacecraft to leave Earth orbit was launched in January 1959, only fifteen months after the lunch of *Sputnik*. Мечта (*Mechta*), later re-named Луна-1 (*Luna-1*), was intended to be a lunar impactor, and was hailed by the Soviet Union as the first 'Cosmic Ship,' in part as a jibe against the USA's Pioneer 1 and Pioneer 2 spacecraft, both of which failed to leave near-Earth space in late 1958. The next decade and a half saw a bevy of lunar missions – the Luna, Pioneer, Ranger, Зонд (*Zond*), Surveyor, Lunar Orbiter, Apollo, and Луноход (*Lunokhod*) programs – consuming the attention of the world's superpowers, as well as hundreds of billions of US Dollars in research, development, manufacturing, and operations. Indeed, the 1960s and 1970s saw a flurry of space missions to a wide variety of deep space destinations, including Venus, Mars, Halley's Comet, and the outer planets.

Planetary exploration has continued since that period, though the ongoing trend has been towards larger, more complex, and more expensive missions that are launched less frequently. The first era of lunar and planetary missions – defined here as the period between the launch of Pioneer 1 in 1958 and the final *Luna / Lunokhod* mission in 1976 – saw an average of more than eight such missions per year, whereas the average since that time has been less than two. A possible shift back towards the earlier paradigm of more frequent government missions – driven largely by then NASA Administrator Dan Goldin's 'Faster, Better, Cheaper' mantra – met an ignominious end with the failures of the Mars Climate Observatory and Mars Polar Lander in the late 1990s.

Regardless of that paradigm shift, all of the lunar and planetary missions conducted during this period share one thing in common: all were government funded. Indeed, the vast majority of them were funded by two governments in particular: the USA and the USSR / Russian Federation. Other governments did not launch such missions until 1985, when both Japan and the European Space Agency launched missions to Halley's Comet. The club of deep space exploration remained with only those four members until China and India joined in 2007 and 2008. Although commercial industry and smaller nations have been launching spacecraft since 1962, we have yet to see such players put together a mission designed to fly to the Moon or beyond.

Commercial industry has, of course, had a large role to play in facilitating the exploration of our solar system conducted by civil space agencies. But with those industrial partners operating under traditional government contractual mechanisms of cost-plus contracts, et cetera, the spirit of entrepreneurialism has not yet been brought to bear on this aspect of the global aerospace industry.

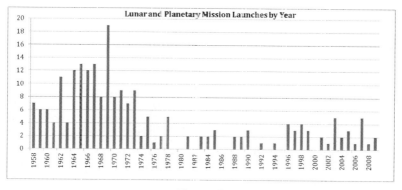

Fig.ure 1

The rate of lunar and planetary missions took a steep drop in the mid-1970s, and remains much lower than the earliest era of such exploration, owing partly to an emphasis on more complex, more expensive missions.

The cost of lunar and planetary exploration has been metastable for essentially the entire history of the Space Age: a very limited pool of government customers is willing to pay the current prices and, as revealed by NASA's brief and unsuccessful experiment with 'Faster, Better, Cheaper,' is relatively insensitive or even disinclined towards minor price decreases, whereas any potential new players that might serve as customers of these missions likely will not emerge until prices drop radically. As a consequence, much as with the price of launch, the price of exploration beyond Earth orbit has remained essentially flat.

THE INTRODUCTION OF NEW PLAYERS

In the 1990s and early 2000s, glimmers of hope for an escape from this metastable condition emerged, both in the form of successful missions and intriguing though failed attempts.

As noted above, most of the history of lunar and planetary exploration has been dominated by the civil space agencies in the USA and in the Soviet Union / Russia. Those agencies provided complete, end-to-end funding for the missions, as well as spearheading either the technical development of the spacecraft or, at a minimum, selecting between the technical paths proposed by a small group of aerospace contractors. With such a small pool of players, both the motivation and the ability to make radical breakthroughs in cost and in capability were constrained. Both agencies performed incredible missions worthy of admiration, but the total appetite for unusual and high-risk ventures (relative to the high levels of risk required of even the safest of lunar or planetary missions) was understandably low.

Two lunar missions successfully carried out in the mid 1990s demonstrated the potential for this pool of players to grow:

CLEMENTINE, 1994

At first glance, Clementine might seem like a typical NASA mission: it was a US government effort to map the Moon and to demonstrate the capability to rendezvous with an asteroid. However, Clementine was led not by NASA but by US Department of Defense's Ballistic Missile Defense Organization. Built largely at the US Naval Research Laboratory, Clementine was the product of a small, skunkworks team at a total cost, including launch and operations, of approximately $80M (in 1994 US Dollars; approximately $115M in 2009 US Dollars). Although the US Department of Defense is highly unlikely to conduct future missions to the Moon, the Clementine mission provides an excellent example of how new players can drive new capabilities and new price points in an otherwise static industry niche.

LUNAR PROSPECTOR, 1996

Like Clementine, Lunar Prospector was a US mission to the Moon that had its origins outside of NASA. Principal investigator Alan Binder notes that Prospector was originally *"conceived as a private mission to demonstrate to NASA, Congress, and the American taxpayer how missions could be done inexpensively, efficiently, and reliably."* Over the eleven years of Prospector's development and operations, the mission was passed from the Space Studies Institute to the National Space Society and eventually into NASA itself; however, the mission maintained an 'outsider' spirit and a skunkworks team. In the end, the entire mission, including launch and operations, cost $65M (in 1996 US Dollars; approximately $88M in 2009 US Dollars) even less than Clementine. Prospector serves as an example of the ability of non-governmental groups to conceive of successful lunar missions, as well as civil space agencies' willingness to accept lower cost mission ideas pushed by external advocates.

SERIOUS COMMERCIAL ATTEMPTS

On the heels of the successes of both Clementine and Prospector, several commercial entities began planning their own missions to the Moon. Such an idea had been pursued before – the Committee for the Future proposed the ambitious Project Harvest Moon in the late 1970s, and explicitly commercial lunar missions have been prevalent in fiction since the time of Verne's *De la Terre à la Lune,* but three commercial enterprises of the early 2000s merit particular attention for the amount of actual work conducted, even though these missions were never completed.

BLASTOFF!

Founded by Internet entrepreneurs Bill and Larry Gross in 2000, BlastOff! conducted serious development of multiple rover missions meant to explore the landing sites of the Apollo missions. With a business model driven largely by entertainment and media customers, including directors James Cameron and Stephen Spielberg, both of whom joined the company as investors, BlastOff! projected revenues of $250M in 2002 Dollars ($296M in 2009 Dollars). BlastOff! raised and spent over US $15M in 2002 Dollars ($18M in 2009 Dollars) more than twenty percent of the budget required to conduct their first two missions, including launches – before the burst of the dot-com bubble and the resulting economic downturn caused the company to cease operations in 2002.

Figure 2
BlastOff! engineers build the mother rover for what was to be the first private mission to the lunar surface. BlastOff! raised more than $15M in pursuit of the mission, but scrapped plans when the economic downturn of 2001 cost them the remainder of their required funding. Source: BlastOff!

LUNACORP

Similar to BlastOff!, LunaCorp planned to send rovers to the surface of the Moon in the early 2000s. However, whereas BlastOff! concentrated largely on a media-driven mission, LunaCorp's was intended to conduct serious science. The company planned to land a 440-pound (200-Kg) rover with a four foot drill and numerous other scientific instruments to the lunar surface, and had aims to operate throughout the lengthy lunar night. The company did pursue some media and entertainment revenue streams, as well, including a sponsorship deal with RadioShack worth $1M in 2000 US Dollars ($1,250,000 in 2009 US Dollars), with additional funds promised in part through the joint production of a LunaCorp video game. However, LunaCorp too fell prey to the economic downturn that followed the dot-com bubble burst.

TRANSORBITAL

Unlike BlastOff! and LunaCorp, TransOrbital planned to develop a lunar orbiter, rather than a rover. Their TrailBlazer spacecraft was to carry high-resolution video cameras to image the lunar surface, with special attention paid to NASA's Apollo and Russia's *Lunokhod* landing sites. A partnership with electronics giant Hewlett Packard generated both near term revenues and the important hardware components. However, TransOrbital also fell short of its funding goals in the midst of the economic doldrums of the early 2000s, succumbing before launching TrailBlazer or any of the company's planned follow-on lander missions.

Though none of those three were destined to leave the surface of the Earth, much less Low Earth Orbit, one commercial spacecraft did reach the Moon in this timeframe – though it wasn't originally planned to do so. The Asiasat-3 communications satellite was left shy of its desired orbit after a failure of its launch vehicle's final stage, rendering the expensive spacecraft useless. However, a new method pioneered by Rex Ridenoure and Ed Belbruno allowed the spacecraft to embark on a lengthy journey that used small increments of delta-v – and therefore small amounts of propellant – to gradually place the vehicle on a spiraling trajectory that eventually allowed *Asiasat-3* to slingshot around the Moon and into its desired orbital slot. Though time consuming, this maneuver demonstrated that such low fuel journeys to the Moon were possible, offering promise for future spacecraft hoping to achieve mass and cost savings. This technique has also been demonstrated by the Japanese lunar probe *Hiten* in 1991 European Space Agency's SMART-1 probe in 2004.

MOON 2.0: A NEW ERA OF LUNAR EXPLORATION

After the end of the first era of lunar exploration in the mid 1970s and a relatively inactive interstitial period that lasted three decades, a new era has at last begun. With exciting activities and a diverse range of actors all across the globe, the promise of this second era of lunar exploration, 'Moon 2.0,' is enormous. Though just recently underway, it offers the likelihood of being more participatory and longer lasting, building on the great foundations of the NASA and Soviet missions of the 1960s and 1970s with a new goal in mind: economic sustainability.

To fulfill this new promise, Moon 2.0 will depend on two critical elements: new reasons to explore the Moon, and a new set of innovators and operators focused on such exploration.

THE MOTIVATIONS OF MOON 2.0

The primary causes of the first era of lunar exploration, and the primary justifications for the significant expenditures undertaken by both the USA and the USSR, can be pithily summed up in two words: flags and footprints. Although phenomenal scientific and engineering advances occurred as a result of these programs, advances from which we still benefit today, national prestige and a desire both to demonstrate military might and to prevent an adversary from claiming the ultimate 'high ground' drove the massive expenditures that made these programs possible. Regrettably, neither national prestige nor even the military imperative proved to be a sustainable motivation for lunar exploration; once each impressive milestone had been claimed by one of the two competing superpowers, funding quickly dried up. It is for this reason that the first era of lunar exploration came to such an abrupt end; the scientific and engineering motivation for visiting the Moon increased, rather than decreased, by each successful mission, but the prestige diminished with each subsequent voyage.

It is unlikely that national prestige will be the primary motivation behind Moon 2.0, despite some handwringing in the USA regarding China's plans for crewed missions to the lunar surface. However, other reasons to return to our celestial neighbor abound.

The scientific rationale for visiting the Moon with orbiters and landers can and has filled entire books; for the purposes of this chapter, suffice it to say that the Moon is scientifically interesting enough that every well established space agency on the planet (and several emerging space agencies, as well) has multiple lunar missions in operation or development, and that the Moon is continually listed as a high priority destination by scientific steering bodies. Concepts such as the International Lunar Network – a proposed group of eight or more lunar landers, built and financed by different civil space agencies, that would be distributed across the lunar surface to conduct coordinated observations – further demonstrate the need for large numbers of lunar missions for purely scientific reasons, as well as the increase in scientific demand when the costs of access are decreased sufficiently to allow new entrants into the field.

The Moon is also an incredibly important destination for the purposes of exploration of other destinations. Although the global space community is frequently divided along the lines of preferred planetary destinations, it is a generally accepted maxim that the exploration of the Moon will allow the perfection of skills and techniques that will facilitate the exploration of

Mars and other destinations farther from Earth. With the majority of lunar approach trajectories requiring only three days of transit time, the Moon offers a nearby sandbox for planetary exploration systems and protocols, and in the event of problems, rescue, escape, and resupply are all dramatically more feasible than they would be at more distant locations. Similarly, teleoperations and communications are much simpler.

The Moon also sits at the bottom of a gravity well far more modest than Earth's, meaning that the lunar surface is particularly attractive as a venue for manufacturing and launch of materials and equipment for further exploration.

This rationale received a massive and important boost with the recent discoveries of the presence of significant quantities of water on the lunar surface. If future missions are able to harvest this water, it may well serve as an off-planet equivalent of the oil fields of the Middle East. Lunar water would of course find myriad uses, including use as a rocket fuel after electrolysis into hydrogen and oxygen.

In all likelihood, both the scientific and exploration motives for lunar landings will ultimately provide real, financial incentive for commercial entities to join governments in the pursuit of the capability to explore the Moon. Indeed, an important cash reward for such capabilities already exists in the form of the Google Lunar X PRIZE. Announced in September of 2007, the Google Lunar X PRIZE offers a total of $30M in prizes to the first privately funded teams to successfully explore the surface of the Moon with a robotic spacecraft.

This incentive prize is explicitly designed to facilitate a lasting, systemic revolution in cost reduction, and thus to expand the possibilities for lunar exploration, rather than promoting just a single mission. Designed in part by veterans of the BlastOff! commercial lunar efforts of the early 2000s, the prize seeks to provide momentum to an emerging market niche, acknowledging the fact that private lunar exploration is difficult concept to pitch to investors prior to serious demonstration of technical capabilities. Ideally, the prize money and the resulting media attention provide sufficient promise to attract both the inventors and the financiers needed to accomplish the first mission or two, which will in turn serve as a proof of concept that liberates future investment.

Although it is the largest international incentive prize in history, the Google Lunar X PRIZE is not the only such prize to address issues related to lunar exploration. The $2M Northrop Grumman Lunar Lander X CHALLENGE and the $750,000 Regolith Challenge, both funded by NASA and awarded in 2009, incentivized on-Earth demonstration of lunar exploration technologies. The successful conclusion of these two incentive prizes, as well as the ongoing success and recognition of the teams that won them, further legitimizes the concept of privately funded missions to the Moon and beyond.

Incentive prizes such as the Google Lunar X PRIZE are an exciting and important component in fostering this new market niche in part because of their proven ability to leverage large financial investments from a diverse range of sources far broader than those that would be available through more traditional research and development models. Incentive prizes have three centuries of history, and statistically leverage a total investment that exceeds the prize purse money by a factor of ten or more. This can be accomplished for multiple reasons:

- In the traditional research and development model, a funding agency pre-selects a limited number of developers – often a single developer – based on the strength of a proposal developed at the beginning of the process. Once this selection process is made, other potential developers generally cease their efforts, meaning that any potential delays or failures on the part of the selected developer will translate directly to delays or failures of the process as a whole. Incentive prizes, by contrast, provide awards after the successful completion of the project, and rely only on demonstrations, rather than proposals, to select recipients. By doing so, incentive prizes achieve parallel innovation, where multiple entities are racing each other to the best or fastest conclusion, and each is spending its own funds and making progress until the prize money is claimed.

- As described above, the pool of entities interested in funding lunar missions has historically been limited to a very small group of government agencies. The introduction of the competitive elements that surround an incentive prize program introduce totally new sources of funding that may have little to do with the actual exploration of the Moon, such as corporate sponsorships and 'ego money,' investment from wealthy individuals interested in the prestige and satisfaction that comes from backing a winning effort that completes a challenging task. With such financiers already backing events such as professional sporting teams and yacht races – many of which will cost these financiers more than it would to conduct a mission to the Moon – such a possibility is both feasible and intriguing.

- Similarly, the teams that compete for incentive prizes often benefit from volunteers and from donations of time, money, and material. A volunteer showing up a NASA center to offer assistance with a lunar mission would likely be thanked and sent away; if that same volunteer were to visit one of the teams competing for the Google Lunar X PRIZE, the result would likely be quite different.

Importantly, though, the primary function of an incentive prize such as the Google Lunar X PRIZE is not to create a single monolithic motivation for a new industry, but rather to highlight, amplify, and give birth to a number of motivations, and to motivate a variety of players to join in overcoming the barriers to entry particular to that pursuit.

THE CAST OF MOON 2.0

While the first era of lunar exploration had two players and the interstitial period saw the European Space Agency and the Japanese entering the fray, the new era of lunar exploration is bearing witness to an explosion in the number and variety of relevant players. Included among them are some national space agencies.

CHINA

China launched its first deep space mission, 嫦娥一號 (*Chang'e 1*), in late 2007. That spacecraft, which successfully completed a year-and-a-half long mission of mapping the Moon from orbit, was the first of several lunar probes planned as part of the *Chang'e* program. A close copy of the first mission will fly as *Chang'e 2* in 2011, and a lander and rover mission is planned for 2013. Including launch and operation, the cost of *Chang'e* 1 is estimated at 1.4B Yuan (approximately $190M in 2009 US Dollars).

INDIA

Shortly following China's first mission to the Moon, India launched *Chandrayaan-1*. Like its Chinese counterpart, this mission is meant to be the first of several Indian missions to the Moon. With a cost of approximately Rs 3,800,000,000 (approximately $76M in 2009 US Dollars), *Chandrayaan-1* is the least expensive mission yet to the Moon. A 2013 lander-rover mission being jointly pursued by India and Russia is projected to cost only 10% or 15% more. *Chandrayaan-1* further demonstrated the possibility of international collaboration by carrying payloads for NASA, ESA, and other international groups, as well as by directly collaborating with NASA's Lunar Reconnaissance Orbiter on measurements and mapping.

JAPAN

Additionally, the Japanese lunar orbiter かぐや (*Kaguya*), launched in 2007, offers hope for a new era of lunar exploration. Though the spacecraft's cost ($474M in 2007 US Dollars, $490M in 2009 US Dollars) differentiates it from its Chinese and Indian counterparts, Kaguya is of particular interest because of the high definition video camera it carried. A collaboration between JAXA, the Japanese civil space agency, and NHK, the Japanese public television station, this HD camera and the public response to the videos it returned demonstrate a global appetite for compelling lunar data generated with public outreach rather than pure science as a first order goal.

PRIVATE INDUSTRY AND NGOs

But the pool of relevant players in lunar exploration need not be limited to government agencies. Private industry is already becoming involved, and as of the time of this writing, twenty-two privately funded teams have already registered to compete in the Google Lunar X PRIZE. (See Figure 3)

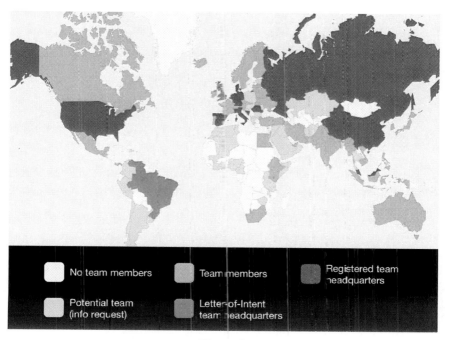

No team members   Team members   Registered team
                                                headquarters

Potential team   Letter-of-Intent
(info request)   team headquarters

Figure 3
The Google Lunar X PRIZE has already helped to identify many of the commercial companies interested in participating in lunar exploration. As of August 2010, twenty-two teams were fully registered in the competition and actively working on their Moon missions; an additional set of 2-5 teams are expected to join prior to the close of registration in December 2010. Many of these teams are multinational, meaning that team members are working in nearly 70 countries around the world.
Source: X PRIZE Foundation

These teams are remarkably diverse in scope: they are headquartered in a dozen nations, with members of the various teams working in nearly 70 nations on every continent save Antarctica. In addition to their geographic diversity, these privately-funded groups represent a remarkable range of members and partner institutions, as they are built around universities, existing aerospace companies, newly minted small businesses, non-profit foundations, and even open source communities.

Of course, not all of the teams competing for the Google Lunar X PRIZE will prove to be viable, but the principle of parallel development recognizes this and indeed celebrates it. Similarly, it is highly likely that other important lunar exploration companies will emerge beyond the list of Google Lunar X PRIZE participants. Nevertheless, this group of teams provides an early glimpse of the very wide range of ventures that might seek to profit from lunar exploration.

After a point, more players will not necessarily be better: the market will reach a point of saturation, after which new additions will likely be a zero sum game or worse. However, the private lunar market is currently so undeveloped and radically under saturated that the addition of new players such as those identified above will likely lead to a much larger range of services, offered with greater regularity, and at lower price points.

THE CASE FOR SUSTAINABLE LUNAR COMMERCE

An increase in lunar exploration would not by necessity mean an increase in lunar commerce. Although private companies certainly played a role and earned revenues during the first era of lunar exploration, one would not really say that that era resulted in any lunar commerce whatsoever. For such commerce to emerge requires both that there is a reasonable base of customers for lunar commerce and related products, and that commercial entities can compete effectively against their non-commercial counterparts, the government-backed 'competition' against these business cases.

STRENGTHS OF COMMERCIAL LUNAR EXPLORATION FIRMS

As discussed above, the strengths of the government-funded missions that dominated both the first era of lunar exploration and the subsequent interstitial period were their scope and complexity. After an initial foray of relatively simple trailblazer missions, the early lunar pioneers packed an enormous amount of instrumentation and capability into each spacecraft, culminating in the crewed Apollo missions – which can lay a plausible claim to being the among the most complex undertakings of all time. This standard of large and complex has proven to work well with the realities of governmental funding cycles: taxpayer support for lunar or planetary missions only comes around every so often, so space agencies and the scientists and engineers who lead individual missions are incentivized to load the maximum amount of capabilities into each such opportunity.

Commercial enterprises are unlikely to compete with governmental missions where the governments are strong because it is highly unlikely that any company that did so would succeed, at least in the short term. Instead, companies are expected to fill in new market niches and to develop capabilities and prices that are complementary to, rather than competitive with, their government counterparts. Where government missions are large, extraordinarily capable, and relatively infrequent, commercial missions are likely to trend to the opposite end of the spectrum: agile, frequent, and specialized.

NEW MARKETS FOR LUNAR COMMERCE

These strengths will make commercial capabilities for lunar exploration appealing to a broad variety of new customers. Given both the wealth of research opportunities available to scientists and engineers who have affordable access to the Moon and similar environments, and the high levels of prestige associated with such exploration, it is highly likely that non-space faring nations will become customers for lunar services at the correct price point – something that is not yet qualitatively known, but which is almost certainly at least one order of magnitude lower than the costs for lunar missions conducted to date.

Less wealthy nations and smaller space agencies have already displayed a predilection for undertaking Earth-orbiting satellite missions for similar reasons, demonstrating their interest and willingness to undertake space missions for both science and prestige when such missions can be conducted affordably, and the historic scarcity of lunar missions will only increase their prestige, and therefore the extent to which they are in demand, in the near term.

Nations need not be the only group to do so; if the price of placing a small instrument in lunar orbit or on the Moon's surface begins to approach some of the other exotic equipment or campaign costs now relatively common in academia, such as field work in Antarctica, equipping a new professor's chemistry lab, purchasing a gene sequencer, et cetera – it is easy to imagine some of those funds being allocated to lunar science and commerce.

Additionally, as those prices break out of their historic metastability, it's highly likely new markets totally unlike anything seen to date will emerge. Companies such as the Google Lunar X PRIZE teams are already pursuing and finding success in such radically new markets, including everything from the carrying of human ashes for a 'burial' on the Moon to a wide variety of entertainment options to be sold via subscription or underwritten by corporate sponsors.

Ego money, as mentioned above, may allow sales of components that have otherwise fulfilled their mission, as was demonstrated when video game pioneer and second generation astronaut Richard Garriott purchased the 'deed' to the Soviet *Lunokhod 2* lander. Some of these revenue streams may not be sustainable in the long run, as their value is at least partially a result of their unique and unprecedented nature; but other revenue streams are likely to emerge once the early adopters prove the feasibility and reliability of such missions.

Although these new markets bring exciting potential, it is likely that in the short term, at least, they will be secondary to markets built upon serving more traditional players, the major space agencies of the world and the large firms who supply them. A striking amount of room for innovation exists in this space as well, but several possible lines of business with these customers can be anticipated:

- Access to the lunar surface has been incredibly rare. Private companies that can provide such access – full lunar delivery services – with reliable frequency and at a tolerable price will likely find a healthy list of customers. A number of payloads already exist as candidates for such delivery, having been orphaned by cancelled missions or been left over as spares or prototypes of payloads that have flown on other spacecraft, such as the flight spares of the optical microscope, the wet chemistry lab, and the robotic arm created to fly on NASA's Mars Phoenix spacecraft. Depending on the price point, other payloads may well emerge or be specifically develop to take advantage of a 'Lunar U-Haul' service. Space agencies large and small are likely customers, and by building upon the models shown through programs such as NASA's Stand Alone Missions of Opportunity Notice (SALMON) and Commercial Reusable Suborbital Research Program (CRuSR), space agencies could fund academic labs and other groups looking to take advantage of this one-way delivery service.

- In the space industry, 'heritage hardware' is big business. Given the high costs associated with the failure of space missions, mission designers are reluctant to incorporate new systems or new components into their plans, even when such new elements carry substantial rewards. Because of this reluctance, progress is often slowed or altogether impeded; when a proven piece of hardware can fulfill the minimum mission requirements, the incentive to take the risk on an unknown quantity is low. If commercial lunar providers are able to offer a low cost, low risk mechanism to demonstrate the functionality and performance characteristics of these unproven elements in space and even on the lunar surface, they stand poised to reap the benefits either through the direct sales of these elements or through fees they collect from their developers via delivery or operational expenses. Space agencies are likely to be customers for such services, and traditional aerospace contractors should be important customers as well, as they seek to prove out hardware and to differentiate themselves from their peers as they bid on large contracts, including those too large for these new lunar companies.

- Given the relative infrequency of government funded planetary exploration missions, and the even lower frequency of missions that make it to the surface of other bodies, rather than orbiting around them, the selection of landing sites is extremely important. Before every mission, large teams of scientists scour the available data and haggle over the optimal landing site, always aware that they need to trade off the quality of the data expected at a given landing site with the danger and difficulty associated with landing and performing there. Often, the attractiveness of a site is inversely related to the ease with which missions can land there, so the balancing act can be a difficult one. With the advent of relatively inexpensive commercial lunar capabilities, these teams will have the option of commissioning one or more low cost missions using disposable robotic explorers to venture to their top candidate landing sites to pave the way for the more capable and expensive government funded missions that will come later.

- The markets shown in Table 1 below have often been based on the assumption that private companies will largely serve as passive delivery vehicles for hardware and components built by their customers. Another class of companies in this emerging niche will likely take a different tact: selling data transmitted back from the Moon, rather than physical items carried to it. In most cases, this will involve an additional layer of complexity for the lunar enterprise itself, as it seeks to develop and operate the sensors. However, this decision carries an upside, as the resulting data can potentially be sold to multiple customers, or monetized in other ways that are unavailable to companies in a more traditional transportation business such as fixed-term usage agreements or subscription based services.

Many of these market niches share the common theme of allowing space agencies and similar players to manage the risk associated with their currently-planned and future missions. Indeed, the hopes for near term success for many of these lunar entrepreneurs lies in enabling government space agencies to do more with relatively fixed amounts of money, rather than poaching funding away from the space agencies. In this sense, commercial industry and government-backed planetary exploration missions are expected to have a relationship that is complementary, rather than competitive. NASA has already begun taking a lead on studying how best to benefit from new commercial capabilities, commissioning an inventory of existing 'orphaned' equipment and assessments of other capabilities likely to align with NASA's mission.

THE SIZE OF LUNAR MARKETS

The commercial lunar industry is still immature, and very few existence proofs exist that can be used to extrapolate total market caps. However, a study performed by the Futron Corporation in early 2009, drawing from interviews with Google Lunar X PRIZE teams, venture capitalists, and NASA officials, provided the firmest numbers available to date, as shown in Table 1 on the facing page.

BEYOND THE MOON – NEAR EARTH OBJECTS

In this emerging new marketplace, lunar exploration is likely to be both more developed – on a relative scale – and more likely to pay near-term dividends than exploration to other destinations further from the Earth's surface than geostationary orbit. Recent trends, including the Google Lunar X PRIZE, have spurred such activity all across the globe, including some lines of business, such as payload slot sales, that are already generating revenues. However, the Moon is not the only destination open to commerce.

Near Earth Objects, including asteroids and comets whose natural orbit brings them into Earth's general vicinity, are scientifically interesting bodies that have been the target of numerous recent government-funded missions. The threat of potential impacts provides an additional imperative to learn more about these objects, and observing them from close proximity, or even landing on their surfaces, offers the best way to harvest the data that we need to understand them.

For commercial enterprises, an even more compelling reason may at some point drive large volumes of business: minerals. Asteroids in the Iron-Nickel family may prove to be treasure troves for companies looking to harvest materials that could be used in space, or potentially even on Earth. The frozen water that makes up much of the mass of comets might be useful for the same reasons that lunar water is so hotly coveted. Of course, the value of both of these is highly dependent on the regulatory stance that will emerge from both existing treaties and, in all likelihood, a new legal canon regarding property rights off-planet. However, it is feasible that both governments and corporations will have a sizeable incentive to come to satisfactory agreements regarding the legality of ownership of spaceport minerals, et cetera, in the near future.

Market	Estimated Market Size (2011-2019)
Full-vehicle / full-mission sales to governments	US$700,000,000
Payload and data delivery services for governments	US$200,000,000 - US$400,000,000
Sales to the private sector, including individuals	US$30,000,000 - US$160,000,000
Entertainment	US$10,000,000 - US$100,000,000
Sponsorship	US$50,000,000 - US$100,000,000
Technology sales and licensing	US$10,000,000 - US$100,000,000
TOTAL	**US$1,000,000,000 - US$1,560,000,000**

Table 1
Although further data are needed to project the size of lunar markets with greater fidelity, a market size analysis conducted by the Futron Corporation provides the first solid estimates of the potential size of the markets that will be opened and filled by the emerging cadre of lunar service providers. Several of the Google Lunar X PRIZE teams, each of which is drawing upon proprietary business plans have commented that the Futron study, while a useful yardstick, likely underestimates some of these markets, especially 'technology sales and licensing' and 'payload and data delivery services for governments.'   Source: Futron Corporation

Regardless of the property debate, it is likely that industry will turn its eyes towards these Near Earth Objects in the relatively near future. Many of the market opportunities open to companies able to visit the Moon will be repeated for these asteroids and comets. Perhaps the companies that emerge as successful on the lunar frontier will be the first to expand to Near Earth Objects, though it is also quite possible that new companies will emerge that are focused from the start on these destinations.

CONCLUSION

Fictional entrepreneurs like Jules Verne's Impey Barbicane (*From the Earth to the Moon*) and Robert Heinlein's D.D. Harriman (*The Man Who Sold the Moon*) have long been imagined to focus their sights on the Moon as means to make a healthy profit, but reality has not yet borne out those dreams. Although the Moon occupied the attention of the world during the impressive first era of lunar exploration – highlighted by the astronaut sorties on the lunar surface through the USA's Apollo program – it did so only thanks to the support of direct government funding. Commerce has not yet taken a foothold on our celestial neighbor.

However, a new day is dawning for lunar exploration. Unlike its counterpart of the 1960s and 1970s, 'Moon 2.0' is shaping up to be international, sustainable, and participatory in its nature – and many private companies from all around the world are seeing ways in which they can generate profits from the exploration of the Moon. With a variety of revenue streams from prize money and sponsorship to the proving of new hardware components and the scouting of future landing sites, these companies are using new methods to build a broad range of systems meant to go to lunar orbit and even down to the surface of the Moon.

In all likelihood, these companies will exist in symbiosis with government space agencies, many of which have the Moon firmly in their own sights for their exploration programs. By developing strengths and capabilities that complement, rather than competing against those developed by civil servants and the traditional contractor base, these new companies are opening a new market niche. Though projections are still preliminary, there are likely to be billions of US dollars in revenues to be earned over the course of the next decade for companies that can demonstrate success.

Should these predictions prove accurate, the sphere of human economic influence will have expanded greatly, and the period of metastability in the price of lunar exploration will have been broken. Other destinations, including asteroids and comets may prove worthy. But for now, the Moon stands poised as a lucrative and tempting financial, scientific, and exploration frontier – calling out to real world businessmen, just as it has to dreamers and poets for centuries.

•••

POST SCRIPT

Just before this book went to press, NASA announced the creation of the Innovative Lunar Demonstrations Data (ILDD) program. Managed at the Johnson Space Center, ILDD will allow NASA to spend as much as US $30.1M purchasing data pertinent to small, low cost missions to the lunar surface. Specifically, NASA is offering firm-fixed price, indefinite-delivery/indefinite-quantity contracts to purchase *"data associated with the design and demonstration of an end-to-end lunar landing mission including: hardware design, development, and testing; ground operations and integration; launch, trajectory correction maneuvers, and lunar braking burn; lunar landing; and other enhanced capabilities."*

With individual firms eligible to earn as much as $10.1M, this program will provide a much appreciated flow of capital to companies such as the Google Lunar X PRIZE teams that are developing the capacity to conduct or support lunar surface missions. Perhaps more importantly, this new program sends a clear signal to both these companies and their potential investors that, regardless of whether NASA maintains its current exploration plan of record or adapts new exploration missions such as those proposed by President Obama, NASA recognizes the valuable insight that private companies can provide into emerging technologies and systems that will benefit NASA as it develops its own plans to explore the solar system, and further, NASA is ready and willing to become a customer of commercial lunar services. The first awards under this program are anticipated in September or October of 2010, with further payments expected over the following two or three years.

WILLIAM POMERANTZ

William Pomerantz currently serves as the Senior Director of Space Prizes for the X PRIZE Foundation. He holds a BA in Earth and Planetary Sciences from Harvard University and a Masters of Science in Space Studies from the International Space University. As Senior Director of Space Prizes, Mr. Pomerantz manages the all of the X PRIZE Foundation's space activities, including the $30M Google Lunar X PRIZE. From 2006-2009, he also managed the Northrop Grumman Lunar Lander X PRIZE Challenge, which concluded with the successful award of $2M in NASA-provided prize purses. Additionally, he oversees the development of Foundation's forthcoming prizes in the field of space exploration.

Mr. Pomerantz is married to Mrs. Diana Trujillo Pomerantz, a Systems Engineer at NASA's Jet Propulsion Laboratory. Mr. and Mrs. Pomerantz both serve as coaches for the Zero Gravity Corporation, joining passengers in weightlessness on parabolic flights.

Additionally, he serves on the Board of Trustees for the Students for the Exploration and Development of Space (SEDS). Mr. Pomerantz is a frequent blogger for the Launch Pad, and blogs occasionally for the Huffington Post, VentureBeat, and Wired Magazine's GeekDad blog.

CHAPTER 3

CHALLENGES FOR THE NEW SPACE ECONOMY

WALTER PEETERS, PH.D.
DEAN AND VICE PRESIDENT FOR ACADEMIC AFFAIRS, THE INTERNATIONAL
SPACE UNIVERSITY, AND
DIRECTOR, THE INTERNATIONAL INSTITUTE OF SPACE COMMERCE

INTRODUCTION

Most sectors requiring a relatively high upfront investment have started off as public, often military funded projects. A typical example is the development of the commercial aeronautical sector with some similarities but also important differences compared to the space sector. Starting with early flights in 1897 performed by Clement Adler (but kept secret due to military financing) the first flights that can be considered as a milestone in aviation took place in Kitty Hawk on 17 December 1903 by the Wright Brothers, also under a military contract, this time under the auspices of the US Signal Corps.

The First World War no doubt boosted the development of aircraft considerably under war conditions, reaching, for example, productions of more than 1000 DH-4 aircraft monthly in USA alone, with plans to double this production rate after 1918[1] [p.125 a.f.]. The availability of this large surplus of aircraft, trained pilots and airports from 1919 onwards led to the birth of the first commercial passenger flights. It is interesting to note that the first regular service offered by the Farman Company between Paris and London, starting as early as 1919, proved not to be financially viable due to high ticket prices. Government support was subsequently provided for such routes from 1920 onwards and commercial passenger flights took off with, among others, the then reputed Franco-Romaine Group with London-Paris-Constantinople routes.

So even if we can note a number of interesting parallels, there are also a number of considerable differences between 'airflight' and spaceflight developments:[2]

DIFFERENCE IN TIMELINE

If we consider the evolution in technological know-how it is rather remarkable that it took only 15 years between the first experimental aircrafts and a commercial passenger service. With the first human spaceflight in 1961, it took until 2001 (more than 40 years) before the first paying passenger, Dennis Tito, could participate in a spaceflight.[1]

GOVERNMENT SUPPORT

Most analysts agree that the birth of commercial air traffic would not have taken place without considerable PPP (Public-Private-Partnership) type governmental support. Besides some isolated attempts, such as the US-DOD supported DC-X development and minor ESA and NASA technology development contracts, the same impetus has not taken place in the space era.

CUSTOMER ORIENTATION

The aforementioned Farman Company fitted the interior of its F60 Goliath planes in accordance with tourist requirements. As one can see, the example from Figure 1, the (five) front seat passengers in particular had an excellent and undisturbed view. Similar customer considerations have only been recently introduced in commercial space tourism projects.

These differences continue to exist strongly in early publications on Space Commercialization. Most publications describe in great detail the technical aspects of present space projects and try to deduce from this the utilization possibilities for a commercial public; market demand is rarely taken as a starting point.

---

[1]   The Japanese journalist Toyohiro Akiyama spent one week on board of MIR in 1990, but as this flight was sponsored by Tokyo Broadcasting Service (TBS) he was not a paying passenger, contrary to D. Tito.

Figure 1
Model of Farman F60 passenger plane (1919)
Source: Musée de l'Air, Le Bourget

Classics in this field, such Goodrich's *The Commercialisation of Outer Space*[3] provide very visionary application examples, but most of the perceived obstacles are dealing with 'how to do business with the government,' describing in detail aspects such as space law and space insurance, all based upon governmental space transportation systems.

Later on, the need to apply open market competition principles, in particular marketing, has been emphasized.[4] This has led to an approach whereby the interaction between politics, economics and technology (the typical tension according to the classical works of Thomas Kuhn) were put in a more balanced concept.

The relatively long lead-time to develop space technologies remained, and still remains, a major obstacle for companies seeking funding in a market that wants to see a positive Net Present Value in four to five years. It makes it difficult to find Venture Capital interested in general and virtually limits early funding possibilities to Business Angels.

More recent works acknowledge the reality that there needs to be a close interaction with government funding and political decisions. Nevertheless, there is a trend to have a more open approach towards space commercialization, which has been strongly fuelled by the opening of international markets after the geopolitical changes that took place at the end of the 20th century. An example of this openness can be found in more recent works on Space commercialization such as the works from Handberg.[5]

Authors are not only pleading for adapting the vested principles evolving from the Outer Space Treaty or based upon 'Guardian' principles such as export control, but highlight the existence of a New Space Economy which is developing independently, even if the political environment is still an important factor which cannot be neglected. Admittedly this is the case for any commercial product, but we have to acknowledge the fact that it is certainly more stringent for an arena such as space with a strong strategic component.

This leads us to think one step further and look at how the commercial opportunities for the New Space Economy can be further developed. Hereafter the obvious discussion on changing the regulatory framework will not be discussed (see other contributions on this in this book) but we will emphasize:

1. Changes needed in the company culture of space companies
2. The resulting new workforce needs
3. The need for developing new markets

CHANGES IN SPACE COMPANY CULTURE

A strongly underestimated factor, in the space arena in particular, is the fact that due to a long-standing tradition of working for government and military projects, many of the vested companies have a deeply rooted business culture adapted to that particular environment.

A number of privatizations over the last few years have highlighted these points whereby employees working under a governmental type of business had to change attitudes at relatively short notice. A notable example of this is Intelsat, which changed between 1998 and 2003 from an IGO (Intergovernmental Organization) to a private company and was acquired by a Private Equity Investor. Each of these changes was accompanied by reorganizations and changes in assignments as well as labor contracts. As an Intelsat executive expressed it as:

> *"Our engineers had to change from focus on process (the best satellites we can build) to focus on product and delivery (the best satellite we can build quickly for a given price)."*

It is probable that a change in methodology or approach was a factor in addition to the formal aspect of such a change.

The space sector was strongly technology driven and therefore also had a strong tendency to technical perfection, including the building in of high redundancies. This effect results from a number of elements inherent to the non-profit sector that is often categorized as:[6]

1. Dominance of professionals
2. Constraints on goals and strategies
3. Importance of political influences
4. Lack of profit measure for allocation of resources

Unfortunately the authors conclude that this often has led, and is still leading, to a tradition of inadequate management controls. The lack of profit measure shall not be underestimated as it deprives the non-profit sector from a very efficient benchmark: measuring profit per unit or cost center. More and more recent managers from non-profit space organizations have therefore introduced other Key Performance Indicators (KPI), being aware that taxpayer's money is involved. This is well reflected in the statement of Dan Goldin when becoming NASA administrator:

If you cannot measure it, you cannot manage it.

As discussed earlier, we can also bring this in context with two different approaches that are often labeled as Guardians and Merchants. The two different cultures are synoptically described as shown in Table 1.[7]

Merchants	Guardians
Shun Force	Shun trading
Come to voluntary agreements	Are obedient and disciplined
Compete	Are loyal
Use initiative and enterprise	Adhere to tradition
Collaborate easily with others	Respect hierarchy
Are efficient and industrious	Are exclusive

Table 1
Tension between a commercial and protective policy environment

The aforementioned work[7] is developing these differences in a policy context, as it strongly reflects the tension between an open, outgoing approach with a minimum of regulations compared to a more conservative approach with export and other control mechanisms. However, besides the policy issue, a similar distinction can be made between the more market-oriented part of an organization and the technology part of it, as per table 2[4] [p. 162].

We clearly need to acknowledge that this tension also exists in any major commercial cooperation, as expressed in the wish for better interdepartmental cooperation shown in Table 2.

The numerous problems with early software versions and recalls from car manufacturers these days clearly show that the optimum is also not reached in other sectors, but the space sector is suffering more due to its historical background.

Most of the companies have inherited the characteristics of the non-profit sector, either as they originally belonged to that sector or they were mainly dealing with that sector and adapted to it. In relation to Tables 1 and 2 there is therefore a strong predominant Guardian and technology overemphasis, also due to the dominance of technological professionals in management positions.

I have a DREAM:
Development by Research, Engineering And Marketing.

Marketing Department	Technology Department
Concentrate on product development	Concentrate on research
Freeze design as fast as possible	Keep options open
Accelerate Time-to-Market	Do extensive pre-testing
Rapid Ramp-up (production)	First start a pilot plant
Enhance customer acceptance	Emphasize technical performance
Keep Proprietary rights	Publish results

Table 2
Tension between marketing and technology interests.

NEW SPACE WORKFORCE NEEDS

The issue of demography and the ageing space workforce has been addressed in many publications and workshops, such as the Space Policy Summit at the World Space Congress in 2002.[9] It shall be noted here that the situation in Europe proved to be a little less alarming, as shown in a study performed by the European Science Foundation (ESF).[10] Evidently the more regulated retirement schemes in Europe are one of the main reasons for this difference, combined with the relatively younger existence of the European space sector.

This ageing effect conversely allows the more commercial oriented space companies to renew the skill set of their workforce. It was therefore a surprise that in a recent survey[11] in Europe nearly 50% of the space companies reported problems recruiting staff with the required skills.

A detailed analysis showed two different categories of recruitment issues. As far as 'hard skills' are concerned, the results of the survey show the different pattern of multidisciplinary backgrounds that are preferred in the present space sector, as shown in Figure 2.

From this figure we note that the space sector in the first place is still looking for specialized engineers, but is also searching increasingly to find engineers and scientists with business management skills.

It is noted that young graduates have sensed this trend and in general are more inclined to obtain multiple degrees in order to position themselves better in the recruitment process. In particular in countries that have adapted the concept of the BMD system (Bologna Agreements), more students feel the need to obtain differentiating Master degrees rather than seeking jobs after obtaining 3-year Bachelor degrees.

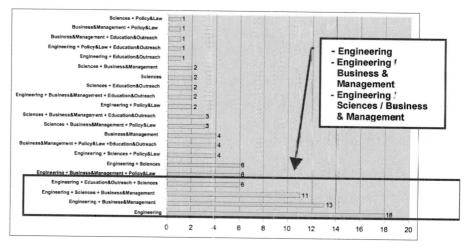

Figure 2
Educational background sought in the European space industry.[11]

Similarly, for the existent workforce, this has led to the creation of a number of executive type programs on request of the space sector, such as the newly introduced Executive MBA (EMBA) in ISU.[12] These programs are geared towards providing mid-career space professionals with technical backgrounds while also providing them with necessary business knowledge.

Probably even more important is the concept of the 'soft skills,' the space sector seeks. From the same survey the sector validated these skills as per Figure 3.

Soft skills are related to personality traits and characteristics and therefore depend on the level of personal and social intelligence. Evidently, they are much harder to measure and quantify compared to the aforementioned hard skills.

We can clearly deduce from Figure 4 that the most appreciated soft skills for the future workforce are mentioned or assumed to be:

1. Analytical / conceptual thinking
2. Communication
3. Creativity
4. Motivation
5. Teamwork

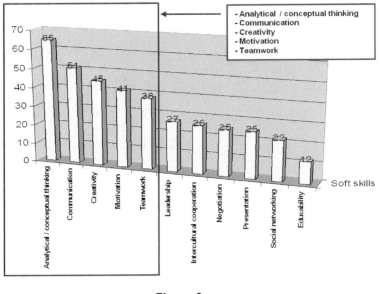

Figure 3
Ranking of the soft skills in function of frequency mentioned.[11]

One of the important issues is the fact that many of these skills are either ignored or only partially covered by classical education curricula. However, communication skills are very apparent at interviews. (If a candidate is not able to 'sell' himself, what is the level of confidence that he will be able to 'sell' the company image or products to the outside world?)

A last point of interest from the survey was the need for future specialists per specific area. This need is reflected in Figure 4.

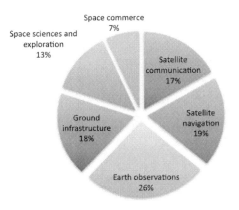

Figure 4
Space application skills required in future recruitment.[11]

Some sectors are evidently not a surprise due to their present commercial success (such as communication and navigation) but there is also a rather high demand for specialists in the field of ground infrastructure. This, again, is an area which is in general less covered in traditional space education curricula, even if, as will be described later, there is a much higher market prospect in ground based value added services than in the space segment itself.

DEVELOPING NEW MARKETS

Developing new markets without obvious benchmarking is difficult. In the space sector we can compare 4 different forecasts from different sources covering the last 3 decades. Space based telecommunication was virtually the only area which was correctly predicted (and therefore does not appear anymore in later forecasts) whereas some areas, such as space tourism, are still in a stage of infancy. Solar power and mining, on Mars, the Moon or other celestial bodies have not yet found the right impulse whereas some other areas have completely disappeared. A good example of the latter category is the idea to dispose of nuclear waste in space, which has luckily completely disappeared after an increased awareness of sustainable development.

1979	1991	1999	1999
Communication	Suborbital Transport	Mars Exploration	Space Tourism
Nuclear Waste Disposal	Space Tourism	Moon Exploration	Solar Power
Manufacturing in Space	Solar Power	Solar Power	Tele-operated Satellite Repair
Space Based Solar Power	Manufacturing in Space	Space Tourism	Industrial Platforms
	Mining		Asteroid Mining
	Colonization		Lunar & Mars

Table 3
Forecasts of commercial markets over time[4] [p.11].

The famous physicist Niels Bohr was therefore rather correct when he stated:

Prediction is very difficult, especially if it's about the future.

Based upon an analysis using expert groups, OECD has performed a series of space market studies and has identified[13] a number of markets which were less obvious some years ago but can become gradually more realistic, namely:

IN THE FIELD OF TELECOMMUNICATIONS

TELEHEALTH

This area will benefit from the ageing of population, where people will be in a position to travel when they are older but will want to be medically supervised when traveling in remote areas. This will require regular, possibly remotely controlled, interventions (e.g., insulin pumps).

ENTERTAINMENT

There are still many possibilities in this area both from a quality point of view as well as from a comfort point of view. Interactive systems via TV, allowing people to choose movies on demand, are one of the many possibilities under examination.

IN THE FIELD OF EARTH OBSERVATION

FIRE MONITORING

With the effects of climate change many areas are sensitive to increased temperatures and are under risk of considerable and devastating fires (e.g., California in 2009). Earlier detection can result in very considerable savings in this field.

URBAN PLANNING RISK ASSESSMENT

Many areas are exposed to higher flooding and other risks, which can be better assessed from space by long-term observations. Also here, better planning can decrease remedial costs.

IN THE FIELD OF NAVIGATION

ROAD USER CHARGING

We can easily relate this aspect to an increased awareness of carbon cycle issues. Better tracking of individual road users will improve the relation and fairness between the costs associated with this versus the direct originators of these costs.

CAR/TRUCK NAVIGATION

Even if many proposals are made there is no direct solution to eliminate transport in the vicinity of and inside towns. What can be done with better navigation systems is to reduce the number of kilometers covered and reduce the number of traffic jams. This will not only reduce cost but certainly also pollution.

IN THE FIELD OF SPACE TRAVEL

SUBORBITAL SPACE TRAVEL

Whereas we immediately think in this context of space tourism, there are logic commercial markets that can evolve from this. The first one is evidently point-to-point (P2P) suborbital travel, where we can already start considering Concorde-like business models, as well as the transport of very time-sensitive cargo (e.g., organs for transplants).

ORBITAL SPACE TRAVEL

Suborbital space tourism will be limited in microgravity exposure and therefore will be restrained as a niche market. Even if it offers more challenges, adventure tourism products will stimulate this market.

In previous forecasts it has been noted that some of these proposed fields will not fully develop, knowledge of space capabilities has evolved in a way that aforementioned areas now seem feasible.

As shown previously in terms of workforce demand, space based infrastructure, admittedly technologically the most noble, is by far not the only market that will be considered. Indeed, some 30% of the space sector's activities are highly visible (human spaceflight, civil and military projects) and catch the majority of the attention from the media. The largest activity, commercial systems and services, remains unknown to the general public.[14] For example, based upon the 2008 Euroconsult figures, telecommunications services are estimated to be more than one order of magnitude bigger ($73B) than the space segment of the telecommunication market ($6.3B).

One of the major problems in space commercialization has been overemphasis on new products, with less emphasis on the other marketing elements like price, promotion and physical distribution. This stems from the space heritage described before inherent to a nonprofit way of thinking, with a dominance of technical leadership.

The New Space economy will need to get used to thinking in terms of attainable markets rather than in terms of total markets (a typical mistake in many business plans).

The Total Available Market (TAM) is the starting point of each qualitative analysis, and takes into account latent demand. However, due to economic and demographic reasons only a part of this market can be addressed, sometimes only a small fraction. We call this the Addressable Market.

In this Addressable Market, each company can achieve a market share, due to competition (we are excluding here monopolistic or oligopolistic markets), which is the Achievable Market.

IN OTHER WORDS
Achievable Market = S1.S2.TAM

WHEREBY:
S1 = the share of the market that can be addressed due to economic or demographic constraints,
S2 = the market share, taking into account competition.
TAM = the Total Available Market

The Achievable Market is therefore in general a much smaller portion of the TAM than many assume, as the first reduction factor (S1) is often ignored.

This is becoming more and more important in view of the more global economy than decades ago. Nevertheless, most companies cannot permit themselves to be present globally and therefore need to make a choice which geographical market they wish to penetrate. One of the aspects that should be considered here is the need to forecast new potential geographical markets.

With fierce competition in western countries, many companies are seeking expansion in the direction of the so-called BRIC countries. BRIC stands for Brazil, Russia, India and China, these countries are often grouped, as it is not clear which of them will have the fastest growth, but surely they are fast growing as a group.

Research teams[15] have identified a new series of countries as the next group of emerging countries, namely (in alphabetic order) Bangladesh, Egypt, Indonesia, Iran, Korea, Mexico, Nigeria, Pakistan, the Philippines, Turkey and Vietnam. This group of countries is labeled as the N-11 (Next 11).

The selection of this group was made on the basis of present performance and Growth Environment Scores (GES), based upon measurable parameters, namely:

1. Macroeconomic stability (inflation, governmental deficit, external debt)
2. Macroeconomic conditions (investment rates, trade openness)
3. Human Capital (education, demography)
4. Political environment (political stability, rule of law, corruption)
5. Technology level (penetration of telephones, internet and PCs)

From these 13 parameters a score is calculated which led to the group of aforementioned 11 countries. Note that leading this group, in order of ranking scores are Korea, Mexico and Vietnam.

Some extrapolations show that for 2050[16] [p. 134]:

1. The N-11 aggregate GDP could reach 2/3rd the size of the G7 by 2050.
2. The shift driving the rising BRIC countries could at the same time shift economic trading towards Asia and therefore additionally stimulate some of the N-11 countries in the region.
3. Incremental new demand from the N-11 could conceivably be twice the G7 demand by 2050.

In terms of space activities the N-11 expected growth after 2040 may lead to a share of these countries reaching the 10% space market range even before 2050.

Many analysts have started to work in this direction and early evaluations are being made on how to explore cooperation not only with the BRIC countries but also with these new emerging N-11 partners.[17] Many of the space programs in some of these countries were less visible until first launches and satellites became publicly known. This is in particular the case for the ambitious space programs of Iran and North Korea, which are now gradually being unveiled.[18]

BORDERS OF THE NEW SPACE ECONOMY

Early in this article it was stated that one of the important aspects of space projects is often large initial investments and resulting long payback times. It is often rather difficult to find large amounts of money, in particular at a stage before the equity break-even point is reached.

Debt financing in the aftermath of the financial crisis is quasi impossible for projects outside the vested space application areas like telecommunications and possibly some early navigation applications. There is no doubt that with the increased risk-aversion over the last few years this situation will not improve, as was discussed at a workshop at The International Institute for Space Commerce (IISC).[19]

Besides the purely financial aspects we shall not forget another important aspect of space, namely the scientific and social dimension.

Many space projects do not have a direct economic return but are very important for humanity in general. Most of these are only made possible with government support and, in particular in the present period of increasing climate driven disasters, are saving thousands of lives.

JUST TO QUOTE SOME EXAMPLES[20]

1. In 2008, 214 million people were affected by natural disasters, with 235,000 casualties and a cost close to $200B. Without good space based meteorological forecasts and effective disaster management the number of casualties would have been considerably higher.

2. The international Cospar Sarsat system provides distress alerts and location data to help search and rescue authorities assist persons in distress. Since the beginning of its operation in September 1982 the system provided alerts leading to the rescue of almost 30,000 persons.

It is interesting to note that at the moment when early privatization plans were announced many authors have pointed out that even in the commercial telecommunication sector there should be room for making resources available in case of a disaster on a priority basis. Early warnings were voiced before the privatization plans of Intelsat and Inmarsat took place[21] and the mechanisms to make such resources available have been discussed in many studies, discussing also the expansion of the present International Charter on Space and Major Disasters.[22]

Recent works on space and commerce are paying increasingly attention to this synergy, whereby the space technologies and space applications are used as a starting point but peripheral areas such as social, philosophical and even artistic aspects are no longer ignored and clearly emphasized.[23]

It is therefore evident that there is no reason to see public funded space activities and commercial space as competitors. Let us think for example about questions of major importance such as:

1. What happened on Mars and what can we learn from it?
2. Is Mars terraforming possible in case we need to leave Earth?
3. How can we protect ourselves against impacts of major celestial bodies that can threaten our existence?
4. And many others related to the origin of life and the universe.

These can only be evaluated and researched by publicly funded, international projects due to the high investment costs with no associated direct financial returns.

One way of distinguishing between different funding sources may be to look at both the financial as well as the social dimension.[24] We can then conclude that there are 4 quadrants, as depicted in Figure 5.

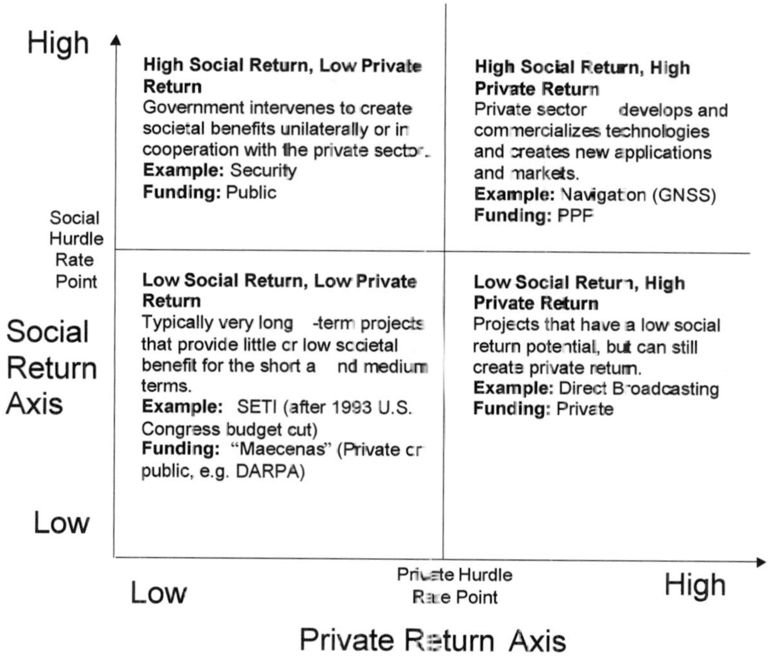

High

High Social Return, Low Private Return	High Social Return, High Private Return
Government intervenes to create societal benefits unilaterally or in cooperation with the private sector. **Example:** Security **Funding:** Public	Private sector develops and commercializes technologies and creates new applications and markets. **Example:** Navigation (GNSS) **Funding:** PPP

Social Hurdle Rate Point

Low Social Return, Low Private Return	Low Social Return, High Private Return
Typically very long -term projects that provide little or low societal benefit for the short a nd medium terms. **Example:** SETI (after 1993 U.S. Congress budget cut) **Funding:** "Maecenas" (Private or public, e.g. DARPA)	Projects that have a low social return potential, but can still create private return. **Example:** Direct Broadcasting **Funding:** Private

Social Return Axis

Low

Low   Private Hurdle Rate Point   High

Private Return Axis

Figure 5
Distinction between public and commercial markets.[24]

It is evident that it is not as simple to calculate a social hurdle rate as a financial one, which is often based upon the Internal Rate of Return. Nevertheless, Figure 5 shows clearly that a number of projects with high level of social return but very low financial return still have a raison d'être and can probably only be financed via public funding due to the aforementioned lack of direct economic return.

The New Space sector has many fields to expand, and with more financial robustness there will be more willingness to enter into areas where an economic return is possibly not to be gained in the short term. However, the limits shall also be considered and part of space exploration, due to its nature, will remain a public endeavor. Most important in this context is that both parties recognize and respect these mutual boundary conditions.

CONCLUSION

The space sector originated from a political environment and therefore has less commercial legacy than many other sectors. As in the case of many nonprofit endeavors there has been a strong technological domination with equally strong emphasis on the product side of the marketing mix.

Although most space companies have separated themselves from direct public governance, such technological behavior is still strongly present in the company culture. A 'Merchant' type of attitude will be required to fully develop the potential of the new Space Economy.

In order to do so, the space sector will need to recruit new manpower with undoubtedly a technical oriented background or passion, but also with a more business oriented attitude. It is worthwhile to mention here that, based upon surveys; the European space sector still faces challenges in finding the right skill set when it comes to manpower. Indeed, the aforementioned survey [11] showed that:

1. Nearly 50 % of the space companies in Europe still have unfilled positions and difficulties in finding the right applicants.
2. Communication skills are the soft skill quoted most frequently for failing recruitment interviews.
3. Besides engineering skills, there is an increasing demand for combination of engineering/science backgrounds with business degrees.

With the prerequisites of company culture adaptation and a new workforce fulfilled, the opening of new space markets will require a more commercial approach. There are still many new space based markets to be developed, mainly in the value chain of applications. Moreover, the present shifts in economic power will also require rethinking strategies which are presently very focused on trading with traditional space powers. Beyond the BRIC countries it will be useful to start considering also the N-11 countries as potential customers, the next generation of emerging space nations.

However, space is still the 'Final Frontier' for humanity, and therefore it also needs further development of knowledge and scientific discoveries. As these elements are not compatible with economic return in the short, even mid-term future, hence there will still be for many decades the need to continue government-funded projects. If the principle is maintained that each sector that is commercially viable is gradually taken over by industry, both worlds will be able to co-exist in full harmony.

•••

WALTER PEETERS, PH.D.

Walter Peeters is Dean and Vice President for Academic Affairs at International Space University (ISU) and Director of The International Institute of Space Commerce (IISC).

Following initial management positions in the construction and petrochemical industries, he joined the European Space Agency (ESA) in 1983 in a number of project control and management functions, among others in the HERMES project in Toulouse, France. Since 1980, he has been involved in astronaut activities as Head of the Coordination Office of the European Astronaut Center in Cologne, with strong involvement in the EUROMIR missions. He joined ISU in 2000, after serving as visiting professor (Non-profit Marketing) at the University of Louvain, Belgium. He was nominated as Dean of ISU in 2005.

He is the author of articles on incentive contracting, project management, space commercialization and organization in the space sector, and wrote the book *Space Marketing* (Kluwer, 2000). Recent research has focused on space commercialization, financing models of space projects and space tourism. He is a contributor to various organizations in the area of space commercialization (Working Group 2000, JAXA, OECD, IAC, IBA, EC).

Recent consultancy assignments include Space Policy (Luxemburg, Estonia), and Space Tourism (Singapore spaceport, Gallactic Suite, Excalibur)

He earned bachelor's degrees in engineering and applied economics at the Catholic University of Louvain, Master of Business Administration at Louvain, and Cornell University, and acquired a Ph.D. degree in Industrial Organization at TU Delft, the Netherlands.

REFERENCES

1. Holley, W., *Ideas and Weapons* (Yale University Press, 1998), p.29.
2. Peeters W., From Suborbital Space Tourism to Commercial Personal Spaceflight, *Acta Astronautica*, 2010. (under publication)
3. Goodrich, J., *The Commercialisation of Outer Space.* (Quorum Books, New York, 1989)
4. Peeters, W., *Space Marketing* (Kluwer, Dordrecht, 2000).
5. Handberg, R., *International Space Commerce,* (University Press of Florida, Gainesville, 2006)
6. Anthony, R. and Young, D. *Management Control in Nonprofit Organizations* (7th ed.) (McGraw-Hill, 2002).
7. Pace, S., *Merchants and Guardians, Balancing U.S. Interests in Global Space Commerce.* Editors: Logsdon, J. and Acker, R. (GWU, Washington, 1999)
8. Moenaert, R. et al., R&D Marketing Integration Mechanisms, Communication Flows and Innovation Successes, *Journal of Product Innovation Management*, 11, (1994) pp. 31-45.
9. Contant, C., The Space Policy Summit, *Space Policy*, 19 (2003): 63-65.
10. ESF, *Demography of European Space Science*, (ESF, Strasbourg, 2003).
11. Doule, O. and Peeters, W., Workforce Policy in the European Space Sector, *Astropolitics*, vol. 7(3), (2009), pp.193-205.
12. See www.isunet.edu
13. [OECD, *Space 2030* (OECD, Paris, 2005)
14. Grimard, M., Is Space Schyzophrenic? *Paper presented at ISU's 14th Annual International Symposium,* (ISU, Strasbourg, February 2010).
15. Goldman-Sachs, *BRICs and Beyond* (Book, November 2007), available under www.goldmansachs.com
16. Goldman-Sachs, *Dreaming with BRICs : The Path to 2050* (Global Economics Paper No 99, Oct. 2003), available under www.goldmansachs.com
17. Peter, N. and Stoffl, K., Global Space Exploration 2025. Europe's perspectives for partnership. *Space Policy* Vol25 (1), (Feb 2009), pp. 29-36.
18. Harvey, B., Smid, H., and Pirard, T., *Emerging Space Powers. The New Space Programs of Asia, the Middle East and South America*, (Springer, Berlin, 2010)
19. IISC, *The Influence of the Financial Crisis Aftermath on Space Financing* (IISC, Isle of Man, 2009), see www.iisc.im.
20. Wagner, A. and Grimard, M., Spacenomics, *Paper presented at ISU's 14th Annual International Symposium*, (ISU, Strasbourg, February 2010).
21. Frieden, R., Should Intelsat and Inmarsat Privatize? *Telecommunications Policy* vol.18 (9), (Dec. 1994), pp 697-686.
22. ISU, *Disaster Risk and Evaluation And Management* (Team project, ISU SSP 2009), available at www.isunet.edu.
23. Olla, P., *Commerce in Space*, (Information Science Reference, New York, 2008)
24. Peeters, W., Gürtuna, O. and Hachem, A., *Classifying and Evaluating Space Projects: A Unified Method For Estimating Social and Private Returns*, (Proceedings of RAST Conference, Istanbul, 2005).

CHAPTER 4

ENTREPRENEURIAL NICHE MARKETS
FOUR CASE STUDIES ON THE DEVELOPMENT OF SPACE COMMERCE

TOM TAYLOR
LUNAR TRANSPORTATION SYSTEMS, INC.

AND

WALTER P. KISTLER AND BOB CITRON
LUNAR TRANSPORTATION SYSTEMS, INC.

INTRODUCTION

Throughout history, trade routes have emerged to serve those pursuing commerce in all its many forms, from the recovery of value from natural resources, to tourism, to manufacturing and agriculture, to migration and exploration. Specialized markets, or niche markets, inevitably develop along trade routes to take advantage of specific conditions and to meet the specific needs that exist there.

During the last thirty years, space commerce has emerged as a commercial reality at various orbital altitudes around Earth, and it too, is conducted along the trade routes that lead to various Earth orbits, along the highway between Earth and the surface of the moon. Space commerce to date has certainly occurred within niche markets, and capturing such a niche market in today's very limited commercial space business usually requires very specialized innovative hardware, as well as an innovative business concept.

This chapter discusses four startup ventures that address 'niche' markets and products in space. We discuss how each started with a business model concept, raised risk capital in various stages (which is sometimes referred to as 'smoke and mirrors'), used its core innovation effectively to produce a profit, protected it with patents and other means, and eventually how a small team of varying talents survived the startup venture environment and absorbed some lessons learned.

1. Since its founding in 1983 by Bob Citron, and with early funding by Walter Kistler, SPACEHAB,[2,3] has created and operated a commercial microgravity module in the space shuttle. The company has progressed through the entire cycle of development, from an entrepreneurial commercial space company to a viable commercial space company that changed its name to Astrotech in 2009, stock symbol ASTC.

2. SPACEHAB raised more than $105M in capital, built two modules in Italy, has flown its module and other company hardware on 24 Space Shuttle missions, and has earned more than a billion in revenues from NASA and commercial customers.

3. GLOBAL OUTPOST was founded in 1988,[4] and proposed to NASA that the external fuel tank of the Space Shuttle could be salvaged and reused. After winning a NASA External Tank Solicitation in the 1980s, (1988) the company confirmed the technical feasibility of its concept by hiring the fuel tank manufacturer Martin Marietta Aerospace, (Michoud Advanced Programs group) in 1988 to conduct the necessary Salvage study. The company received a letter from NASA on February 19, 1993 confirming technical feasibility. The salvage concept used the space shuttle to attach a propulsion control package to the ET in orbit and the reboost of the salvaged ET 5 times for an orbital life of ~55 years at a cost of ~$200M.

4. The Kistler Aerospace Corporation was started in 1993 by Walter Kistler and Bob Citron and almost created an innovative, fully reusable launch vehicle (RLV) with traditional aerospace equity partners and $860M in private capital and $40M of NASA funding. Originally designed to offer affordable launch for replacement satellites for Teledesic and other emerging space

based cell phone networks, which were to dominate the emerging cell phone market. One other mission for the fully reusable launch vehicle, called the K-1, was to reduce the salvage cost of the ET to ~ $40M. The company raised over $900M in mostly private Equity Risk Money and built launch hardware in partnership with traditional aerospace organizations.[5,6]

5. Lunar Transportation Systems, Inc. was started in 2004, and intends to support lunar resource recovery operations to permit NASA to move on to Mars and beyond without being slowed down with the necessity of continuing support for lunar exploration operations.[7,8]

Each of these companies addressed a niche market, had a strong technical and managerial startup team, raised money, partnered with traditional aerospace companies to achieve its own operational and business goals, and pursued cooperation with NASA. In this chapter we will describe them in detail, and explore what happened and what can be learned by other would-be entrepreneurs.

TERMINOLOGY USED IN THIS CHAPTER

ET - External tank in a variety of upgrades to 138 ETs over a 40 year history, not reusable

SPAB - SPACEHAB, INC. stock symbol (SPAB), recently changed name to Astrotech (ASTC)

GOI - GLOBAL OUTPOST, Inc

KAC - Kistler Aerospace Corporation

LTS - Lunar Transportation Systems, Inc.

NSTS - National Space Transportation System, including SRBs, ET, Orbiter and launch facilities

SRB - Solid Rocket Booster

Shuttle - The reusable fly back orbiter vehicle of NSTS

BTF - Basic transportation frame, used in four versions of the LTS vehicles

NICHE MARKETS IN SPACE

This is a special time in our species' history, an era in which we begin to move off the home planet and seek opportunities and livelihoods elsewhere in space. With the potential for economic value to be derived from available resources, private investors can and will support high-risk, niche-market ventures that have the potential for appropriate return on investment.

These niche markets[1] in space will likely develop in ways that are similar to how they have developed on Earth, along early commercial trade routes that emerge in the course of exploration beyond Earth. These niche markets will be the foundations upon which entrepreneurs will build businesses capable of raising the risk capital needed to build aerospace hardware, or provide services that in the end will earn profits and generate a return for investors.

This is a very different business scenario than the one that has predominated in the space industry for the last half century, the one in which aerospace companies supplied hardware to NASA for its science and exploration activities on behalf of the taxpayer-customer. As NASA refocuses on a new space mission, development of space commerce is properly falling to private sector.

In the current environment, new startup ventures for space commerce are likely to require specialized and often very innovative hardware to function in the very demanding rigors of space. The entrepreneurs themselves may sometimes create this hardware, or it may be designed and fabricated by traditional aerospace companies, or by new, emerging ones that are formed to exploit this new niche.

To launch such a business successfully, a good entrepreneurial startup team is essential. Unless one of the founders is already wealthy (as is the case with a number of today's emerging commercial ventures, such as SpaceX) the entrepreneurs will have to raise capital.

From the perspective of venture investor, the quality and experience of the management of the team will be more important that the actual concept or business model itself, as most venture capitalists would prefer to back a 'second rate idea developed by a first rate startup team' than the reverse. The reasoning is that a first rate team can always improve its ideas, but a second rate team may not be able to do so.

SPACEHAB, INC.

The SPACEHAB Module is carried in the Space Shuttle payload bay, and provides a microgravity experiment capability for $2M in Mid-Deck Lockers within a pressurized volume.[9, 10]

A mid-deck locker is a storage module, originally designed to contain an astronaut's toothpaste, accessories and clothing on the Space Shuttle. Some early, battery powered research experiments were also stored in these lockers, operated by the astronauts in the mid-deck volume below the pilot's flight deck.

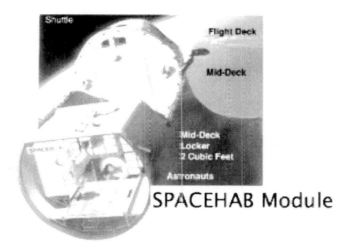

Figure 1
The Mid-Deck Pressurized Module in the Space Shuttle offering Microgravity Research Capability in space at 1/10th the previous Customer Cost.

Figure 2
The SPACEHAB Module in late 1980s with Chet Lee, former President, left, Walter Kistler, early investor, and Tom Taylor, co-inventor, at the SPACEHAB Florida Facility. Photo by Bob Citron.

The SPACEHAB innovation was to expand the capability to more than 60 additional mid-deck experiments in a small, pressurized module located in the Space Shuttle payload bay. SPACEHAB provided additional electrical power, a container for the researcher's experiment and communications plus additional support supplied by the company in cooperation with NASA. An initial $400M NASA Contract for 200 Mid-Deck lockers with a lease arrangement for shuttle transportation allowed low cost access to microgravity for commercial and government researchers around the world. Not only was the cooperation between NASA and the private SPACEHAB company innovative, but the resulting cost was also an order of magnitude less for commercial customers and NASA researchers.

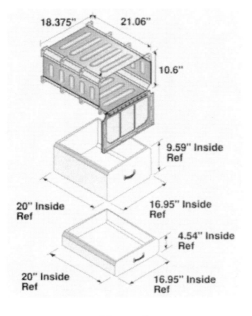

Figure 3
The mid-deck locker.

THE BUSINESS CONCEPT

The Business Concept was to provide a commercial service module in low earth orbit consisting of plug-in Mid-Deck volumes of 2 cubic feet. It was manned and supplied with power, communications, and microgravity.

The SPACEHAB module enabled ~2,000 early microgravity researchers to get a head start on their access to space in the shuttle payload bay and to quickly repeat and refine experiments using the same hardware on future shuttle launches leading to the Space Station.

The unique features included an order of magnitude reduction in cost compared with a similar Spacelab Module in the shuttle offering the same access to microgravity. The SPACEHAB Module was built for one-ninth the cost of traditional aerospace hardware, as documented by Price Waterhouse.[11]

Figure 1 depicts a SPACEHAB Module in orbit with astronauts working with experiments in microgravity in orbit.

Figure 2 shows Chet Lee, former President of SPACEHAB, Walter Kistler, and Tom Taylor. Early investor Bob Citron and Tom Taylor were co-inventors of the module in U.S. Patent.

THE LESSONS LEARNED

1. The early SPACEHAB Module concept was exhibited at 12 International Aerospace Conferences and became known within the global aerospace industry, but global recognition of the concept was less important than its innovative design, unique approach to cost reduction and fabrication progress in Torino, Italy.

2. Offers to buy the company were received from major aerospace companies, but an assessment of the value of the future market was difficult for both sides. Meanwhile, a larger firm wanted to buy the startup company at a low price, while the entrepreneurs wanted a fair price based on the future value they expected.

   a. The discussions broke down after 8 months.
   b. At the time, the entrepreneurial team was operating in a plant owned by the larger firm, so the firm simply kicked the entrepreneurs out.
   c. The larger firm also put a team of about 30 engineers on a project to replicate the SPACEHAB concept, but later stopped when they apparently realized that SPACEHAB had filed for a U.S. Patent.
   d. The larger firm also faced a bad public relations scenario.

3. SPACEHAB then requested other American aerospace companies to build the two 10' long modules, but were rejected because it was believed that a big ISS Module Contract was about to be released by NASA, and none of the major firms wanted to risk losing an opportunity to bid on a huge NASA contract if that had already accepted the smaller contract from SPACEHAB. American designers and major aerospace fabricators probably still fear that working for or with entrepreneurs may reduce their opportunities to win large government contracts.

4. SPACEHAB then looked internationally for help, and settled on Aeritalia, a Torino, Italy based contractor (to avoid confusion with the airline Alitalia, Aeritalia was later renamed Alenia Spazio). One member of the SPACEHAB team had previously worked with Aeritalia. Earlier, Aeritalia produced the ESA Spacelab Module pressure shell, and subsequently produced two SPACEHAB modules (with some technical help from McDonnell Douglas) at a cost to SPACEHAB of $105M.

5. During the course of about 200 marketing meetings and events, SPACEHAB was offered as a less expensive alternative, but this could not be proven until SPACEHAB was actually in operation.

    a. This market-based business model is very different from how NASA operates. In NASA's model, aerospace firms are paid to do Phase A through Phase D design and engineering contracts to define the hardware that they will later bid on to manufacture.
    b. Through this process innovation (including cost reduction) is a negative inducement, and hence a cause of high hardware and operations costs.

6. The commercial SPACEHAB Module was required to be a truncated circular shell design to permit astronauts the capability of latching the payload bay doors in orbit should the automatic door latches failed to work. The full circular ESA-supplied Spacelab Modules had a NASA safety waiver unable to be obtained by an American entrepreneurial company. The European Space Agency financed and fabricated the Spacelab Module and the related equipment was given to NASA free in exchange for access to the Space Shuttle services. The truncated SPACEHAB module was more expensive, but stimulated other innovations including experiment windows that looked into space from the flat top and allowed Mid-Deck lockers to be prepared, attached, and integrated cost effectively on the ground.

7. SPACEHAB pioneered many enhancements to NASA's two-cubic-foot mid-deck locker volume to draw researchers in with a 10-fold decrease in cost for a 'microgravity research' volume in the shuttle. SPACEHAB provided electrical and other services, while NASA provided some astronaut assistance on orbit.

8. Mid-deck lockers in the shuttle were priced at $2M each. Transferring them to ISS raised the price to approximately $5M, and required changing the mid-deck volume to fit into a Space Station rack, which in most cases excluded relaunching the ~2,000 previous fabricated research hardware inserts that were

fitted to the mid-deck units. This unfortunately meant that customer-fabricated research hardware was less able to fit in the new volumes.

9. SPACEHAB's stock price rose from 5 cents per share to nearly $15 per share over a decade. (This 300 times increase in the stockholders' original investment is the reason that venture capitalists invest in startups.) Private investors were able to recover their investment plus a significant gain. In an understated way, this suggests that opportunities for wealth enhancement for private investors are available in the commercial space industry.

10. This shows that a relatively non-technical entrepreneurial startup team can enter the technical aerospace industry, use private funds, hire others to design and fabricate the hardware, and create a successful commercial business at a significantly lower cost (an order of magnitude) than NASA.

11. A significant portion of the cost reduction resulted from the ability of SPACEHAB to hire about 150 of the NASA staff and subcontractors who were needed to perform the work.

   a. By comparison, NASA required a staff of about 1350 to manage Spacelab Module flights, although it should be noted that Spacelab was three times larger, 30' long, and filled the payload bay completely, while SPACEHAB was 10' long.

   b. The 10' long SPACEHAB Module allowed NASA to cost effectively use the remaining shuttle payload bay for other payloads.

   c. With the order-of-magnitude cost reduction available in a previously non-commercial environment, other things also occurred. This new, lower cost level allowed NASA to spend the money saved (90% of the previous cost) to use the commercial SPACEHAB Module service on other NASA project, which increased the overall level of activity in microgravity research funded by NASA.

   d. On the commercial side, the cost reduction of a mid-deck locker space from $20M per locker to $2M per locker stimulated the rental of about 2,000 mid-deck lockers, with many flown multiple times because of the additional benefit of more frequent repeat flights. This stimulated researchers to explore what might happen in a new environment like microgravity, which tends to be a 'research the unknown, fly a little, learn from it' environment.

The early SPACEHAB experiments focused on pioneering research to explore a different gravity and its effects on all basic science laws and on basic industrial processes. Purely commercial researchers explored proprietary innovation, mostly without peer review, and were able to uncover a variety of new phenomena in every field, from combustion science to protein crystal growth. Some researchers explored new solar cells capable of being produced from lunar materials to how best communicate between the researchers on the ground to the astronauts in space helping the experiment. A Google search for the term 'spacehab experiments' provided 65,500 results.

STS-77 in March 1996 included a Crystal Growth by Liquid-Liquid Diffusion investigation that was intended to grow protein crystals by diffusing one liquid into another; and a National Institutes of Health-C7 (NIH-C7) experiment to evaluate the effects of space flight on muscle and bone cells from chicken embryos. Kyser Thebe, an Austrian startup firm and later a successful customer of SPACEHAB, indicated that the reduced cost to the customer was a major economic driver in the growth of their space business and the success of their company.

The transfer of the mid-deck locker research projects to ISS raised the price to the customer because the dimensions of the container changed, which forced additional cost onto customers. While cost to the research customer is a huge issue for small and medium sized research organizations, it is sometimes ignored in government facilities where cost growth is treated differently, but it is the small and medium organizations that are usually the most innovative.

> *(Editor's note:* Please see Chapter 8, *An Open Source, Standardized Research Platform for the International Space Station* for additional discussion of the mid-deck locker.)

GLOBAL OUTPOST, INC.

The External Tank (ET) of the Space Shuttle achieves about 99% of full orbital velocity, before being jettisoned and forced back into the atmosphere where most of it burns up upon re-entry. The ET is about 20% by weight and some of its thicker aluminum alloy components fall into an ocean disposal area north west of Hawaii.

THE BUSINESS CONCEPT

The proposed GLOBAL OUTPOST, Inc. (GOI) Business Concept calls for preserving the External Tank after launch, taking the ET into orbit, and salvaging it for other uses in space.

To get the shuttle near to orbital altitude, each ET (weighing 58,000 lbs empty) has invested transportation energy in it, and this investment can have value if a productive use for the ET can be found in orbit.

How much value does the salvaged ET in space have, and what is the cost to salvage it? GLOBAL OUTPOST submitted a proposal, and was one of three winners in a Reagan Administration 1988 NASA Solicitation focused on the ET in space.[12, 13,14,15]

One winner dropped out almost immediately, while the other two placed cash deposits for five ETs transported free to orbit by the space shuttle.

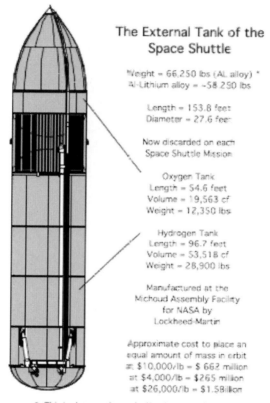

The External Tank of the
Space Shuttle

Weight ~ 66,250 lbs (AL alloy) *
Al-Lithium alloy = ~58,290 lbs

Length = 153.8 feet
Diameter = 27.6 feet

Now discarded on each
Space Shuttle Mission

Oxygen Tank
Length = 54.6 feet
Volume = 19,563 cf
Weight = 12,350 lbs

Hydrogen Tank
Length = 96.7 feet
Volume = 53,518 cf
Weight = 28,900 lbs

Manufactured at the
Michoud Assembly Facility
for NASA by
Lockheed-Martin

Approximate cost to place an
equal amount of mass in orbit
at $10,000/lb = $ 662 million
at $4,000/lb = $265 million
at $26,000/lb = $1.58 billion

* This is data on the early Aluminum version and the
Aluminum-Lithium version saving ~ 8,000 pounds

Figure 4
The External Tank technical information is the latest of a series of upgrades and design changes over the series of ~130 each External Tanks fabricated at the NASA Michoud Assembly Facility near New Orleans.

One example of ET use is a shown in Fig.4. In this scenario, the ET jettisons the Aft Cargo Compartment (ACC) Shroud at an appropriate time on ascent, and the ET is salvaged in orbit.

The 100' long Liquid Hydrogen tanks are joined with a 25' diameter connector ACC module to form a 300' diameter ring, and provide a partial gravity 25' diameter torus volume for living on long trips in space.

This is one of the few modifications to the ET design that would be required.

The Liquid Oxygen tanks are used for utility purposes at each node, but are not shown.

The 10 (each) Liquid Hydrogen tanks near the center of the Torus provide 100' long 'flying Volumes' 25' in diameter with trampolines at each end.

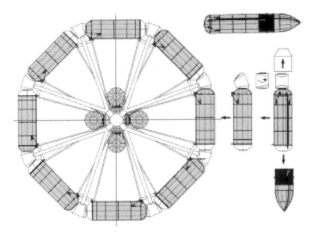

Figure 5
The eighteen ET Torus is capable of rotating at 2-3 RPM to provide ~ 1/5th Earth Gravity and 10 each center 100' long free flying volumes with Trampolines at each end.

GLOBAL OUTPOST hired the ET fabricator, Martin Marietta Aerospace (MMA), Advanced Programs Group at the Michoud Assembly Facility to assist in the technical confirmation of proposed ET salvage concept.   The design called for a change in the operational software sequence that controlled the separation of the ET from the orbiter, delaying separation until the orbiter was in orbit. A simulation run at NASA-JSC run by astronauts was successful and confirmed the salvage and separation software delay could be accomplished.

The salvage mission required using a portion of the orbiter payload bay to transport a reboost package and place it on the ET before separation to ensure that the ET did not re-enter the Earth's atmosphere in an uncontrolled manner. The NASA ET reboost package solution cost $200M and used the shuttle robot arm to place a propulsion device on the ET for reboosting the ET orbit.

The reboost package supported a 55-year life for the ET in orbit, reboosting it periodically to raise the ET orbit at intervals to provide orbital make-up.

A 1988 Global Outpost NASA Enabling Agreement, now in Revision 3 was signed; GOI placed a cash deposit with NASA for five ETs in orbit, and MMA assisted GOI in extensive technical discussions with NASA HQ and NASA-JSC. GOI paid MMA and NASA-JSC to review the technical procedures and salvage mission, and received a letter dated 19 Feb 1993 which stated the NASA-JSC *"appears technically feasible"* and *"the ET salvage mission was technically acceptable."*[16].

Figure 6
The interior of the ET is 27.6'. The interior padding is shown on the right is by Space Island Group.

THE STARTUP PHASE

The startup phase for GLOBAL OUTPOST, Inc. (GOI) involved raising capital from 32 private investors, placing a cash deposit with NASA, and discussions and marketing studies with potential customers and support organizations including SDIO, DOE, the Russian TOPAZ II reactor organization, (The Kurchatoff Institute of Atomic Energy), University of Maryland (MIPS) research grant program, as well as commercial customers including Space Island Group, Japanese organizations and others.

Many customers were interested, but few could afford the $200M salvage operations cost.[17] The opportunity for salvage may still exist, and the GOI President became the first employee in an entrepreneurial startup team called the Kistler Aerospace Corporation creating a reusable launch vehicle that could potentially reduce the cost of ET salvage to ~$40M.

THE LESSONS LEARNED

The process revealed that customers who liked the ET concept, and had uses in orbit for the ET, did not have the money to pay for salvaging it.

Other solutions could get the cost down to $40M with a Kistler Aerospace K-1 Reusable Launch Vehicle or other rockets. Figure 4 depicts one innovation possible with ET salvage by taking the 100' long LOH tank and combining it with an Aft Cargo Carrier (ACC) launched connector module to create a partial gravity torus, ~ 300' spun at 2-3 RPMs could produce ~20% of Earth's gravity and become a standard transport volume for humans to explore the universe and use as nodes around a variety of planets and moons.

With passenger transport, an [18] ET Torus Facility in orbit could be profitable, given the possible extension of the shuttle and the ability to salvage future ETs. The long-term artificial gravity might be helpful to NASA in creating larger crewed vehicles with a reusable design for exploring and homesteading our solar system.

The real commercial market pull is the commercial tourist transportation for passengers to and from the Torus location and could evolve into a huge Earth to Orbit commercial transportation industry within the next decade.

The saving of money on space projects was ahead of its time in the 1980s and 1990s. Few in the traditional aerospace environment were concerned about cost to the customer. Space commerce, even with cost reduction innovation, was still too expensive for those interested in mankind's movement off planet in numbers beyond a few NASA astronauts. Given the potential extension of the shuttle use beyond 2010, the ET innovation may still be possible.

The ET inside volume is difficult to imagine, but Figure 5 depicts a 20'section of the 27.6' diameter ET interior.

KISTLER AEROSPACE CORPORATION

Walter Kistler and Bob Citron founded Kistler Aerospace Corporation in 1993. Tom Taylor was hired as the first employee, so Tom and his family moved to Las Cruces, NM to prepare to use the White Sands Missile Range for launching a fully reusable launch vehicle (RLV) and in the process became the first customer to express interest in the commercial spaceport later called Spaceport America.

KAC participated in the Environment Impact Studies for the spaceport, and attended to answer some early town meeting questions from ranchers concerned about potential damage to their cattle.

THE BUSINESS CONCEPT

The Business Concept, invented by Walter Kistler, is a fully reusable launch vehicle that consumes propellant, but does not destroy the rocket in the launch process. The first stage rocket called the Launch Assist Platform (LAP) boosts the orbiter stage to 138k feet and separates to propel the first stage return back toward the original launch site. The first stage lands 5-10 minutes later at the original launch site, using large parachutes that deploy at about 70,000 feet to reduce the re-entry velocity, and air bags to reduce ground impact.

Burt Rutan of Scaled Composites (now famous as the designer and builder of the Virgin Galactic spacecraft system) was an early subcontractor on the KAC Project, and built several early innovative hardware items.

Figure 7
The 150' long K-1 RLV rolls out from a horizontal processing building on right on rails to be tilted upright and loaded with propellants.

After the first stage lands it is transported in the horizontal position into a preparation building to prepare for the next launch.

The orbiter stage continues to orbit and delivers its payload, and then goes to 'sleep' until the Earth turns a full 24 hour rotation to permit landing at the same launch site on the same orbital inclination trajectory. The orbiter stage also lands with parachutes and airbags at the original launch site.

New payloads are then fastened to the orbiter with eight bolts, and the 150' long mated K-1 RLV rolls out to the launch pad on rails to be tilted up for fueling and launch.

Fig. 6 shows the resulting design.

THE STARTUP PHASE

The startup phase continued from 1993 to 2005 with the firm raising money, and hiring design and fabrication work from traditional aerospace contractors, including Northrop Grumman, Aerojet, Lockheed Martin, Draper Labs, Irvin Aerospace and others.

Reduction of cost and reusability were key production goals. Over time the design evolved to use Russian NK-33 and Nk-43 rocket engines, composite structures, aluminum cryogenic tanks, and innovative software development. The large cargo parachutes were the only major hardware component that required a new technology development and testing program, as the other major RLV components were pre-existing aerospace hardware applied in a reusable way.

The company raised a total of $860M in private equity financing without government help or customer commitment.

Figure 6 depicts the K-1 vehicle vertical at the launch site. KAC won one of the NASA's Commercial Orbital Transportation Services (COTS) demonstration program, but was unable to raise an additional $500M to complete the fabrication and the program of five test launches.

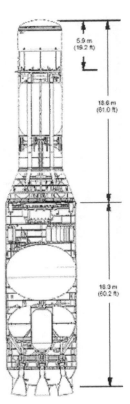

Figure 8
The RLV Costs more to build, but costs less refurbish and operate.

THE LESSONS LEARNED

1. We learned that a fully reusable launch vehicle could be built with private funds. 2 vehicles were about 75% assembled for approximately $900M.

   With an anticipated K-1 launch cost of $17M to $20M per launch carrying 12,500 lbs to low Earth orbit (LEO), success of the project would have started the space transportation industry down a path toward other launch innovations that would have significantly reduced the cost of commercial space transportation.

Assuming that the unmanned K-1 vehicle was capable of launching every two weeks after refining the turn around operations, then a fleet of five K-1s would have been capable of launching more tonnage per year than the entire rest of the market. Admittedly, the K-1 was a small-payload vehicle in the Delta II Class of expendable launchers, but reusable launch vehicles can bring cost reduction to a government supported launch industry that has steadily increased in cost over time. While the K-1 never proved the $17M launch price was achievable, such a cost was 39% of the existing the Delta II Class of expendable launcher at $70M, when compared side by side with the $17M K-1 over a 12 launch sequence as shown in Figure 5. The Delta II recently was quoted at $100M per launch.

Entrepreneurs can never entirely predict that they are going to reduce the cost of a project by an order of magnitude in a highly technical industry such as aerospace, but previous ventures, like the SPACEHAB described above, have indeed produced that kind of order of magnitude cost reduction.

Comparing Reusable Launch Vehicle & Expendable Launch Vehicle Costs

Launch	1	2	3	4	5	6	7	8	9	10	11	12
K-1 RLV						Replace parachutes			Refurb high speed parts-engines			
Vehicle Cost	250	0	0	0	0	0	4	0	0	10	0	0
Relaunch	5	5	5	5	5	5	5	5	5	5	5	5
Cumulative	255	260	265	270	275	280	289	294	299	314	319	324
Expendables			Breakeven			K-1 ahead over $500m						516
Vehicle Cost	65	65	65	65	65	65	65	65	65	65	65	65
Launch	5	5	5	5	5	5	5	5	5	5	5	5
Cumulative	70	140	210	280	350	420	490	560	630	700	770	840

Figure 9
Comparison of the costs of an RLV and a Delta II rocket in similar payload class, launching 12 each in Earth-to-orbit missions

2. It may be unfair to compare a vehicle that has not launched with one that has, but Figure 9 shows a reusable launch vehicle compared with an expendable rocket of the K-1 and Delta II Expendable Launch Vehicle class, with the following assumptions:

    a. 12 launches each
    b. K-1 frame designed for 50-100 launches
    c. Engines refurbished after 10 launches and replaced after 20

    d.   Parachutes last 7 cycles, and are then replaced at a cost of $4M.

    e.   The RLV saves $516M over the 12 launches.

Figure 7 depicts a vertical launch, but because the K-1 is processed in the horizontal position, this significantly reduces preparation time. The RLV may launch twice a month while an expendable may take 2-3 months to erect vertically on the launch pad, so the time to perform the launches is different and the time value of money is not well depicted in the above cost comparison.

3.   The RLV costs about 4-5 times more to produce than an expendable and carries components designed to be reused, which weigh more than expendable parts, but the RLV uses components that are mostly pre-tested after the first launch.

4.   It takes four launches for the cost breakeven to occur between using an RLV and an ELV in this case.

5.   The launch sites are also different, and probably cost different amounts. The simple comparison shows ~ 40% reduction in launch costs.

LUNAR TRANSPORTATION SYSTEMS, INC.

Commercial lunar transportation architecture can start small and grow as the market emerges, which is the way most breakthrough businesses develop in the private sector. Expendable transportation architecture can be the early solution for a new commercial lunar transportation system, and then evolve toward a reusable, more affordable system that will be required to support and sustain an emerging lunar commerce that will then permit NASA to move on toward exploration of Mars and beyond.

    Lunar Transportation Systems, Inc. (LTS) proposes a transportation architecture that uses 4 variations of a Basic Transportation Frame (BTF). Each frame is fitted with components that permit each version to perform specific tasks.[18,19]

    This architecture is characterized by modularity and extreme flexibility, leading to

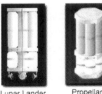

Lunar Lander   Propellant Transporter

Payload Dispenser   Propellant Dispenser

Figure 10
The Four LTS versions of the Basic Transportation Frame (BTF) hardware provide opportunities for reuse in space.

reduced development costs and enabling a system more capable of evolution as the market changes and grows.

The new architecture can be seen on YouTube at http://www.youtube.com/watch?v=26Y5w0vqtIU. [20,21]

A hard look at this concept will show that it enables NASA to meet its strategic objectives, including sending small payloads to the lunar surface in a few short years, sending larger payloads to the lunar surface in succeeding years, and sending crews to the Moon and back to the Earth by the middle of the next decade.

The architecture is based on the concept of refueling a fleet of fully reusable spacecraft at several locations in cislunar space, which create the equivalent of a two-way highway between the Earth and the Moon.

In the startup phase the LTS hardware is abandoned on the moon to deliver early payloads and later grows with propellant depots. The use of the hardware for a different purpose at the destination can also contribute to cost reduction.

Figure 10 depicts lunar surface logistics. The moon is 20 times further than any logistics support of a remote base on Earth, so lunar logistics is not just about transportation to the moon, as there will also be a need for use of the LTS hardware in surface operations. Lunar logistics involves managing the movement, planning and control of the flow of goods and materials to, from, and on the moon, and deals with the procurement, distribution, maintenance, and replacement of materiel and personnel.

An affordable transportation system is the first objective of a sustainable commercial trade route supporting mankind's first off-planet base. An equal requirement is a market or commercial reason for being there. The initial markets will be on the moon's surface and later in space.

THE BUSINESS CONCEPT

The business approach calls for the use of existing ELVs, which are already commercially available. As 70% of the energy required for a lunar trip is used in getting out of the gravity well surrounding Earth, the first 200 miles, this new lunar architecture utilizes ELVs to bring a new fleet of reusable spacecraft, lunar payloads, propellants, and eventually crews from the Earth to Low Earth Orbit. The LTS reusable spacecraft could do the rest of the job, taking payloads from LEO to the lunar surface and back.

This commercial strategic roadmap permits a 'pay as you go' and a 'technology development pathway' that allows NASA to achieve a series of its strategic objectives as funding and technology developments permit. This approach reduces recurring mission costs by advancing in-space transportation technology, and later, resource utilization, because this is less costly than investing in new Earth to orbit transportation.

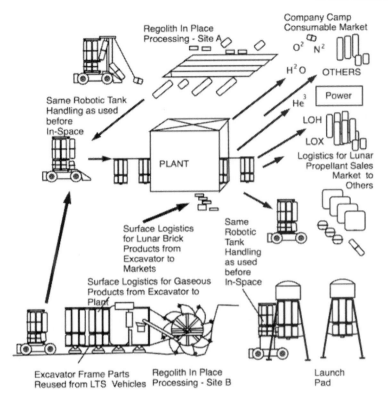

Regolith In Place Processing - Site A

Company Camp Consumable Market

O^2 N^2

H^2O OTHERS

He^3 Power

LOH

LOX

Same Robotic Tank Handling as used before In-Space

PLANT

Logistics for Lunar Propellant Sales Market to Others

Surface Logistics for Lunar Brick Products from Excavator to Markets

Same Robotic Tank Handling as used before In-Space

Surface Logistics for Gaseous Products from Excavator to Plant

Excavator Frame Parts Reused from LTS Vehicles

Regolith In Place Processing - Site B

Launch Pad

Figure 11
The Surface Logistics can profit from the reuse of LTS hardware components.

The initial design of reusable spacecraft was based on the K-1 RLV or the payload capabilities of Delta II Heavy class launch vehicles or other vehicles with an 11' diameter payload shroud. In fact, the diameter of the Earth to orbit vehicle payload bay defines the diameter and size of the LTS vehicle system. The larger the diameter of the initial payload, the more capable and efficient the LTS highway scale-up becomes.

Lunar Lander spacecraft can deliver payloads of up to 8 metric tons from LEO to the lunar surface, depending on where and how frequently they are refueled on their way to the Moon. This architecture is capable of delivering 800kg to the lunar surface directly from LEO without the need to refuel in space, or delivering payloads of 3.2 metric tons to the lunar surface with refueling at L1 only. Comparable payloads can be returned from the lunar surface to the Earth with refueling at one or more of those locations.

This initial system is not meant to transport crews to and from the Moon, but as a technology development testbed to prove the reliability through repeated non-critical cargo missions, leading a crewed Earth-Moon transportation system.

If a 33' payload diameter could be derived from the existing NSTS or current space shuttle program vehicles and was available to commercial ventures, then the entire process of the trade route development and LTS vehicle deployment would be significantly accelerated.

KEY FEATURES

SCALABILITY

This new Lunar Transportation System vehicle is scalable, which means it can be used in Earth to orbit stages with payload diameters from 11' to 33'. A follow-on fleet of larger spacecraft, designed to fit the payload capabilities of Delta IV Heavy class launch vehicles, can transport payloads of up to 30 metric tons from LEO to the lunar surface, depending on where and how frequently they are refueled on their way to the Moon.[5] These larger spacecraft are capable of transporting crews to the lunar surface and returning them to the Earth, and also have the capability to provide heavy cargo transportation to support a permanent lunar base.

COST REDUCTION

The non-recurring costs to develop this Earth-Moon transportation system are much lower than the cost of developing systems that use more traditional architectures because there are fewer unique pieces of technology to develop, and in addition LTS relies on existing launch systems, and a significant reduction in lunar mission costs comes from the reusability of the major elements of this system.[21]

The largest cost in operating this system, 70%, or more, is the delivery of the original LTS spacecraft to LEO. The next large cost is the delivery of propellants to the reusable LTS vehicles, and the lunar payloads from the Earth to LEO, so if propellants can be manufactured on the Moon, then Earth-Moon mission costs may be reduced by 60% or more, and allow affordable round trip operations of reusable vehicles.

These payloads could be other commercial vehicles, while commercial launch vehicles in a variety of sizes could transport individual cryogenic propellant fuel tanks to a propellant depot. The different propellants required for various spacecraft systems use tanks that could service several classes of emerging commercial vehicles.

While existing NASA vehicles are expensive to operate, the development cost of a significant new launch capability represents at least 100 launches of existing EELVs and many years of lunar transportation operations.

If and when reusable Earth to LEO launch vehicles become available, lunar mission costs may be reduced further by 60% or more.

SCHEDULE

Because this LTS concept relies on existing technologies and existing ELVs and only requires the maturation of several enabling technologies, LTS could deliver payloads to the lunar surface relatively quickly and well within NASA's schedule for robotic and human lunar exploration.

THE BOTTOM LINE

This lunar architecture is based on concepts that reduce lunar mission life cycle costs and technical risks, improve reliability and eventually crew safety by demonstrating reliability through cargo-only transport until the vehicles are proven by many years of operations.

Figure 10 shows lunar logistics hardware made from discarded fuel tanks and BTFs, to become part of the lunar surface commercial logistics systems that can potentially reduce costs, accelerate early lunar mission schedules, and allow for routine, frequent delivery of lunar payloads on a two-way highway between the Earth and the Moon. Cost reduction is part of the ultimate goal, using the most affordable and efficient transportation hardware on each leg of the trade route in both directions.[22-23]

THE STARTUP PHASE

The 2004 startup of Lunar Transportation Systems, Inc. began with multiple conceptual innovations by Walter Kistler, followed by the formation of the LTS Corporation and the continued exploration of the potential market opportunity. The company participated in Roadmap Conferences and presented proposals to NASA Centers, but with mixed reception.

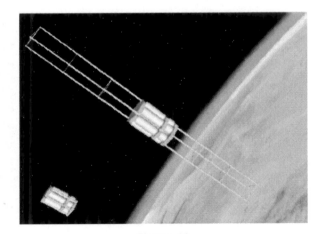

Figure 12
The LTS Basic Transportation Frame (BTF) provides for the reuse
of hardware for Truss Units and future propellant depots.

The company engaged some former Lockheed Martin employees to assist in the proposal and design process.

The Kistler Aerospace K-1 Vehicle was used as a prototype for early LTS designs with an 11' diameter by 17' long payload bay. However, design work showed that the LTS Payload needed to be a vehicle in LEO, which is actually very scalable, and can fit into any payload bay diameter from 11' to 33'. 18,22,23

Figure 11 shows the LTS Basic Transportation Frame (BFT) as a system of rotating concentric tubes, expanded longitudinally to become a truss. The finished truss uses the structural strength within the BTF for the second reuse of the same BTF mass or discarded hardware.

THE LESSONS LEARNED

1. A key lesson learned from previous entrepreneurial ventures is the importance of protecting the firm's intellectual property. The aerospace industry is a sophisticated marketing environment, with traditional companies working to retain dominance and not wanting to decrease the cost of entry for competing commercial companies. Rockwell, for example, tried to overrun the startup SPACEHAB by quickly designing a competing module with similar characteristics, but abandoned the effort, when they heard the small company had applied for and later was awarded U.S. Patent 4,867,395 (a copy of which is available free from www.pat2pdf.org).

    The cycle of interest by Venture Capitalists is normally five years, including the time frame in which they receive their return on investment. But in five years the lunar market has yet to define any commercial opportunities capable of utilizing an affordable transportation system, or even defining a market for commercial participation.

2. Entrepreneurship has become more expensive and more difficult over the 32 years of activity by the authors. The reasons are many, including International Traffic in Arms Regulations (ITAR), which keeps American aerospace products expensive compared to readily available aerospace products from other nations.

    There is a cyclic back-and-forth swing of support and encouragement from NASA to commercial efforts. NASA's inability to mesh existing innovations, private financing, and entrepreneurial development methods that have flourished in the commercial world puts extra pressure on start-ups. Entrepreneurs are rarely acknowledged in NASA procurement documents, and NASA doesn't pass on to entrepreneurs all the

Bid/Proposal, IRAD and other cost advantages given to traditional aerospace companies.

3.   The degree to which NASA and government recognize and help entrepreneurs and commercial space ventures has varied over the years. At one time there was an Associate Administrator with 'Commercial' in the job title printed on the door, and there are other periods, when 'commercial' has seldom been mentioned, although we note a significant upsurge in interest in space commerce since 2009.

4.   Without NASA or a major lunar effort by other governments or companies, it is very difficult to finance the entrepreneurial ventures described here. Private investors always ask, 'What does NASA think of your venture?' It took us 3 years to find, understand and solve that problem at SPACEHAB.

CONCLUSION

The entrepreneurial startup process for space ventures has changed significantly over the last 30 years. SPACEHAB was a small company start-up that slipped through the cracks to become successful by applying start-up techniques to commercial aerospace. In recent years, however, it has become much more difficult for a startup company to slip through today's narrower procurement cracks, all of which is complicated by bigger NASA budgets that include fewer dollars focused on actually saving money, or targeted to entrepreneurs that advocate saving money.

Today, the high cost of getting to orbit is the significant barrier to the development of space, and has driven even American companies to try and launch systems developed by other nations. Our hope is for a transportation system to rise from the ashes of the current confused situation, and to stimulate cooperation between commercial aerospace entrepreneurs and NASA. The next vehicle may be a Shuttle Derived Vehicle (SDV), and by using the existing Shuttle hardware and applying innovation to all aspects of its operations, operating costs can be significantly reduced, which will stimulate the development of many major space commerce markets that are now emerging, including these nine:

- Lunar trade route logistics & surface development
- Assemble affordable orbital solar collectors:
  materials & depot logistics
- NASA-JSC bigger Solar System exploration assembly in orbit
- NASA-MSFC exploration engine development and test to orbit
- Second generation depots on lunar trade route
- More robust Orion life boat transported unmanned
- Space tourist support and facilities in orbit, ET profit center

- VASIMR engine testing for Mars logistics missions
- Asteroid missions and homesteader support - two way support logistics.

The four entrepreneurial examples discussed in this chapter all applied innovation to reduce operations costs for space ventures. In fact, the innovations came from very small businesses started by serial entrepreneurs, whose only chance of success was by lowering costs. The four companies raised $1.2B in private equity, and most of the money was paid to major American aerospace companies for hardware design and fabrication, although when American companies wouldn't take our money, we turned to companies in other nations.

Now the leaders of many nations recognize the importance of the emerging space commerce markets and they are very aware that the nations that capture those markets will build national wealth and consolidate their central positions in important global markets.

Entrepreneurs are forming teams of innovative small companies, and joining together to accelerate the use of private financing to forge the trade routes beyond humankind's first planet. Our hope is that the four stories presented in this chapter will help these entrepreneurs to succeed.

•••

ACKNOWLEDGMENTS

Thank you to Walter Kistler and Bob Citron for being the huge risk takers you are, and for enabling three of the four companies discussed above to come into being. The early money is always the most difficult to obtain for entrepreneurs, and without money entrepreneurs don't move off the starting line into the ever-changing world of commercial space.

THOMAS C. TAYLOR

Thomas C. Taylor is an entrepreneur, inventor and a Professional Civil Engineer in the commercial aerospace industry. His goal is building commercial space projects including an unmanned transportation cargo service to and from the moon's surface with Lunar Transportation Systems, Inc.

Since 1979, Tom has helped to form 22 entrepreneurial aerospace startup companies with four successful commercial space startup companies raising a total of $1.2B in private equity financing. These four actually completed the commercial space startup process and evolved into meaningful private commercial space companies, but each took almost a decade to unfold.

Tom enjoyed working in the trenches for 4 to 12 years on each of these commercial space successes with Walter Kistler and Bob Citron, the founders of most of the successful startups, as described in this chapter, including SPACEHAB, Inc., Kistler Aerospace Corporation, and Lunar Transportation Systems, Inc., an unmanned logistics service anticipating commercial cargo to the moon's surface at commercial rates with scalable hardware. Started in 2005, LTS proposes a privately financed logistics service for commercial lunar development. The goal is a sustainable commercial transportation system for the moon to support government and commercial efforts.

WALTER P. KISTLER

Walter Kistler holds about 50 patents worldwide and has invested time, innovative energy and early money for emerging entrepreneurial ventures in America and abroad. Trained in physics, Walter was instrumental in starting and financing Spacehab, Inc., the Kistler Aerospace Corporation, and Lunar Transportation Systems, Inc. among other startup ventures.

ROBERT A. CITRON

Bob Citron was the spark behind and founder of many aerospace and space ventures including Spacehab, Inc., the Kistler Aerospace Corporation, and Lunar Transportation Systems, Inc. Bob is a graduate aerospace engineer from UCLA, a serial entrepreneur, and early pioneer in space businesses.

REFERENCES

1. Wikipedia Search, 'Niche Markets,' A niche market is the subset of the market on which a specific product is focusing on, http://en.wikipedia.org/wiki/Niche_market

2. Citron, R. and Taylor, T.C. "An Early Low Cost Alternative for Manned Orbital Research," *AFSC/NSIA Cost Reduction and Cost Credibility* Workshop, Denver, CO.,1986. Proposed a SPACEHAB pricing structure an order of magnitude below present pressurized Spacelab Module research.

3. Citron, R. and Taylor, T.C. "SPACEHAB: A Pressurized Payload Bay Space Station Testbed Module - An Early Low Cost Developmental Lead-in for Space Station," *AIAA Space Station in the 21st Century*, Reno, NV, Sept. 3-5, 1986. Proposed SPACEHAB Module as low cost lead-in Space Station testbed module.

4. Mellors, W.J., Taylor, T.C. and Wilson, J.E. (1989), "The Global OUTPOST Program - Commercial Services in Low Earth Orbit," *40th Congress of the International Astronautical Federation*, Malaga, Spain, Oct 7-12, 1989, IAA-89-711.

5. Mueller, G., U.S. Patent 5,927,653, "Two-Stage Reusable earth to orbit aerospace vehicle and transport system," Patent Appl. 08/632,786, Filed: April 17, 1996.

6. Mueller, G., Lai, G., Taylor, T., U.S. Patent Appl. 10/682,761, "Commercial experiment system in orbit,"

7. Walter Kistler, Bob Citron, and Thomas C. Taylor, Lunar Transportation Systems, Inc., *1ST SPACE EXPLORATION* Conf., www.aiaa.org/events/exploration, 30 Jan -1 Feb 05, Disney's Contemporary Resort • *Walt Disney World*® Resort, FL, "Commercial Transportation Mission Overviews" Proposed LTS hardware sys for lunar logistics to and from the moon.

8. Kistler, W., Citron, R., Taylor, T., USPTO Patent Number 7,118.077, "Platform and System for Payload Mass Transfer in Space." Issued Oct 10, 2006

9. Citron, R. and Taylor, T.C. "SPACEHAB: A Pressurized Payload Bay Space Station Testbed Module - An Early Low Cost Developmental Lead-in for Space Station," *AIAA Space Station in the 21st Century*, Reno, NV, Sept. 3-5, 1986. Proposed SPACEHAB Module as low cost lead-in Space Station testbed module.

10. 1Citron, R. and Taylor, T.C. (1986), "SPACEHAB: A Space Station Testbed Module," *AAS Annual Meeting*, Harvest House, Boulder, Colorado, Oct. 26-29, 1986. Proposed SPACEHAB Module & a payload services division as low cost lead-in Space Station test-bed module scenario.

11. Price Waterhouse Study, "Analysis of NASA Lease of and Purchase alternatives for the Commercial Mid-deck augmentation module," 1991, http://en.wikipedia.org/wiki/Space_logistics, Concluded cost savings with SPACEHAB,

12. Taylor, T.C., "Commercial Operations for the External Tank in Orbit," 18th Goddard Memorial Symposium, Washington, D.C., AAS 80-89, March 1980. Proposed an External Tank Derived Commercial Service Platform in orbit.

13. NASA Solicitation 1988, "ETs as a Possible Commercial Resource," CBD announcement 1 June, 1988, follow-up to President Reagan National Commission on Space, May 1986.

14. 14NASA GOI Enabling Agreement and cash deposit for five ETs in orbit transportation free, Signed 20 April 1993, Rev. 3, Agreement No. 1564-0001-00A, Covered technical confirmation costs at NASA-JSC and resulted in a 19 Feb 93 "appears technically feasible" NASA letter on ET salvage in orbit.

15. Taylor, T., GLOBAL OUTPOST, Inc., U.S. Patent Application for a "Salvage Hardware Apparatus and Method for Orbiting Hardware," U.S. Pat. No. 5,813,632, ET Salvage discussions with NASA-JSC & MMA Tech. studies & discussions

16. NASA Letter dated 19 Feb 1993, NASA-Hqs and NASA-JSC technical confirmation and result of GOI paid review by NASA-JSC in a 19 Feb 93 "appears technically feasible" NASA letter on ET salvage in orbit.

17. Martin Marietta Aerospace, Michoud Advanced Programs Group, Contract Study awarded by GLOBAL OUTPOST for the technical studies related to the salvage of the ET in orbit, 1988-93

18. Taylor, Thomas C., Kistler, Walter P, & Citron, Robert B., "To the Moon: Commercially," LOGISTICS SPECTRUM Magazine, Expanded reprint Volume 40, Issue 4, Oct-Dec 2006, ISSN 0024-5852, Soc. of Logistics Engineers (SOLE) Pub.

19. Lunar Transportation Systems, Inc., an entrepreneurial startup company in commercial space offering potentially affordable access to the lunar surface via a commercial logistics architecture, Start-up Team of Walter P. Kistler, Bob Citron and Tom Taylor, 2004, raised private equity, U. S. Patent 7,114,682, 7,118,077, 7,156,348

20. Lunar Transportation Systems Animation, 7:14 minutes, 2006, http://www.youtube.com/watch?v=26Y5w0vqtIU

21. Taylor, T., Kistler, W., Citron, R., Lunar Transportation Systems, Inc., "Lunar Commercial Logistics Transportation," *Rutgers University, Rutgers Symposium on Lunar Settlements*, 3-8 Jun 07 Discussed Lunar Resource Recovery and Logistics Transportation including on the surface in support of mining operations

22. Taylor, T., Kistler, W., Citron, R., Lunar Transportation Systems, Inc., India IAC 07, Session on Space and Society E5.1 Innovating Through Technology Spin-in and Spin-off, IAC-07-E5.1.01, Paper 59. Title: "Innovating Public Private Partnerships And Dual-Use Technology," LTS invites the Entrepreneurs of the world and their respective nation's space agencies to join international Alliance focused on Innovation in all aspects and join with us in organizing an "Innovation Alliance" to assist Society in moving off this Planet Earth. The Alliance would unite entrepreneurs

around the world to join with their Space Agencies, if they have one, and use innovation to create commercial opportunities, open new trade routes, stimulate space commerce and become a space faring planet.

23. Taylor, T., Kistler, W., Citron, R., Lunar Transportation Systems, Inc., Lunar Exploration Analysis Group Conf. 1-5 Oct 07, Houston Hobby Hilton, Session: Commerce: Incremental Steps from Earth to Lunar Enterprise, Title: "Commercial Transportation and Lunar Mining," Paper Abs 2 p & VGs 40 ea. avail from author, Discussed LTS concept & support of Lunar Resource Recovery with Logistics Transportation including on the surface in support of mining operations.

CHAPTER 5

SPIN-OUT AND SPIN-IN IN THE NEWEST SPACE AGE

MICHAEL SIMPSON, PH.D.
PRESIDENT, THE INTERNATIONAL SPACE UNIVERSITY

INTRODUCTION

For the aspiring space entrepreneur, rocket science may be the biggest obstacle. This is definitely not because rocket science is impossibly difficult. Since at least the time of Robert Goddard, we have known that however difficult it is, it is not impossible.

In fact, rocket science is an obstacle as much because of the impression it gives and the aura we have erected around it, as because if its inherent complexity. For some people, rocket science and space activity are the same, and both are seen as too rigorous and unforgiving for any but the best capitalized and most technologically powerful businesses to venture forth into the markets they are creating.

Although this chapter does not hope to make any part of the space sector look easy, it does seek to open the eyes of cautious entrepreneurs and business planners to the enormous potential for a very wide range of enterprises to participate. The operative theme here is that the human experience of space, whether it be through machines of human creation or through direct human presence, has gotten so complex, its appetite for technical and procedural solutions so ravenous, and the economic resources available to it so limited in proportion to the vastness of the objectives, that there is no choice but to incorporate good ideas developed elsewhere.

For many people this concept is referred to as "spin-in:" the transfer of technology developed for uses outside of the space sector to meet needs identified inside it. Although there is by no means a standard use of this term (NASA for example often uses it to refer to a kind of partnership or co-development of technologies between internal teams and industrial partners), spin-in in the sense I have defined it above is increasingly discussed in Europe. Since it gives us a convenient short-hand for a concept that could be a profitable pathway by which to enter the space market, 'spin-in' will be used here in its European sense.

Although easily enough defined on its own, spin-in, in the context of the space sector, is best understood in relationship to its far better known and better-publicized companion concept, spin-off. Since the early days of the space era, spin-off has been invoked as one of the major benefits of large national investments in space technology. Research and development undertaken to push human horizons beyond the obviously finite limits of the Earth inevitably made discoveries that could be useful in more terrestrial pursuits. Thus, materials, medical breakthroughs, energy solutions, information technologies, industrial processes, and many more such capabilities developed for use in space applications could be re-programmed and re-deployed for other very down to Earth uses.

As we will see later, this argument has become so strong that several often cited examples of spin-off are, in fact, among the more interesting examples of spin-in. The lesson here being that spinning-in a product, idea, or technology may not only gain you a niche presence in the space market, but it might also help you gain additional market visibility and penetration in terrestrial applications. Hence, while the aura of rocket science may be an obstacle to the over-cautious entrepreneur, once you have spun something into a space project, it is likely to benefit from the public's admiration for products that are 'space proven.'

With that in mind let's begin with a quick survey of the idea and underlying business opportunities of spin-off before turning the concept around to see how business can be done by infusing outside developments into a space sector that can use them.

SPIN-OFF

A recent search on the NASA web site (www.nasa.gov) revealed 24 hits for the term, spin-off. The European Space Agency (ESA) site (www.esa.int) yielded an astonishing 2940 hits, aided in part by its effort to bring content to its readers in the national language of all 18 member states. Digging a bit deeper however, it is clear that there is much more to the results of these searches than hits and click rates.

Both agencies have backed up their interest in spin-off as a friend-raising strategy by well documented and elaborately illustrated publications testifying to practical successes in actual business situations.[2] A few hours studying these materials would be well advised not only because applying a space developed technology to a new terrestrial use can be a good investment (there are after all still more customers on Earth than there are off it!), but it can also be a good training ground for the habits of mind necessary to see how the process could work in reverse.

An example from Europe is useful here. In June 2009 the European Space Agency's (ESA's) Technology Transfer Program Office (TTPO) posted an entry on its web site concerning the RIVOPS (Remote Intuitive Visual Operations System) implemented by the EATOPS company, a French-Dutch start-up at ESA's business incubation center in Nordwijk, The Netherlands.

See (http://www.esa.int/esaCP/SEM56L1OWUF_Improving_0.html)

The firm was reported to have adapted a technology that ESA had developed for monitoring and controlling multiple parameters affecting safe satellite operations to meet the needs of the off-shore drilling industry. This short piece contains a number of insights into the complex synergies that make spin-off ventures matters of great interest for space agencies and entrepreneurs alike.

First, although the RIVOPS system was deeply rooted in 'proven ESA technology,' Alexandre Van Damme from EATOPS is clearly listed as a co-inventor. Whether spun-off or spun-in, technologies are rarely transferred between sectors without some modifications being required by their new uses. One should expect that it is necessary to work with partners in either case. Emotionally, this may be harder for spin-in, where you must inevitably expect others to seek to transform your input in line with their perception of their needs, or their understanding of the lessons that their experience with space projects has taught. While this does not have to mean that you cede all control, it does mean that a strategy of maintaining absolute control is unlikely to make such a deal work.

Second, for the space agency, the reward of spin-off is clearly one of public benefit. Quoted in the piece, Bruno Naulais, ESA Business Incubation Manager gets right to the point. *"This is an excellent example of how space technology can benefit society."*

With spin-off, space agencies can fully expect that a short, rich example can show an attentive public that money invested in the agency's

---

1. European Space Agency Technology Program Office, *Down to Earth, How space technology improves our lives*, September 2009; and NASA Innovative Partnerships Program, *Spinoff, 2009 ed.*, Developed by Publications and Graphics Department, NASA Center for Aerospace Communication.

work does more than fund satellites and missions to far away places. The implicit payoff for the agency is public support for continued appropriation of government funds. For the time being, agencies may not see equivalent benefit in spin-in and may even see it as a 'competitor' to internally developed technologies. This means that the strategies for building a partnership bonded by perceptions of mutual benefit are often much different depending on whether the spin is 'off ' or 'in.'

Third, the 'technology' transferred in this case was already a well-honed concept involving the clustering of parameters critical to safe and effective satellite operations. A lot of the movement of value between the space sector and its economic partners takes the form of concepts or intellectual property. Although often incorporated into significant pieces of hardware, this property may involve new science, new engineering, or new ways of operating. Sometimes it involves all three, but it can often be of great value even if it involves only one. A brilliantly conceived physical tool can fail in practice because it has not yet been linked to the right way of using it. A wonderfully engineered system can fail because the technology incorporated into a single component is not equal to the demands placed upon it in critical circumstances. In the first case the shortcoming is the lack of an operating method; in the second the need for a design or manufacturing innovation. In both, the need for a solution has created a market, and this will be the case no matter what direction the technology is spinning.

Certainly, NASA shares the same understanding of the importance of spin-off. Since 1976 it has issued an annual publication devoted to the theme that should be required reading for anyone hoping to profit from meeting a market need through technology transfer with the space sector, whether spun-in or off, or a little of both. The 2009 edition is available at the following link:

http://www.sti.nasa.gov/tto/Spinoff2009/pdf/spinoff2009.pdf

In 208 short pages, it provides a yearly insight into the kinds of technologies NASA has developed and the uses to which creative business have converted them.

It does more, however. It also provides a quick insight to the huge array of subjects in which NASA is interested. Ranging from health to industrial productivity with plenty more in between, the catalogue of spin-offs generated in the past year is proof that NASA is far more than rocket science, and provides encouragement that if so many of NASA's ideas can find uses outside of aeronautics and astronautics, then there is a good chance that outside ideas could find a use inside the space sector as well. With 24 editions of Spin-off already issued, it is likely that whatever industry is closest to your heart, there is an example of previous synergy to provide inspiration and incentive to persevere. The European Space

Agency's equivalent publication, cited previously, is called *Down to Earth, How space technology improves our lives.*

Don't expect to find a companion volume on Spin-in, however. It doesn't seem to be in the culture, yet. There is a case to be made that it is equally beneficial to society and perhaps even more useful to the general economy by providing economies of scale, but it can also be interpreted either as the introduction of inexperience into missions with no room for failure, or equally sinister in the minds of some, it could be viewed as threatening competition in a world where publicly funded laboratories seek to demonstrate their usefulness or even indispensability in face of regular budget reviews.

Unfortunately, unlike spin-off, which promises to improve the chances for renewing funding for public laboratories, spin-in can seem like a threat to funding in a zero-sum game. The possibility that it might also be a chance to get more done with the relatively small budgets allocated to space agencies and procurement officers is only slowly gaining credibility with decision-makers and publicly-supported researchers.

Although we will never completely abandon the discussion of spin-off, it is time to focus on spin-in and its possibility to open the door to space commerce for small firms and large alike.

SPIN-IN

Years ago as a young assistant scoutmaster on a campout, I heard the scoutmaster comment that the dehydrated orange flavored drink mix we used to mix up a high vitamin C breakfast beverage was 'space-age technology.' Called Tang, this stuff had supposedly been developed for the needs of astronauts in NASA's 1960s Gemini program. This was the truth as I understood it for many years until I learned that the original patent for Tang had been issued in 1957, a good 7 years before Gemini.

The real story was that NASA wanted a good dehydrated mix that could be added to drinking water for the Gemini astronauts, and had found one that already existed on the commercial market. They did modify it a bit by adding potassium to replace astronauts' electrolytes, but the basic product was clearly spun-in rather than spun-off.

Similar stories exist for Teflon and Velcro, two widely known products. These examples should help you understand that NASA and other space customers buy good ideas when they meet their needs. Any visitor to the American module on the International Space Station soon recognizes that a lot of items that would be otherwise floating about in microgravity are firmly attached to one surface or another by the same Velcro that keeps things in their place 300 km below on earth.

The key to your ability to build business out of this reality is to keep in touch with all the needs confronted by the space sector and to review the capacity of your products or competencies to meet those needs. To add some structure to this review we will look at several categories of such products or competencies that could help forge a business relationship with the space sector.

INTELLECTUAL-PROPERTY

Space activity is an insatiable consumer of ideas. Working at or beyond the limits of current knowledge or experience, the sector often needs to look beyond itself to make sense out of the environments, challenges and opportunities confronting everything from ongoing operations to unique, one-off missions.

A simple anecdote is useful to illustrate how terrestrial ideas, experience, or research results can be critical as space projects confront the new conditions imposed by the space environment. From the earliest days of space flight anything put into space is confronted by a condition that Earthly designers need rarely account for: microgravity.

Microgravity is the phenomenon that permits astronauts, and anything else that isn't tied down, to float freely in the space station. It results from the fact that the station and its contents are in free fall while in orbit, managing to not come crashing back to earth only because their forward velocity is so great that they effectively keep falling over the horizon.

The problem was that until Sputnik made it to orbit in 1957, there had been few ways to test the principle of microgravity, or its effects on materials on Earth.

As we prepared for the advent of access to orbit in the late 1950s it was possible to test some of the effects through the use of sounding rockets or drop towers. Sounding rockets rising to several kilometers of altitude could contain experiments that produced data during the time it took the expended rocket to fall back to earth. Drop towers, which were very high structures in which experiments could be subjected to free fall for a few seconds at most, provided the opportunity for greater experimental control but suffered from the fact that objects accelerate as they fall meaning that adding additional amounts of time to the free fall period required building exponentially taller towers. In both cases the costs of running the experiments were high enough that those designing the tests wanted the best understanding possible before they initiated them so as to maximize the new information they could obtain.

Fortunately, experiments and experience in microgravity preceded the space age by at least two centuries.

Two hundred ten years before Sputnik took its beep generator to orbit, William Watts had put microgravity to work in the United Kingdom. Confronting the desire of the British military to produce the most perfectly round musket balls possible, Watts erected what he called the *"Shot Tower"* in 1747. The principle was simple. Lead heated to a liquid state at the top of the tower was poured through a mesh and allowed to fall. With the temperature carefully controlled the lead would have solidified by the time it arrived at the bottom of the tower. More importantly, thanks to the behavior of liquid in microgravity, the lead arrived as perfectly shaped spheres.

With this painfully terrestrial technology having been well documented, it was available years later as space-focused engineers and scientists began to consider how to evolve their experiments and develop their equipment to function as desired in the free fall conditions of orbit.

Given the amount of time between Watts' idea and its implicit value in providing first principles to those charged with space mission planning, it is no surprise that he never received royalties. But in today's faster-moving R&D environment, there is good potential for knowledge developed to meet an Earthly need to then spin-in usefully and profitably to the space sector. This should provide an incentive to review the ability of your intellectual property to meet challenges within that sector and to participate in the space activities market.

INNOVATION

When searching for ways to apply what you already know to a need in the space sector, don't forget that products you have proven to work well in meeting customer needs on Earth may have a whole new range of uses beyond it as well. In this case in particular, however, the adage that innovation and adaptation go hand in hand is especially true.

Innovating from the basis of an earth-proven product requires careful attention to how the space environment differs from the conditions the product confronts on Earth. High radiation, hard vacuum, thermal stresses that can subject objects to variations of hundreds of degrees Celsius from one side (facing the sun) to the other (in shade), high vibration on launch, and highly limited energy budgets are just some of the major differences that have to be taken into account.

INNOVATION EXAMPLE: CISCO

One recent success story in adapting terrestrial technology to the space environment involves a company that has hardly been a household name in the space business: Cisco Systems. Working under a mission statement that calls on the company to *"Shape the future of the Internet by creating unprecedented value and opportunity for our customers, employees, investors, and ecosystem partners,"* Cisco has earned a reputation in internet routing and related services in a very Earth-centered business.[3] In fact as the year 2000 ushered in the new millennium, the high volume, high value internet router part of Cisco's business was Earth-bound as well.

By 2003, however, that had begun to change. Using a production model router, a lot of innovative human capital, and less than $1,000 of modified hardware, the company launched a demonstration payload designed to show that its gear had what it took to perform in space. With results reported frequently at major space conferences over the next several years, it became clear that the router was functioning as designed, surviving frequent, intentional stops and reboots, and slowly earning the respect needed for project managers to rely on it or its derivatives when designing spacecraft architectures to support mission critical functions.

The next logical step occurred in November 2009 when Cisco's IRIS (Internet Router In Space) rocketed into orbit as a hosted payload of Intelsat's IS-14 satellite. Two months later the company announced that the router had completed its in-orbit test and had successfully become the first terrestrial-standards based Internet Protocol router to be deployed on a commercial geostationary satellite.

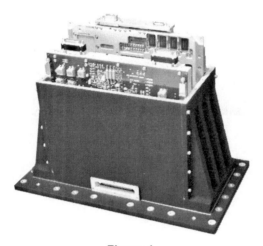

Figure 1
Cisco IRIS Router
© Cisco Systems, Inc.

In spite of the numerous space-specific adaptations needed to achieve this result, Cisco's IRIS stands as an excellent and informative example of the potential for spin-in by demonstrating several key principles.

---

2.   "Frequently Asked Questions: What is Cisco's Mission Statement," Cisco Systems Investor Website: http://investor.cisco.com/faq.cfm?SH_No_JavaScript=yes

1.   The first pre-requisite for project success was identifying a need within the space sector for which a terrestrially proven technology could promise a cost effective and reliable solution.

     a. In a news release on January 18, 2010, Cisco emphasized that the need they had identified could be addressed by an innovative use of their router and internet expertise: *"IRIS offers several enhancements over conventional satellite technology. With IRIS, users will be able to experience a true mobile network – one that helps enable them to connect and communicate how, when and where they want, and that continuously adapts to their needs without a reliance on predefined, fixed infrastructure."* [4]

     b. The same release emphasized that by placing a radiation resistant and reliable IP router in geostationary orbit they would be able to enhance mobility for their clients. They also noted that the same software upgrade capability appreciated by systems administrators on Earth had been built into their on-orbit router. This essentially meant that software associated with the router could be updated as needed, just as has been the case with ground-based systems, providing a level of flexibility and responsiveness not previously available aboard satellites.

2.   The second key element was identifying the business case that supported the spin-in technologies over actual or possible competitors.

     a. IP services from space have been available up to now through the use of teleports which receive downloaded data and route it to customers. Cisco's release made it clear that they believed their technology has a decided advantage over that competitor. In fact, it promises to save bandwidth, energy, and complexity problems associated with teleport based, 'double-hop' technology.

     b. Emphasizing important government uses for their services, Cisco also made it clear that they had identified their initial market while pursuing new market opportunities with *"satellite manufacturers, system integrators, and end users"* who seek to serve markets *"outside traditional ground-based networks."* Implicit in this is that even

---

3.   "Cisco's Space Router Successfully Operates in Orbit," Cisco Systems, Inc. news release, January 18, 2010

individual customers may be able to access IP processed content directly.

c.   Perhaps even more importantly, the IRIS project was a step forward in making networks in general more robust, a long-sought goal of the company. With the added capability of in-space routing, one more truly independent element was added to network redundancy since most calamities that could put a terrestrial network element out of service would not simultaneously affect an element in orbit.

3.   The Cisco release provides one more critical insight into identifying and acting on a spin-in opportunity by showing the vision to include space applications in implementing a company's strategic objectives:

a.   Quoting Steven Boutelle, vice president, Cisco Global Government Solutions Group, the Cisco release makes it clear that this is exactly how the company views this initiative. *This milestone is another step in our strategy to expand borderless networks into space and redefine how satellite communications are delivered. This technology can help transform satellite communications around the world by reducing latency and increasing the efficiency.*

b.   Also quoted was Arnold Friedman, senior vice president, Sales & Marketing, Space Systems/Loral, who made it clear that Cisco's new router fell squarely in the category of innovation, saying, *Commercial satellites offer a best value solution for quickly deploying important and innovative space-related technologies, such as IRIS.*

c.   On March 16, 2010, The Society of Satellite Professionals International (SSPI) honored Cisco with an award for innovation in technology development and applications for the IRIS project.

4.   A number of other lessons need to be drawn from this example of successful spin-in.

a.   Spinning-in a product is not the same as off-loading inventory. The 2009 IRIS router was not exactly off the shelf. It was built by a partner, SEAKR engineering of Centennial Colorado, space qualified, and radiation hardened to meet the rigors of space flight at the altitude necessary for geostationary orbit: about 24,000 miles.

Cisco's Internetwork Operating System (IOS) controls its multiple functions.

b.   Many space applications will require your business to gain space awareness and insight before the spin-in can be successful. Cisco has been working toward this goal for nearly a decade and learning every step of the way. It is precisely for this reason that the International Institute of Space Commerce (http://www.iisc.im/) was founded on the Isle of Man in 2008 and conducts workshops and seminars at various locations including the International Symposium on Personal and Commercial Spaceflight (http://www.ispcs.com/) in Las Cruces, NM, and the International Space University in Strasbourg, France. Another useful source of space information useful to the entrepreneur is the annual Space Investment Summit (http://spaceinvestmentsummit.com/)

c.   Picking space savvy partners facilitates the market entry. In bringing IRIS to the successful conclusion of its test phase, Cisco teamed up with Loral, SEAKR, and Intelsat, all space proven companies. Whether it feels entrepreneurial or not, space ventures favor partnering with others, and sharing with them some of the fruits of innovation.

(Editor's note: Please see the following chapter for additional information about Cisco IRIS.)

A SECOND EXAMPLE

Another example of applying a non-space technology to a space sector need was reported in a paper presented to the International Astronautical Congress in 2003 by Raitt, v. d. Heide, Kruijff, and Hermanns.[5] By drawing its principal illustrations from the textile industry, their work shows how seemingly far afield from 'rocket science' the space sector can go in seeking the technologies it needs.

With a host of terrestrially developed technologies, the textile industry proved especially useful in providing tethers and tether management hardware. Drawing examples from the experience of a Students for the Exploration and Development of Space (SEDS) project and from the second Young Engineers Satellite (YES-2) mission, the authors demonstrate how equipment used commonly in the textile industry was used to solve engineering challenges associated with the eventual

---

4.   D. Raitt, E.J. v.d. Heide & M. Kruijff, F. Hermanns, "Space Spin-in from textiles: Opportunities from Tethers and Innovative Technologies," IAC-03-U.2.b.09

deployment of long tethers in support of space missions. Here the spin-in contribution took the form of machinery widely used in a non-space application. The primary innovation involved was recognizing that the equipment could meet the need, but as in the Cisco case, modifications were necessary to adapt the equipment to the space environment.

Raitt, et. al. capture the relationship between spin-in and innovation quite well in their conclusion:

> Although spin-off from the space sector to the non-space sector has hitherto been the norm, there is a growing need and demand within the space industry for innovations coming from industrial sectors outside the space field. This implies conducting a technology watch for innovations in relevant non-space sectors.[6]

What they do not make clear is that for entrepreneurs seeking to maximize the opportunity for their product to find its niche in the space sector, the technology watch that matters most is the one they conduct themselves among the technologies they or their firms control.

INDUSTRIAL PROCESSES

So far we have seen how spin-in can result from intellectual property and innovative adaptations of existing products and machinery. Now we will look at an example of how it can result from industrial processes and acquired manufacturing expertise.

By now it should be obvious that whatever product, idea or service you hope to spin-in to the space sector, it will be subjected to quality control standards and tests generally exceeding anything it would face in a terrestrial use. The inherent quality you bring to market may be sufficient to meet these tests or it may need to be space-hardened for its new application. Some earth-bound technologies, however, may already be the best that they can be given the state of the manufacturing art. In such a case it can be worth allowing your personal technology watch to explore their potential for use in or for the space sector.

If there is a poster child for this type of spin-in, it is the Magna-Steyr company of Austria. Long a major supplier of parts to the automobile industry, Magna-Steyr is particularly renowned as a supplier of automobile seats. Knowing the relationship between the seats they supplied and the safety of their occupants, Magna-Steyr placed extraordinary emphasis on the quality of its welding and the skill of its welders. With a well established   business-to-business   relationship   with   automobile

---

5.   *Ibid.*, p. 5.

manufacturers, Magna-Steyr paid no more attention to space activity than would any outside observer interested in pushing back the frontiers of the unknown. But that turned out to be just enough.

In the normal course of looking for new business, an interesting request for proposal caught Magna-Steyr's eye. Bids were being solicited for the production of the cryogenic feed lines for the Ariane launch vehicle. This was in fact VERY close to 'rocket science' and might have been quickly passed by except for one of the critical specifications in the RFP: welding, very, very good welding. The welding standard specified was one in which relatively few firms were certified, but Magna-Steyr was one of them. Encouraged that a skill that they had mastered was on the critical path, they bid for the job and won it.

Of course an important process of learning about the demands that would be placed on the feed line system followed. The steep learning curve of understanding the world of the super cold and the effects that liquid Hydrogen and Oxygen could have on the feed lines and their joints had to be climbed. In time, it was climbed, and a company that had once been primarily a supplier to the automobile industry became a partner in the manufacturing of one of the world's most reliable launch vehicles.

It also became something more. It became an intentional developer of space related products and the holder of one of the more important patents in the production of slush hydrogen, a super cold form of hydrogen gas seen as a potential fuel for hypersonic aircraft.

THERE ARE SEVERAL LESSONS FROM THIS EXAMPLE

1. If you have a state of the art quality certification, expect that some space-related RFP's are going to reference it in their specifications.

2. Once you are established as a supplier to the space market, expect to find more opportunities as you climb the learning curve.

3. Just because you enter the space sector through spin-in, don't overlook the possibility of spinning-off some of your newly acquired space-based expertise into the core businesses you started in. (In a world tired of fossil fuel and its side effects, slush hydrogen and its safe storage have some rather interesting innovative possibilities in the automotive sector.)

4. Opportunities for technology transfer and especially for spin-in are not confined to companies operating in the major space faring countries, or, for North American readers in those provinces or states most identified with the space sector. Firms operating in smaller markets may in fact have an advantage since

they have often developed expertise in managing and expanding an important niche.

LOOKING FORWARD

The challenge of looking at examples of how something has been done in the past is that it can leave an impression that all the worthwhile opportunities have already been seized. Like the psychological hurdle of 'rocket science,' the feeling that you have 'missed the wave' can be a crippling, though self-imposed barrier to entry.

There are probably numerous opportunities remaining in the very same industries we have already looked at, but with the objective of showing some emerging opportunities in the space sector that we have not already covered, let's look at some places where spin-in is likely to have a big contribution to make in the decades to come.

MINING

Although Earth has been mercifully spared any cataclysmic impacts from asteroids in recent decades, we know that several past impacts have been extremely powerful. Although the likelihood of an impact is small, several countries including the United States and Italy have invested significant sums in trying to identify, classify, and count asteroids that pass close enough to Earth to present a non-zero probability of impacting us.

This effort was given a bit of a dramatic boost by the 100th anniversary of the Tunguska event, where we believe an asteroid about 40 meters in diameter exploded in the atmosphere over Siberia in 1908 causing extensive damage over a physical area larger than Los Angeles.

With several thousand such objects now identified, predictions of the total number of Tunguska sized asteroids that will ultimately be catalogued ranges as high as 500,000.[7] There may be opportunities for spin-in technologies to address the threat these objects may pose, but there is an even more interesting implication in knowing that Earth orbits in a kind of cosmic rock quarry.

Spectroscopic analysis shows that many of these objects are rich in mineral ores that on Earth are becoming scarcer by the year. Nickel and iron are commonly mentioned, but materials that are much more rare such as titanium have also been identified in extra-terrestrial rocks. Given that some of these 'rocks' are mountain-sized behemoths (although certainly not solid titanium!), the potential for eventually mining them is increasingly discussed.

---

6. Association of Space Explorers International Panel on Asteroid Threat Mitigation, *Asteroid Threats: A Call for Global Response, Executive Summary*, 2008, p. 3.

So where is the spin-in? Mining itself is an area of expertise that has been only marginally tapped by the space sector. Although tools like the drill bits that have served the Mars rovers, Opportunity and Spirit so well have been brought into the sector, the opportunities presented by future off-Earth mining operations promise a potential market of immeasurable size. Especially if the mining operations are driven by private capital in quest of return, there is going to be little interest in completely reinventing the mining industry in order to begin harvesting mineral-rich asteroids crossing or coming close to Earth's orbit.

There is already evidence that this possibility is attracting the attention of people with mining expertise. The Colorado School of Mines organizes an annual symposium on the subject[8]; AfriSpace, a new organization in South Africa is looking at applying mining technology off planet; and Korea's Hanyang University in Seoul has been working steadily on the challenges inherent in what is called In Situ Resource Utilization (ISRU) and other extreme technologies such as robotic excavation[9].

ISRU is the idea that future human communities off-Earth, whether on the moon or Mars or somewhere else, could at least partially sustain themselves by using material they could find in place. This material could range from oxygen chemically bonded into lunar regolith, to water beneath the Martian surface. In all these cases, solutions to the discovery and extraction of the desired material could be opportunities to spin-in expertise, equipment, and technology from Earth-based mining.

INTERIOR DESIGN

The transformation of small spaces into pleasant environments is going to be essential in any future development of space tourism. Private citizens who have made the trip so far have more nearly matched the profile of traditional adventurers or private explorers by whom the rigors and inconveniences of space travel have been accepted as part of the price of adventure. To grow appreciably, any space tourism industry will have to move beyond this hardy band.

Spacecraft heading to orbit and destinations awaiting them there will need to offer as pleasant an environment as possible under the limitations of physical volume and security. Here, of course, there is terrestrial expertise aplenty in the automobile industry, as anyone who has successfully designed the interior of a passenger car or truck cab, especially

---

7.   Planetary and Terrestrial Mining Sciences Symposium (PTMSS),
     http://www.isruinfo.com/
8.   Kim Jae Won, "HYU, Touching Down on Space," *Weekly Hanyang News*,
     http://www.hanyang.ac.kr/controller/weeklyView.jsp?file=/top_news/2010/03
     4/english2.html

a high-priced one, could have something to offer in the design of a spacecraft.

The potential for spin-in would not be limited to this industry of course. Designers of yachts, cruise staterooms, and pied-a-terre apartments would all have opportunities here, as would those who supply the materials. There would be plenty to learn about ensuring that techniques were space-safe and space-adapted, but the fact remains that an emerging space industry of potentially substantial proportion would greatly benefit from the expertise of a whole professional class whose work has been heretofore confined to non-space applications.

Given the 'space-proven' cachet we discussed early in this chapter, managers of luxury brands could quickly find that spinning-in their expertise serves also to give them space-themed marketing opportunities on Earth.

TELEMEDICINE

Design will not be the only need of a space tourism industry. With more and more people going to space in good ordinary health but without the rigorous physical attributes for which we have so far selected our professional astronauts, we can expect to see a wider range of medical conditions presenting themselves in the orbiting population. Since it is unlikely that any business plan will be able to provide for a physician on every flight, telemedicine technologies developed on Earth will have spin-in possibilities.

These services are likely to range from simple consultations with passengers anxious to have new sensations or reactions explained, to more extensive assistance to crew members seeking to provide preliminary care in more serious situations. Medical services will also have opportunities prior to flight and in the period of adaptation following, where spin-in expertise may play a role. In these cases the most important expertise may be that of the passenger's own personal care physician who should be the one most familiar with the traveler's personal medical circumstances.

With medical services in remote areas of Earth increasingly augmented by remote assistance from specialists some considerable distance away, there may be increasing opportunities for institutions providing such services to contract with the emerging personal space flight industry to ensure that the needs of future passengers are addressed and that the liability of the space flight providers is managed. When the possibility of tele-surgery, robotically performed, becomes a proven reality, the technologies involved will likely have numerous opportunities to spin-in to space service, at least in low Earth orbit.

Lastly, any Earth-based surgical techniques, such as laparoscopy and arthroscopy, which reduce the amount of bleeding will be of interest to space surgeons seeking to intervene in microgravity.

DATA PROCESSING

As chip technology puts more and more data processing capability on smaller and smaller devices, the weight-sensitive space industry presents a great potential demand. To meet this sector of the demand, producers will certainly need to address the sensitivities to radiation tolerance and energy consumption as well, but even if adapted, winning technologies will have a great deal of Earth-centered legacy to rely upon. The story of Cisco's IRIS project recounted earlier demonstrates this possibility.

There is another side of the data processing opportunity however, that may hold even more promise. Amazing amounts of data are being generated daily by spacecraft already functioning in Earth orbit or beyond. Added to this is terrestrially generated data from sensors designed to improve our knowledge of the space environment generally and of the objects we have placed into it.

Today there are opportunities for spinning-in data-mining and image processing technologies because of the sheer size of the databases being generated, and the limitations on financial and human resources confronted by nearly every space project. To get a sense of the magnitude of the problem consider a couple of examples from NASA's recent history.

When the near-Earth asteroid Apophis was discovered in 2004, the limited number of observations available made the potential error in the calculation of its orbit rather large. This led to the conclusion that there was a disturbingly large probability that the space rock that was 250 meters in diameter could hit Earth on a future pass. Hoping to make their predictions more accurate, scientists poured over data sets from the Spaceguard project, which had tasked NASA with locating potentially hazardous objects much bigger than what they had just found. With clues to where they should look coming from their initial orbital calculations, they were able to narrow the search enough to find several more detections in the data. With these data they were able to refine their calculations and considerably reduce their assessment of the probability of impact in the near term. This was good news, of course, but for our purposes here the lesson is that there was useful data waiting to be found in data sets too large to have yet been fully mined for the information they contained. With data mining capability growing rapidly for Earth-based uses, the possibility of squeezing usable information out of oversized data sets in the space sector holds some tantalizing opportunities.

Another example of the 'too much data to handle problem' comes from the Mars rover program. The rovers have now generated an enormous wealth of image data alone, not to mention all the other scientific data they have sent back to Earth. The image volume is so large that NASA has made the data available in real time, recognizing that in many important cases images downloaded during the night for analytical teams in California are already processed and posted to amateur websites by the time the rover teams arrive at work in the morning.[10] This represents an enormous savings of time for the project team, and in many cases means that they have access to visual information that they would never have had the time or money to process themselves. In this case the technologies spun-in are image processing capabilities broadly available to the general market.

Although you cannot readily build a business plan around free services delivered by passionate volunteers, the possibility of more advanced image processing capabilities delivering value-added services for a fee on data that costs you nothing certainly seems worth investigating. After all, the business plans of companies currently marketing personal navigation devices are built on the solid foundation of GPS signals being made available to everyone at no cost.

SO WHAT IS IN IT FOR YOU?

As you prepare to pursue your spin-in opportunities, plan on having plenty of work to do. Identifying your opportunities, finding a receptive ear with prospective customers, making the adjustments necessary for your product to be space worthy, and going through the process of proving it can meet the rigorous requirements of space service will all take time, investment, and perseverance. The process of identification alone will not only require investing substantial time, learning what the space industry is all about and what it needs, it will also require that you look closely at your products and core competencies to see how they stack up against what you are learning about space sector demand.

But if your interest in a profitable business is matched by a desire to be part of the industry that is most likely to be laying the foundation for the most fundamental changes in the way humans live, solve problems, and experience the future, then the work will be worth it, as it will have cleared the way for you to become part of the newest space age … the one in which you don't have to be a powerful country or a giant corporation to make big things happen.

•••

---

9.   See www.unmannedspaceflight.com, a British site which does a masterful job of making rover images available on the web very shortly after their data stream arrives from the red planet.

DR. MICHAEL K. SIMPSON

Dr. Michael K. Simpson became President of the International Space University in May 2004. His academic career extends over 32 years and four continents. He has also been president of Utica College and the American University of Paris with a combined total of twenty years of experience as an academic chief executive officer. He has lectured in political science, international relations, business management, international law, leadership, and economics at Universities in the United States of America, France, China, the United Kingdom, and Australia.

Dr. Simpson received his Bachelors Degree magna cum laude from Fordham University in 1970 where he was elected to Phi Beta Kappa. He has also been elected to academic honor societies in the fields of political science and business management. After graduating from Fordham University, Dr. Simpson accepted a commission as an officer in the U.S. Navy where he served as an Oceanographic Watch Officer, Communications Officer, Leadership and Management Instructor, Repair Officer, and Political Military Action Officer. In 1993 he retired from the Naval Reserve with the rank of Commander. He holds numerous commendations including the Defense Meritorious Service Medal.

Dr. Simpson completed his Ph.D. at The Fletcher School of Law and Diplomacy of Tufts University, holds the Master of Business Administration from Syracuse University; and two Master of Arts degrees from The Fletcher School. He has also completed two prestigious one year courses in Europe: the French advanced defense institute (Institut des Hautes Études de Défense Nationale) and the General Course of the London School of Economics.

He is a board member of the Space Week International Association, a member of the Board of Governors of the National Space Society in the United States and an observer representative to the UN Committee on the Peaceful Uses of Outer Space. In 2005 he served as a participant in the workshop on *Humanity and Space the Next Thousand Years* hosted by the Foundation for the Future and from 2006-2008, he served as a panel member of the Association of Space Explorers workshop on mitigation policy for threats from near earth objects and currently serves on the commercial Spaceflight Safety Committee of the IAF. He is a co-founder of the International Institute for Space Commerce and a founding trustee of Singularity University. He is a corresponding fellow of the International Academy of Astronautics.

Seeing universities as nodes in an interconnected lattice of educational opportunities, Dr. Simpson has been responsible for concluding partnership agreements with Universities in Australia, Asia, North America, the Middle East, and Europe and has brought ISU into the Space Education Consortium in the United States as the only international partner in that body.

During his tenure as President of the International Space University, the school's already widely respected curriculum has been enhanced to include more material on satellite operations, management challenges of space projects, personal spaceflight, entrepreneurship, space policy, and prospects for commercial activity in space. An ISU Executive MBA enrolled its first students in June 2009.

The International Space University is headquartered in Illkirch-Graffenstaden in the urban community of Strasbourg, France. It offers three Masters Degrees, including the recently inaugurated Executive MBA. Each year from June through August it offers a prestigious, 9-week long session known as the Space Studies Program (SSP) that prepares high potential participants for rapid advancement in the space sector. The school also offers a number of short professional development courses tailored to the needs of space agencies and businesses.

He is also the author of Chapter 22 of this volume, *To Plan for a Century: ISU's Vision of Education in Space.*

REFERENCES

1. European Space Agency Technology Program Office, *Down to Earth, How space technology improves our lives,* September 2009; and NASA Innovative Partnerships Program, *Spinoff, 2009 ed.,* Developed by Publications and Graphics Department, NASA Center for Aerospace Communication.
2. "Frequently Asked Questions: What is Cisco's Mission Statement," Cisco Systems Investor Website: http://investor.cisco.com/faq.cfm?SH_No_JavaScript=yes
3. "Cisco's Space Router Successfully Operates in Orbit," Cisco Systems, Inc. news release, January 18, 2010
4. D. Raitt, E.J. v.d. Heide & M. Kruijff, F. Hermanns, "Space Spin-in from textiles: Opportunities from Tethers and Innovative Technologies," IAC-03-U.2.b.09
5. *Ibid.,* p. 5.
6. Association of Space Explorers International Panel on Asteroid Threat Mitigation, *Asteroid Threats: A Call for Global Response, Executive Summary, 2008, p. 3.*
7. Planetary and Terrestrial Mining Sciences Symposium (PTMSS), http://www.isruinfo.com/
8. Kim Jae Won, "HYU, Touching Down on Space," *Weekly Hanyang News,* http://www.hanyang.ac.kr/controller/weeklyView.jsp?file=/top_news/2010/034/english2.html
9. See www.unmannedspaceflight.com a British site which does a masterful job of making rover images available on the web very shortly after their data stream arrives from the red planet.

CHAPTER 6

THE SPACE-BASED INTERNET

Editor's note:
In the previous chapter, Michael Simpson discussed the Cisco IRIS project as an example of spin-in. To provide more information on IRIS, the following was compiled from materials that were downloaded from a number of Cisco web sites. It was also reviewed by Cisco for accuracy. Figure 1 & 2 are reproduced here courtesy of and with the permission of Cisco Systems, Inc.

OVERVIEW

As commercial endeavors expand into space, the need to communicate goes with them. Most of the entrepreneurs, scientists, explorers, and tourists who journey to space will expect to remain in more or less constant contact with the rest of human civilization, which will require a significant communications infrastructure.

Businesses will require constant exchange of data, while space-inhabitants will want their YouTube videos, and live feeds from Earth's critical elections or its great sporting spectacles. They'll also want immediate access to the latest tweets from their favorite celebrities, and the latest news from their parents, children or grandchildren.

Increasing the capability of Earth and space-based communications networks therefore becomes a significant enabler of space commerce. A modest but perhaps important step forward is the recent development of a radiation-tolerant internet router that, for the first time, implements internet-protocol-based network services directly onboard a satellite.

Cisco's prototype router, Internet Routing in Space (IRIS) is a hosted payload on Intelsat 14 (IS-14), launched on November 23, 2010 and operating since then in GEO orbit.

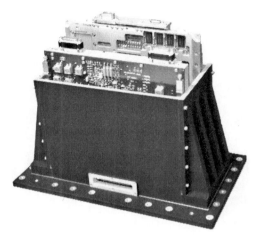

Figure 1
Cisco IRIS Router
IRIS is a radiation-tolerant router that
implements network services directly onboard a satellite.
© Cisco Systems, Inc.

The IRIS router is a technology demonstration created by Cisco at the request of the U.S. Department of Defense to validate the feasibility of locating internet switching equipment in space in order to seamlessly converge space and ground communication networks.

The DoD tests have been completed, and a report on test results is pending, but was not issued as of the publication of this book. Following the completion of testing, Cisco has been providing access to IRIS to commercial and government customers to help them understand how it may impact their needs in the future.

SWITCHING IN SPACE

Before it was possible to locate a router in space, all internet switching gear was located on the ground, so all internet transmissions were of necessity routed through ground-based stations, increasing transmission delays and reducing network flexibility. The purpose of IRIS is to enable satellite transmissions to be routed directly from one satellite to another, thereby increasing the efficiency of both on and off-Earth communication networks, and making additional capabilities available to all space travelers and inhabitants.

IRIS also has the potential to make existing satellite networks more efficient by reducing the extra communications steps that must presently be used with non-internet-protocol satellite systems. Further, many currently existing satellite networks were designed to operate only with one type of communications signal, and thus satellite networks designed for television signals typically do not interoperate with those designed for telephone. However, as communications media are converging on internet protocol standards, the ability of different satellite networks to communicate directly with one another offers the possibility of improving the efficiency of network operations.

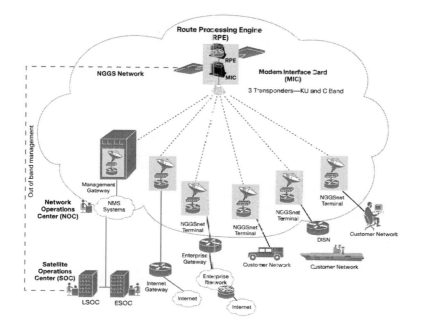

Figure 2
Cisco Space Architecture, referred to as "Next Generation Global Services" (NGGS) links a variety of sites through satellite ground terminals to increase communication efficiency and reduce costs.
© Cisco Systems, Inc., 2009

IRIS creates a converged space-ground network that ensures every voice, video or data session travels on the most efficient path, whether through space or on the terrestrial network or a combination of both. This is intended to optimize the end user experience while reducing the volume of bandwidth needed to accomplish communication tasks.

In many space commerce scenarios, space-based routers will enable manned and unmanned spacecraft, space stations, and satellites to be in direct communication with each other, offering increased communications capability to commercial operators by extending the point-to-point communications network beyond Earth. They will also enable telecommunications, video, and data to be transmitted by a single satellite.

To manage costs for end users, Cisco uses its standard software tools, called IOS, which are already deployed on millions of ground-based routers throughout the world.

Using IOS for space applications should make it easier for commercial teams to design and develop systems and equipment destined for space, and perhaps the resulting cost savings will further enable the emerging commercial space sector by reducing or entirely eliminating what might otherwise be a significant development cost for new space hardware. It's also expected to reduce in-space operating costs.

More information on Cisco's space initiative can be found at http://www.cisco.com/web/strategy/government/space-routing.html.

•••

CHAPTER 7

A Tourist's Perspective on Space

Michael A. Blum
Chief Operating Officer, Hedgeye Risk Management

I, Michael Blum, am a venture capitalist for Richard Branson.

Well, not really. After all, billionaires like Branson don't need me to finance them.

But figuratively it is nevertheless true, because I have bought my ticket for a ride on Virgin Galactic's suborbital SpaceShipTwo.

By purchasing a ticket I not only put myself on a path to fulfill my childhood dream of going to space, but I'm also doing what I can to support the nascent commercial space industry. I'm betting on the success of Virgin Galactic, and I also believe that affordable and safe access to space will likely be available to hundreds of thousands, or even millions of people in the coming decades. For now, I'm also a tiny bit of proof that a market for these journeys exists.

MY DREAM

When I was 6 years old my first grade teacher turned on the television so we could watch the launch of one of the first Space Shuttle missions. From the amazing moment that the Main Engines ignited and my classmates and I saw this marvel of technology rise into the Florida skies, I knew I wanted to be an astronaut. On that day, so did most of the other kids in that classroom.

But becoming an astronaut turned out to be virtually impossible for me. Take a look at the opening chapter of Colonel Mike Mullane's great book *Riding Rockets*, and pay particular attention to his description of the astronaut selection process. See if you share my admiration for him and also if you feel a bit of inadequacy – I know I couldn't have done that, and no amount of self-confidence would have made it so.

So I had to find a different way. Alas, a $25M trip to the International Space Station, à la Dennis Tito, is definitely beyond my financial means, and so it turned out to be entirely fortunate for me, and for a great many others, that entrepreneurs including Richard Branson believe in the market for commercial space travel. They're creating businesses to enable people like me to experience something we had only once dreamed of.

Figure 1
Blum's future spacecraft, Virgin Galactic SpaceShipTwo.
Image provided courtesy of Virgin Galactic.

Branson is not alone, of course. His technology partner in Virgin Galactic, Burt Rutan of Scaled Composites, is providing the hardware to match Branson's entrepreneurial and marketing vision. And there are other ventures, including Elon Musk's SpaceX, and Robert Bigelow's Bigelow Aerospace, and their dedicated teams are setting about to fulfill my childhood dream, because it is a dream that they also share.

WHY DO SO MANY PEOPLE WANT TO GO TO SPACE?

There's the romance of it, the lure to see the Earth differently, from above. There's a wonderfully romantic feeling attached to the idea of looking out a porthole back onto the home planet, of seeing it floating there so effortlessly in the vast expanse of darkness around it that is the universe, and watching the tiniest of blue slivers, our atmosphere, stretch across the horizon. This very sight has humbled those lucky few who, like Mullane, had the right stuff and the good fortune to get chosen to ride on big rockets. Well the rest of us want a look too.

And there's politics. One of the earliest ticket holders on a now defunct space tourism venture once mentioned that she would have happily given her ticket away to the leader of any nation who asked for it, simply so that the leader could experience first hand that in fact nothing separates us from one another; that borders are lines on maps but should not divide people, or make them forget the oneness of humankind.

OH, AND THE ADVENTURE!

The lure of experiencing the seemingly final frontier, a trip to space allows us mere mortals to experience sensations that otherwise are barely attainable. Is your idea of fun a supersonic flight, alas, now a great rarity since the Concorde has been mothballed? And high G-loads, followed by weightlessness and then more G-loads on reentry? This is as good a reason as any to buy a ticket.

AND THE PIONEERING SPIRIT?

To be among the first 1,000 or 10,000 humans to leave the planet will be an honorable badge of achievement to recount to future generations, who shall then perhaps be inspired to reach further and set their own higher standards for themselves and their descendants in their journeys to come.

DRIVEN INTO SPACE

But perhaps the single most important motivation for me, the reason above all others that I plunked my deposit down with Virgin Galactic and took my place in line, was expressed by Elon Musk, the founder of Space Exploration Technologies. He noted that when we think of the truly important events in history, we need to think in a geologic time scale. The rise and fall of empires has no geologic significance, nor do even our great historical documents such as the Magna Carta or the Constitution.

Beyond civilization's events, it was life's destiny to leave the oceans and colonize the surface of the Earth, and this is the single most important event in our geologic history.

Scientists are unsure why life evolved beyond its sole habitat in the world's oceans, but what is clear is that the realm of land and air posed countless challenges to the early aquatic creatures. Gravity, new sensory stimulation, including light, sounds and smells that did not exist in the water, the search for food, and of course the need to exchange oxygen and carbon dioxide for respiration, the steps onto land were not easy. Nor were they necessarily obvious.

SO WHY DID IT HAPPEN?

Did competition for survival drive these organisms from their ocean home? Was it opportunity? Or was it simply the availability of new habitats and niches? Could it have been an innate drive to explore?

The answer may remain forever hidden from us, but by thinking in a geologic timescale one cannot but come to the conclusion that the same drive, the same forces, the same imperatives that led the ocean's creatures to colonize the land will inevitably lead humans to colonize the solar system, and perhaps many more solar systems beyond our own.

In my small way I will also be part of this.

THE NEED FOR INSPIRATION

Today's kids seem more interested in the latest video games and iPhone Apps than in space, but this was not always so. At the height of the Apollo Program, NASA and its contractors employed over 400,000 people, average age 28, all dedicated to the single cause of putting a man on the moon. This challenge inspired widespread excitement and enthusiasm in people not only in the United States, but also around the world.

Where is today's younger generation? Today, the average NASA employee is 47.

But ventures such as Virgin Galactic and SpaceX have the potential to reignite the fire of excitement in our children, to demonstrate that a career in engineering or science may lead to a great success not only for the individual, but for society as well. And perhaps you'll make a fortune too.

All of these factors – romance, politics, adventure, the pioneering spirit, evolution – have played a role in my decision to buy a ticket on Virgin Galactic. Today, as I wait impatiently for my turn, I cannot say which aspect appeals to me more. Perhaps I will be able to tell you after I return. And then we can discuss it all after you return from your journey.

And after millions of us have seen the Earth from outer space, and when millions more live their lives on other planets and space habitats, what then will they say about evolution, and adventure, and politics, and romance?

This is what my ticket on Virgin Galactic gives me the opportunity to be part of.

•••

MICHAEL A. BLUM

Michael A. Blum is the Chief Operating Officer at Hedgeye Risk Management. Prior to co-founding Hedgeye, Michael was Founder and Chief Operating Officer of Falconhenge Partners. The firm was integrated into Magnetar Capital in April 2006. Before moving to Wall Street, Michael spent 7 years in Silicon Valley, eventually joining PayPal, the world's leading electronic payment system, where he served as Country Manager, Germany and eventually oversaw the firm's business in SE Asia and the Pacific. PayPal sold to eBay for $1.5B in 2002. Michael is an Astronaut-in-waiting with Virgin Galactic, and received his Bachelor of Arts in Economics and International Studies (honors) from Yale University.

(Editor's note: Michael Blum's trip on Virgin Galactic is currently scheduled for 2012.)

CHAPTER 8

AN OPEN SOURCE, STANDARDIZED RESEARCH PLATFORM
FOR THE
INTERNATIONAL SPACE STATION

CHRISTOPHER K. CUMMINS
CHIEF FINANCIAL OFFICER, NANORACKS LLC

In the not too distant past, anyone who wanted to manipulate or analyze data for a scientific or engineering project would need to know low level programming languages, especially if there was a real sensor or hardware in the loop. Consequently, 8086 machine language was commonly taught in physics and engineering programs. But with the advent of scientific programming environments like MatLab™, Mathematica™ or R, most researchers no longer need to take the time or suffer the brain damage required to acquire such arcane knowledge. Instead, they can employ a relatively simple and widely used scientific programming environment so that they can focus on being creative about their research. While these programming environments are simple and flexible, they allow for very complex applications. And since the users themselves generally write the application programs, they are free to share their work for free or to charge for it.

Space research is just now crawling out of the equivalent of the machine language era. Until very recently, only a handful of specialists around the globe understood space research hardware, and in most cases their expertise was confined to a specific launch vehicle or to the Space Station. As a result, all space research hardware was custom designed and fitted, a painstaking and expensive process.

Even today, standard operating procedure requires custom designed research hardware built with great care, and should a client require the use of a different launch vehicle or even a different part of the space station than the one for which it was originally designed, the time consuming and expensive process of redesigning and redeveloping the hardware to national space agency specifications must begin yet again, most likely with a new team of engineers.

The auto industry deployed large scale mass production a century ago, so why has space research been so slow to create and benefit from an open source, standardized platform for scientific research? In essence, industrial standardization so common in everything from cars to laboratory hardware has never before been necessary in space research: a Russian scientist would fly experiments only on Russian vehicles; an American only on NASA vehicles.

But as the era of segregated, national space programs is clearly over, the time for standardization of the research infrastructure has arrived.

In the past neither time nor cost were overriding concerns, but this is no longer the case. A single research project funded by NASA may well ride up on the last of the space shuttle flights, be re-flown on a Russian Progress resupply vehicle, and then be installed and activated in U.S. National Laboratory on ISS. Later, a follow-on experiment might be flown on SpaceX's DragonLab, not to mention also launch on an Indian or Japanese launch vehicle. Other research projects may soon get their first microgravity exposure on an American suborbital vehicle, manned or unmanned, and then be accommodated on a private orbital platform like that from Bigelow, or perhaps even on the distant time horizon it will benefit from an entire Chinese infrastructure of vehicles and platforms.

In all cases, time and cost are critical deciding factors that enable or perhaps prevent a scientist from conducting an experiment at all. Therefore, it makes complete economic and operational sense to assure that the research hardware is built only once, allowing the researcher to focus on the scientific objective of the payload rather than on the 'box,' just as using a scientific programming environment enables researchers to quickly and easily write programs to address their scientific objectives, rather than dwelling ad nauseum in the depths of machine language programming.

Other industries serve as helpful examples of standardization. When freight is sent from Asia to North America, it doesn't matter which airline or even cargo ship is chosen: the pallets are a standard size and the shipping rules are the same, which assures the fastest development time, optimal standardization, and lowest cost.

Figure 1
The NanoRacks Platform

My colleagues and I created NanoRacks for just this reason. NanoRacks is a company whose purpose is to flourish by introducing commercial standardization to space research hardware and operations. We believe it is imperative that researchers should not have to re-design and re-build custom made hardware just because their launch vehicle is from Orbital Sciences while a future version will be flown onboard the Progress, and when the hardware gets into orbit it may first be used in the Russian lab, then the Japanese lab, and then the U.S. lab.

NanoRacks intends to provide the benefits of a standardized research platform, which is indeed what the entirety of space industry should be aiming for as well. We did not invent the idea of standardization on space station, as starting around the turn of the century NASA introduced the Express racks that are designed to produce a commercial interface, and that is what NanoRacks is further exploiting by reaching out to a broader community.

Founded in August 2009, NanoRacks has accomplished an amazing amount in its first year. NanoRacks designed and deployed two research platforms (NR-1 and NR-2) on the International Space Station in the U.S. National Laboratory. These first two racks are similar and each can house 16 CubeSat sized payloads.

The CubeSat form factor was chosen specifically because it is well known to a growing number of corporate and university researchers and engineers worldwide. Measuring 10 cm by 10 cm by 10 cm and weighting in at less than 1Kg, the CubeSat has been proven in the microsatellite industry to be a productive standard. Despite their small size, CubeSats are designed to operate as free flying satellites.

Whether one flies with India, Russia, the US, or other nations, many different types of launch vehicles can now host CubeSats, and customers can also build satellites that are multiples of a single CubeSat form factor (1U or 2U or 4U).

As a result of the success of the CubeSat standard, a supplier market for structures, power supplies and communications systems has also grown to accommodate the standard. The typical CubeSat derives power from solar arrays, deployed after launch, and ground communications are provided by the user/operator using a low power radio.

Standardization in the CubeSat marketplace also came about with the development of the *Poly Picosat Orbital Deployer* (P-POD) launch vehicle integration system, a standardized interface between CubeSats and launch vehicles.

Today there are dozens of CubeSat development teams around the world, and among the technologies being developed are new thruster systems, miniaturized avionics, communications systems, passive and active attitude control systems, and power systems. Some development teams are graduating to more complex platforms, and there are early studies being made for planetary missions.

At the moment, in fact, the number of projects is far greater than available launch slots, which presents a problem for CubeSat developers, but may be an emerging opportunity for launch providers.

New companies are emerging to service this market, including kit manufacturers and subsystem vendors, and one quick count found at least 34 participating institutions (universities, national labs, and corporations) as well as a handful of suppliers of applicable hardware and software.

If a similar community could be developed that would drive market growth and innovation for the International Space Station and other orbiting research platforms, the results would likely be a significant expansion of current space commerce.

This is the business model behind the NanoRacks Research Platform

The NanoRacks Research Platform provides a standardized CubeSat-like development environment for ISS researchers. A student, a researcher, or a business developer can design payloads that fit within the CubeSat form factor, now known as a CubeLab™. A student may want to design a single 1U project, whereas a corporate researcher might wish to make use of a 2U or 4U payload for pharmaceutical research. Using this form factor, the NanoRacks payloads can be accommodated on any launch vehicle, and the 'plug and play' model requires the standardized hardware to be built only once.

Using an off-the-shelf CubeSat kit to build a CubeLab™, users can develop experiments, integrate the experiments with the CubeLab™, and deliver the 1 kg project for flight aboard any available vehicle visiting the ISS. Each CubeLab™ module simply plugs into one of the 16 standard USB connectors in each rack, which thus provides structural, electrical and data connectivity in one simple operation. NanoRacks takes care of the interfaces to the rest of the station and the rest of NASA.

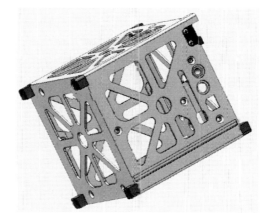

Figure 2
CubeLab™ Frame

Power is supplied to the NanoRacks Platform via a standard power connector that plugs into an ISS EXPRESS Rack, and data connectivity is handled via an ISS EXPRESS Rack Laptop. The company also schedules the astronaut time required for connecting or disconnecting the CubeLabs™, and in a departure from a long standing NASA policy, NanoRacks (and NASA) are responsible for hardware safety, but NOT for payload success.

Hence, the likelihood of success is not a selection criterion. Rather, it is a commercial model where the researcher has responsibility for experiment success.

The key question, of course, is whether there is sufficient market demand for the system opportunities at a profitable price point. To date, no commercial system on the ISS has demonstrated a profit, so why should NanoRacks be different?

One element of our answer is our low price point. A commercial customer can fly to the ISS to perform a research project for thirty days at a price of $50,000 per 1U, and the price is lower for student projects. Previously, there was not a mechanism in place to accept small, simple payloads on the ISS at a price that made economic sense. On the Russian Mir, the price would have been upwards of $200,000.

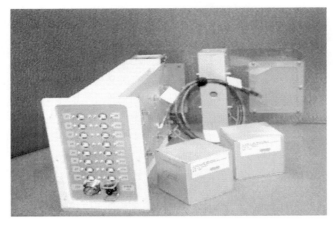

Figure 3
NanoRacks Platform with payloads ready to plug and play.

At this price, a customer is able to 'tinker' with the design and endure failures before hitting on a success.

Another aspect of the answer is the rapidity and frequency of getting experiments onto the space station. A new experiment can take as little as 6 months to go from payload reservation to operation aboard the Space Station, and repeat experiments can be accomplished in even less time.

We anticipate between 4 and 6 missions a year, which means new plug and play CubeLabs™ will replace old CubeLabs™ every 2 to 3 months.

Using our current financial assumptions and market projections, we expect an occupancy rate of about 70% in 2014 which is about three and half times our break even occupancy rate.

NanoRacks platforms are an open architecture system, and much as the open architecture of personal computers and software created enthusiastic and large markets, we anticipate that an open architecture space science system will lower costs and free researchers from dependence on a proprietary, expensive system.

Good communities are also central to good open standards. Our goal is to become a focal point for customers wanting to use space stations for lower cost, smaller projects. Like many of the newer scientific programming environments mentioned in the introduction, we expect to see a set of toolbox- or toolkit-like CubeLabs developed, which will provide basic research utilities such as imaging and measurement. NanoRacks will develop some of these, and we're enthusiastic for third parties to develop others.

Similarly, many researchers may want to create permanent NanoRacks-class research facilities for sustained and repeatable research. In particular, commercial researchers are likely to demand the assured ability to conduct repeated experiments as a foundational issue before they are willing to commit corporate funding. For example, the new capabilities offered by the NanoRacks Research Platform may be extremely attractive to newly funded stem cell researchers who are likely to want to exploit differences in how cells organize themselves in microgravity versus how the cells organize on Earth.

Hence, NanoRacks Platforms will enhance the ability of the ISS to conduct repeat experiments, while further lowering costs to researchers by providing the ability to exchange sample containers instead of returning entire CubeLabs.

We'll know that NanoRacks has truly succeeded when there are a great many users who 'Think in Zero G,' and who associate NanoRacks with their successes. That will occur because we've given them the chance to learn what zero gravity really means through inexpensive, repeated experimentation. They will have adapted to an environment without up or down, without convection, where properties such as elasticity are often more important than density, and where a glob is a more natural liquid form than a puddle. Then who knows what they'll discover and invent!

The goal of NanoRacks is to develop an extensive, international community of researchers who use ISS as a fully functioning multidisciplinary laboratory, much as has been the case with CubeSats. We anticipate that the use of the NanoRacks Research Platform can be both a stepping stone to future commercial free-flyers such as the one announced by SpaceX, and as an end product in and of itself. The resulting establishment of a cadre of young space science researchers in the near term will serve as a major resource for future exploration activities.

•••

CHRISTOPHER K. CUMMINS

NanoRacks' CFO/COO Christopher K. Cummins is an experienced financial innovator with an aerospace background who has been involved in the financing side of commercial space since 1981. Prior to being a pioneer in developing fund-linked products at Citigroup, Mr. Cummins consulted to various aerospace companies and worked at NASA/JSC developing cost and schedule estimates for the ISS. Mr. Cummins holds a MS in Statistics from NYU, a MBA from Yale, and a BA in Physics and in Government from Cornell. http://www.nanoracksllc.com/

CHAPTER 9

MANUFACTURING FOR SPACE FROM A SMALL COMPANY'S POINT OF VIEW
A CASE STUDY

HELMUT KESSLER, PH.D.
MANAGING DIRECTOR, CVI TECHNICAL OPTICS LTD.

THE COMMERCIAL SPACE ENVIRONMENT
HISTORICAL DEVELOPMENT

Rockets first saw use in military applications in ancient China in the 13th century, and they saw intermittent development thereafter in China and then with greater focus in Europe. It was, however, only in the late 19th and early 20th century that the 'Father of Russian cosmonautics,' the Russian Constantin Tsiolkovsky, developed the theoretical basis for rockets as means to escape the Earth's gravity and explore space. Further groundbreaking work was undertaken by the American Robert H Goddard and the German Herman Oberth.

The Second World War saw the first use of rockets as ballistic missiles with the German V2 rocket designed by Wernher von Braun. Von Braun had been an active member of one of the German rocket societies founded as a result of general enthusiasm for rocketry kindled by Oberth's work. Eventually von Braun's work culminated in the design of the Saturn V rocket that enabled the Moon landing.

Following the Second World War and the resulting Cold War, the main emphasis of rocket development was on national security rather than space exploration. With the USA confident of its technological supremacy, astronomy and space exploration were pushed into the background until the Soviet Union launched Sputnik, the world's first satellite, in October 1957.

Shocked by this development, the 'space race' began with both the USA and the Soviet Union applying considerable funds and resources to their space programs. While the political system in the Soviet Union did not allow private enterprise, the USA's political system encouraged it, though initially all use of space was scientifically oriented.

The 10th of July 1963 saw the launch of the first communications satellite, Telstar, built by AT&T's Bell Laboratories on behalf of the USA's NASA, the UK's General Post Office and the French National Post, Telegraph and Telecom Office. The first publicly available television broadcast was undertaken on the 23rd July 1962.

Following this milestone, the April 1965 launch of 'Early Bird,' the world's first commercial communications satellite, marked the beginning of a new era. It was built by built by Hughes Aircraft Company and used by a commercial company, Communication Satellite Corporation (COMSAT) (now Boeing Satellite Systems) and marked the beginning of the commercial use of space, driven by private entrepreneurship.[1]

PRIVATE SECTOR ACTIVITIES IN SPACE

The main private sector activity in space, and so far the most profitable, is telecommunications. Since the second half of the 1990s, however, several other space-related, private sectors have developed:

1.   Commercial launch services
2.   Satellite navigation
3.   Remote sensing
4.   Telemetry, tracking, control monitoring and data collection
5.   Space tourism

While these sectors are making an increasing contribution to the space industry, the majority share of activity is still provided by government driven investments.   However, especially in the telecommunications sector it has become clear that governments are moving more and more to a regulatory role, dealing with international treaty provisions and safety aspects, rather than the direct finance of space activities.

At the same time, governments are still one of the main drivers for space use for national security and space exploration, areas where private activity is either unwanted for security reasons, or where it does not make commercial sense.[2]

OVERVIEW OF SPACE INDUSTRIES

In terms of its historical development, the space industry must still be considered very new. The participating companies are a mix of large corporations with a space industry division as well as many smaller and medium-sized companies involved in space related activities to different degrees, depending on the sector.

Generally, the large firms are the main contractors to government-operated space programs as a result of their extensive experience in government contracting, while the smaller and medium-sized companies are sub-contractors and suppliers.

The breadth of technology required for space commerce and exploration gives rise to a large variety of typical products and services offered by these subcontractors. Some examples are:

1. Specialized electronic components
2. Specialized mechanical solutions
3. Optical systems and components
4. Software development
5. Finance for private space ventures
6. Space-related insurance brokerage
7. Technology brokerage
8. Legal advice for space-related activities

While private enterprise is seeing growth in all these areas and is thereby gaining economic importance, it is nevertheless still the case that there is still a very strong inter-dependency between private enterprise and governments.[2]

CASE STUDY: CVI TECHNICAL OPTICS LTD.

COMPANY OVERVIEW AND PRODUCT PORTFOLIO

Founded in 1972, CVI Technical Optics Ltd. is part of the global CVI Melles Griot Group headquartered in New Mexico and operating in the US, Europe, and Asia. CVI Technical Optics became part of the CVI Melles Griot Group in 2000, and has benefitted from substantial capital investment, enabling the company to expand both sales and product range. With a headcount of approximately 50 employees in the Isle of Man, CVI Technical Optics is a typical small to medium-sized enterprise (SME), but with the backing of a large parent company. The Isle of Man itself is an environment that strongly embraces and encourages space-related business.

Within the CVI group of companies, CVI Technical Optics Ltd. specializes in the manufacture of high quality, high laser damage threshold (LDT) components that are applied in a large variety of applications such as:

1. Industrial applications such as laser cutting, marking, and welding
2. Medical applications including tattoo and hair removal
3. Aerospace, defense and space applications
4. Research and development applications
5. Semiconductor applications.

An example of a CVI innovation in a space application is a vacuum compatible coating that can also withstand large temperature swings. The demand for such coating is growing due to the increased use of optical components in satellites, which requires them to be able to withstand use in the space environment, in a vacuum and under circumstances that very often involve large temperature swings as a result of the satellite facing towards the sun or away during its orbit.

Figure 1
Substrate inspection under halogen light.

The risk for an optical device under these circumstances is that the optical coating can craze, or develop small surface cracks, and thereby render the component useless. On a slightly less dramatic scale, the optical flatness of the component changes, resulting in the instrument's precision bring compromised.

Use of optics in space thus requires these issues to be solved, necessitating an improvement in optical surface polishing and coating processes that provide better adhesion of the optical coating to the substrate.

The developed process is now also being used in Earth-bound applications, as it offers the same advantages (vacuum compatibility combined with resistance to large temperature swings) for large optical components as they are being used in the world's most powerful laser systems, those involved in high laser power research.

CVI Technical Optics benefits from an experienced and long-standing workforce with many staff members having worked for the company for more than 10 years, and an annual staff turnover of less than 4%. This, combined with customer requirements that constantly push component specifications to the technologically possible limits, has over the years enabled the company to become a world leader in the manufacture of some specific components such as Fabry-Perot etalons and optically contacted polarization cubes.

Continued capital investment has at the same time enabled the company to remain competitive in its core markets through both innovation and introduction of lean manufacturing techniques.

For many SMEs, this is an important balancing act, as the 'bread-and butter' business needs to be maintained in a profitable fashion to provide the funds for development of new products and production methods, not all of which are initially customer funded.

MANUFACTURING FOR SPACE: BENEFITS AND CHALLENGES

Space is a hostile environment and hence all equipment manufactured for space is required to meet demanding specifications. Apart from the hostility of the space environment itself, the remoteness of the location where the equipment is going to be used makes reliability paramount. Once a piece of equipment has been launched – an expensive undertaking in itself – it is expected and required to work because any exchange of components is generally not possible.

CVI Technical Optics Ltd. manufactures components for the space industry, such as optical mirrors, windows, lenses and polarizers. These optical components are supplied to contractors or sub-contractors who then integrate the components into a system or sub-system for the payload of a spacecraft.

Optical components used for space applications can range from almost standard components to very specific components designed and manufactured to extremely tight tolerances, which depends on the system or sub-system they are being used in. During the development phase of spacecraft bus or payload systems or sub-systems, it frequently occurs that specifications are assigned to components without any further thought, the system or sub-system designer simply assuming the manufacturability of the given part.

Only when manufacturers are being contacted regarding procurement of the component does it then emerge that certain aspects of the specifications are unachievable, even in some rare cases to the point where the specification contravenes the laws of physics. In such cases, a cost-efficient solution must be found. Cost efficient here means both with a view to the manufacture of the component itself, and also with a view to a potential re-design of the system or sub-system, and the consequent cost involved with that.

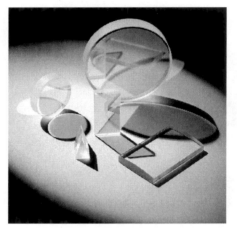

Figure 2
Various Laser Optics.

In these situations, SME-sized component manufacturers can have a distinct advantage over their larger competitors because many of the people in the firm have the detailed technical knowledge of what is and is not possible. In the case of CVI Technical Optics Ltd., most of the senior staff have risen through the company's ranks through in-house promotion, they are also often the ones who negotiate with the customer and are very familiar with the manufacturing process and its limits and cost-drivers. This means that they can contribute significantly in the design/negotiation process of looking for a new solution when the original design has been found to be unfeasible.

As a result, negotiations about the manufacturability of certain specifications and possible alternatives can be held very efficiently. The manufacturer of the system or sub-system can gather the relevant staff from their side, while two or three members of staff from CVI Technical Optics Ltd. are generally able to assess all requirements and answer all possible questions. Hence, even after the first meeting the achievable specifications are generally clear, and a way forward has been established.

This solution is generally either the manufacture of a component with altered, yet acceptable specifications, or a substantial re-design of the system or sub-system on the basis of the discussion and the decisions taken.

Hierarchies in SMEs are generally very flat and the ways of communication are direct, so decisions can be taken quickly, thereby speeding up the decision-making process, especially when time is short.

Often the changed specifications that move a component into the realm of manufacturability are generally at the leading edge of what is technologically possible. As a result an SME like CVI Technical Optics Ltd. will generally benefit from the manufacture of such a component, as new avenues of manufacturing in both materials and process will more often than not have to be taken. After the successful manufacture of the relevant component, many of the new techniques learnt will be applied to the every-day manufacturing of other components, thereby increasing the technical capabilities and efficiency of processes of the company overall.

More often than not, terrestrial market applications for components or derivatives thereof can be found. This will then make a good case for further capital investment, allowing the company to take another step forward. As a result, even a small quantity of components manufactured for space applications will generally have a significant impact on the overall technological advancement of the product portfolio and, through improved efficiency of processes, will also reap financial benefits.

An example of a process developed for space-related optics that was then transferred with great success to Earth bound applications was mentioned above regarding the vacuum and large temperature swing compatibility of optical components.

Another example comes from a project where a high extinction ration optical polarizer was required, which again had to work in the space environment. Traditionally, optical cue polarizers consist of two prisms, where the prism of one hypotenuse of the prism is coated and then cemented to the hypotenuse of the other prism using optical cement. Once light passes through this component, the vertically and horizontally polarized components of the light are separated.

Unfortunately, conventional optical cement is not able to withstand high laser power or cosmic radiation. While it would survive cosmic radiation for a limited amount of time, on longer missions the optical cement would discolour and drastically reduce the functionality of the polarizer, jeopardizing the instrument.

To find a solution for this requirement, CVI Technical Optics developed optically contacted polarizaton cubes, in which the prisms are coated as before, but the surfaces are kept so flat that the two hypotenuses can be contacted together simply by molecular (van-der Waals) adhesion, thereby eliminating the use of optical cement. This makes the component stable even for prolonged use in the space environment.

At the same time, elimination of the optical cement also means that the cube polarizer can withstand high laser power, making it a useful alternative to plate polarizers traditionally used for high power applications. Especially when used in the field, the cube has the advantage of being much easier to align, saving service time and thereby maintenance costs. As a result of these advances, optically contacted cubes are now widely used within the laser industry.

Optical components manufactured for space applications generally require much more rigorous testing than Earth-bound components for the above-mentioned reasons. While the tests are generally harder, there is also often greater variation in the tests required..

While many defense-related optics require salt-spray testing to ensure that the component can cope with use in a marine environment, this is rarely required of optics destined for space. On the other hand, many Earth-bound industrial applications do not require any components to be radiation resistant, something that is of paramount importance in the space environment.

Use of non-radiation resistant optical windows in space applications, for example, will create color-centers in the component substrate and cause it to become non-transparent, so the system or subsystem it is being used in will most likely fail to function properly.

Component testing is a challenge that many SMEs face.. In fact, the testing requirements are often the biggest challenge SMEs manufacturing for space application face. Since SMEs generally have limited test equipment, both in terms of the type of specification that can tested as well as the number of test bays available, the required certification of a component can often be more costly and difficult to achieve than its actual manufacture because this must be paid for outside.

Not only does much of the testing tie up valuable metrology equipment for considerable amounts of time, but the necessary documentation in itself is very often extensive. The size of the company more often than not does not warrant the employment of a specific member of staff for such tasks, but the function of ensuring proper documentation will generally fall on the quality assurance manager, who will also deal with all other aspects of quality within the company.

Hence it is the case that not only is testing equipment used for long periods, but also manpower to monitor and record test results. This is not always reflected in the achievable sale price of the component, and can hurt the SME when the final delivery and invoicing are completed, and total costs are aggregated.

The QA documentation issue is part of a wider documentation issue associated mainly with the space industry. In most cases the documentation required when tendering for space-related work is rather extensive and requires a significant amount of time to be spent on it.

Especially in an SME, this means that manpower is diverted from other sales and technical areas of the company to enable the tender paperwork to be compiled properly as per the customer's requirement.

Using the relevant manpower naturally has a monetary cost side, but especially for an SME, where key people very often 'multi-task', there is a significant opportunity cost associated with such work. In fact, this is often the biggest hurdle in the way of 'the next step up' for an SME.

As the components will be used in space, a meticulous record of manufacturing and testing needs to be maintained. The scope of the required documentation in most cases far exceeds the scope required under standard requirements for Earth applications. For example, while the optical surfaces of standard components generally have to meet standard cleanliness ('scratch-dig') criteria, the customer will in most cases accept a report that simply states whether or not the component passes the requirement.

For space applications, a map of the surface, generated by inspection under a microscope, is generally required. As a result, the per–surface inspection time can easily increase from 10 minutes to around 30-45 minutes, depending on the level of accuracy.

Further, the nature of much of the additional documentation such as surface mapping requires the work to be carried out by a senior member of staff, but only when the volume of work in this area grows above a certain level can it be justified to employ a specific member of staff for such tasks. Expanding the workforce is a financial expense and by committing to this expansion, the SME needs to be certain that the required revenue can be generated. Especially when the staff headcount is very low, each additionally employed member of staff, especially when in a more senior position, adds noticeable percentage increases to monthly overhead.

Being prepared to take this risk, and knowing when to take it, depends on the forecast of future revenues and relates directly to the degree of risk that the owners of the company are prepared to take.

MANUFACTURING FOR SPACE: THE FUTURE

It is clear that space-related industries are not only here to stay, but that the commercial use of space is constantly expanding. With it goes the need for systems and sub-systems for spacecraft bus and payloads, which themselves are made up of individual components.

From this point of view, there will be significant growth in the opportunities for SMEs to get involved in the manufacture of components for space applications. CVI Technical Optics Ltd. is firmly committed to manufacturing components for space applications due to the synergies for the overall product portfolio, discussed above, which far outweigh the challenges.

Further, many components required for space applications have stringent requirements combined with generally low production quantities, and are hence less and less suited for manufacture by large companies with established and hard to change manufacturing processes. This is where the SMEs benefit from their higher agility and decision-making processes. The coming years should therefore see an increase in the number of space-related components manufactured by SMEs.

The challenge for most of them, including CVI Technical Optics Ltd. will be to move to the next step and become a manufacturer of sub-systems. Under most of the current tender procedures this will be a difficult and risky step, so only a few companies will be likely to take the step in the first place, or achieve this transition. In many cases, change will be initiated from potential customers and will ultimately be driven by their willingness to increase purchasing risk while lowering costs. This tradeoff shows a significant change from the days when government agencies were the only one procuring these components and systems; the logic of the competitive marketplace is progressively coming into space commerce as well.

Furthermore, with cost pressures running through all parts of the manufacturing sector, it has to be emphasized that an early involvement of component manufacturers will reduce design cost due to reducing the cost of potential re-design of parts of a system or sub-system. Dialogue at the earliest stages between all parties involved in a potential project will be beneficial.

Since the exchange of data is cheaper and easier than it has ever been, many hurdles that in the past prevented a closer collaboration from day one have been overcome. One can therefore only hope that improvements in this area will be made over the coming years as the needs for close collaboration in the development of new generations of commercial space hardware expand as the overall industry of space commerce also expands.

•••

DR. HELMUT KESSLER

Dr. Helmut Kessler lives in the Isle of Man where he is the Managing Director of CVI Technical Optics Ltd. a company belonging to the CVI Melles Group. He was born in Hannover, Germany and it was there that he also went to school, which was followed by National Service in the German army. Following that, he studied physics at the University of Hannover. His diploma thesis investigated optical coatings for the UV and VUV light range. Having obtained his diploma, Dr Kessler went on to study for a PhD, which he completed in 1995 with a thesis on laser spectroscopy of molecules.

Dr. Kessler then moved to the Isle of Man to work for the company that is now CVI Technical Optics Ltd. where he progressed to become Managing Director.

Apart from his interest in optics, Dr Kessler has a strong interest in space research and exploration and enjoys finding engineering solutions for space related applications of optical components. He is currently studying for an executive MBA with the International Space University.

Dr Kessler is married with one child, and in addition to spending time with his family, his hobbies include classic cars and photography.

REFERENCES

1. http://www.boeing.com/defensespace/space/bss/factsheets/376/earlybird/e bird.html
2. W. Peeters, *Keys to Space*, McGraw-Hill Inc, US 1999, ISBN 0070294380

CHAPTER 10

THE EMERGING ORGANIZATIONAL FRAMEWORK FOR THE SPACE COMMERCE ENTERPRISE

MICHAEL WISKERCHEN
DEPARTMENT OF MECHANICAL & AEROSPACE ENGINEERING, UC SAN DIEGO
AND DIRECTOR, THE CALIFORNIA SPACE GRANT CONSORTIUM

INTRODUCTION

At the end of the first decade of the 21st century, the American space program is going through particularly turbulent times. Many believe that America has lost its vision and focus, and that we will consequently abdicate our leadership role in space exploration and innovation to other international space faring nations. There are many indicators that if we continue on our present path this will certainly happen.

As a participant in and as an observer of the American space program for over forty years, my intent here is to provide personal insights on the evolution of the U.S. space 'culture' from its Apollo era to the present, with the thought that many positive aspects of this evolution could provide a path to enable the space commerce enterprise to rapidly emerge and thrive.

Likewise there are a number of deeply rooted political, financial, and social issues that could impede progress in development of the U.S. as a leader in space commerce, and these also bear examination.

While you might question whether a life-long space scientist and educator can adequately address these cultural issues, I believe that a professional scientist, trained as I am to observe nature and model its actions, should be able to accurately document observations about culture, as indeed social scientists do as a matter of course.

Hence, I will attempt to identify some of the major drivers that have influenced and indeed shaped the culture of the American space effort in the past, and others that will do so in the future. Hopefully this will provide clues as to the direction the space commerce enterprise should take to be successful, and it also may point us in the direction that the U.S. must take to retain its leadership.

The background for all of these observations consists of two critical points that should be kept in mind as you read this chapter.

The foundational concept relates to the significance of space commerce. Along with many others, I believe that leadership in space commerce will be a critically important goal for America to achieve. There are two major reasons why. First, the sheer magnitude of the commercial opportunity is so enormous that leadership in space commerce will inevitably mean some significant degree of leadership in Earth commerce. And second, the technical capacity to engage in space commerce will enable leadership in technologies that will likewise be critical to the success of any nation.

To put it bluntly, to forego leadership in space commerce is to forego leadership among nations.

The second foundational concept is that the endeavor to go to space and to accomplish some mission, program, and now commercial objective is absolutely filled with new challenges, with problems in engineering, science, and management that require dedicated and talented individuals to solve. Preparing to travel to and in space, to live in space, and to accomplish any sort of meaningful work in space is an intellectual challenge of the highest order. Further, there is no single organization anywhere in the world that has the necessary talent to solve all these challenges, or indeed to solve nearly any of them.

Consequently, in the process of accomplishing its greatest feats and even many of its seemingly more mundane ones, NASA has always relied on the deep and profound expertise of a huge ecosystem of individuals and organizations. Identifying that talent, engaging it through contract and partnership, and managing the process for maximum effectiveness should be and is indeed a core competence of the organization, and it is a skill of the highest order that should and must be cultivated and harnessed in support of the emerging commercial movement.

Let me again put it bluntly. All the engineering talent in the world will not get you there if you don't have the complementary skill set to manage the optimal deployment of that talent. The Organizational Framework referred to in the title of this chapter is therefore every bit as requisite to successful space commerce as the knowledge of rocketry, guidance, control, life support, or indeed the principles of business.

What follows, then, is a discussion of some organizational principles that I feel will be particularly important to success in space commerce, and in which I have more than a little experience that I would like to share.

A THEORY OF BUREAUCRACY

Early in my career at NASA, when I was young, brash, and determined to make the space enterprise absolutely perfect, one of my high level bosses explained to me his theory of the natural aging of a government agency (or bureaucracy). His theory was that a newly formed agency could accomplish great things and progress rapidly for a decade or two, at which point the accumulation of bureaucratic rules and regulations would converge to inhibit almost every action. He noted that this organizational process naturally happens because a 'critical mass' of key agency personnel would inevitably recognize an immediate problem, and just as quickly arrive at consensus on a rule or regulation to address the problem.

The difficulty with this process, of course, is that long after the immediate problem is solved and the rule or regulation is not needed, you will again never coalesce the 'critical mass' consensus necessary to eliminate the rule or regulation, and the resulting accumulation of rules would serve to stifle future progress.

He went on to state that the two 'bellwether' areas of the agency to watch were procurement and personnel, as you arrive at the point where so many rules and regulations are permanently in place that you can't hire or fire anyone, nor you can't procure anything efficiently. He concluded by noting that this continues until the agency either ceases to be functional and is terminated, or reaches such a crisis level that it is reborn.

After all these years and lots of confirming evidence, I tend to subscribe to this theory. Now that NASA has just reached its fiftieth birthday, where do you think we are in this process? Indeed.

THE KEY QUESTIONS, THEN, ARE

1. What are other factors do we need to consider?
2. And given a relentless process of bureaucratization, what is the best path forward?

The space commerce enterprise is so new and there are so few successful examples that it is hard to establish an adequate set of 'DOs' and 'DON'Ts' for success. It is clear that successful space commerce businesses will involve public – private partnerships of some sort, and will necessarily be international in scope. National leadership will come from nations that develop innovative organizational and management models for the international enterprise and are on the forefront of harnessing worldwide information and networking technologies.

These are the issues that I will discuss in the remainder of this chapter.

HISTORICAL PERSPECTIVE

WHAT CAN WE LEARN FROM THE APOLLO AND SHUTTLE ERAS?

As a starting point let's examine some key similarities and differences between the Apollo and Shuttle programs as to their impacts on the space culture (i.e. the people, their attitudes, and organizations).

In both cases, it is important to look at the political and economic climate that existed prior to their beginning, as well as the mood of the general population.

Throughout the late 1940s and the 1950s, the intense Cold War rivalry with the Soviet Union had a huge impact on American culture. Not long after the Second World War, the Defense Department launched a serious research push into the fields of rocketry and upper atmosphere sciences to ensure American leadership in technology, and in 1950 fear of Soviet domination led to the creation of the National Science Foundation (NSF). Through the NSF, the federal government sponsored research, primarily at American universities.

NSF struggled constantly with Congressional concerns about its usefulness since it was focused on funding basic science rather than national defense directed R&D.

When the Soviet Union shocked and awakened the world with the launch of Sputnik 1 on 4 October 1957 they had, in military terms, taken the dominant 'high ground,' and the launch shook the widespread American belief that the U.S. was superior to all other others in math and science. Americans suddenly feared that Soviet schools were superior to American ones, and Congress reacted by passing the National Defense Education Act (NDEA).

As a high school student in the late 1950's, I well remember how average citizens were deeply worried about nuclear attack, how we had bomb shelters and practice drills. The NDEA, signed into law less than a year after Sputnik, on September 2, 1958, provided funding to United States education institutions at all levels.

The NDEA authorized funding for four years on eight program titles, with the funding increased each year. Key features of the legislation included a student loan program intended to increase the flow of talent into science, mathematics, and foreign language careers, a 'National Defense Fellowship' for graduate study toward a college teaching career, and a wide array of programs to enhance pre-college teacher training and public understanding of science and technology. I, and many of my future NASA colleagues, benefited significantly from the NDEA Program.

President Dwight D. Eisenhower had approved a plan to orbit a scientific satellite as part of the International Geophysical Year (IGY) for the period from July 1 1957 to December 31 1958, a cooperative effort to collect scientific data about the Earth, and then on 1 October 1958, Congress and the President created the National Aeronautics and Space Administration (NASA), with the intent to pursue both scientific and direct military goals.

During this period the number of American students attending college increased significantly. In 1940 about one-half million Americans attended college, about 15 percent of their age group. By 1960, however, college enrollments had grown to 3.6 million students, and by 1970, 7.5 million students attended colleges in the U.S., or 40 percent of college-age youths.

Between 1958 and 1968, Congressional support for NDEA, NASA, the Department of Defense (DoD), and NSF R&D budgets grew steadily. As an expression of Cold War fears, NASA's Apollo Program accounted for a considerable proportion of federal expenditures and peaked in 1968. Over its life, Apollo investments totaled $25.4B, a huge sum for that era.

The amount of money involved provoked both concern and opposition. In the mid to late sixties the DoD initiated several studies (including Project Hindsight in 1969) that questioned the funding of pure science versus very targeted applied research based on national interests and priorities. The Vietnam Conflict also created a climate where defense research and procurements directed the flow of money to the defense industry and its targeted R&D.

As Apollo moved closer to achieving its ultimate goals, NASA began to consider its subsequent endeavors. In October 1968, and thus even before the first Apollo moon landing in 1969, NASA began early studies of space shuttle designs. The Shuttle program was formally launched on January 5, 1972, when President Nixon announced that NASA would proceed with the development of a reusable Space Shuttle system.

As with the Apollo program, the Shuttle program had many constituencies, including NASA, DoD, White House, Congress, and aerospace industry, and they had varied ideas of what it should do and how much it should cost. NASA wanted a cost-effective reusable launch vehicle that could service Low Earth Orbit (LEO) missions (i.e., large space station and free-flyer missions) for science and exploration. The DoD, particularly the Air Force, wanted a space transport vehicle to carry and service both military astronauts and large military satellites into equatorial and polar orbits. The White House and Congress wanted a cost-effected space capability as a follow on to Apollo to keep the U.S. in a Cold War space leadership position. The public, however, was effectively disengaged.

During the post Apollo period, budgetary constraints and compromises between federal agencies were the dominant drivers of the system design. Design changes, budget issues, waffling support, and contractor in-fighting plagued the Shuttle program from the start. Although the Cold War influence was still in play in the 70's, the Vietnam conflict received most of the attention of politicians and the public.

Hence, budgetary constraints and organizational compromises greatly influenced the design philosophy that had been applied so successfully during Apollo. During Apollo the design methodology, aided by adequate annual funding, revolved around identifying a set of technologies for each subsystem and testing and evaluating each before that technology was incorporated into the final design.

Unlike Apollo, where the singular focus was putting a man on the moon, the wide spectrum of goals expressed by the military and NASA led to a design that was not optimal for any of them. The annual budget constraints forced a departure from the proven Apollo systems engineering design methodology, so instead of extended design and test cycles, subsystem technology options were selected based primarily on the perceived costs at a very early stage of design and test. The Shuttle thermal protection system – the infamous tiles - was a prime example of a decision taken although the options had not been properly examined. Consequently, the technology risks and the long-term operational cost issues were not fully understood, and the system plagues the Shuttle program to this day.

In the transition from Apollo to Shuttle, the overall mission was therefore diverted from building a world-class space infrastructure for science, space exploration, and military purposes, to one focused primarily keeping Congressional appropriations at a consistent and manageable level. In this political arena, you enter a never-ending cycle in which mission budgets and plans are up for discussion, and for politically motivated changes, on an annual basis. I believe that this scenario, which emerged in early 1980s, was the start of the Congressional 'earmark' problem that continues to plague NASA.

As a result, NASA's earmark problem has grown to 3% of its annual budget.

Why does it matter? Because major NASA decisions are made according to how many jobs will be created or lost in a particular geographic area, making NASA a pawn in a political battle between the

White House and the political parties in Congress. Alas, you cannot effectively manage a highly technical program with 3% of your annual budget being manipulated by the winds of political whim.

The evolution of the space program workforce is also an important topic. As I noted above, the implementation of the NDEA and NSF programs had a large impact by expanding the available science and engineering workforce that was then tapped by the Apollo program. Apollo was a new, stimulating, and exciting area for young, bright, and eager technically-trained people to participate in, and the NASA organization they came to work in was a new agency without any bureaucratic personnel issues. Hence, it was not unusual to see 25 to 30 year old engineers leading engineering, science, technology, and operations aspects of Apollo. In fact, this was occurring throughout industry, government, and academia.

Universities received federal support to establish major R&D laboratories on their campuses, and NASA's Space Act Agreement (SAA) authority allowed for a unique environment of shared resources, both personnel and facilities, between the government, industry, and academic institutions.

My own career was shaped by that capability. I received my Ph.D. (Space Physics) in the early 70s, but I and had a difficult time landing a job in the space program. Luck and persistence eventually led to an outstanding opportunity to work at a NASA-sponsored laboratory at the University of Arizona, and in 1978 I was offered the opportunity to join NASA Headquarters in the Office of Space Science.

I am relating this part of my career since it is important to how things have changed since the late 70's.

On my arrival at HQ, my boss told me that it was considered important to recruit young engineering and science professionals from organizations outside the government into NASA since they brought new ideas and a sense of what the outside science and technical community was thinking. During that period about 30 percent of the NASA HQ science professionals rotated in and out of the agency, serving 2 to 4 years and then returning to their respective universities or private organizations.

He explicitly told me that I should not spend more than five years in my new government position, because changing positions was essential to remaining in touch with the real world outside the government, and this would prevent me from becoming 'bureaucratic' in my decision-making. At the time I didn't fully understand what he was trying to convey, but on reflection now I know it to be true.

Today the cadre of science professionals who rotate in and out of NASA is a very small percentage of the personnel. It could be argued, however, and a few of my long time NASA colleagues do make this point, that NASA is so engaged today in the annual political budget struggle that bringing in 'political novices' from the science and technical communities would cause NASA to ultimately lose most of its budget battles. On the other hand, I contend that if you lose contact with the key outside communities you have trouble knowing when you need to stand your ground on a program decision, or when you should compromise. Too often, compromises are made that are eventually detrimental to program goals.

Our quick review of history would not be complete without a discussion of the International Space Station (ISS) and its turbulent birth. NASA's dreams of developing the space station, stalled for years by the difficult birth of the Space Shuttle, finally came true in January 1984. President Reagan gave the official green light to the ambitious project, which envisioned a permanently manned facility in orbit by 1991 with a diverse set of allies, including Europe, Canada, and Japan as partners. I became intimately involved in 1985 when I served on the International Task Force for the Scientific Uses of Space Station (TFSUSS), and the following year I was also hired as a consultant on the NASA Space Station Operations Team.

After three years of intense discussions and design meetings that were held in various parts of the world, the Space Station design was coming together as a very functional space laboratory when political and budgetary realities appeared. Neither the budgetary support from Washington nor the interest of the general public were evident, which forced NASA to begin a cost-cutting redesign which eliminated many features that had been deemed essential just a couple of years before.

Since the TFSUSS team had been disbanded, NASA never bothered to ask potential user communities about the impacts of these design changes, and yet even with this cost-cutting effort behind it, it turned out that the Space Station was still not viable in terms of cost and political support.

Meanwhile, in 1992 Russia entered the scene to address the issue of the quick and cost-effective emergency return from the station by incorporating the veteran Soyuz vehicle, and in 1993 the U.S. and Russia agreed to a joint program between the Space Station and the Mir-2 projects. If anyone had told us in the mid 70s or early 80s that we would be partnering with the Russians on a major space venture it would have been deemed ludicrous, and yet there we were. Today it is good to keep these lessons in mind as we discuss international space commerce partnerships with countries such as China and India.

The International Space Station is now nearing completion and will soon be open to commercial business. Will ISS be able to transform itself from a NASA-managed engineering project to a viable multi-discipline application environment that engages with international space commerce partners? What elements of our space program history will be beneficial to this transition, what barriers must be overcome, and what are the needed elements to stimulate a thriving space commerce environment?

DRAMATIC CHANGES IN THE WIND FOR SPACE COMMERCE

In parallel to the background of Apollo, Shuttle, and the Space Station is the history of space commerce in the US. From the 80s until today space commerce has been a small adjunct activity under the management of the federal government. It was, and remains, a very difficult environment in which to carry out commercial activity.

In the early days of SkyLab, Shuttle, and the Russian Mir, results from research in life-sciences, pharmaceutical, and material science research strongly indicated the value of a microgravity environment from a research perspective. But space transportation costs and therefore access to and from space, interference from government managers, and the lack of adequate investment capital were the major barriers. The government controlled the transportation to and from space, they controlled the use of the space laboratory, and they controlled and managed the flight schedule and most of the operations.

Hence, it is not surprising that most business entities simply could not participate under these circumstances, and commercial use of the ISS or other earlier space laboratories has languished.

However, since the mid-90s a new era of space commerce has begun to emerge. On the government side, the ISS was being completed and was gradually opened for 'business' as the largest international scientific project in history. The ISS draws upon scientific and technological resources of 16 nations, including the United States, Canada, Japan, Russia, Brazil and the 11-member European Space Agency, and is the world's only continuously inhabited outpost and laboratory in space.

In December 2005, the U.S. Congress designated the ISS as a National Laboratory (ISSNL), providing new opportunities for government and private supported R&D in space. The ISSNL designation opens the door for utilization of the ISSNL by other Federal entities and by the private sector through partnerships, cost-sharing agreements, and other arrangements as well. It supports the development of a Commercial Orbital Transportation System (COTS); and develops a science, technology, engineering, and mathematics (STEM) workforce development environment.

Going forward, the ISS provides an unprecedented opportunity to achieve advances in research knowledge, commercial development, and education in the United States. But this depends on whether the federal government, and particularly NASA, can loosen its ultra tight grip on the management and operations of both the enabling space transportation systems and the ISS laboratory itself. Both factors will determine whether the ISS capability flourishes as a scientific and commercial venture.

Also at the end of the 1990s, Mircorp, a private Russian venture in charge of the Mir Space Station, began soliciting potential space tourists to visit Mir in order to offset some of its maintenance costs. Dennis Tito, an American businessman and former JPL scientist, became their first customer, but when the decision to de-orbit Mir was made, Tito managed to switch his trip to the International Space Station through a deal between MirCorp and U.S.-based Space Adventures, Ltd., despite strong opposition from senior figures at NASA.

Space Adventures subsequently facilitated flights for the world's first private space explorers, who paid in excess of $20M each for a 10-day visit to the ISS. Although space tourism has been discussed for decades, these private space flights have exited the worldwide community and have created a viable customer base for future suborbital and orbital flights.

Dissatisfaction with all of the many obstacles associated with government managed and dominated space transportation and space laboratory capabilities have stimulated a push by the private sector to enter the space transportation and space laboratory marketplace. These private sector enterprises are characterized by their insistence on being primarily privately financed, and their view of the government as only one segment of their potential customer base.

Over the past five years the number of companies that have entered this market has been growing rapidly. They span the orbital and suborbital marketplace with products that include vehicles, human and payload rated capsules, and orbital laboratories. These private capabilities are either in the proposal, development, or test stages. Without a doubt they have caught the attention of both the public and governments around the world.

MAINTAINING A US LEADERSHIP IN THE EMERGING SPACE COMMERCE MARKETPLACE

Throughout the history of the space program it has always been a balancing act to define the appropriate roles and responsibilities of the government, the private sector, and academic institutions. Invariably, imbalances cause inefficiencies that lead to a diminished leadership role in the world. In this era of globalized markets, access to space and space commerce are not limited only for the former super powers, as many nations aspire to a space faring presence, among them China, India, and Brazil.

The key to U.S. leadership is going to be linked to innovation. This is innovation in the broadest sense, for the U.S. must develop innovative organizational structures that not only harness the extensive capabilities of both private and public entities, but also must equally embrace partnership opportunities with international resources, public and private as well.

Innovation in education and workforce development at all levels is essential to success, just as innovation in technology development and technology transfer to applications is utterly necessary to sustained leadership.

This is particularly true in the area of worldwide network communications and information technology as it applies to space operations, management and customer services. In the 1985 to 1987 time frame, while chairing the international TFSUSS committee on ISS payload operations, I coined a term that I called, *"Telescience."* Simply put, Telescience is the ability of a geographically distributed (worldwide) research team to design, build, test, integrate into a launch vehicle and space laboratory, operate in space, analyze the research results, and publish those results without ever having to leave their own research institutions. In the mid 80s and early 90s, this was only a dream, but shortly after it would be realized with advances in worldwide high bandwidth networks and information technology. Space commerce needs to employ these technologies as other Earth bound industries have done.

ESSENTIAL ELEMENTS FOR A SUCCESSFUL BUSINESS MODEL FOR SPACE COMMERCE

WHO IS THE CUSTOMER?

Although I wouldn't classify myself as a skilled businessperson I have had the opportunity to observe and work with many people who are, who have created successful businesses involved with space. The successful ones have all focused on a four set of questions:

1. Defining the customer,
2. Obtaining investment capital,
3. Putting strong management in place, and
4. Resolving the myriad of operational questions that inevitably must be addressed in any activity as complex as space-related business.

AMONG THE KEY CUSTOMER-RELATED QUESTIONS ARE THESE:

1. Who is the customer for the product or service that my space commerce business provides?
2. Does the customer have a recognized need and the resources to purchase my products or services?
3. Is there a near-term customer base that will provide near-term cash flow?
4. Is there a developed path to grow the customer base with new and innovative products?

Most new space commerce businesses have a lot of difficulty coming up with sound answers to these questions, largely because the government has been the predominant customer, and it has been a marketplace that was simply too costly for a non-government customer to afford; only the very wealthy have been non-government players, as we saw with the initial space tourism customers, multimillionaires all.

The commercial space transportation industry, for both suborbital and orbital applications, is also struggling with the customer questions. I have had discussions with many of them, and they all look at the growing backlog (possibly several thousand worldwide) of university R&D payloads as a good initial customer base. These are science and engineering payloads that have been developed by university personnel over the past ten years that require a space environment to complete the research effort. Either the cost or launch vehicle availability has halted the completion of the research. I point out to them that universities do have a need for such services, but unless the government funds them they have no funds to build, integrate, or operate payloads. In other words, the universities are 'NOT' direct customers; we are back to the government being the true customer.

There is also a backlog of industry-financed R&D payloads waiting to fly, and if the cost of services can be brought down to an appropriate (cost-effective) level, then they may become a real customer. The microgravity environment of suborbital and orbital space is required by an array of industrial users including those interested in biotechnology, material processing, microelectronics, nanotechnology, and space physics. Since the availability of such a cost-effective capability has not been there, a quantitative analysis of the size of this industrial customer base is not known.

But cost is not the only issue for industry customers. Timely delivery of services is often more critical. An example of this is the biotechnology industry, which has a clearly defined need for suborbital and orbital microgravity research platforms. There is compelling evidence that the unique microgravity environment of spaceflight provides important insight into a variety of fundamental human health issues, with tremendous potential for the commercial development of novel enabling technologies to enhance human health here on Earth. These research areas include: Infectivity & Infectious Diseases; Cell Tissue Engineering; Biological Processes in Aging; Biophysical Reactions to Weightlessness; and Macro-molecular Crystallization. If commercial space services can shorten the time required to conduct research or the development products for delivery to their world market, then the biotech industry will be a highly motivated customer, and there are many examples waiting in the wings (see http://alliancespace.net - ISS Entrepreneurial Paradigm - Biotech Workshop)

WHO PROVIDES THE START UP INVESTMENT CAPITAL?

Many small, space-related startup companies begin their enterprise with funding from 3F and CC resources. 3F equals 'Family, Friends, and Fools,' while CC means 'Credit Card' investment. These are obviously high-risk approaches motivated by tremendous entrepreneurial commitment in the face of great unknowns. Many of the small suborbital rocket companies and payload integration companies got their start in this manner.

Some startups rely on independently wealthy family and/or friends, such as Elon Musk's SpaceX organization, which draws capital from Musk's prior life as a highly successful technology entrepreneur. Also angel investors, who are space enthusiasts, have financed some startup businesses. Others are enticed by government agency sponsored Small Business Innovation Research (SBIR), and Small Business Technology Transfer (STTR) programs. As examples of such projects funded by NASA can be seen on the website:

http://sbir.gsfc.nasa.gov/SBIR/SBIR.html.

And for some with a well-developed business plan and a willingness to turn over a considerable portion of their company, then venture capital is a viable path. These are rather rare, in that venture capital considers commercial space to be too high of a risk in terms of short-term return on investment.

Over the past 10 years another investment strategy has been employed by a number of technology companies which could also become a viable path for the space commerce industry. This indirect approach is based on an R&D partnership with a research university. Although the amount of federal and state government R&D dollars flowing to universities has fluctuated over the past several decades, the total amount allocated to space-related R&D areas is still sizeable.

Initially there were some problems with these partnerships, since issues of Intellectual Property (IP) sharing and ownership could not be easily resolved, but solutions to those problems have now been devised and are in place at most research institutions. A good industry–university partnership will provide a viable means to utilize government sponsored research facilities, access to world class researchers, and an inside view of multiple emerging technologies with the potential for IP licensing. This does come at a cost, but frequently that can be negotiated in terms of providing scholarships/fellowships to university research students. If done right, as I will discuss that in the next section, this is a tax deductable process for industry and a highly valued resource for the research institution. The University of California, in its partnerships with the biotechnology, microelectronics, nanotechnology, and information technology industries has seen and worked with these issues (see California Institutes for Science and Innovation in next section).

This is only an initial set of issues to be addressed by the emerging space commerce business sector.

EMERGING TRENDS IN PUBLIC - PRIVATE PARTNERSHIPS

Leadership among nations and in business today is often linked to the capacity to stimulate and manage innovation, and this will certainly also be true for the emerging space commerce enterprises. Public–private partnerships can play a significant role, and indeed they have a history in this endeavor. Most of the approaches that we are familiar with today were initially targeted as economic or innovation drivers by either state or federal government agencies. Some were primarily directed at non-space related technology innovation while others were initiated directly for the space program. During the past ten years several new public–private partnership models have also been developed that could have direct implications for space commerce enterprises.

CALIFORNIA'S INSTITUTES OF SCIENCE AND INNOVATIONS

In 2000 the California Institutes for Science and Innovations (Cal ISIs) were established as an ambitious statewide initiative to support research in fields that were recognized as critical to the economic growth of the state, including biomedicine, bioengineering, nanosystems, telecommunications and information technology. The Cal ISIs were conceived as a catalytic partnership between university research interests, private industry, and state and federal support to expand the state economy into new industries and markets, and *"speed the movement of innovation from the laboratory into peoples' daily lives."*

Today, four research centers operate as partnerships among the University of California system, state government, industry, and federal sponsored research, and each involves structured collaborations among campuses, disciplines, academics, researchers, research professionals, and students.

Each institute is hosted by at least two University of California (UC) campuses, with one campus usually taking a lead role:

1. California Institute for Quantitative Biological Research (QB3) is hosted by UC San Francisco, UC Berkeley, and UC Santa Cruz;
2. California Nanosystems Institute (CNSI) is hosted by UCLA and UC Santa Barbara;
3. California Institute for Telecommunications and Information Technology (CalIT2) hosted by UC San Diego and UC Irvine; and

4. Center for Information Technology Research in the Interest of Society (CITRIS) is hosted by UC Berkeley, in collaboration with UC Davis, UC Merced, and UC Santa Cruz.

Collectively, the partner companies and organizations involved in these institutes number in the hundreds, and they are now pursuing a wide range of research initiatives ranging from the design of energy efficient 'smart buildings,' to developing medical breakthroughs in STEM cell research that promotes advances in the prevention and cure of a number of diseases, to next generation information technologies for memory and computation, or developing and implementing worldwide computer network architectures and visualization environments that are having broad applications in distance learning, collaborative work environments, and the understanding of large, complex data sets. In addition, all four Institutes have developed educational and training programs that are impacting the preparation of the next generation of scientists and engineers in the United States.

As world-class centers using multi-disciplinary strategies and state of the art facilities to focus on the development of cutting edge technologies, the Cal ISIs are clearly an important new model that could play a significant role in the emerging space commerce enterprise.

EACH ISI HAS HAD TO ADDRESS SIGNIFICANT QUESTIONS AND CONCERNS ACROSS A WIDE RANGE OF ISSUES INCLUDING:
1. How to sustain an adequate level of ongoing funding?
2. How to become integral to industry's internal R&D and workforce development efforts?
3. How Intellectual Property (IP) is managed and shared?
4. How they are integrated into the universities in terms of budget, administration and academic programs? and
5. How to interact and partner with international entities?

Two successful Institutes that have addressed these questions are QB3 and CalIT2. QB3 has developed significant partnerships with the two large California biotechnology industry associations (BayBio – San Francisco area and BioCom – San Diego area). The two biotechnology industry associations represent over 500 companies - many are multinational corporations. This same partnership orchestrated the passing of a California bond initiative ($3B) that created the California Institute for Regenerative Medicine (a world-class STEM cell research capability).

CalIT2 has also made significant progress in convincing the communication networking and information technology industry to utilize the university facilities as a home for their internal R&D. Also they have been very successful in establishing relationships with a number of other countries (Japan, Australia, and several European Countries, to name a few).

One of the founding intentions of the institutes was that they would be funded equally by private, federal, and state sources, and this has been a success, with more than $75M raised in nearly equal proportions from all three sources.

Although the Cal ISI model has been fairly successful in developing and transferring R&D from the laboratory to products, I believe that the model has yet to reach its full potential. It appears that neither industry nor government have fully embraced the model, and the reason seems to be that it requires a culture shift from the way they operate now. And while culture shifts are slow processes particularly for government organizations, we have nevertheless seen some significant progress.

Being a member of the UC San Diego Jacobs School of Engineering that houses CalIT2, I have been able to see, day to day, dynamic progress of CalIT2 programs. The telescience that I dreamed about and planned for ISS in the mid 80s has become reality with CalIT2 research. High bandwidth networks capable of spanning the world, ultra-high resolution display environments (Highly Interactive Parallelized Display Space - HIPerSpace) to explore, fuse, and visualize complex scientific data sets, and virtual reality environments where complex systems can be simulated, bring telescience to life. I am thrilled at the prospect of applying these technologies to the ISS National Laboratory.

Recently, the thought occurred to me that this same data fusion and visualization technology, along with the simulation environment, could be an innovative way to address many of the issues facing space commerce today. In particular, collecting worldwide market data and building a decision support system that the commercial space industry could use to establish functional business plans and strategies would be especially valuable. The investment capital community could also utilize these technologies to realistically simulate a commercial space scenario to predict success or their return on investment. Simply put, these knowledge support technologies could revolutionize the way business decisions are made. It may be a dream today, but how long before it becomes reality?

In applying this model to the space program and space commerce there will also be cultural and operational issues to address. NASA's dominance and management of the existing space infrastructure is obviously one of the largest barriers to employing the model for space commerce. The agency's heavily politicized environment is filled with regional parochialism (i.e., creating and saving jobs as the primary motive for implementing programs) and, as noted, has promoted the excessive earmarking of federal monies to garner regional political clout. On an international scale this political barrier has the potential to push the U.S. to a second tier level in space commerce as compared to other emerging space nations.

NASA INSTIGATED AND MANAGED PUBLIC – PRIVATE PARTNERSHIPS

REINVIGORATING NASA SPACE ACT AGREEMENTS

In the National Aeronautics and Space Act of 1958 under which NASA was formed, Congress uniquely authorized NASA to enter into and perform contracts, leases, cooperative agreements, or other transactions as may be necessary in the conduct of its work, and on such terms as it may deem appropriate, with any agency or instrumentality of the United States, or with any state, territory, or possession, or with any political subdivision thereof, or with any person, firm, association, corporation, or educational institution.   No other federal agency has such a flexible partnership authority.

Hence, we see that here from the very beginning there is a profound awareness, actually written into law, which recognizes that the talent needed to get America into space would come from many different organizations, and would require unique organizational approaches to gathering and deploying that talent effectively.   This does give you some appreciation for the insight of both those who prepared the Space Act, and those who voted it into law.

In NASA terminology, such agreements are known as Space Act Agreements, or SAAs. Under its Space Act authority, NASA has entered into a great number of SAAs with diverse groups of people and organizations, both in the private and public sectors, in order to meet wide-ranging NASA mission and program requirements and objectives. These agreements constitute Agency commitments of resources, including personnel, funding, services, equipment, expertise, information, or facilities, to accomplish the objectives of joint undertakings with an Agreement Partner. The Agreement Partner can be a U.S. or foreign person or entity, an educational institution, a Federal, state, or local governmental unit, a foreign government, or an international organization. The Space Act further provides authority for Reimbursable, Non-reimbursable, and Funded Agreements, and to engage in international cooperative programs pursuant to the Agency's missions.

For many years I have personally studied, implemented, and utilized SAAs, and I have found them to be the singular federal procurement mechanism that allows the government to actually be an effective working partner with profit and non-profit entities in the sharing of personnel, facilities, and funds. A recent example of an effective use of the SAA involved a partnership between NASA Ames Research Center (ARC),

SpaceX, and the Space Grant Education and Enterprise Institute (SGEEI - non-profit facilitator organization). SpaceX, one of the rapidly emerging commercial space transportation companies, needed (for their Dragon capsule) the heat shield expertise and technology that NASA ARC possessed. Negotiating a SAA directly between NASA ARC and SpaceX became entangled with a number of time consuming legal and procurement issues until SGEEI offered a solution. SGEEI already had a SAA in place with NASA ARC to support the commercial space and educational activities at the NASA Ames Research Park. The SpaceX project certainly involved commercial space and it was not difficult to engage the educational aspects into the project. Under the reimbursable SAA, NASA personnel were assigned to SGEEI, graduate fellowships were provided for students from several California Space Grant affiliate campuses, and SGEEI provided the overall project management. Within a year of our initial discussions, the SpaceX Dragon Capsule implemented a heat shield that was derived through this SAA mechanism. In addition, the students that were involved have become familiar with both NASA Ames and SpaceX as future employers. This is a win-win situation for all of the partners.

As discussed above, SAA authority includes a government personnel provision called the Intergovernmental Personnel Act (IPA) that allows agency employees to be assigned to and work for non-profit and/or profit organizations while remaining civil servants. Depending on the circumstances, these agency employees can be funded by the agency or the outside entity. The IPA provision also enables employees from outside organizations to serve for 2-4 years within a federal government agency, and it was this provision of the Act that first enabled me to work at NASA HQ while I was still an employee of the University of Arizona in the late 70s and early 80s.

I have found that the IPA process is an excellent way to transfer operational and organizational knowledge and technology both into and out of the agency.

It is also an important and effective tool in shifting the cultural thinking inside the government by bringing talented individuals from diverse organizations to work together, sharing their various viewpoints and experiences, and blending these together to discover how to accomplish their shared goals.

During the first thirty years of NASA existence SAAs were widely used, but unfortunately as the Agency has become more bureaucratic in its approach to both procurement and personnel, the use of SAAs has been considerably reduced as the process for approval of SAAs became very legalistic and cumbersome.

SAAs should be employed extensively to promote public–private partnerships among academic institutions, industry and government, and I believe they will become increasingly necessary as NASA seeks to share its expertise with the private sector through the process of space commercialization.

OTHER ONGOING NASA MANAGED PARTNERSHIP PROGRAMS

NASA INNOVATIVE PARTNERSHIP PROGRAMS

From its early Apollo years to the present, NASA has found that it needed to stimulate directed R&D to generate the new knowledge needed to satisfy its mission goals.   Similar to the Department of Defense's DARPA program, directed agency personnel at agency facilities can do R&D internally and it can support academic/industry R&D, as well as a combination of both.   In recent years many of these partnership have been managed through the NASA Innovative Partnerships Program (IPP).   The IPP provides the organizational structure for acquiring, maturing, infusing and commercializing technology and capabilities for NASA's Mission Directorates, Programs and Projects through investments and partnerships with Industry, Academia, Government Agencies and National Laboratories.

IPP CONSISTS OF THREE MAJOR PROGRAM ELEMENTS:

1. The IPP Technology Infusion includes the Small Business Innovative Research (SBIR)/Small Business Technology Transfer (STTR) Programs and the IPP Seed Fund.
2. The IPP Innovation Incubator includes activities such as Centennial Challenges and new efforts to facilitate the purchase of services from the emerging commercial space sector;
3. IPP Partnership Development includes Intellectual Property management, technology transfer, and new innovative partnerships.

As NASA has become more bureaucratic it has turned more inward, and funding for the IPP program has become very limited, making it nearly impossible for the program to make a significant difference for the emerging space commerce enterprise. I believe that the IPP effort is too small to make the impact it could and should, and that it should be significantly expanded in order to make NASA's accumulated knowledge more readily available to the private sector.

In addition to the lack of adequate annual and sustained funding, a key missing organizational element becomes apparent. To make IPP work well, it is best to have a neutral, unbiased facilitator or manager to oversee public–private partnerships.   This entity cannot be a 'card carrying' member of the government, industry, or academic organizations.   They must be viewed instead as a neutral 'friendly facilitator' working for the shared interests of the government, and industry, and academia with respect to broader mission goals, not narrower institutional goals.

Why is such an organizational element so important? First, its sole purpose is to form and manage public–private partnerships to accomplish a defined set of goals with clearly defined metrics for success. The partnership triad must fully trust the organizational element and place their partnership resources in the management hands of the facilitator organization to ensure that institutional agendas do not compromise the broader goals.

THIS INDEPENDENT ORGANIZATIONAL ENTITY WOULD PROVIDE THE FOLLOWING:

1. Clear understanding as to the needs of the public–private partners and what their risk/reward conditions are;
2. Knowledge of the resources (personnel, facilities funds) available to the partnerships;
3. A reliable and trusted facilitator/manager of Intellectual Property (IP) and resources that the partnership will share;
4. And an excellent conduit for developing the workforce needed by the partners.

In the present IPP situation no organization is adequately fulfilling this function, and this should be remedied as the commercial space movement grows and NASA is asked to provide its expertise to commercial ventures.

COMMERCIAL SPACE TRANSPORTATION AND INTERNATIONAL SPACE STATION PARTNERSHIPS

In 2005 I helped to organize a dynamic group of commercial space advocates to meet together and explore the many aspects of the budding commercial space industry. The diverse group included individuals from the supply side (aerospace industry), the demand side (current and potential users of 'space' for scientific and commercial purposes), researchers, space entrepreneurs, NASA, the venture capital community, and a variety of related commercial space stakeholders.

This group developed shared insights concerning the demand and supply aspects for commercial space ventures, the venture capital point of view on investing in commercial space enterprises, and the research community's interest in employing commercial space as a research venue. This meeting enabled the commercial space community to explore various business models, to initiate plans for developing the market, to create standards for commercializing space, to identify the core issues for making space accessible on a more consistent basis, and led to the formation of a public–private alliance organization called the Alliance of Commercial Enterprises and Education for Space (ACES). An organization I am part of, the Space Grant Education and Enterprise Institute, played the role of the 'friendly facilitator' organization.

The general purpose of the ACES team was and remains to engage in a new business model for accomplishing research and development in low-earth orbit consistent with the present and future goals of the U.S. space program. The performance based public–private partnership was structured to aggressively pursue science, technology and commercial development programs with clearly defined roles for government, industry, and academic partners.

Out of this initial workshop and four years of subsequent efforts (see http://alliancespace.net), two significant constraints have been identified that continue inhibit the commercial space venture from thriving. These are accessible and cost effective suborbital and orbital transportation, and a fully functional and cost appropriate suborbital or orbital microgravity laboratory facilities. The operational infrastructure is also lacking a modern 'Telescience' capability.

This effort set into motion many of NASA's partnership efforts for commercial space transportation, both suborbital and orbital, and for the commercial utilization of the International Space Station National Laboratory. In 2008, as a result of this activity, I had the opportunity to lead a team of public and private biotechnology organizations in creating the Biotechnology Space Research Alliance (BSRA), a San Diego-based collaborative, intended to stimulate participation in the ISSNL by validating its capabilities as a unique and cost effective research environment for breakthrough biomedical and biotechnology discoveries.

The BSRA intends to advance the development of the low Earth orbit environment for all users, scientific, technological, and commercial, in order to engender scientific knowledge, technological capability, and commerce on Earth as a gateway to 21st Century exploration and development of space.

The BSRA was structured to increase collaboration between scientific and commercial researchers at the National Institutes of Health (NIH), National Science Foundation (NSF), Department of Energy (DoE), and Veterans Administration (VA), and life science companies located in the greater San Diego area (where there is a rapidly maturing cluster of these firms), and to advance biotechnology research and commercial development on the ground and in space.

During this period NASA showed considerable reluctance to fully embrace these partnerships with adequate funding or attention. This reluctance was driven by the perceived need to focus most resources on NASA's Exploration (Constellation) Program, then in development.

Although the ISS had, by this time, been designated as a national lab, and funding for commercial space transportation had been set aside, these initiatives did not receive consistent NASA support, and were clearly seen as the intent of Congress rather than the intent of NASA management. In fact, many NASA personnel viewed being assigned to these commercially related programs as a career–limiting move, and they avoided them diligently.

With the Obama Administration in the White House in 2009, the many questions pertinent to continuation of the Shuttle program beyond 2010, extension of ISS operations beyond 2015, the expansion of the commercial space transportation capabilities, and a rethinking of NASA's long-range mission for space exploration were all being considered. This began to coalesce when Obama established a Commission to review the human spaceflight program. The Augustine Commission issued its final report in October 2009, and firmly sets commercial space on a new path beside a new vision for American space exploration efforts.

At time of this writing in the spring of 2010, an intense 'discussion' is raging between the White House, Congress, the aerospace industry, and various segments of NASA on implementing the Augustine Commission and White House recommendations.

Many have questioned whether the new Obama Space Plan lays out a clear strategy for human spaceflight with concrete timelines and goals such as NASA benefitted from during Apollo. Some feel that a lack of urgency and specificity will not sustain a new vision, and without a sustained vision the programs (including the commercial space aspects) and the skills, and workforce that go with them, will wither.

At the same time, many segments of the space community and many in Congress adamantly oppose strengthening commercial space transportation capabilities, an objection that seems to be driven primarily, and sadly, by the fear of job loss in a given Congressional district, or loss of lucrative contracts by various aerospace contractors.

On 15 April 2010, President Obama, in response to these expressed concerns, enunciated a new vision for NASA space exploration that:

1. Initiates a set of stepping-stone achievements in space that will take us further and faster into space, allowing us to reach a range of destinations including lunar orbit, Lagrange points, near-Earth asteroids, and the moons of Mars, and eventually Mars itself. This sequence of missions will begin with a set of crewed flights to prove the capabilities required for exploration beyond low Earth orbit. After these initial missions, our long-duration human spaceflight technologies will enable human explorers to conduct the first-ever crewed mission into deep space to an asteroid, thereby achieving an historical first; venture into deep space locations such as the Lagrange points (potential sites of

fuel depots that would enable more capable future missions to the Moon, Mars, and other destinations); and then send humans to orbit Mars and return them safely to Earth.

2. Increases investments in ground-breaking technologies that will allow astronauts to reach space faster and more often, to travel further distances for less cost, and to stay in space for longer periods of time.

3. Systematically tackles the hard problems of space exploration – from protecting our astronauts from radiation to developing advanced in-space propulsion – so that we can push the boundaries not only of where we can go in space but also what we can do there to improve our lives here on Earth.

4. Extends the life of the International Space Station, likely beyond 2020, and

5. Jumpstarts a new commercial space transportation industry to provide safe and efficient crew and cargo transportation to the Space Station, projected to create over 10,000 jobs nationally over the next five years.

While this Space Plan identifies space commercialization as a key element, it does not provide clear milestones through which this commercialization should be achieved. As such, emerging space commercialization can be at the mercy of annual political winds and consequently will garner fluctuating general public support. This is not the best position from which to obtain or organize steady support to advance the commercial space enterprise.

SPACE COMMERCE AND WHAT LIES AHEAD

Over the past 50 years I have had the unique privilege of participating in and observing the evolution of the space program both in the United States as well as other parts of the world. I have witnessed successes and failures, and I have tried to understand and learn from both. A fascinating aspect of this is to observe how humans and their organizations develop and maintain risk/reward systems as part of their 'cultures.' Recently I was having a discussion about my thoughts on culture change within the space program with a university colleague, a highly regarded sociologist, and his comment to me was, *"You are not a plasma physicist but an amateur sociologist."*

As I had not seen myself in that image, amusingly, I at first thought it was a terrible thing for him to say, but I have come to see that there is more than a little truth in it. Now let me take the role of amateur organizational and cultural sociologist for the commercial space program.

POSITIVE INDICATORS

Here are some key elements that will propel the space commerce enterprise forward. Recent actions of Congress to designate the International Space Station (ISS) as a national laboratory and the extension of its operations past 2015 are positive signs for commercial space. The new White House Space Plan also promotes the commercial ISS applications and emphasizes the development of a vibrant commercial space transportation capability.

In addition, NASA is gradually relinquishing its absolute management control of the launch operations and space operations to commercial entities.

The emergence of a number of public–private partnership models for engaging universities, state and federal government, and industry in interdisciplinary R&D will benefit the commercial space enterprise considerably. This could be particularly true for the orbital and suborbital commercial transportation programs, as well as in the microgravity research payload area.

These partnerships would also create an effective mechanism for training the next generation workforce for the commercial space sector. The development of a 'friendly facilitator' organization will be critical to forming such partnerships and as noted, that is being modeled and tested in several areas already.

Investments in commercial space are also starting to progress past the 3F funding stage, although the importance of self-financing by wealthy entrepreneurs and Angel investors remains critical.

Adequate and sustained funding by the federal government for delivery of payloads to either orbital and/or suborbital commercial space is not a reality as of yet, nor is there sufficient infrastructure in space to support commercial operations, but there is notable progress. And while investment or venture capital funding is only on the horizon for many space commerce ventures, as the customer base becomes established, the perceived risk will decrease and a reliable return on investment can be determined. From my viewpoint, private investments will probably begin to accelerate in approximately three to five years.

NEGATIVE INDICATORS

One of the fundamental concerns for the present and future U.S. space program is whether we have lost our political and public will to adequately support a world-leading space program. We presently have nothing like the Cold War threats to stimulate sustained efforts. Our primary Cold War adversary is now our strategic partner in space, and although China may be viewed as a political and ideological adversary, it is also viewed as a key economic partner, as it holds a large and growing potion of our national debt and produces a huge percentage of the products sold in the U.S.

Without a serious rival, local and regional political and economic interests will negatively impact any national program. In my years of studying organizational dynamics, I refer to this as *"Tribal Localitis,"* a cultural disease that causes local or regional organizations to refuse to cooperate or support anything outside their immediate tribal region or culture. The high level of 'earmarking' on federal and state budgets is a prime example of this, and it is a critical problem to overcome if the U.S. is to take a leadership position on commercial space.

Although we have been producing report after report about the decline in the U.S. education system, particularly as regarding Science, Technology, Engineering, and Mathematics (STEM) education, little decisive budgetary actions have been taken. Compared to other industrialized nations, the educational STEM pipeline in the U.S. is in total disarray, and the negative impact to our national and economic security, although very real, is not perceived by the general public as an imminent threat.

Therefore it has not been a high priority topic during local, state, or federal elections. It should be. The U.S. needs a new National Defense Education Act to address the same issues that were addressed in 1958. Without such an initiative, our leadership role in space and world-class innovation will be lost.

Unfortunately, I do not see a solution to this particular problem. Corporate and 'Wall Street' culture look at recognizable impacts on a quarterly basis, while the government looks at impacts in a two or four-year election cycle. But benefits from STEM education reforms will only be fully evident as making a difference in a time frame of several decades, and disturbingly, this disjoint of time frames threatens to keep this issue off of the corporate and government radar screens.

CONCLUSION

Lets review some of the key ideas presented in this chapter that might impact the future of space commerce. We have examined the evolving organizational structure of both public and private entities along with the possible impacts from emerging technologies and the growing international commercial space marketplace. We have also discussed how the political and subsequent budgetary shifts have fluctuated from the time of Apollo to the present.

KEY DRIVERS

Here a some of the key drivers that I think will aid or hinder the full emergence of the commercial space enterprise:

1. The space commerce market is growing rapidly in areas, ranging from suborbital and orbital transportation systems to multi-disciplinary science and technical payloads and their operations to space tourism.
2. New public–private partnership models are emerging that will address investment resources and sharing of resources, IP management and licensing, shared R&D environments, and workforce development.
3. NASA and the Federal Government are showing a willingness to turn over space-related operations and space transportation to the private sector – a serious demand from the emerging space commerce sector.
4. Innovative networking and information systems technologies have emerged that will enable a worldwide space commerce enterprise to thrive and grow, and
5. The most serious threat to an American commercial space enterprise is whether the political and public will is sufficient to provide sustaining support over a number of years.

I believe all of the organizational models and changes that are necessary to stimulate a vibrant and growing U.S. commercial space enterprise are already available to us.

Whether our government and corporate leaders are ready to actively embrace the necessary culture changes is an open question, but like many others it is very disturbing to me to think that we will discard these opportunities and let other countries take the leadership role in space commerce simply due to the lack of understanding, or the lack of the will needed to take the right steps forward.

•••

MICHAEL WISKERCHEN

 Michael Wiskerchen is a faculty member in the Department of Mechanical & Aerospace Engineering at UC San Diego and Director of the California Space Grant Consortium (a NASA sponsored K-12, undergraduate, and graduate educational program). Over the past 35 years, Dr. Wiskerchen has had a diverse academic and research career in aerospace-related science and engineering while in government, industry, and academic organizations. His recent efforts have been focused on the development, application, and operations of aerospace-related projects involving an alliance between industry, university, and government partners.

He has published or presented over 100 articles on space-related research, human capital development, and organization modeling. He is recognized as a national leader in hands-on career training programs at the high school, university, and industry levels. These programs emphasize the effective use of state-of-the-art distance learning (Internet based multimedia curriculum) techniques in a collaborative environment involving students and academic, industry and government mentors.

He is also a member of the ATWG leadership team.

CHAPTER 11

SPACE-RUSH
A NEW WAY FORWARD FOR SPACE EXPLORATION & SETTLEMENT, ALIGNED WITH PRESIDENT OBAMA'S NEW SPACE VISION

BRUCE PITTMAN
DIRECTOR OF FLIGHT PROJECTS AND CHIEF SYSTEM ENGINEER,
NASA EMERGING COMMERCIAL SPACE OFFICE

AND

DR. DANIEL J. RASKY
DIRECTOR, NASA EMERGING COMMERC AL SPACE OFFICE AND
NASA SENIOR SCIENTIST

INTRODUCTION

Since the days of the Apollo program, most of NASA's manned exploration activities beyond LEO have used what could be called a 'mission' based approach. This approach requires that the astronauts take all of the resources required for the mission from Earth, at great expense and difficulty, while providing little (if any) infrastructure for future missions. This approach also relies solely on government funding and direction, with private enterprise engaged only as subcontractors.

In February 2010, President Obama made radical changes to this historical approach to manned space exploration, including canceling the Constellation program's Ares 1 and 5 rockets, the Orion capsule, and the Altair Lander.

Some of the highlights of the President's report include:

- Extending the life of the ISS until at least 2020.
- Relying on private, commercial space companies for crew access to low-Earth orbit.
- A new focus on technology development for exploration and commercial space, and
- Adoption of a 'flexible path' architecture for human spaceflight, with multiple destinations including near Earth asteroids, Lagrange Points, and eventually the moons of Mars and Mars itself.

There has been considerable controversy concerning this significant change in direction and approach. Many have suggested that this means that the US is giving up on manned spaceflight and returning to the Moon, but we strongly disagree. The Augustine Committee report clearly indicates that the NASA Constellation program was *"on an unsustainable trajectory"* and would not succeed in returning astronauts to the surface of the Moon until late in the next decade, perhaps by 2028, if then.

The new approach put forward by the President is much more than just technology development. It is a strategy for embracing the challenge of sustainable exploration and settlement, ones that goes beyond 'flags and footprints.' It's the difference between the Lewis & Clark expedition and building the transcontinental railroad.

As we have seen from other periods of human expansion, including the settling of the American West, the door to expansion and development opens when the government establishes a minimum level of infrastructure, which in the case of the West was railroads and forts, after which entrepreneurs and settlers quickly followed. This then enabled a significant reduction in the resources required by the hardy pioneers who followed, and reduced the difficulties they faced.

When deliberate actions are undertaken to engage private enterprise (e.g., the Pacific Railway Act and the Homestead Act of 1862), entrepreneurs then flock in and find ways of making productive use of the new resources that the frontier offers. These entrepreneurs also bring the benefits of the frontier back to the settled communities, providing proof of the value of the new terrain, and creating additional excitement. Taken together, establishment of infrastructure and engaging private enterprise set the stage for very effective and rapid expansion and development. For example during the California gold rush between 1848 and 1850, the population of San Francisco grew from 1,000 to 35,000 and the cost of a housing lot skyrocketed from $16 to $45,000.

This route to rapid expansion and development is as true today as ever, as we see with the recent opening of an important technological frontier, the Internet. It was the government, specifically the Department of Defense's Advanced Research Projects Agency (ARPA) that put in place the first high-speed data lines between powerful computers in the US to support government and university researchers in the late 1960s and 1970s. Had this high-speed data transfer capability remained the sole province of the government, few of us outside of select government and university scientists would ever have known of its existence, or its utility.

But the door to this high-speed network was opened to resourceful entrepreneurs in the 1980s, and the Internet was born. Few could have anticipated the enormous economic and public benefit that accompanied the advent of e-commerce and search engine technologies. Today, the internet advertising industry alone adds $300B to the US economy, amounting to 2.1% of US GDP, and this from an industry that did not exist 15 years ago. As with many others, we believe that the economic benefits to be had from the commercial development of space could be significantly larger.

Figure 1
NASA illustration showing commerce and habitation on the moon.

A New Way Forward for Exploration

In laying out a path for space exploration for this new millennium, it is essential to learn from the past and use an effective strategy to enable rapid expansion and economic development. Such a strategy has critical tasks for both the government and private enterprise.

The government must enable the demonstration of critical capabilities, the gathering of critical knowledge, and the development of key infrastructure. Once these initial activities and developments are accomplished, the government must not only allow but actively encourage private sector engagement and investment to enable timely, cost effective, and productive uses of the new space frontier that show a direct benefit to the people here on Earth.

This may include new services such as space tourism and entertainment, new knowledge such as fundamental new understandings of biology and materials, new products including new medicines, vaccines, and materials, and new resources including space based power. This will enable the general public to understand and appreciate the economic and social value of space, which in turn help to maintain NASA's relevance. We call this infrastructure based, private enterprise engaged strategy for space exploration 'Space-Rush.'

Five categories of infrastructure can be identified that would greatly reduce the resources required for space commercialization, and hence the difficulties that space entrepreneurs will encounter:

1. Optimized Transportation
2. Power and Communications
3. Fuel and Water
4. In-situ Resource Utilization
5. Crew Accommodations

Each of these categories is examined below, including a strategy for establishing it, and options for engaging private enterprise for the initial stages, optimization, and broad utilization.

With the capabilities from these infrastructure elements in place and private enterprise effectively engaged, the potential for important new products and benefits for Earth would be greatly increased.

OPTIMIZED TRANSPORTATION

NASA has tried repeatedly to develop a 'next generation' replacement for the Space Shuttle over the last two decades, and the story reads like a litany of missed opportunities. The National Aerospace Plane (X-30), VentureStar (X-33), X-34, National Launch System, the Space Launch Initiative, and most recently Constellation and the Ares 1 and 5 all started and failed. Billions of dollars have been spent, and millions of man-hours expended, with very little to show for it. Tragically, few of these vehicles got even an inch off the ground.

Albert Einstein noted that a sure sign of insanity was when people keep doing the same things over and over but expect to get a different result, so we must ask what we can learn from these experiences that will help us get it right this time? It's time for us to take this to heart and try some new approaches in space transportation development, with the goal to develop an affordable and reliable orbital space transportation system, one that actually gets to space.

We need to think beyond getting to Low Earth Orbit (LEO), and open space for public access and commercial development, including access to the Moon and beyond. This means considering four different transportation requirements:

* Earth to Orbit (ETO) and return
* Orbit to Orbit (OTO), including LEO to Geo-synchronous (GEO),
* Earth orbit to lunar and Mars orbit, and finally
* Orbit to Extraterrestrial Surfaces (OTES), including the lunar surface, asteroids, Phobos and Demos, and eventually Mars.

While NASA has been focused almost exclusively on rocketry and ETO transportation, in addition to rockets there are many intriguing propulsion options that have not been explored to any significant degree, including laser propulsion, in which ground or space based lasers are used to propel a vehicle to orbit, and spinning tethers that could be used to rendezvous with reusable suborbital rockets. Both of these concepts could reduce the size, complexity, and cost of launch vehicles.

One of the key goals for optimized space transportation is to develop fully reusable vehicles that will significantly reduce the cost of space travel.

Technical performance is not the key to reusable vehicles. The Space Shuttle is an example of a vehicle that, while refurbishable, is expensive to operate and maintain. Even with the significant reductions in maintenance staff between 1995 and 1999, the Shuttle still requires 1800 workers to keep it operational.

In the design phase for next generation vehicles, emphasis must be placed on efficient maintainability and operability so that space systems operate more like commercial airlines, and less like experimental aircraft.

Several suborbital vehicles are now under construction with the goal to travel to 100 km or more on a routine basis; some are even planning multiple flights per day with a ground crew of fewer than 10. These companies include XCOR Aerospace, Armadillo Aerospace, Masten Space Systems, Blue Origin, and Virgin Galactic.

Fuel depots are another option that has recently received a good deal of attention because of the Augustine Committee review of US Human Space Flight Program. The concept is straightforward: a fuel depot is a filling station in space, so instead of taking all the fuel you need for your space mission, you take only enough to get to the depot, where you refuel just as you refuel your car on road trips. This allows the fuel for the depot to be launched on less expensive, reusable launchers, and as secondary payloads on missions that have excess payload margin.

Fuel depot technology has advanced significantly, and we now have the technology to store liquid oxygen and even liquid hydrogen for extended periods of time in space with very low boil-off, a key requirement for storing fuels on orbit for long duration.

Using a fuel depot allows the launch vehicles needed for space missions to be significantly smaller, potentially eliminating or at least reducing the need for a heavy lift vehicle.

There is also an interesting synergy between the development of fuel depots and reusable launch vehicles (RLVs). The key to keeping costs down on reusable launch vehicles is frequency of flights. If fuel depots are resupplied by commercial RLVs then this will help provide the demand needed to close their business case.

(*Editor's note:* A somewhat less optimistic view of the fuel depot concept is presented in Chapter 13, *Prospects for In-Space Re-Fueling.*)

OTO transfer is conceptually much simpler than ETO travel. OTO can be subdivided into a couple of categories. The first of these is LEO to GEO transport. The idea of a reusable space tug to provide LEO to GEO transportation has been studied for decades. The Orbital Transfer Vehicle (OTV) and its several derivatives were studied by NASA, Lockheed, and Boeing in the 1970s and 80s, but were never developed for budget and programmatic rather than technical reasons. OTVs could also make use of fuel depots, and they could also utilize aerobraking to slow OTVs down by using the Earth's atmosphere to slow the OTV down when it returns from GEO to LEO.

The original NASA concept was to house OTVs at a space station. Payloads would be launched from Earth on an ETO vehicle that would dock at the Station. There, the payload would be removed and attached to the OTV. The OTV would then take the payload to GEO orbit, where it would be released. The OTV would use its aerobrake to return to the station.

A velocity change of about 4 km/sec is required to get from LEO to GEO, as well as a required plane change to the angle of orbit. Coincidently, this is the same velocity change that is needed to get to Low Lunar Orbit (LLO) from LEO (4.04 km/sec) (see figure 2). Therefore the same type of OTV that is used for Earth orbit and GEO could also be used to transfer payloads to and from lunar orbit.

In additional to chemical propulsion, advanced propulsion technologies offer the potential of improved performance that could open up the solar system for commerce and settlement. Ion propulsion technology has already been demonstrated in space with the Deep Space 1 and Dawn missions to the Moon, Mars and the asteroid belt. Although the thrust is low, often a fraction of a pound, the propulsion efficiency (Isp) is very high, and as it runs continuously, after weeks or months very high velocities can be achieved. This is fine for cargo, but not useful for transporting people.

There is also a particular problem when leaving LEO due to the extended time the vehicle spends in the Van Allen radiation belt.

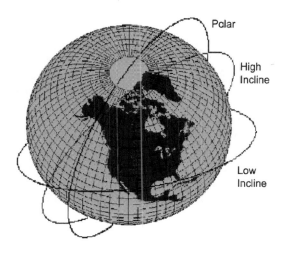

Figure 2
General categories of orbital inclination planes.

What is needed is another option that could be used to propel the OTV from LEO to GEO or LLO.

To open up the solar system, what is needed is a high thrust system that also has high Isp, and there are a few possibilities that could be quite attractive. Former astronaut Dr. Franklin Chang Diaz and his company Ad Astra have developed the VASIMR (Variable Specific Impulse Magnetoplasma Rocket) concept, which will produce both high thrust and high specific impulse. A VASIMR prototype has been tested in the laboratory up to 200-kilowatts, and worked as expected.

Ad Astra has signed a Space Act Agreement with NASA to fly the VASIMR engine on the International Space Station. A 200MW VASIMR engine could propel a manned mission to Mars in less than 40 days, compared to the 270 days it would take using chemical propulsion. We will discuss how to achieve these power levels in the next section.

The last transportation segment to consider is from OTES and back. A good example is LLO to the lunar surface. Since there is no air on the moon, a hypergolic propulsion system similar to what was used on

Surveyor and Apollo could be used, and there are interesting options to consider. One possibility is to harvest rocket fuel from the lunar soil in a process called in-situ resource utilization (ISRU).

Figure 3
Human Mission to Mars with a Nuclear Powered VASIMR engine.
Illustration courtesy of Ad Astra.

As the Moon is ~45% oxygen by mass, rather that transporting oxygen from Earth to the lunar surface at great expense, extracting the oxygen required for the return trip from the lunar soil is an attractive option. Twenty-seven different possible processes have been identified for performing such an extraction.

A great benefit of this approach is that by-products of oxygen extraction include iron, silicon and titanium, all of which are of course valuable materials.

Another, more technologically advanced option would be a Lunar Elevator that would go from the Earth/Moon L1 point to the Lunar surface, a distance of 56,000 km. While building a space elevator on Earth is beyond the current capabilities of materials technology, this is not the case on the Moon with its lower gravity and lack of atmosphere. A cable would be lowered from L1 to the Lunar surface and a climber vehicle attached to the cable. Using beamed power (laser or microwave), the climber would ascend the cable, completing the journey in a matter of a few days at very low cost. The process would then reverse, and cargo and people would descend from the L1 terminus to the Lunar surface.

Technologies including mass drivers and rotating tethers will be the subjects of further R&D for their possible application to the Moon, where they may be particularly well suited.

A mass driver is a long electro-magnetic accelerator with a series of coils through which a conducting payload canister is accelerated. It is kind of like a linear motor. A rotating tether is like a two rocks rotating on a common string. If the string is cut at the right time they will go flying off in opposite directions. In orbit, one would go to a higher orbit and one could be re-entered into the atmosphere.

Devices such as these may ultimately make the mining of such high value materials such as Helium-3 (which we will discuss in the next section) economically viable.

POWER AND COMMUNICATIONS

Power and communications are the next essential infrastructure elements. One concept that has particular potential for both government initiation and private enterprise is in-space power beaming. Using current US government capabilities in high-power lasers, and US industry's large satellite design capabilities, several hundred-kilowatt space power stations could be designed and constructed incorporating new high efficiency photovoltaic solar cells and other relevant technologies. These space power satellites could then beam power to locations of space activities, such as the lunar surface or Lagrange points. These space power stations could also serve as communications hubs, transferring broadband data to and from points of interest.

A government directed demonstration program could accomplish the necessary initial infrastructure for these space power and communication stations. One very useful activity would be to construct a demonstration space power and communication station to support NASA's lunar surface missions. With successful demonstration of the necessary technologies and systems, construction and deployment of operational power and communication power stations could be handed off to industry.

Borrowing from the NASA Commercial Re-Supply (CRS) program for the ISS, an agreement could be offered through which the government agrees to purchase minimum levels of power and data communication from the stations.

To go beyond the moon will require large amounts of power for such systems as the VASMIR. Power levels from 100MW to 10GW would be required to truly open up the solar system for exploration, commerce and settlement.

Power systems for space propulsion differ in two key ways from terrestrial, stationary counterparts. The first is that output power is not the only consideration, as energy density measured as kilowatts per kilogram, is also a vital factor. The other key difference is that getting rid of waste heat is much more difficult in space than on Earth, so energy conversion efficiency becomes important. In space both conduction and convention are not viable for getting rid of waste heat, and this leaves only radiation, but the radiators required to dispel waste heat can add a very severe mass penalty to the design of a vehicle, and also severely handicap its performance.

In the past, the primary mechanisms for providing power to space systems has been solar energy and nuclear fission. Solar energy is typically collected by solar cells that convert incoming photons into electricity. This works well for power levels up to 10-100 kilowatts, but for higher power levels the arrays become very large. But as one travels outward from Earth's orbit toward Mars, the energy flux (energy/unit area) from the sun decreases, requiring an increase in the size of the solar array required to produce the same amount of power.

Nuclear fission is the other approach that has been used. Radioisotope Thermoelectric Generators (RTGs) have been used on all of the unmanned outer planet probes, including Pioneer, Voyager, Galileo, and Ulysses. These devices generate heat from the nuclear decay from the fissionable material, typically plutonium, and then convert this heat to electricity using thermocouples. The energy conversion efficiency of these devices is very low (3-7%), but they are very simple and reliable. These systems work well for low power levels less than one KW, but do not scale well.

However, there are other technologies under development that can help meet these challenges. Two options discussed here are Nuclear (fission) Thermal Rocket (NTR), and A-neutronic Fusion Rockets (AFR). The concept for a NTR is to use the fission reactions in the reactor core as a heat source, run fluid through the core to heat it up and then expand this hot gas/plasma out the back as fast as you can. From the late 1950s through the early 1970s the US spent $1.4B on solid-core nuclear rocket R&D, and more than 20 NTR reactors were designed, built, and tested at the Nevada Nuclear Test Site at Jackass Flats Nevada.

These engines achieved exhaust temperatures of 2,350-2,550 K using graphite fuel and an Isp of 825-850 seconds with burn durations from 62 minutes to over 4 hours, and an engine thrust to weight of ~3. The technology of these engines was relatively mature in 1970s, and some work has continued by companies such as Aerojet as recently as 2002, so it may not be a significantly difficult feat to develop such an engine for space applications. The public relations difficulty, however, concerning launching nuclear material is another matter altogether.

The second option is the AFR, which differs from the conventional approach to achieving fusion that the US has pursued for the last half century. This conventional approach attempts to burn a mixture of tritium (a radioactive gas) and Deuterium (DT), both of which are isotopes of hydrogen. This fuel combination is the easiest one in which to induce fusion (13.6 keV required), but even if DT fusion is achieved, it presents several drawbacks, including the fact that 80% of the energy released in this reaction comes out as energetic (14 MeV) neutrons and only 20% comes out as charged particles. These high-energy neutrons cause many problems, including inducing radioactivation (the neutron flex changes the atomic structure of the of the surrounded structure) that causes the material to become radioactive as well as degrading material strength. The only way these neutrons can be turned into useful energy is to thermalize them (using a large blanket of liquid lithium for instance) and then running this hold fluid through a steam cycle to produce electricity. Due to materials limitations, the Carnot efficiency of such processes is very low (<20%), and it produces a very large waste heat problem for any space application.

Fortunately, there has been significant recent progress in a different approach, a-neutronic fusion. A-neutronic fusion differs from conventional fusion reactions in that neither of the fuel elements is radioactive, and the resulting fusion products are charged particles. Two a-neutonic reactions are of particular interest for space applications, DT and He3 (D-He3), and Protium (ionized hydrogen) and Boron (P-B11). D-He3 is easier to burn – 58 keV compared to 123 keV for P-B11. Since this is a more difficult technical challenge, new approaches need to be tried to reach these high energies. However, the US Department of Energy (DOE) has repeatedly refused to provide significant support to these advanced concepts despite numerous calls by Congress to do so. Some efforts are nevertheless under way, but most are under funded, which of course limits their progress.

Another interesting a-neutronic fusion concept is inertial electrodynamic fusion (IEF). P. T. Farnsworth and Robert Hirsch developed the basic concept for IEF in the 1960s as a spherical accelerator. Electrostatic potentials are used to accelerate the particles to velocities where their momentum can overcome the coulomb barrier and fusion can occur. Materials limitations prevented the Farnsworth/Hirsch device from producing net power, until in the 1980s when Dr. Robert Bussard modified the Farnsworth/Hirsch device and replaced their electron grid with a magnetically-insulated 'magrid.' Over the next two decades with funding from the Navy (although none from DOE) Bussard's company EMC2 was able to demonstrate many of the fusion requirements for a practical fusion device, including producing 109 fusion reactions/sec at very low voltage (10 kV). Unfortunately, Dr. Bussard passed away in 2007, but his work is being carried on by Dr. Richard Nebel.

In 2009 the Navy awarded EMC2 a $12M contract that, if all the options were exercised, would demonstrate PB11 fusion in 2012. Dr. Nebel predicts that the next power producing system could be demonstrated by 2020, a system that could be capable of producing hundreds of megawatts to gigawatts of electrical power, with no radioactivity, and at conversion efficiencies as high as 95%.

Shortly before his death Dr. Bussard made a presentation at the International Space Development Conference on space applications using IEF technology, and he predicted that IEF could power a colony on Mars capable of housing 1200 people with 50 tons of supplies each, for under $20B.

Several other a-neutronic fusion concepts have received public or private funding, including efforts by Tri Alpha and FRC machine, Lawrenceville Plasma Physics and their Dense Plasma Focus, Magnetized Target Fusion at Los Alamos National Lab, as well as a Sandia Labs and Prometheus II Ltd. PLASMAK™ device. Each of these devices has unique advantages and challenges, but experimental work has been done and the results have been encouraging enough to continue development. Most if not all of these concepts could provide the energy levels and propulsion performance that could open up the solar system for commerce and settlement.

FUEL AND WATER

As previously noted, space fuel depots could constitute an important new space infrastructure. A primary function will be to store liquid oxygen and hydrogen, as well as other expendables, including water. Ample supplies of hydrogen and oxygen enable you to produce water easily in standard fuel cells that also then provide electrical power. A space depot could therefore be an important source of fuel, water and even food grown in space based greenhouses, which would support a wide range of activities of interest to both government and commercial firms. With access to the lunar surface or suitable asteroids, in-situ resource utilization (ISRU) techniques could employed to provide additional sources for fuel, water, and even building materials.

Government demonstrations of space depots should be the first step, and when the techniques and technologies are proven the government could then turn over construction and operational of space fuel depots to industry. As with power and communication contracts, minimum government purchase agreements for fuel, water, and even food, could provide a guaranteed market to ensure and stimulate commercial adoption of these facilities.

Recent discoveries by NASA's Moon Minerology Mapper (MMM) on board India's Chandrayaan-1 Lunar Orbit, and by the US Lunar Reconnaissance Orbiter (LRO) and Lunar Crater Observation and Sensing Satellite (LCROSS) probe, reveal data that suggest that there is at least 600 million tons of water contained in ice sheets 1 to 3 meters thick on the moon's north pole. This invaluable resource could be used to support a variety of purposes, including providing oxygen to breathe, water to drink and grow crops, and hydrogen and oxygen for propulsion and many other industrial purposes, including re-supply of orbiting fuel depots.

IN-SITU RESOURCE UTILIZATION (ISRU)

Living off the land has historically been the key to opening up new frontiers. When American settlers moved west of the Mississippi they came upon the Great Plains with not a tree is sight. To create shelter they could have hauled wood to build traditional houses, but that would have been prohibitively expensive. Instead they used local materials such as sod and adobe to build a new kind of structure that could keep cool in the summer and warm in the winter. Similarly, space settlers will need to learn to live off the resources that they find wherever they go.

While the moon is mostly oxygen, it also contains other valuable materials including iron, silicon, aluminum, calcium, magnesium, sodium, and titanium. The data from LCROSS from the Oct. 9, 2009 impact shows definitively that there is water ice in the permanently sheltered charts on the poles of the moon as well as other economically valuable materials.

The abundance of solar radiation on the moon could be readily applied to breaking down the compounds into a useful form. For example, as noted above, 27 different processes have been identified for extracting oxygen from the lunar soil, and a great side benefit of many of them is that the by products are iron, silicon, and titanium, all of which are very valuable in their own right.

The asteroids are also sources of mineral wealth. While most of the known asteroids are located far from Earth in orbit between Mars and Jupiter, there is a class of asteroids called Apollo objects which have orbits that come very close to and in some cases cross the orbit of the Earth. These objects are a potential source of raw materials, but they also pose a threat because a collision with even a small object (100 m) could be catastrophic, suggesting that it is important to learn more about this objects for profit and also for protection.

Hence, Congress has tasked NASA with *"detecting, tracking, cataloging and characterizing near-Earth asteroids and comets in order to provide warning and mitigation of the potential hazard of such near-Earth objects (NEOs) to the Earth."* In response, NASA established a program to identify and track NEO's greater than 140 meters in diameter.

As of August 2009, 6,244 such objects had been cataloged. Asteroids make up the majority of these objects, and there are two major types: 1) metallic and 2) carbonaceous chondrites. A typical metallic asteroid is composed of iron and nickel, both valuable elements. A single 1 km wide metallic asteroid could provide the earth with enough iron and nickel to meet the current world demand for 2 - 3 years. Carbonaceous chondrites, on the other hand are made of silicates, oxides and sulfides, but more importantly a significant portion of them contain water (from 3-22%) and other volatiles.

From an energy point of view, many of these NEOs require even less delta V to reach them than is required to land on the moon, which would conceivably make it possible to mine these objects for valuable materials elements, and then return them to cis-lunar space for use and economic benefit.

CREW ACCOMMODATIONS

Expandable space habitation modules can be purchased today from commercial providers such as Bigelow Aerospace. The Bigelow expandable space habitat is a success story that should be noted and copied. The design of this deployable habitat was adapted from a NASA advanced technology program called Transit Habitat, run by Johnson Space Center in the 1990s, with the intention to design an interplanetary vehicle to transfer humans to Mars. The Transhab concept that emerged from this project was intended as a replacement for the already existing International Space Station crew Habitation Module. But while the ISS habitation module is a rigid structure, inflatable modules can be launched in a compact form. When fully inflated, Transhab would expand to 8.2 meters in diameter (compared to the 4.4 meter diameter of the Columbus ISS Module).

Controversy arose during Transhab development due to delays and increased costs of the ISS program, and the National Space Society issued a policy statement recommending that NASA cease development of Transhab. Finally in 2000, House Resolution 1654 was signed into law banning NASA from conducting further research and development of Transhab, but an option to lease an inflatable habitat module from private industry was included in the bill.

Since that time, Bigelow Aerospace has purchased the rights to the patents developed by NASA, and is pursuing a similar scheme for a private space station design. The company has launched the Genesis I and Genesis II pathfinder spacecraft, with plans for additional experimental craft culminating in their BA 330 production model. Bigelow plans to launch the first series of expandable modules to orbit in 2014, and to welcome the first inhabitants in 2015. By 2020 he could accommodate as many as 24 people in orbit at one time.

The government may be interested in purchasing expandable habitats for space, and even for lunar sorties and outposts it would seem to be a very effective approach to crew accommodation. Developing and using ISRU to help provide oxygen, fuel, building materials and even food would be a natural extension of this concept. Continued government supported for research and development on advanced technologies and concepts, for crew accommodations and life support systems would also be a smart investment. As history has shown many times, government developed concepts, like Transhab, that are proven and then transferred to industry, can lead to rapid and significant benefits for the government, industry, and the general public.

SUMMARY

History tells us that infrastructure-based exploration led by the government, with active engagement of industry, provides the best opportunity for economic expansion in the space frontier. As the expansion of the railroads and Internet shows, this strategy offers the best means of providing the necessary foundation for development while engaging the entrepreneurial spirit of the private sector for economic and social benefit.

The 'Space-Rush' strategy described here recommends focusing on four critical infrastructure elements:

1. Optimized Transportation,
2. Power,
3. Fuel, Water and Materials, and
4. Crew Accommodations.

Using government-funded demonstrations, followed by guaranteed purchase agreements to assure minimum demand while engaging private entities provides a proven path for success.

Important activities that could be pursued immediately include space fuel depot development, in-situ resource utilization experiments, space power beaming demonstrations, and expandable crew accommodation purchases. Re-establishment of long-range government funded technology programs should also be pursued to assure that new and improved technologies are continually under development.

With 'Space-Rush' we will finally begin to open space to rapid and beneficial development for the government, industry, and the general public.

•••

BRUCE PITTMAN

 Bruce Pittman is the Director of Flight Projects and Chief System Engineer at the NASA Emerging Commercial Space Office at the Ames Research Center, where he supports programs ranging from suborbital human-tended research, orbital applications and research, low cost, responsive access to space, and lunar commercialization. He has been involved in high technology product development, project management and system engineering for over 30 years.

He started his career at NASA Ames for 11 years on projects including Pioneer Venus, the Infrared Astronomy Satellite (IRAS), the Cryogenic Grating Spectrometer on the Kuiper Airborne Observatory, the Space Station Freedom Technology Advocacy Group, and several advanced studies programs. He has also worked with NASA as a contractor on projects including the NASA Emerging Commercial Space Office (2005-present), Commercial Orbital Transportation Services (2006-2007), International Space Station Commercialization (2005-2006), High Speed Civil Transport (1997-1998), Program and Project Management Initiative (1988-1993), the Space Exploration Initiative (1989-1991) and Space Shuttle Processing (1987-1988).

Mr. Pittman has also been a founder and member of the startup team of early stage growth companies including SpaceHab, Kistler Aerospace, New Focus, Product Factory, Prometheus II Ltd., and Industrial Sound and Motion.

Mr. Pittman has a BS in Mechanical Engineering from U. C. Davis and a MS in Engineering Management from Santa Clara University. Mr. Pittman is an Associate Fellow of the American Institute of Aeronautics and Astronautics (AIAA) a member of the AIAA Commercial Space Group and founder and first chairman of the System Engineering Technical Committee. He is also a member of the organizing committee for the Space Investment Summit series, a member of the Aerospace Technology Working Group (ATWG), and President of the Silicon Valley Space Club. He has authored or co-authored more than 3 dozen papers on a technical, management and business topics in aerospace and high technology. In addition to his technical work Mr. Pittman is also a member of the adjunct faculty in the Graduate Engineering School at Santa Clara University.

For his technical work Mr. Pittman has been awarded 2 NASA Special Achievement Awards, four NASA Group Achievement Awards, and the AIAA Distinguished Leadership Award.

DR. DANIEL J. RASKY

Dr. Daniel J. Rasky is the Director for the Emerging Commercial Space Office at NASA Ames, and also a Senior Scientist with NASA. He is a Co-Founder and Director for the Space Portal whose mission is to "Be a friendly front door for emerging and non-traditional space companies." He recently completed a one-year Interagency Personnel Assignment (IPA) with the Space Grant Education and Enterprise Institute (SGEEI), where he served as a Senior Research Fellow supporting a number of emerging space companies and other organizations. This included provided expert consulting to SpaceX on the design and development of the heatshield for their Dragon capsule. SpaceX has chosen to use the PICA heatshield material, invented by Dr. Rasky and associates at NASA Ames, for Dragon.

Dr. Rasky is an internationally recognized expert on advanced entry systems and thermal protection materials, with 25 years of experience in advanced entry systems and materials for NASA (20 years) and the US Air Force (5 years). Dr. Rasky has made significant contributions to flight hardware on seven NASA missions, including co-inventing the PICA heatshield material that enabled the NASA Stardust comet sample return mission, and is the primary heatshield for the Mars Science Laboratory (MSL) lander mission.

Dr. Rasky is the recipient of the NASA Inventor of the Year Award (the first ever for NASA Ames), the Senior Professional Meritorious Presidential Rank Award, the NASA Exceptional Achievement Award, the NASA Exceptional Service Medal, twelve NASA Group Awards, and eight Space Act Awards. He has 6 patents, 64 publications, is an Associate Fellow of the AIAA and Senior Member of the ASME.

REFERENCES

1. D. Schrunk, B. Sharpe, B. Cooper, M. Thangavelu, *The Moon: Resources, Future Development and Settlement*, Springer Publishing, NY, 2008
2. G. Sanders, M. Duke, NASA In-Situ Resource Utilization (ISRU) Roadmap, Final Report, May 2005
3. NASA 2008 Authorization, HR 6063.
4. *Pioneering The Space Frontier*, The Report of the National Commission on Space, 1986.
5. D. Wingo, *MOONRUSH: Improving Life on Earth with the Moon's Resources*, Apogee Books, Ontario, Canada, 2004.
6. S. Ambrose, *Nothing Like It In The World: The Men Who Built The Trans-continental Railroad 1863-1869*, Simon and Schuster, NY, 2000.

CHAPTER 12

HEAVY LIFT LAUNCH
HOW BOOSTERS WORK, THEIR HISTORY, AND THE ROLE OF HEAVY LIFT IN SPACE COMMERCIALIZATION

THOMAS E. DIEGELMAN
NASA

AND

THOMAS C. DUNCAVAGE
NASA

BOOSTER SYSTEMS:
WHY LIFT SYSTEMS AND THEIR PLANNING ARE CRITICAL TO THE COMMERCIALIZATION OF SPACE

The current crisis in American human spaceflight has generated a great deal of concern and confusion in the general public, as well as in the aerospace sector, regarding booster systems, how they are developed, and what might be the best path forward for the United States and the rest of the world.

While there is little argument that the United States needs to have diverse and cost effective lift capability, there is debate regarding whether the approach to this necessary system is a national asset or an international asset with national components.   This discussion has political, policy technical and commercial aspects that also have significant implications for the commercial space sector.

The human rated launch system, in particular, is facing a serious predicament. The resolution and resultant policy implications have serious long term consequences.

Simply put, the ability of the United States to play a significant role in the commercialization of space would be considerably limited if it did not have adequate launch capabilities, and further, the idea that commerce and trade are fundamental to the sustainability of a nation is accepted as a fact.

Therefore, in this chapter we begin with a discussion of the technical mechanics of booster systems, and then consider the policy implications and choices as they pertain to the development of commercial space.

THE PHYSICS: HOW A LAUNCH BOOSTER SYSTEM WORKS

The intent of this section is to acquaint the reader with the terminology of launch systems. It is based on the work of Robert A. Braeunig, and of course a more detailed version may be found at his web site.[1] Most classical texts on rocket propulsion use similar nomenclature.

Providing a concise overview here requires an extensive degree of simplification, so the reader who is knowledgeable about the underlying science and technology is asked to forgive the omissions. The intent is to support an effective discussion of boosters, their history and their likely evolution in the future, particularly with respect to how commercialization, which heretofore was not a factor, makes its impact felt.

---

[1]   http://www.braeunig.us/space/propuls.htm
"Rocket Propulsion", compiled and edited by Robert A. Braeunig, 1997, 2005, 2007, 2009. This web site is also the source of Figures 1 – 6.
For the interested reader, more complete information on rocket propulsion can be found in the classic reference, *Aircraft and Missile Propulsion, Volume I and II: Thermodynamics of Fluid Flow and Application to Propulsion Engines*, by M.J. Zucrow, Professor of Gas Turbines and Jet Propulsion, Purdue University, 1958, which was at one time a standard college course reference book. Although long out of print, it is sometimes available on-line for purchase.
The reader may also refer to *Elements of Propulsion, Gas Turbines and Rockets*, by J.D. Mattingly, 2006, AIAA Education Series, AIAA, and *Aerothermodynamics of Gas Turbine and Rocket Propulsion*, 3rd ed., by G.C. Oates, 1997, AIAA Education Series, AIAA.

ROCKET ENGINES AND THRUST

A typical rocket engine consists of the nozzle, the combustion chamber, and the injector, as shown in Figure 1. Thrust is the force that propels a rocket or spacecraft, and is measured in pounds, kilograms, or Newtons. Physically speaking, thrust is the result of pressure that is exerted on the wall of a combustion chamber.

Figure 1 shows a combustion chamber with an opening, the nozzle, through which gas can escape. The pressure distribution within the chamber is asymmetric; that is, inside the chamber the pressure varies little, but near the nozzle it decreases somewhat. The force due to gas pressure on the bottom of the chamber is not compensated for from the outside. The resultant force, F, is therefore due to the difference between internal and external pressure, and the resulting thrust occurs in the direction opposite to that of the gas jet, and pushes the chamber upwards.

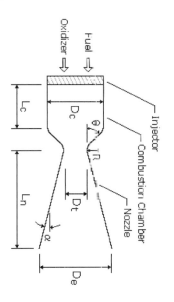

Figure 1
A Typical Rocket Engine

The burning of propellants takes place at high pressure in the combustion chamber. The chamber must be strong enough to contain the high pressure generated by, and the high temperature resulting from, the combustion process. Because of the high temperature, the chamber and nozzle are usually cooled. The chamber must also be of sufficient length (Lc) to ensure complete combustion before the gases enter the nozzle.

NOZZLE

The function of the nozzle is to convert the chemical-thermal energy generated in the combustion chamber into kinetic energy. The nozzle converts the slow moving, high pressure, high temperature gas in the combustion chamber into high velocity gas of lower pressure and temperature. Since thrust is the product of mass and velocity, a very high gas velocity is desirable. Nozzles consist of a convergent and divergent section. The minimum flow area between the convergent and divergent section is called the nozzle throat. The flow area at the end of the divergent section is called the nozzle exit area. The nozzle is usually made long enough (or the exit area is great enough) such that the pressure in the combustion chamber is reduced at the nozzle exit to the pressure existing outside the nozzle. It is under this condition, Pe=Pa where Pe is the pressure at the nozzle exit and Pa is the outside ambient pressure, that thrust is maximum and the nozzle is said to be adapted. This is also called optimum or correct expansion. When Pe is greater than Pa, the nozzle is under-extended. When the opposite is true, it is over-extended.

Therefore, because atmospheric pressures vary by altitude, a nozzle is designed for the altitude at which it has to operate. At the Earth's surface, at the atmospheric pressure of sea level (0.1 MPa or 14.7 psi), the discharge of the exhaust gases is limited by the separation of the jet from the nozzle wall. In the cosmic vacuum, this physical limitation does not exist. Therefore, there have to be two different types of engines and nozzles, those that propel the first stage of the launch vehicle through the atmosphere, and those that propel subsequent stages or control the orientation of the spacecraft in the vacuum of space.

SPECIFIC IMPULSE

The specific impulse of a rocket, Isp, is the ratio of the thrust to the flow rate of the weight ejected, that is:

Isp = F / q g0

Where F is thrust, q is the rate of mass flow, and g0 is standard gravity (9.80665 m/s2).

Specific impulse is expressed in seconds. When the thrust and the flow rate remain constant throughout the burning of the propellant, the specific impulse is the time for which the rocket engine provides a thrust equal to the weight of the propellant consumed. Some typical values are given in Table 1.[2]

---

[2] This is known as the Tsiolkovsky rocket equation.

Engine type	Scenario	SFC in lb/(lbf·h)	SFC in g/(kN·s)	Specific impulse (s)	Effective exhaust velocity (m/s)
NK-33 rocket engine	Vacuum	10.9	309	330	3,240
SSME rocket engine	Space shuttle vacuum	7.95	225	453	4,423
Ramjet	Mach 1	4.5	127	800	7,877
J-58 turbojet	SR-71 at Mach 3.2 (Wet)	1.9	53.8	1,900	18,587
Rolls-Royce/ Snecma Olympus 593	Concorde Mach 2 cruise (Dry)	1.195	33.8	3 012	29,553
CF6-80C2B1F turbofan	Boeing 747-400 cruise	0.605	17.1	5,950	58,400
General Electric CF6 turbofan	Sea level	0.307	8.696	11,700	115,000

Table 1
Specific Impulse of various rockets.
http://en.wikipedia.org/wiki/Specific_impulse

Note that for the different engine types, particularly engines that do not require or function on chemical reaction, the values and characteristics of the Isp are wildly different. Careful interpretation and examination of details is required to reach valid conclusions from this high level data.

Engine	Effective exhaust velocity (m/s, kg·m/s/kg)	Specific impulse (s)	Energy per kg of exhaust (MJ/kg)
Turbofan jet engine (actual V is ~300)	29,000	3,000	~0.05
Solid rocket	2,500	250	3
Bipropellant liquid rocket	4,400	450	9.7
Ion thruster	29,000	3,000	430
Dual Stage Four Grid Electrostatic Ion Thruster	210,000	21,400	22,500
VASIMR	290,000	30,000	43,000

Table 2
Effective exhaust velocities.
http://en.wikipedia.org/wiki/Specific_impulse

For a given engine, the specific impulse has different values on the ground and in the vacuum of space, because the ambient pressure is involved in the expression for the thrust. In evaluating engine performance it is therefore important to state whether specific impulse is the value at sea level, at high atmosphere, or in a vacuum.

LIQUID FUELED ROCKET ENGINES

Liquid fueled rocket engines and the associated booster systems require tanks for two commodities: fuel and oxidizer. The fuels are liquid phase as the name implies, but can be also cryogenic. Oxidizers may be oxygen, always cryogenically tanked, but may not involve oxygen at all if the propellant and oxidizer are what is known as hypergolic, or upon mixing, spontaneously decompose to 'combustion' products. Table 3 shows some of the more common fuel / oxidizer pairs.

The table also shows monopropellant entries. These are essentially decomposed over a catalyst bed or can be heated to cause 'combustion' or decomposition. All of these reactions are exothermic, giving off heat and energy to be turned mechanically into thrust.

Nitric acid / hydrazine-base fuel
Nitrogen tetroxide / hydrazine-base fuel
Hydrogen peroxide / RP-1 (including catalyst bed)
Liquid oxygen / RP-1
Liquid oxygen / ammonia
Liquid oxygen / liquid hydrogen (GH2 injection)
Liquid oxygen / liquid hydrogen (LH2 injection)
Liquid fluorine / liquid hydrogen (GH2 injection)
Liquid fluorine / liquid hydrogen (LH2 injection)
Liquid fluorine / hydrazine
Chlorine trifluoride / hydrazine-base fuel

Table 3
Typical Fuels For Liquid Rocket Engines.
Shown as Fuel/Oxidizer.

Liquid bi-propellant rocket engines can be categorized according to their power cycles, that is, how power is derived to feed propellants to the main combustion chamber. Described below are some of the more common types.

Gas-generator cycle: The gas-generator cycle, also called open cycle, taps off a small amount of fuel and oxidizer from the main flow (typically 3 to 7 percent) to feed a burner called a gas generator. The hot gas from this generator passes through a turbine to generate power for the pumps that sends propellants to the combustion chamber. The hot gas is then either dumped overboard, or sent into the main nozzle downstream.

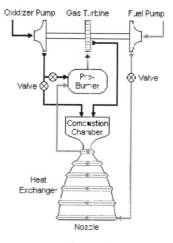

Figure 2
Staged Combustion

Increasing the flow of propellants into the gas generator increases the speed of the turbine, which increases the flow of propellants into the main combustion chamber, and hence, the amount of thrust produced.

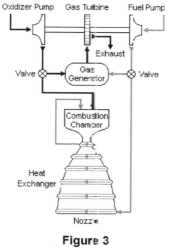

Figure 3
Gas Generator

The gas generator must burn propellants at a less-than-optimal mixture ratio to keep the temperature low for the turbine blades. Thus, the cycle is appropriate for moderate power requirements but not high-power systems, which would have to divert a large portion of the main flow to the less efficient gas-generator flow.

As in most rocket engines, some of the propellant in a gas generator cycle is used to cool the nozzle and combustion chamber, increasing efficiency and allowing higher engine temperature.

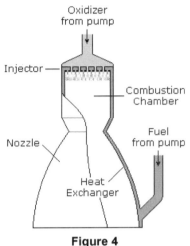

Figure 4
Regenerative Cooling

HOW THE ENGINE IS COOLED

Regenerative cooling is the most widely used method of cooling a thrust chamber, and is accomplished by flowing high-velocity coolant over the back side of the chamber's hot gas wall to convectively cool the hot gas liner. The coolant with the heat input from cooling the liner is then discharged into the injector and utilized as a propellant. This is shown in Figure 4.

Earlier thrust chamber designs, such as the V-2 and Redstone, had low chamber pressure, low heat flux and low coolant pressure requirements, which could be satisfied by a simplified 'double wall chamber' design with regenerative and film cooling. For subsequent rocket engine applications, however, chamber pressures were increased and the cooling requirements became more difficult to satisfy. It was necessary to design new coolant configurations that were more efficient structurally and had improved heat transfer characteristics.

This led to the design of 'tubular wall' thrust chambers, by far the most widely used design approach for the vast majority of large rocket engine applications. These chamber designs have been successfully used for the Thor, Jupiter, Atlas, H-1, J-2, F-1, RS-27 and several other Air Force and NASA rocket engines. The primary advantage of the design is that it's lightweight and accrues a large experience base. As chamber pressures and hot gas wall heat fluxes have continued to increase (>100 atm), still more effective methods have been needed.

SOLID ROCKET MOTORS

Solid rockets motors store propellants in solid form. The fuel is typically powdered aluminum, and the oxidizer is ammonium perchlorate. A synthetic rubber binder such as polybutadiene holds the fuel and oxidizer powders together. Though lower performing than liquid propellant rockets, the operational simplicity of a solid rocket motor often makes it the propulsion system of choice. There is also an emerging technology that has the oxidizer injected into the solid propellant chamber and therefore the solid rocket motor can, unlike its oxidizer / fuel blended cousin, be turned on and off by use of the oxidizer control.

SOLID FUEL GEOMETRY

A solid fuel's geometry determines the area and contours of its exposed surfaces, and thus its burn pattern. There are two main types of solid fuel blocks used in the space industry, cylindrical blocks with combustion at a front, or surface, and cylindrical blocks with internal combustion. In the first case, the front of the flame travels in layers from the nozzle end of the block towards the top of the casing. This so-called 'end burner' produces constant thrust throughout the burn. In the second, more usual case, the combustion surface develops along the length of a central channel. Sometimes the channel has a star shaped, or other, geometry to moderate the growth of this surface.

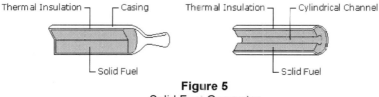

Figure 5
Solid Fuel Geometry

The shape of the fuel block for a rocket is chosen for the particular type of mission it will perform. Since the combustion of the block progresses from its free surface, as this surface grows, geometrical considerations determine whether the thrust increases, decreases or stays constant.

In Figure 6, we see fuel blocks with a cylindrical channel (1) develop their thrust progressively. Those with a channel and also a central cylinder of fuel (2) produce a relatively constant thrust, which reduces to zero very quickly when the fuel is used up. The five-pointed star profile (3) develops a relatively constant thrust that decreases slowly to zero as the last of the fuel is consumed. The 'cruciform' profile (4) produces progressively less thrust. Fuel in a block with a 'double anchor' profile (5) produces a decreasing thrust that drops off quickly near the end of the burn. The 'cog' profile (6) produces a strong initial thrust, followed by an almost constant lower thrust.

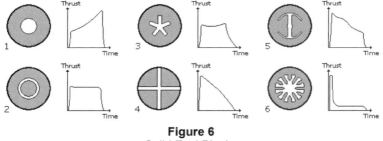

Figure 6
Solid Fuel Blocks

BURN RATE OF SOLID ROCKET BOOSTERS

Regression, typically measured in millimeters per second (or inches per second), is termed burn rate. This rate can differ significantly for different propellants, or for one particular propellant, depending on various operating conditions as well as formulation. Knowing quantitatively the burning rate of a propellant, and how it changes under various conditions, is of fundamental importance in the successful design of a solid rocket motor.

Propellant burning rate is influenced by many factors, the most significant being: combustion chamber pressure, initial temperature of the propellant grain, velocity of the combustion gases flowing parallel to the burning surface, local static pressure, and motor acceleration and spin. These factors are discussed below.

Burn rate is profoundly affected by combustion chamber pressure. The usual representation of the pressure dependence on burn rate is the Saint-Robert's Law,

$$r = a P_c^n$$

Where 'r' is the burn rate, 'a' is the burn rate coefficient, 'n' is the pressure exponent, and 'Pc' is the combustion chamber pressure. The values of 'a' and 'n' are determined empirically for a particular propellant formulation and cannot be theoretically predicted. It is important to realize that a single set of 'a' and 'n' values are typically valid over a distinct pressure range. More than one set may be necessary to accurately represent the full pressure regime of interest.

Example 'a' and 'n' values are 5.6059* (pressure in MPa, burn rate in mm/s) and 0.35 respectively for the Space Shuttle SRBs, which gives a

burn rate of 9.34 mm/s at the average chamber pressure of 4.3 MPa or roughly 3000 lbs / in2
  * NASA publications give a burn rate coefficient of 0 0386625 (pressure in PSI, burn rate in inch/s).

MONOPROPELLANT ENGINES

By far the most widely used type of propulsion for spacecraft attitude and velocity control is monopropellant hydrazine. Its excellent handling characteristics, relative stability under normal storage conditions, and clean decomposition products have made it the standard. The general sequence of operations in a hydrazine thruster is:

When the attitude control system signals for thruster operation, an electric solenoid valve opens, allowing hydrazine to flow. The action may be pulsed (as short as 5 ms) or long duration (steady state).

The pressure in the propellant tank forces liquid hydrazine into the injector, it then enters as a spray into the thrust chamber and contacts the catalyst beds.

The catalyst bed consists of alumina pellets impregnated with iridium. Incoming hydrazine heats to its vaporizing point by contact with the catalyst bed and with the hot gases leaving the catalyst particles. The temperature of the hydrazine rises to a point where the rate of its decomposition becomes so high that the chemical reactions are self-sustaining.

By controlling the flow variables and the geometry of the catalyst chamber, a designer can tailor the proportion of chemical products, the exhaust temperature, the molecular weight, and thus the enthalpy (heat content) for a given application. For a thruster application where specific impulse is paramount, the designer attempts to provide 30-40% ammonia dissociation, which is about the lowest percentage that can be maintained reliably. For gas-generator application, where lower temperature gases are usually desired, the designer provides for higher levels of ammonia dissociation.

Finally, in a space thruster, the hydrazine decomposition products leave the catalyst bed and exit from the chamber through a high expansion ratio exhaust nozzle to produce thrust.

Monopropellant hydrazine thrusters typically produce a specific impulse of about 230 to 240 seconds.

Other suitable propellants for catalytic decomposition engines are hydrogen peroxide and nitrous oxide However, their performance is considerably lower than that obtained with hydrazine, a specific impulse of about 150 s with H_2O_2 and about 170 s with N_2O.

Monopropellant systems have successfully provided orbit maintenance and attitude control functions, but lack the performance to provide a large, weight-efficient change in velocity (ΔV) maneuvers required for orbit insertion.

Bipropellant systems are attractive because they can provide all three functions with one higher performance system, but they are more complex than the common solid rocket and monopropellant combined systems.

A third alternative is dual mode systems. These systems are hybrid designs that use hydrazine both as a fuel for high performance bipropellant engines and as a monopropellant with conventional low-thrust catalytic thrusters. The hydrazine is fed to both the bipropellant engines and the monopropellant thrusters from a common fuel tank.

Cold gas propulsion is just a controlled, pressurized gas source and a nozzle. It represents the simplest form of rocket engine. Cold gas has many applications where simplicity and/or the need to avoid hot gases are more important than high performance. The Manned Maneuvering Unit used by astronauts is an example of such a system.[3]

STAGING OF MULTI-STAGED BOOSTERS

Multistage rockets allow improved payload capability for vehicles with a high ΔV requirement, such as launch vehicles or interplanetary spacecraft.

In a multistage rocket, propellant is stored in smaller, separate tanks rather than a larger single tank as in a single-stage rocket. Since each tank is discarded when empty, energy is not expended to accelerate the empty tanks, so a higher total ΔV is obtained. Alternatively, a larger payload mass can be accelerated to the same total ΔV. For convenience, the separate tanks are usually bundled with their own engines, with each discardable unit called a stage.

Multistage rocket performance is described by the same rocket equation as single-stage rockets, but must be determined on a stage-by-stage basis. The velocity increment, ΔVi, for each stage is calculated as before,

$$\Delta V_i = C_i LN\left(\frac{m_{oi}}{m_{fi}}\right)$$

Where 'm_{oi}' represents the total vehicle mass when stage 'i' is ignited, and 'm_{fi}' is the total vehicle mass when stage 'i' is burned out but not yet discarded.

---

[3]   Suggested reading on the simplicity of solid rockets coupled with some technological innovations, including a detailed review of the military interest, development and employment of the solid rocket launcher is found in *Journal Of Propulsion And Power*, Vol. 19, No. 6, November–December 2003; "Solid Rocket Enabling Technologies and Milestones in the United States," Leonard H. Caveny, Robert L. Geisler, Russell A. Ellis, and Thomas L. Moore, Chemical Propulsion Information Agency, Columbia, Maryland 21044.

It is important to realize that the payload mass for any stage consists of the mass of all subsequent stages plus the ultimate payload itself. The velocity increment for the vehicle is then the sum of those for the individual stages where n is the total number of stages.

$$\Delta V_{total} = \sum_{i=1}^{n} \Delta V_i$$

We define the payload fraction as the ratio of payload mass to initial mass, or mpl / mo.

For a multistage vehicle with dissimilar stages, the overall vehicle payload fraction depends on how the ΔV requirement is partitioned among stages. Payload fractions will be reduced if the ΔV is partitioned sub optimally. The optimal distribution may be determined by trial and error. A ΔV distribution is postulated and the resulting payload fraction calculated. The ΔV distribution is varied until the payload fraction is maximized.

After the selection of the ΔV distribution, vehicle sizing is accomplished by starting with the uppermost or final stage (whose payload is the actual deliverable payload) then calculating the initial mass of this assembly. This assembly then forms the payload for the previous stage and the process repeats until all stages are sized. Results reveal that to maximize payload fraction for a given ΔV requirement:

1. Stages with higher Isp should be above stages with lower Isp.
2. More ΔV should be provided by the stages with the higher Isp.
3. Each succeeding stage should be smaller than its predecessor, and
4. Similar stages should provide the same ΔV.

These design 'rules of thumb' are uniformly reflected in the discussion to follow, but with the caveat that the extent of application is modified by the optimization that was done on the stages and total system as a routine part of its design. Said another way, these rules of thumb will not provide sufficient guidance to build a customized launch booster. Mission profiles and side issues such as whether or not a system is 'human rated,' a term that is discussed later, are important drivers as well. Table 4 shows the relative performance of some well known launch systems.

The column labeled 'mass ratio' is the ratio of lift off to delivered mass. This might be considered in the future to be the metric for commercial launch systems as the ratio has a 1:1 relationship to the cost per pound of delivered mass to any orbit class, be it LEO, GEO, or lunar. Note that even 40+ years after successful missions in Apollo, the Saturn V (which was human-rated) is still nearly the performance of the Ariane V, (which was not human rated). That masterpiece of design, created essentially by the Peenemunde staff with support from the American industrial base, remains unrivaled, and will be a benchmark for a long time to come.

Vehicle	Takeoff Mass	Final Mass	Mass ratio	Payload fraction
Ariane 5 (vehicle + payload)	746,000 kg (~1,645,000 lb)	2,700 kg + 16,000 kg (~6,000 lb + ~35,300 lb)	39.9	0.975
Titan 23G first stage	117,020 kg (258,000 lb)	4,760 kg (10,500 lb)	24.6	0.959
Saturn V	3,038,500 kg (~6,700,000 lb)	13,300 kg + 118,000 kg (~29,320 lb + ~260,150 lb)	23.1	0.957
Space Shuttle (vehicle + payload)	2,040,000 kg (~4,500,000 lb)	104,000 kg + 28,800 kg (~230,000 lb + ~63,500 lb)	15.4	0.935
Saturn 1B (stage only)	448,648 kg (989,100 lb)	41,594 kg[3] (91,700 lb)	10.7	0.907
Virgin Atlantic GlobalFlyer	~181,000 kg (400,000 lb)	1,678.3 kg (3,700 lb)	6	0.83
V2	13,000 kg (~28,660 lb) (12.8 ton)	not available	3.85	0.74
X-15	15,420 kg (34,000 lb)	6,620 kg (14,600 lb)	2.3	0.57
Concorde	~181,000 kg (400,000 lb)	not available	2	0.5
Boeing 747	~363,000 kg (800,000 lb)	not available	2	0.5

Table 4
The relative performance of some well known launch systems.

THE HISTORY OF BOOSTER SYSTEMS IN THE UNITED STATES, AND THEIR MISSIONS

Since their initial operational capability in the 1950s, space access launch vehicles have undergone nearly as many capability classification definitions as the vehicle series have had vehicle variants. Evolution of the vehicles has resulted in what today is generally accepted as 'rules of thumb' rather than clear distinctions with hard metrics. Moreover, orbital altitude, eccentricity, and inclination plane are independent variables that greatly effect on-orbit mass delivery for any launch system.

This is often perplexing, so the intent here is to develop an understanding of how a booster system, or space launch vehicle operates, linking this to the history of vehicle evolution.

Launch vehicle systems are tailored by the vendor to accommodate the greatest market share of their customer's target operational payloads and orbits. This accounts for much of the confusion when it comes to comparative vehicle capability based on top-level nomenclature.

There are three primary lift categories to consider as a baseline: low, medium, and heavy. However, there are only two lift categories to consider when dealing with access to space for human beings, namely medium and heavy lift.

For the sake of brevity, the discussion here centers upon payload delivery mass only, principally to circular Low Earth Orbit (LEO) at inclinations between 28 and 52 degrees. It is important to note that LEO metrics have direct bearing on accepted mission profiles for exploration beyond LEO, principally because payload mass is parked in LEO before transfer insertion to points beyond LEO, including the Moon and other Solar System destinations.

There are currently three American rocket systems capable of medium and heavy lift, Delta, Atlas, and Titan. (In addition, the Russian Proton and the ESA Ariane are also heavy lift systems.)

ATLAS

Atlas V is an active expendable launch system. Atlas V was formerly operated by Lockheed Martin, and is now operated by the Lockheed Martin-Boeing joint venture United Launch Alliance.

Figure 7
Early Atlas Family
Referred to as Atlas 1 or Atlas A-F Series

Each Atlas V rocket uses a Russian-built RD-180 engine burning kerosene and liquid oxygen to power its first stage and an American-built RL10 engine burning liquid hydrogen and liquid oxygen to power its upper stage.

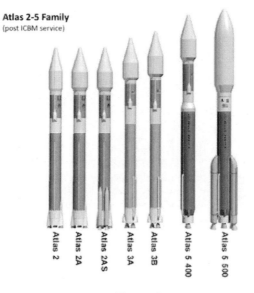

Figure 8
Atlas 2 – 5 Family

DELTA

The original Delta rockets used a modified version of the Thor, the first ballistic missile deployed by the United States, as their first stage. The Thor was designed in the mid-1950s. Subsequent satellite and space probe flights soon followed, using a Thor first stage with several different upper stages. The fourth upper stage used on the Thor was the Thor 'Delta,' delta being the fourth letter of the Greek alphabet. Eventually the entire Thor-Delta launch vehicle came to be called *"Delta."*

NASA intended Delta as *"an interim general purpose vehicle"* for communication, meteorological, and scientific satellites and lunar probes during the early 1960s, and planned to replace Delta with other rocket designs when they came on-line. Due to its reliability, however, Delta remains very much in use. Delta rockets are currently manufactured and launched, as with Atlas, by the United Launch Alliance.

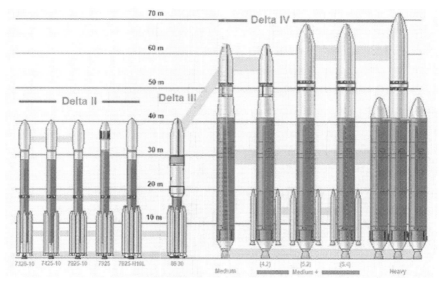

Figure 9
Delta Series (post IRBM)

Delta II   Delta III   Delta IV (heavy)

Figure 10
Delta Launch Vehicles Currently Operational

Figure 11
Delta Launch Vehicles Currently Operational

TITAN

As of 2006, the Titan family of rockets is no longer in use. The high cost of using hydrazine and nitrogen tetroxide fuels, along with the special care that was needed due to their toxicity, proved too expensive compared to the higher-performance liquid hydrogen or RP-1-fueled vehicles (kerosene), with a liquid oxygen oxidizer. Titan is owned by the Lockheed Martin company, which decided to extend its Atlas family of rockets instead of its more expensive Titans. The final Titan was launched from Vandenberg Air Force Base on 19 October 2005, carrying a secret payload for the National Reconnaissance Office (NRO). There are about twenty Titan II rockets at the Aerospace Maintenance and Regeneration Center near Tucson, Arizona, that are set to either be scrapped or used as monuments

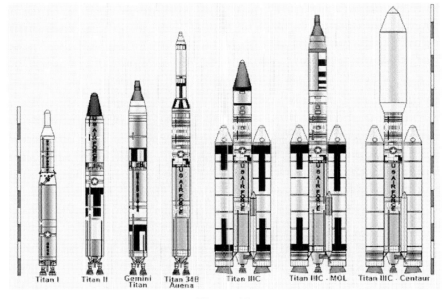

Figure 12
Titan Family of Missile and Launch Vehicles

CATEGORIES OF BOOSTER ROCKET SYSTEMS

In and across the booster 'Lift Categories,' there are three Rules of Thumb that guided the definition of the booster systems.

THE FIRST RULE OF THUMB: MEDIUM AND HEAVY LIFT

Traditional medium lift to LEO is roughly 10,000 – 40,000 lbs; plus or minus 5,000 lbs. 50,000 lbs is considered the absolute maximum in the 'traditional' medium lift category systems.

The medium lift category covers the most ubiquitous launch systems, which have collectively conducted a tremendous variety of diverse missions, including human spaceflight. They span nearly half a century of payloads from every conceivable customer base to virtually all points above Earth's atmosphere, including unmanned probes that have explored nearly all of the Sun's planets. Some have even ventured beyond the solar system itself.

Today, medium lift rocket propulsion systems are common, with several countries possessing domestically produced systems of similar capability.

However, some terminology pertaining to the first rule of thumb has morphed. Yesterday's 'medium lift' isn't always applied today, and the upper bracket of traditional medium lift is often referred to as 'heavy' lift.

The reason for this is that 'heavy' lift was a term that initially applied only to human exploration, principally beyond LEO, which is to say

Apollo. The first and arguably only true heavy lift rockets were the Saturn series, which were developed for the sole purpose of sending humans beyond LEO.

The originator of the early NASA booster systems was the military, which meant that the Saturn series of rockets set the heavy lift standard in both civilian and military space. For nearly half a century and still counting, the Saturn V remains unchallenged as the record for throw weight to LEO. It could place a whopping 250,000 lbs into a 28 degree inclination LEO orbit per launch.

In the decades since the Saturn first flew, 200,000 lbs to LEO has remained a traditional lunar reference mission minimum requirement for human exploration. The planned Ares V booster (estimated 300,000 lbs to LEO) substantially exceeds that. If funded for development, the Ares V would be, by far, the most powerful launch system ever developed, and would open up the entire solar system to human exploration. It would also provide a catalyst of unquestionable value to the prospects of space commercialization.

Looking at the Saturn as compared with other launch systems tells a story in itself, as seen in Figure 11.

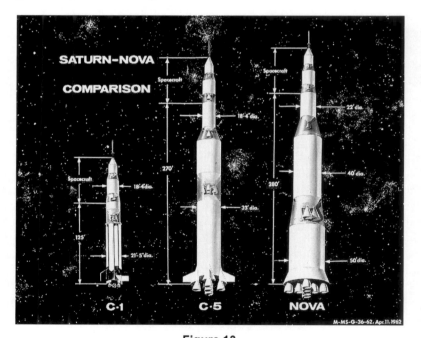

Figure 13
1962 graphic comparison of Saturn C-1, C-5 and proposed NOVA launch vehicles. NASA – Marshall Space Flight Center
http://mix.msfc.nasa.gov/IMAGES/HIGH/9902050.jpg

An interesting detail concerning the Saturn program is that the Saturn V was not the end of the evolutionary cycle for this behemoth. There was a planned Mars rocket that would have also been a very heavy lift capability for the lunar missions, called the Saturn VIII or *"Nova."* Few details remain as to its projected performance, but a visual comparison shown in Figure 13 hints that this is well over 500,000 lbs to LEO.

THE SECOND RULE OF THUMB: LIFT TO LUNAR

As noted, traditional heavy lift systems are based on the lunar exploration reference mission profiles established for Apollo, which is 200,000 lbs or more to LEO.

While the Space Shuttle stack is technically a heavy lift system, the Orbiter returns to earth, which means that the current Shuttle system can deliver a maximum on-orbit payload of less than 50,000 lbs. This is one of the driving reasons why cargo versions of the Shuttle stack (SSME's bolted to a payload can instead of to the Orbiter) were much studied in early ISS evaluations as well as in preliminary exploration systems architectures.

Traditional heavy lift terminology has also morphed since the retirement of the Saturn series in 1975. Based principally on military lift requirements, the upper limit of traditional medium lift category is increasingly referred to as 'heavy' lift and is often confused with exploration 'heavy' lift. This is an important distinction and serves to clarify Rule of Thumb 3.

THE THIRD RULE OF THUMB: LIFT TO LEO

Human access to ISS – or comparable adventures in the commercial arena - from U.S. facilities requires 30,000 – 50,000 lbs of lift to LEO.

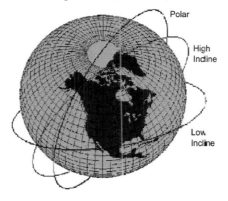

Figure 14
Earth Orbits
High inclination orbits require more energy to achieve compared with low incline orbits, because the Earth's spin helps a spacecraft achieve orbit at low incline.

Lift requirements for human access to ISS complicates the LEO scenario because of the space station's relatively high orbital inclination (51.6 degrees) and the consequential additional energy required to get there when compared to low inclination LEO orbital planes (U.S. traditional 28 degrees).

This is the flashpoint of discussion for U.S. based human launch systems because with the cancellation of Ares I, only two American launch systems outside of further Shuttle service could conceivably transport crews to ISS – Delta IV Heavy and Atlas V Heavy.

Neither of these vehicles are Saturn class at this time, although there is much discussion over maximum developmental limits that, if realized, could make both Delta and possibly Atlas true Saturn class launch vehicles. Figure 15, taken from Boeing literature on Delta IV, shows what could be done to 'grow the family' to very high useable payload size.

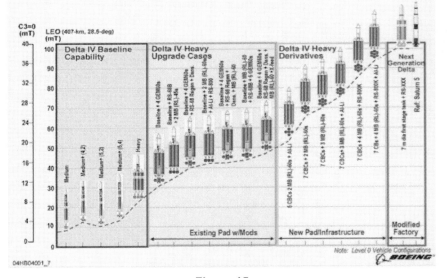

Figure 15
Delta IV Baseline and Upgrades

For the time being, it is sufficient to say that any vehicle capable of delivering 50,000 lbs to the ISS should satisfy current Orion command and service module lift requirements. The challenge is to connect launches and accumulated operational experience with a growth plan for the launcher that tracks and slightly leads the forecast need for lift capability.

As suggested by Figures 16 and 18, the difficulty is not confined to the launch system but spills over into the launch pad and the ground infrastructure as well. Accumulated experience in all aspects of the system is essential to developing long term reliability, and therefore confidence on the part of commercial customers.   These points are illustrative of the nature of this business, and the difficulties of operating from a position of policy and pragmatism; the results may be economically and technically disastrous.

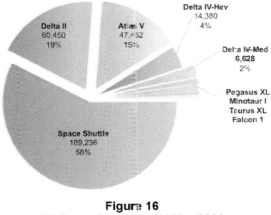

Figure 16
US Space Deliveries, 2005 – 2009
Payload Mass Launched (kg)

HEAVY LIFT LAUNCH FOR SPACE COMMERCE

In the short term, which is defined here as the next five to seven years, there are only three American solutions that could satisfy the above launch requirements for NASA, military, or commercial missions:
1. Extending the Space Shuttle Program
2. 'Human Rating' for the Delta IV Heavy.
3. 'Human Rating' for the Atlas V heavy.

(A definition of 'human rating' is provided below.)

Extending Space Shuttle operations is not impossible at this late juncture, but because such an undertaking would require substantial logistical contract re-instatement and may quickly prove to be cost prohibitive when compared to human rating heavy versions of either Delta or Atlas. Shuttle continuation remains a very contentious issue on those grounds.

The shutdown of the Shuttle Program is significant for many reasons, including operations work force stability, cost of payload per pound, loss of a human rated vehicle availability, and others. However the principle concern is the gap left in the launch market, as shown in Figure 11.

Clearly the supposition that transition from government to commercial launch systems can be smooth, painless, and swift would not be an accurate conclusion based upon this Figure. The path may be long, arduous, and difficult, especially in the current fiscal situation and business climate, projected to last well beyond 2012.

HUMAN RATING

Human Rating refers to the suitability of a launch system for transporting humans. As stated in the latest NASA led forum on Human Rating, the definition is:

> *"A human-rated system accommodates human needs, effectively utilizes human capabilities, controls hazards, and manages safety risk associated with human spaceflight, and provides, to the maximum extent practical, the capability to safely recover the crew from hazardous situations.*
>
> *"The overall objective is to provide the safest possible design that can accomplish the mission, given the constraints on the program, mass, volume, schedule, and cost."*[4]

NASA NPR 8705.2

This definition leads to several connected, deliberate, and nearly irrevocable decisions. First, engineers and managers must always concern themselves with these questions:

- What is the failure mode set that would threaten significantly human life on-board?
- What are the limits that must be designed in, such as g force limits, maneuvers rates, accessibility, operability, and the like?
- What is the over-system-design capable of in terms of reliability, in on and off nominal situations?

In the un-manned arena, the primary criterion is 'mission success.' If one translates that into booster design, the ability to not destroy the launch pad, have adequate range safety, and effective abort scenarios (destruction of vehicle) at any point causes only the loss of the booster system and the payload, but there is no loss of life. There are no repercussions except an upset customer.

In human spaceflight, the metric is 'safety of the crew, the vehicle, and mission,' in that very specific and non-negotiable order. Once we

---

[4]   *Aerospace America*, AIAA monthly publication, August 2010, Page 26 – 41.

inject humans into the equation, we see that the design has radically different requirements and attributes. Escape from a malfunctioning booster is one such requirement; the ability to retrieve a crew from abort scenarios is mandatory. G forces also become an issue, something that is difficult (as previously discussed) in solid rockets, since the solid rocket burn rate is not controllable once ignited.

And the complications are additive. A theoretical example is a booster is doing 3 g's and the requirement to have an escape system for the crew that puts separation distance adequate for booster destruction g force requirements at 11 g's (not uncommon for escape systems). The additive effect is 14 g's - very significant, and lethal.

A practical example is that John Glenn rode an Atlas in the Mercury program. At the time the success rate for Atlas was under 50%, and the destruct rate for boosters was around 20%. This launch system was so unstable that the launch silo crews received hazardous duty pay. It is not conceivable that this situation would repeat itself in the quest for the commercialization of space, the return to the moon or a mission to Mars today, because the social tolerance for this risk level and the sense of immediacy from the Russian Sputnik that promulgated the decision to use this unreliable booster in 1963 could not be repeated today.

Therefore, despite a family evolution much like the Atlas, Titan, and Delta families the Ariane Program, shown in Figure 17, having no history of human cargo, was not designed to do so, and therefore would require yet another variant to approach the human rating issue.

Figure 17
Ariane Launch Vehicles

Given the maturity of the design, this is largely impractical. Why? Because if there is an integrated optimized design that has mass-to-orbit as the metric, everything from choice of toxicity of propellants to upper limits of g forces are required to be rethought. Looking back to 1963, John Glenn, in true test pilot fashion, took on a mission that had a very good chance of taking his life. While test pilots of this ilk are still out there, the society and the organizations like NASA have lost the stomach for this kind of risk. History, then, must be viewed carefully so as not to mislead as to what is currently feasible from a social, cultural and technology perspective.

It is interesting that the NASA Forum on Human Rating did not come up with anything new that conflicted with or added to the NPR 8705 requirements. What was decided amounted to recognition that this is a very real design factor that will influence the cost of the total system, and certainly will be an issue when routine commercial space access is being considered.   Human rating is going to be a seminal issue in the development of systems to serve as the transportation system in the space commercialization adventure.

This is an additive complexity to the evolution of commercial launchers and the commercialization of space. We sit today on the cusp of a direction change in space faring. It is inevitable that a transition to commercial service providers will occur, but the question is, When will the probability of success for commercial launch systems even come close to the success factors that the current Russian and American human rated space launch systems enjoy today?

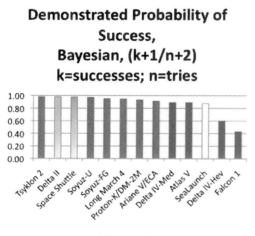

Figure 18
Demonstrated Probability of Success

Moreover, looking at how long it took to get these systems reliable to the current degree, at a commercially viable cost, what does this mean for the commercial arena? These are unanswered and critical questions that policy change alone cannot force in reality.

The simple Demonstrated Probability of Success analysis shown in Figure 18 indicates that the likely gap is closer to 10 years than 5 years, as that's how long it is likely to take to accumulate enough launches on any new system to assure reliability to any sufficient degree, irrespective of what capital, technology and initiative is expended by the commercial sector. In the unforgiving realms of space, it is not appropriate or supportable to 'push the limits' with reckless abandon.

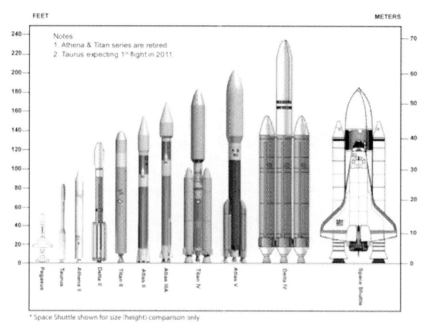

Figure 19
Current U.S. Launch Vehicle Family

A brief glance at the current suite of vehicles, as shown in Figure 19, indicates clearly the satellite market has a rich set of choices. The human spaceflight area, however, has very few. In fact, the human space segment, post Shuttle, is in need of not only a new very heavy lift launch system, but an interim upgrade and certification of some existing non-human rated 'cargo' vehicles. Why does this dichotomy exists at all?

A BRIEF HISTORY OF LAUNCH VEHICLE DEVELOPMENT

All U.S. and Soviet / Russian launch vehicles originated as military systems whose primary mission was to deliver nuclear weapons. Both the

Russians and Americans built upon knowledge and systems captured from German rocket experts immediately following World War II.

The first U.S. and Soviet systems were long range artillery rockets (like the Redstone), and were all largely based on improvements to the WWII V-2 series. Although its range was only 200 miles, the V2 was groundbreaking and unmatched in capability for its time, and it is widely regarded as the first 'strategic' ballistic missile. It of course was not human rated and intended for military uses only.

Increasing the range and payload capacity of these rocket delivery systems for nuclear weapons was the next step for launch systems, and they had advantages over aircraft delivery in three primary areas: 1) enormously faster response, 2) no flight crew risk, and 3) are virtually impossible to intercept in flight. Increasing the range and payload capacity of these launch vehicles was a central factor in the United States achieving strategic advantage its adversaries.

In this case, a human rated system (aircraft) was completely replaced by a non-human rated system (rocket), with attendant stark differences in the infrastructure, the risk profiles, and the delivery focus.

It is important to note that, while much effort was made to miniaturize tactical fission weapons, because strategic nuclear weapons of the early period (1950s and 1960s) were generally large and heavy, the 'bigger is better' rule applied to ICBM launch vehicles. The trend continued with the development of the first thermonuclear (fusion) weapons because they were huge by comparison to fission weapons.

Human rated systems must accommodate a lot of life support gear, a necessary and unavoidable launch mass. The best design case is miniaturization and outstanding design that minimizes booster lift requirements. However, if a brutally large launch weight capacity system is available, such as the Saturn V, Aries V, or the C-8 Nova, the design optimization, complexity, and even reliability of that life support gear can be relaxed in favor of redundancy, and its associated weight can easily increase.

This is yet another difference between the historical launch system evolution and the future commercialization arena. The driving forces are radically different, and if history is used in an uninformed way it could lead to disastrous programmatic decisions.

Range distinctions, which is related to booster capability, evolved quickly, and were classified into three main groups: 1)artillery rockets, range 50-200 statute miles, 2) Intermediate Range Ballistic Missile (IRBM), range 200-3,000 statute miles, and 3) Intercontinental Ballistic Missile (ICBM), range 3,000-10,000 statute miles.

Only categories 2), and 3) had influence in the space launch arena. However, the technology of all three groups is to a degree cross-cutting and there was significant influence shared by emerging technologies in areas such as computing hardware and the emergence of digital flight systems.

SUMMARY: THE NEXT GENERATION OF HEAVY LIFT SYSTEMS

A short summary of the continuously serving and therefore successful launch system vehicles reveals the following:

- Space Shuttle: The world's only human rated, reusable, winged spacecraft. About to be retired.
- Delta: Began IRBM from NATO land bases
- Delta II: The series marked Delta's departure from weapons delivery service. Used for military and civilian satellite launch.
- Delta III: Added lift capability to missions & customers accrued during series II service.
- Delta IV: Follow-on to series II with the added prospect for use as a human launch system.
- Atlas: Started as the USA's principal ICBM of the late 1950s and early 1960s. It evolved away from weapons delivery service in the mid 1960s. Series I-V evolved similarly to and as a prime competitor of Delta.

In this chapter we have discussed the history and the technology that not only explains how the national and international community has arrived today with the arsenal of launch systems available as we approach the departure point for the commercialization of space.

We have also discussed technical and socio-cultural challenges, the lexicon of rocketry and what is meant by such key terms as 'heavy lift,' and the significance of human rated, heavy lift system for space commerce.

Looking forward, the longer term view 25 years out will certainly see the development of new heavy lift systems, but in the short and medium terms the issues remain quite challenging, as cheap, reliable access to space is not yet a reality.

Our view is that the emergence of space commercialization has loftier motivation and more constructive intent than the adapted weapons systems that are the mainstays of our current heavy lift capabilities, but it will take demonstrated markets of significant size in order for the technical development costs to be borne by the commercial sector, as well as significant innovation to develop new systems that bring the costs down. An order of magnitude cost reduction is of course too much to ask, and yet from a commercial perspective this is exactly what the emerging generation of entrepreneurs is asking for. And as generation of bright rocket scientists are well aware of these goals, they are working at them, in both public and private employment, in the US and in other nations.

THOMAS E. DIEGELMAN

Tom Diegelman has been in the aerospace community for over 35 years, involved in research, development and operation of training simulators, ground based flight control installations and facility operations. Tom started his career with Cornell Aeronautical Laboratory as a research engineer, working on early versions of shuttle handling quality study simulations and shuttle shock tunnel testing.

Tom moved to Houston in the late 70's to join Singer / Link Flight Simulation and worked in the Shuttle Mission Training Facility (SMTF) as a model developer, and later a manager of simulation projects. In 1988, Tom joined NASA to lead the $170M redesign of the SMTF. Assignments at NASA / JSC include projects in advanced mission control technology, technology development, and facility operations control. He served as Facility Manager for Mission Control for 3 years before accepting an account manager position in the Technology Transfer Office, developing partnerships and Space Act Agreements.

The design of the training facility for the Constellation Program culminated his nearly 30 years of experience at JSC in Jake Garn astronaut training facility. Tom was elected to Seabrook City Council in 2006, and served two terms, during which he worked closely with the Port of Houston Authority on the Seabrook / Bayport Terminal Facility issues. Tom is a member of Baytran, a non-profit organization promoting inter-modal transportation solutions in the Houston / Bay Area, and continues to be involved in local, state and federal government on behalf of the space technology community.

He is also coauthor Of Chapter 16, *A Space Commercialization Model: Ocean Ports and Inter-Modal Transportation.*

THOMAS C. DUNCAVAGE

Tom Duncavage holds a Bachelor's degree in Physics from Providence College. He is a graduate of the United States Navy Test Pilot's School, Patuxent River, Maryland and is a National Security Fellow of Syracuse University's Maxwell School. He has over 3000 tactical and flight test hours in over 20 U.S. and foreign military and civil aircraft. Mr. Duncavage has served in various positions of technical, managerial and tactical leadership throughout his 31 year professional career both as a Marine Corps officer and as a federal civil servant. He is the founder of NASA's Concept Exploration Laboratory, a recipient of the NASA Exceptional Service Medal, an associate member of the William P. Hobby Center for Public Policy, and currently serves as the NASA Visiting Executive to the Bay Area Houston Economic Partnership.

CHAPTER 13

PROSPECTS FOR IN-SPACE RE-FUELING

KEN YOUNG
BOOZ-ALLEN HAMILTON

AND

JEROME BELL
BIODRI TECHNOLOGIES / SPACE LEGACY LLC

INTRODUCTION

Concepts for relieving the terrible mass-fraction penalties of launching out of Earth's gravity well by re-fueling spacecraft on-orbit have been proposed for decades (Reference 1). Certainly it makes theoretical sense to avoid carrying all needed mission propellants (as well as other vital fluids and/or gases) from liftoff to the final orbit by 'topping off' at an in-space 'filling station.' which is clearly analogous to the re-fueling of cars on an Interstate highway on a long auto trip.

Indeed, analogies have been drawn to the Pony Express in the 1880s and to steam engine trains before that. In those cases, the 'fuel' (feed and water for the ponies and wood and water for the engines) was generally available in situ at the way station; later, for coal-driven and then diesel trains, and finally, automobiles, the fuel was produced elsewhere and delivered to re-fueling locations.

This analogy is usually applied to concepts for on-orbit depots, wherein cryogenic or storable propellants are produced on the ground, transported by rocket-tankers to an orbital storage depot, where it is then available for transfer into upper stages and/ or orbital maneuvering vehicles (OMV). Two other concepts, 'in-situ production' (ideally, also, 'on-demand') of cryogenics at the depot, and 'in-space re-fueling from the ground' (analogous to 'mid-air re-fueling of aircraft') have also been proposed.

This chapter will address the considerable technological, operational and economic challenges for all of these concepts at a very high, qualitative level, and also assesses the prospects of commercialization of such depot/re-fueling systems. In addition, we will discuss potential technology demonstrations or study projects that might help to focus the logical and cost-effective way forward to such an 'in-space refueling system' as part of future space infrastructures.

CONCEPTS AND THEIR CHARACTERISTICS
CONCEPT SCENARIOS (FOR ILLUSTRATIVE PURPOSES ONLY)

CONCEPT A SCENARIO: CRYOGENICS
A cryogenic propellant storage and transfer facility is launched (or assembled after several launches) in a Low Earth Orbit (LEO) at an inclination of approximately 29 deg and an operational altitude (might be assembled lower) of about 200 to 220 nautical miles. Actual altitude depends on drag characteristics and the operating period in the solar cycle. The facility would consist primarily of cryogenic tanks for storage of LH2 (or Methane, CH4, or another such fuel) and LOX that are well insulated and shielded, as well as also possibly actively cooled to prevent any significant boil-off over a period of months.

A photovoltaic energy system of medium capability (30-60 KW) driven by articulating solar panels (200-400 m2) should suffice for power. The structure has an accessible docking port with cryo fluid transfer plumbing to supply propellants to visiting customer vehicles, such as Upper Stages (Centaur, PAMs, etc.) with payloads (e.g., comsats), Orbital Transfer Vehicles (OTV) or Earth Departure Stages (EDS). These Stages, with Automated Rendezvous, Proximity Operations, Docking and Undocking (ARPODU) capabilities, would arrive from later launches into lower insertion orbits, then rendezvous and dock temporarily at the depot for re-fueling and/or 'topping-off' propellants.

Reference 2 has an interesting proposed approach to such a concept, and a variation that avoids the considerable challenge of cryogenic 'boil-off' would be to use more storable propellants. However, the 'market' for such storables in potential 'customer' vehicles would have to be examined and justified as having an economically viable customer base. The preference for cryogenic propellants, particularly LOX and LH2, is that the performance efficiency, as measured by the engine Isp (specific impulse) is about 25-30% greater than storables. Table 1 summarizes Concepts A, B, and C as to their key characteristics.

CONCEPT B SCENARIO: WATER-BASED

This scenario is similar to Concept A in terms of orbit and basic function, but the depot resource would be 'water-based.' That is, large quantities of properly-treated water (probably containing chemical catalysts such as potassium, sodium or chlorine) would be periodically delivered to the facility, which would be capable of electrolyzing the water to produce H2 and O2 gases, then liquefying them into LH2 and LOX.

Ideally these cryo propellants would be created 'on-demand' and transferred (within a few hours) to the customer vehicle. Obviously, there would also be a need for some cryo storage capability, if only to use for the depot's own orbit maintenance propulsion system. The large water tank storage requirement and the energy source needed to provide the huge (>500 KW) electrical demand for electrolysis and liquefaction (Ref. 3) would drive the size and mass of the depot, which might have to be much larger than that in Concept A.

CONCEPT C SCENARIO: A GROUND-BASED SYSTEM

A ground-based re-fueling system would be fundamentally different from a space depot. This concept postulates a launch booster/upper stage-tanker (or fleet of them) that delivers propellants (cryos or storables) to the already on-orbit customer vehicle(s) loitering in LEO, waiting to be re-fueled. Ideally more than one of these waiting customer vehicles would be waiting in a rendezvous-compatible orbit for cost-efficiency reasons.

The tanker vehicle would rendezvous with them (one at a time, in probably significantly different, but compatible, orbits) and facilitate the re-fueling. The tanker would then return to the ground and be recovered and recycled for future reuse. An early version of this scenario would be to discard the empty tanker with a safe, controlled re-entry and ocean disposal.

The relatively low energy power requirement (<20 KW) would probably allow for use of batteries and/or fuel cells (possibly even using the cryo vent gases in the cryo propellants case) and/or a small photovoltaic array. Perhaps the key driving requirement on the re-fueling tanker design would be the capability to perform Automated Rendezvous, Proximity Operations, Docking/Undocking (ARPODU), with sophisticated guidance, navigation, and control, avionic, attitude control and propulsion systems, as well as a sophisticated standard (common) docking or berthing mechanism, and standard propellant transfer interfaces. The technological onus is on the tanker system rather than on the customers' vehicles, although they would have to be adapted with common docking and fuel transfer interfaces.

Concept/Type	Propellant	Energy Source/KW Requirement	Mass/Area (approx.)
A-Cryogenic/ Storable Propellant Depot	LH2 or CH4/LOX	Photovoltaic/30-60	~50,000kg/200m2
B-Water-based/Cryo Produced by Electrolysis Depot	GH2/GO to LH2/LOX	Photovoltaic or Nuclear /500-1000	<50,000kg/1000m2 PV or <50m2 Nuclear
C-Ground-based In-Space Refueling Tanker S/C	LH2/LOX or Storables	Batteries+PV/<20KW	<15,000kg/<50m2

Table 1
Concepts and Key Characteristics

MAJOR TECHNOLOGY CHALLENGES FOR EACH CONCEPT AND CRITICAL TECHNOLOGY DEVELOPMENT

CRYOGENIC TRANSFER IN A MICRO-G ENVIRONMENT

Concepts A, B and C: If cryogenic (typically LH2 and LOX) propellants in large quantities are to be rapidly transferred to the tanks of a customer's vehicle such as an orbital transfer stage, then that capability in a micro-g environment must first be successfully demonstrated. As of this writing, that has not been accomplished, although several experiments are being planned as part of the new NASA's Flagship Technology Demonstration approach (see Section 4 of Ref. 4). Indications are that some docked thrusting or possibly tethered rotation may be required to facilitate rapid transfer, which would further complicate the process (Ref. 5).

Storable propellant transfer has been accomplished, and indeed, it has been done for years on the ISS, and before that, on the Russian space stations Salyut and MIR, although very large quantities and high rates have apparently not been achieved. The attitude control aspects of transferring large masses of cryogenic liquids rapidly could also present significant challenges to avionics, due to the large center of gravity shift between the docked vehicles. An approach that has been suggested as an alternative to actual fluid-flow transfer is to somehow exchange entire propellant tanks, a full tank for a near-empty one. The vehicle design and the operational challenges of such a scheme seem quite daunting, and will be touched on later.

LONG-TERM (WEEKS OR MONTHS) ON-ORBIT CRYOGENIC STORAGE, CONCEPT A (CRYOGENICS)

If cryos are delivered to an on-orbit depot to be kept ready for customer re-fueling, then obviously provision must be made for long-term storage before eventual re-fueling of a customer vehicle. Due to the dynamic thermal environment (Earth shine as well as solar radiation) cryo 'boil-off' has proven to be a very significant challenge (References. 1, 2 and 5).

The latest in-orbit Centaur firing (using cryo propellants, of course) was a mere nine hours after insertion. Alleviation techniques may well involve other technological challenges, such as improved tank insulation materials, complex shielding structures, power-hungry active cooling systems, and even sophisticated depot orientation control avionics and propulsion. As with the cryo transfer technology, none of the solutions for these challenges (if there are some) has yet been demonstrated on-orbit. References 1 and 2 as well as the recently announced plans (Reference 4) for NASA's Flagship Technology Demonstration missions specifically address cryo transfer and storage tests.

Although these proposed tests are predicated on technologies that have been judged to be 'mature' (i.e., at the Technology Readiness Level (TRL) of around 6 or 7), it is the opinion of the authors that cryo transfer and long-term storage in space technology is actually at a lower TRL, perhaps 4 or 5. Testing such technologies in a simulated space (micro-g) environment (normally required for TRL 6) has proven unfeasible, so an exception must be made; hence, the proposed mission, FTD#2 (Ref. 4), in the 2015 timeframe. This first test would only demonstrate cryo (LOX and CH4) transfer between two tanks in the same vehicle, or intra-vehicle. Whether the results of such a test can be extrapolated to predict inter-vehicular transfer success will remain to be seen.

ON-ORBIT LARGE QUANTITY WATER ELECTROLYSIS AND GASEOUS H2 AND O2 LIQUEFACTION, CONCEPT B (WATER-BASED)

If water is to be electrolyzed first into GH2 and GO2, and then liquefied into LH2 and LOX cryogenic propellants in large quantities, and then rapidly transferred ('on-demand') to the tanks of a customer vehicle such as an orbital transfer stage, that capability in a micro-g environment must first be successfully demonstrated.

As of this writing, large quantity electrolysis has not been accomplished, although small amounts (5-10 kg/day) of GO2 have been produced by the Oxygen Generation Assembly (OGA) for crew breathing on the ISS since 2007 (Reference 6). Unfortunately the energy requirement for such chemical phase change systems is extremely large: the approximate power required for the OGA to produce about 10 lbs of O2 per day is about 2.6 KW.   Although it is probably not a totally linear conversion, that would suggest that 2000 lbs of O2 would require more than 500KW.

And then the GO2 must be super-cooled and liquefied! Experiments in such micro-g electrolysis and liquefaction technology may be considered as part of the new NASA's Technology approach, although that is uncertain at this writing.

ENERGY SOURCE

CONCEPT A (CRYOGENICS)

Because a depot that only takes on delivered cryo propellants, stores them for possibly long periods (weeks or months), and then has to facilitate their transfer to customer spacecraft, is not a particularly energy intensive operation, the primary energy source could probably be photovoltaic solar panels of 'reasonable' size. Articulating panels approximating the pairs on the ISS that can produce between 50-60 KW should suffice. The need for considerable shielding and/or active cooling to prevent excessive 'boil-off,' however, could complicate the size and location of such rotating arrays. Fuel cells, making use of the available, vented GH2 and GO2 could be used in combination with smaller solar panels.

CONCEPT B (WATER-BASED)

Because of this depot's requirement to electrolyze water to gaseous H2 and O2 and then liquefy them to cryogenics, a very large amount of energy (>500KW) is needed. Solar panels capable of reliably producing that much energy, roughly 10 times more than the ISS system is actually capable of, have never been built and assembled in orbit, much less operated and maintained.   Even if it is physically possible, assembly, maintenance (both on the rotating joints and panels and on the depot's orbit to counter large aerodynamic drag effects) and operation of the vast, rotating arrays make the concept unfeasible in the authors' opinion.

Hence, an alternate large energy source, such as a small, safe nuclear reactor is postulated.   NASA Glenn Research Center and the Atomic Energy Commission have developed such a prototype reactor in a joint project, and one the size of a 50-gallon keg is said to be capable of producing 40 KW. A NASA Technology Demonstration Project is planned in the 2012 timeframe. (Ref. 7) The cost and environmental/safety issues involved, however, may make nuclear a non-option.

CONCEPT C (GROUND BASED)

The ground-based tanker/re-fueler spacecraft, launched into orbit and then maneuvered to rendezvous with two or more (for efficiency) customer vehicles to re-fuel them, would likely be required to stay on-orbit for only a few days or a week or so, thus it's own energy needs could probably be provided by a combination of batteries and a small solar panel array set similar to the current Progress. Fuel cells driven from available (venting) GH2 and GO2 are another possibility.

OPERATIONAL CHALLENGES FOR EACH CONCEPT

INITIAL CONSTRUCTION/ASSEMBLY

Concepts A and B (depot) – Due to the large and complex nature of a cryogenic-tank–farm depot, especially for Concept B, where processing mechanisms for electrolysis and liquefaction are required, the refueling facility will probably have to be assembled in orbit.

On the other hand, if a sufficiently capable Heavy Lift Vehicle becomes available as part of a future space infrastructure, then one or two launches may be sufficient to deliver a complete facility. Concept A requires a long-term storage capability, but the facility itself would probably be smaller overall than the Concept B structure. It will no doubt have to deploy a thermal shield, and if the energy source were articulating solar panels then it would likely require several temporary crew/robotic assembly missions.

The ISS experiences in assembly operations/disciplines will be extremely valuable, but nonetheless the operational costs to both train for and execute the assembly will add greatly to the depot's Life Cycle Costs (LCC). In the case of Concept B, it is likely that several assembly missions will be required to integrate and test out the complex facility. This is certainly the case if an attempt were made to use a huge acreage of solar panels to provide the massive energy (>500 KW) required for electrolysis and liquefaction. The authors believe that such a design is unfeasible, as noted above, indicating that some other energy source would be needed.

The size and tankage capacity of a propellant depot would be determined by performing a detailed analysis of the potential customer mission base and their anticipated propellant requirements, both as a function of the needed energy (Delta V) and the mission frequency/schedule timing. In the case of Concept A, a limiting factor may well be the maximum time that cryo propellants can be efficiently stored on orbit, which is presently not known. In addition, the launch vehicle capabilities for both initial depot assembly and re-supply (tankers) of propellants could also be limiting factors.

Since Concept C employs Earth-based tanker spacecraft, it would not have an orbital assembly challenge, but instead would require fairly complex launch window timing, along with rendezvous and proximity operations requirements, which are also factors under Concepts A and B. Thus, Concept C would be clearly less cost intensive for initial operations. If the re-fueling tankers are not recoverable and re-usable, however, then ongoing costs for new tanker vehicles, depending on the customer demand, could quickly escalate.

GROUND/LAUNCH OPERATIONS

Based on extensive previous ground operations experience it is already known that the handling, loading and safeing of volatile cryogenic propellants (especially LH2) are difficult and hazardous. In addition, during the actual launch, if the spacecraft payload consists primarily of tanks of these cryos, there are the added range safety concerns (even for non-crewed launches) because of larger blast envelopes and off-nominal trajectory impact zones downrange.

In fact, these dangers constitute a major argument in favor of Concept B, in which the payload would be essentially water, as its ground handling requirements, even when treated with catalyst chemicals, is both far less hazardous and less costly.

AUTOMATED RENDEZVOUS, PROXIMITY OPERATIONS, DOCKING/UNDOCKING (ARPODU)

As Concepts A and B are depots in a specific orbital location, it would be necessary for customer spacecraft to come to that location to re-fuel, much like automobiles coming to the filling station off the highway. The bulk of the requirements for ARPODU, then, falls with customer spacecraft, although the depot facility itself would provide for traffic control and communication, as well as the necessary docking port (or grappling for berthing) systems to facilitate re-fueling requirements.

It would therefore be necessary to assure compatible and interoperable ARPODU interfaces between the depot and the visiting spacecraft. These will be discussed below.

In the case of Concept C, the launched tanker/re-fuel spacecraft would be the active ARPODU vehicle, so the reverse onus is true, but interoperable, compatible systems such as automated rendezvous and proximity operations beacon targets and docking/berthing mechanisms will be necessary on the customer spacecraft. Perhaps the most taxing system requirements on the re-fueling tankers are those of automated ARPODU capabilities, including robust propulsion and attitude control systems to enable multiple rendezvous and refuelings in differing customer spacecraft orbits, which may vary in both altitude and orbital planes.

While single re-fueling missions from the ground would likely prove to be economically inefficient, multiple rendezvous and proximity operations missions have already been successfully accomplished with the Space Shuttle, so a similar versatile tanker capability is reasonable to postulate.

ORBITAL LOCATION, ORBIT MAINTENANCE, LAUNCH WINDOW, TRAFFIC MANAGEMENT/COLLISION AVOIDANCE

The orbital location (inclination) of the depots in Concepts A and B would be market driven, as they would be based where the most projected customer vehicle traffic would transit. It would be likely, therefore, that depots serving for US-launched missions would be located near the due East inclination (approximately 28.5 deg).

Potential traffic at this inclination for LEO-starting missions would consist of upper stages, such as modified/re-designed Centaurs, or PAMs (Payload Assist Modules, but with liquid propellants rather than the now-common solids) carrying payloads such as communication satellites destined for GEO. Other Earth Departure Stages (EDS) bound for Beyond Earth Orbit (BEO) might provide the occasional customer. The bulk of this traffic would be commercial Comsats, estimated at about 24 per year (Ref. 8), as well as government funded missions (NASA, DOD, NOAA, etc.).

While the ideal orbital altitude for a depot would be very low, in the range of 100-150 nautical miles, orbit maintenance necessary to counter aerodynamic drag, as well as rendezvous phasing considerations to increase customer vehicle catch-up capability and broaden launch window durations would probably require that the depot orbit be in an altitude range of at least 190-220 nautical miles. At this 'popular' combination of inclination and altitude range, the risk of orbital debris collisions would be relatively high, so depot maneuverability and guidance, navigation, and control systems (GN&C) requirements for both drag compensation and collision avoidance/traffic management would be important and possibly very costly.

And even at 190-220 n.mi., the propellant costs for altitude maintenance will be significant and would probably be comparable to the costs experienced with the ISS. During the Solar Cycle Max periods, for about two years of every 11 years, a higher orbit, such as 220 n.mi. to 250 n.mi., may be required. Attitude maintenance must also be considered, since that has proven to be a significant propellant cost to the ISS and similar structures.

If designed well, use of Control Moment Gyros (CMGs) for most attitude operations might suffice, but small thrusters with long moment arms (such as used on the ISS for roll control) can significantly reduce attitude control propellant costs.

Long-term maintenance of the depots, as critical on-orbit systems fail, lose efficiency or become obsolete, could prove extremely costly since repair missions are likely to require human skills and/or robotic capabilities and the appropriate supporting mission infrastructure (launch vehicles, crewed spacecraft, EVA systems, specialized training, etc.). Another long-term maintenance cost for Concepts A and B, of course, is the resupply of cryogenics and water, respectively. Hence, a resupply tanker system, with its launch boosters, must also be an integral part of the life cycle infrastructure. This requirement has led the authors to suggest that an evolutionary approach, starting with Concept C tankers, should be seriously considered.

A later development could be a smaller A or B depot in the sun-synchronous (near polar) inclinations, around 97-99 deg, to support re-fueling for stages taking Earth-observation payloads out to the operational altitude range around 500 n. mi. While fuel costs to reach that altitude are not excessive, re-fueling at a lower altitude would permit much larger payloads such as bigger observation platforms to be delivered efficiently to the sun-synchronous orbit altitudes. It is more likely, however, that such a depot would serve as a robotic servicing platform for repair and fluid/gas resupply in conjunction with an Orbital Maneuvering Vehicle (OMV) that would come and go while servicing the sun-synchronous satellites.

INTEROPERABILITY AND ADAPTABILITY CHALLENGES

A challenge to re-fueling concepts A and B is issue of interoperability and adaptability of potential customer vehicles such as existing upper stage Centaur and solid-fuel PAMs. Modifications for ARPODU could include, for example, an international standard docking or berthing interface, as well as for propellant and propulsion systems (solids or storable systems converted to cryos) and the necessary fuel transfer plumbing have already been mentioned.

A related issue is the actual physical location(s) on customer vehicles of payload/payload adapter and/or the required docking/berthing interface, plus the routing of the transfer plumbing. Typically, most current upper stages locate the payload (normally a satellite or a LEO or BEO spacecraft) on the front end, usually protected inside a shroud or adapter at launch until deployed at the mission destination. The rear end of the upper stage has the propellant tanks, engine and engine bell, and, in some cases (like Centaur) it initially fires to place itself and the payload into orbit.

If this upper stage is to approach and temporarily attach at the depot for fluid transfer, where should the docking or berthing port and the transfer plumbing be located, with all the necessary quick disconnect valves and umbilicals, etc.? The obvious place would seem to be along a side of the space craft, but not only does that impose added proximity ops navigation and attitude/translation control requirements, but such re-designs, along with structural side-load constraints, might actually preclude docking as a cost effective possibility.

Another consequence of adding ports and plumbing to current upper stage rockets would be the significant shift of the center of gravity, which would thus affect avionics and GN&C for not only the ARPODU but also possibly the main engine thrust vector control.

Hence, a berthing system may be more feasible. Berthing is accomplished by a depot-grappling device, such as a robotic arm similar to those on the Shuttle and ISS. If the depot were not crewed (or 'man-tended'), then the entire operation would have to be completely autonomous or remotely controlled from the ground. While this is not an impossible solution, it certainly adds significant Life Cycle Costs (for added ground and communications interfaces and operations).

A less costly solution would therefore be to locate the depot at the ISS, where common docking and grappling/berthing capabilities already exist and have been successfully demonstrated, but the ISS is not at the ideal inclination, as it is located at 51.6 deg. This might not be a 'show-stopper' for re-fueling of BEO vehicles, although even those missions would still incur needless weight-to-initial-orbit and ARPODU performance penalties, but GEO and some LEO missions would certainly incur very significant performance losses. Safety issues, at least for cryo depots at the ISS, would also be a factor.

In terms of adaptability, the significant modifications that would be required for current upper stage vehicles, as noted above, leads the authors to conclude that for Concepts A and B, entirely new upper stages (possibly also having OMV and/or OTV capabilities) must be designed integrally with any such re-fueling system infrastructure. [Conceptually, the OMV has been proposed several times in the past as a short range robotic 'space tug' that could move payloads about in the vicinity of the Space Shuttle and/or Space Station. The OMV would use a separate propellant / propulsion module that would be returned to Earth by the Shuttle for refueling. Similarly, the Orbital Transfer Vehicle would be a reusable space tug, powered by Lox/LH2 engines and equipped with an aerobrake allowing it to be returned for refueling and reuse at an orbiting space station or propellant depot.]

That would certainly be the case if the model was to swap-out propellant tank 'modules' using a robotic mechanism to replace a near-empty tank with a full one. Complete re-design of conventional upper stage vehicles would obviously be necessary, as well as development and demonstration of the robotic mechanism(s) and the complex operations required.

While this is not impossible, but considering a current technology readiness level of only 2 or 3, and the added weight of the necessary structures, such a performance overhead would seem to negate the desired objective of using cryo propellants in the first place, at least in the coming decades.

For Concept C, as noted above, the technological interoperability and adaptability onus is on the tanker/re-fueler vehicle, which would obviously be a completely new design. However, customer vehicles would still require relocation of their payload-carrying design, as well as berthing fixtures and fluid transfer plumbing modifications. Although the customer vehicle would be the 'passive' partner in this ARPODU scenario, and thus not require complex new GN&C and avionics, the docking/berthing interface and transfer plumbing accommodation changes would still be major. Thus, even the ground-based tanker concept would necessitate new customer vehicle designs, as contrasted with merely adapting current upper stages.

ECONOMIC CONSIDERATIONS AND CHALLENGES

POTENTIAL MARKETS (BOTH GOVERNMENTAL AND PRIVATE/COMMERCIAL)

A cursory look at potential markets in LEO/GEO leads the authors to suggest that GEO payloads such as communication satellites and observation (intelligence and weather) satellites, both commercial and government (military, NASA and NOAA), may offer the most promise in terms of future traffic volume. Current projections (Ref. 8) are for about 24 such payload missions per year, or about 2 every month. Thus, a depot or ground-based tanker service that could re-fuel the upper stages of the Centaur/PAM class would enable much larger such payloads (with bigger antennae and power arrays, more redundant systems, etc.) to be placed in GEO. No quantitative or qualitative assessment of such future traffic/market possibilities has been done as of this writing, although a hypothetical scenario will be examined below. A less likely LEO market, but one still worthy of consideration and analysis, may exist for Sun-synchronous-type Earth observation (commercial, NASA / NOAA, and military) missions.

HYPOTHETICAL SCENARIO TO ESTIMATE A ROUGH ORDER OF MAGNITUDE (ROM) MARKET PRICE AND RETURN ON INVESTMENT (ROI) FOR CONCEPT C

According to a Euroconsult Report (Ref. 8) on the projected GEO satellite market for the next ten years, about 24 comsats per year may be launched. The average cost to build one satellite will be about $100M, and the launch cost will be about $50M. The average weight of the satellite, including its GEO stationkeeping fuel, will be about 8000 lbs, although the trend is toward heavier payloads of 12,000 to 15,000 lbs. ('Stationkeeping' refers to the fuel required to maintain the satellite's desired orbit.)

Heavier comsats are preferred for at least three reasons:

1. Since the GEO longitudinal 'slots' are highly valued it is better to have one larger sat versus two or more 'neighboring' smaller sats, because of radio/TV frequency interference and collision concerns. In addition, long-term operations and maintenance costs are lower.

2. Larger sats can contain more broadcast capabilities, including bigger arrays, larger antennae, broader bandwidth, etc.

3. More redundant systems and more stationkeeping fuel mean not only more reliable but longer useful satellite lives, thus increasing and prolonging revenue streams

Hypothetically, then, if a Concept C, ground-based tanker re-fueling service were postulated to capture one third of the projected annual market, or 8 satellites per year, a ROM pricing and ROI can be estimated. Assuming that the 8 customers were willing to be scheduled in pairs (a week or so apart) for launch, their upper stages (say a modified Centaur) could be re-fueled in LEO by the same tanker vehicle, and then their larger satellites could be boosted to their equatorial, GEO orbit. If these customers were willing to pay about 15% more than their current costs for the re-fueling, then a positive ROI can be postulated for the tanker service.

For example, assuming the two GEO customers wish to build larger sats, increasing from 8,000 lbs to 14,000 lbs, they would probably only have marginally higher building costs of around $105M. They could be launched with their upper stages (off-loaded to about 1/2 full of cryo) and a 6,000 lbs heavier comsat payload for roughly the same $50M each. If the tanker vehicle system, weighing at its launch only about 15,000 lbs, with about 12,000 lbs of transferable fuel, could be launched for about $20M on a smaller, cheaper launch system, perform the two re-fuelings in LEO and then be deorbited into a safe ocean entry, the charge for each re-fueling could be about $13M, returning a $5M profit, assuming a $1M mission cost for the tanker service.

The GEO customers would be paying about $18M extra each, but they would have almost twice the comsat capability in GEO. Since their current launch system costs about $6,250 per pound, it would cost about $37.5M for the additional weight, (if in fact the launch vehicle could even lift that much extra weight), the net savings to the comsat operator is nearly $20M.

This hypothetical case, of course, does not consider the capital investments, estimated in the range of $400M, required for the initial tanker system and the modified upper stage systems infrastructures.

Amortized at \$5M per mission and at 4 missions per year, and assuming no government subsidies, it would take 20 to 25 years to amortize the development cost of the tanker system. And while there is no guarantee that a small launcher for the tanker could be found for \$20M, some fledgling commercial launch services today have projected such prices.

Having worked through all three scenarios, the authors therefore conclude that a reasonable ROI is not currently possible for any of the postulated concepts, as both of the two depot infrastructures and their LCCs would likely be even more costly.

RECOMMENDED STUDY PROJECT/TECHNOLOGICAL DEMONSTRATION APPROACH

While this chapter has taken only a very top-level and mostly qualitative look at the daunting challenges facing a realistic approach to an economically viable On-orbit Re-fueling infrastructure, other concepts may also exist and be worthy of detailed examination.

Perhaps other propellants, such as storables or solids, or even ion-engine resources should continue to be studied. Recent NASA plans for a Flagship Technology Demonstration Program include missions to demonstrate transfer and long-term storage on orbit of cryogenic propellants (first, LOX and methane, then LH2), as well as other technologies involved, such as ARPODU and power systems.

The authors believe such demonstrations are worth the considerable investment, as long as, in parallel, the entire cryo (or other propellant) re-fueling concepts and their long-range possibilities are studied in-depth for at least 6 to 12 months. Particular emphasis should be placed not only on the technical and operational challenges, but also on the LCC and associated schedule and cost risks. Realistic future market/traffic analyzes, particularly with respect to private or commercial markets, seem critical to any chance for projecting a believable ROI.

The study team should be composed of knowledgeable experts not only from NASA and other government agencies such as DoD, NOAA and the DOE, but also academia and private industries, such as chemical/energy companies and spacecraft/launch providers.

CONCLUSIONS

This chapter has discussed three concepts for Re-fueling Spacecraft On Orbit, and their considerable technological, operational and economic challenges. The major challenges are summarized here.

TECHNOLOGY

The on-orbit transfer and long-term storage of cryogenic propellants is the biggest challenge. This technology maturity level is no higher than TRL 5, and perhaps lower. Fortunately, considerable real flight experience and data from the decades that the Centaur has been successfully flying exists, but very little has been done to extend such missions to gain knowledge to extrapolate or apply it to this challenge.

Solving the transfer and storage challenges is key, of course, for Concept A. It is also key, but possibly to a lesser extent, on Concept B if 'on-demand' on-orbit production of cryos from water can be reliably achieved. Even then, the challenge remains to provide adequate power for the required electrolysis of water and the liquefaction of gaseous O2 and H2. Nuclear power, even with its high cost and attendant environmental and safety issues, seems to be the only possible solution to that enormous power requirement. Concept C, with its relatively short-termed on-orbit missions of a week or two, may also have cryo storage 'boil-off' problems, leading to costly active-cooling and relatively high power requirements.

DOCKING OR BERTHING

The second technological hurdle for all three concepts is not so much the requirement for ARPO, but that of docking or berthing itself, with its challenging impacts on the costumer upper-stage vehicles' structural designs and their GN&C systems (for Concepts A and B, particularly) and on the tanker service vehicle for Concept C. The biggest challenge would seem to be proximity operations and the subsequent actual docking or berthing, as that must be either completely autonomous or remotely-assisted by ground control. Similar technology has been operational for years on the ISS. A related challenge, of course, is that of systems interoperability, particularly with respect to assuring international standards for proximity operations 'homing' systems and related navigation aides and sensors, as well as for common docking/berthing mechanisms and fuel transfer plumbing.

ECONOMICS

The biggest problems seem to be the apparent lack of a substantial customer market, along with the high capital investment required to build a re-fueling system infrastructure. A customer traffic rate of only 8 to 12 missions per year (mostly to GEO, allowing for a few government missions also) is too few to realize a positive ROI.

And while our hypothetical scenario was calculated with frankly very optimistic assumptions about launch prices and vehicle and customer satellite re-design costs to show a positive ROI of S5M per year, this illustrates how difficult it may be to recover capital investments over a 20-25 year period.

In addition, the probable high operations and sustaining maintenance costs, especially for the depot concepts, would seem to make recovery of their LCC a high risk venture. A big problem with the ground-based tanker approach is obviously the recurring launch and new tanker replacement costs in the event that tankers cannot be designed and built cheaply for entry, recovery and re-use.

Given all these major challenges, as well as many lesser but significant ones touched upon herein, it's clear that an in-depth, cooperative study project involving government, international partners, private enterprise (both potential providers and customers), and academic participants be conducted in parallel with the upcoming NASA Flagship Technology Demonstration Program.   Indeed, that Program should probably lead the study. Life cycle costs, technical and schedule risks and realistic space traffic/market analyses should be emphasized.

And for the depot approach, particularly, the urge to follow a 'build it and they will come' credo should be strongly resisted. Since a depot must always have a tanker re-supply system as an essential part of its infrastructure, prudent thinking would seriously consider an evolutionary 'ground-based tanker' approach initially. The ultimate success of such an endeavor would clearly hinge on the LEO/GEO commercial space market customers.

In summary, then, the authors believe that the prospects for a cost-effective, commercial, in-space re-fueling system are at present very low, and entail extremely high risks.

•••

KEN YOUNG

Ken was born in Austin, Texas. He received an Aero-Space Engineering degree from the University of Texas in 1962. He was employed by the NASA Manned Spacecraft Center (now Johnson Space Center) in June, 1962 and subsequently worked on all U.S. human space flight programs (from Mercury to Constellation). During Gemini, Apollo, Skylab and ASTP, Ken was a trajectory expert, mission planner and a rendezvous specialist. Ken served as a real-time flight dynamics advisor in the Mission Control Staff Support Rooms throughout Gemini, Apollo and Skylab. Ken became Chief of the Flight Planning Branch prior to the first Space Shuttle launch in 1981.

He retired from NASA in late 1987 and went on to work or consult for several NASA-JSC contractors, including Grumman, Northrop, Loral, Lockheed Martin, SAIC, Bigelow and Booz-Allen Hamilton, where he now is a consultant on the Constellation Program.

JEROME (JERRY) BELL

Jerome (Jerry) Bell, a native Houstonian, earned his Bachelor of Science Degree in Aerospace Engineering from the University of Texas, Austin in 1963. Following 9 months of Employment with the McDonnell Aircraft Company in St. Louis working in aerodynamics supporting the Phantom 2 Aircraft Program, he accepted a position with NASA Manned Space Craft Center (now Johnson Space Center) where he worked as a civil servant for over 42 years until retirement in 2006.

He has worked on every manned space program from Project Gemini in various technical and Program Management capacities and Program Phases including Program formulation, requirement and concept development, operations, and technology in selected areas. Jerry has served as a JSC representative to Several Agency wide activities including the NASA Space Station Task Force Concept Development Group at NASA HQ, Non Advocacy review teams, Proposal review and Source Board technical support, DOD's Technology Reinvestment Program, and Operations Requirement Development Manager within JSC Exploration Program Office (Space Exploration Initiative proposed under George H. W. Bush).

Since retirement, he has joined BioDri Technologies / Space Legacy LLC as technical advisor providing coordination and independent advice/recommendations with regard to activities between BioDri and NASA. In this capacity, Mr. Bell has acquired a degree of understanding about antimicrobials and their potential space applications and issues.

REFERENCES

1. "Technology Requirements for an Orbit Fuel Depot - A Necessary Element of a Space Infrastructure," NASA/TM-101370, A. Stubbs, R. Cohen, A. Willoughby, Oct. 1988.
2. "A Practical, Affordable Cryogenic Propellant Depot Based on ULA's Flight Experience," B. Kutter, F. Zegler, G. O'Neil, B. Pitchford, AIAA 2008-7644, Sept. 2008.
3. "Hydrogen Basics," *Home Power #32*, A. Potter, M. Newell, Dec/Jan 1992.
4. "Flagship Technology Demonstrations NASA Request For Information," NNH10ZTT003L, May 17, 2010.
5. "Technologies for Refueling Spacecraft On-Orbit," D. Chato, NASA/TM-2000-210476 (AIAA-2000-5107), Nov. 2000.
6. "New NASA System Will Help Space Station Crews Breathe Easier," A. Beutel, L. Madison, J. Morcone, NASA News Release 07-159, July 17, 2007.
7. "NASA Steps Closer to Nuclear Power for Moon Base," T. Malik, Space.com website, posted 08/06/2009.
8. "Space Forecast Predicts Satellite Production Boom," (Euroconsultof Paris Report), P. de Selding, Space News.com website, posted 6/15/2009.

CHAPTER 14

USING THE INTERNATIONAL SPACE STATION AS A TEST BED FOR THE COMMERCIAL SPACE MARKETPLACE

JEFFREY MANBER
MANAGING DIRECTOR, NANORACKS LLC

The international space exploration industry faces two related and bewitching obstacles to its long-term programmatic health. The first is a U.S. administration that views exploration through the lens of the overall economic and political problems afflicting the American economy. In other words, no blank check is forthcoming for NASA, given the nation's deep fiscal woes. And this political reality is an international issue, since no matter what might be said in public, it remains true that America is the critical instigator of major space exploration programs of this and perhaps the next generation as well.

The related problem is the high cost of the sole major operational international space program, the International Space Station (ISS). Often overlooked by space supporters is the fact that one of the lessons still to be learned from the space station is finding the means to lower the cost of operating it, and lowering the cost of the next NASA exploration program as well. By this I mean truly lowering the costs, not simply pushing them onto new international partners.

Those from outside the industry, including politicians, investors, corporations and the public, are often stunned to learn the magnitude of the current costs, which caused even a surprised NASA to end funding for space station research and to pour every last dollar into construction.

The budgetary numbers associated with the orbiting outpost are indeed astronomical. Industry estimates routinely suggest that over $100B has been spent for the design, construction, and operation of the space station, and launches of the U.S. space shuttle are pegged at over half a billion dollars per. (In contrast, Japanese launch costs for the new H-II transfer vehicle (HTV) come in at over $200M, and France's Automated Transfer Vehicle (ATV) at about $300M.)

These numbers defy any previous civilian international research effort. The high speed super collider, for example, that straddles the border between France and Switzerland and involves dozens of nations and hundreds if not thousands of scientists in cutting edge subatomic particle physics, is estimated to have cost $10B – less than 90% the cost of the space station.

Figure 1
The International Space Station

The unprecedented price tag of the ISS is a very real problem today, because it is precisely the cost of the space station, and the inability of

NASA to grapple with the issue, that has dampened the enthusiasm of politicians and voters to support the undertaking of the next great space exploration. It is not an academic point in a time of high joblessness that five scientific projects having the same price tag as the super collider, employing logarithmically far more scientists and engineers would cost federal governments half the budget of ISS and even less than that for a Mars mission. And it is not just the high costs of space exploration that constitutes the problem – it is also the inability of any major space program to be realized on time and on budget.

The ISS, orbiting right now over half a dozen national capitols, is a blinking reminder that something is fundamentally wrong with how we structure space operations; a new era of exploration must no doubt follow a far lower cost structure.

The opposite is also true: if we stay on the present course, then the developed nations will be hard pressed to continue big ticket exploration projects, leaving the field to the developing nations with lower hardware and structural costs.

The goal of this chapter is therefore straightforward: to discuss the need for ISS members, but especially for NASA, to use the now-operational space station not only as a test bed for unique manufacturing, the growth of pharmaceutical drugs, and production cite for new alloys, but also as a laboratory of a different sort, one in which the proven strengths of the consumer marketplace, ranging from competition to open trade, are employed at long last within a NASA controlled program. Until then, Western nations will find themselves in an exploratory cul-de-sac, heading nowhere fast.

Specifically, I suggest that the members of the ISS must undertake three steps to bring international space programs in line with other civilian manufacturing and market sectors:

1. Allow free and open competition for all space station goods and services.
2. Encourage the cross ownership of national space companies.
3. And finally, moving forward, transition to open competition for programs beyond low earth orbit.

The implementation of these market-facing and market-making steps would transition us from an ISS space program that is static and expensive to one that reaps the cost efficiencies and robustness of the private sector. Yes, it could be painful, messy and uncomfortable. Safeguards for technology transfer would have to be enacted, and certain space agencies would find themselves as regulators more than operators.

But the result would be a far safer and stronger space station and a far more capable space market in low Earth orbit, one which will no doubt prove a cost-efficient model for future programs to the asteroids, the Moon and Mars.

But before moving on, let us take a moment to salute the achievements of the builders of the ISS. It is a huge international undertaking, years in the making, involving almost a hundred rocket launches, the sacrifice of seven astronaut lives, and unprecedented coordination among different nations.

I know well that sensitivities arise when criticizing such a majestic and, dare one say it, poetic edifice in orbit. A recent public description by me of NASA's 'tin ear' for international politics drew in response an email from a space station astronaut condemning my comments, and urging me to show more appreciation for the accomplishments of the men and women who have lived onboard the ISS, and the good they have accomplished. I do appreciate that, and very much so.

But appreciation for their fine contributions does not in any way mitigate the space station's unfortunate shortfalls, and to ignore these shortfalls would in fact do a disservice to all those who dream of the next steps in space exploration. At fault is not the actions and decisions of the astronauts and engineers, but rather of American politicians both in Congress and the White House, both Democrat and Republican.

Let's begin by stating the obvious about the structure of the ISS: sadly, this bastion of the new frontier, the outpost of the future of humanity, is overseen by an international consortium of governmental agencies using procurement methods that are known in every other sector to be completely outdated. This conglomerate of national governments operates with all the parochial interests, economic inefficiencies, and cumbersome regulations characteristic of government purchasers.

What is so frustrating is that these same governments acknowledge they should do less and less of the operations in terrestrial markets, and most realize that allowing foreign vendors to participate decreases the costs of domestic programs, while increasing reciprocal and beneficial opportunities for trade. From aviation to mail delivery, from automobiles to defense, from applied research to the Internet, Western governments have in recent decades sought to carefully lower the barriers of protectionism to encourage competition from a global pool of commercial vendors.

The market anachronism of the ISS, operated on a high-cost, nationalistic, and monopoly basis, is impossible to justify. There is a European section of the station, built entirely by European manufacturers. There is a Russian section of the station, built entirely by manufacturers from Russia. There is a Japanese section of the section, built, yes, entirely by manufacturers from Japan. And the American section is the same, with the wrinkle that Russian companies were brought in – with beneficial results.

Where else in America do such nationalist trade practices still exist for an operational program? Japanese subways run under, and Swedish trains take us between, our cities. The American infrastructure is maintained by a spectrum of private companies, government organizations and some in-between, but all following commercial practices. Yet not a single company runs any part of the space station – only government agencies. Nor could international companies even bid on construction, as this was left to national or regional players.

Cost efficiencies, bountiful in all other major non-military markets, are absent from the space station. Foreign companies compete to supply energy for the nuclear power needs of industrialized nations, and operate foreign electrical and water projects, and some also own large pieces of them.   Multi-national   construction   companies   are   involved   in developmental projects from Japan to North America to Africa and Australia.   America's   most   sensitive   data   is   stored   in   computers manufactured in Asia, and even in the highly nationalistic markets for oil and gas, nations across the political spectrum work with commercial firms that have access to huge pools of money and sophisticated knowledge. And where governments have barred all commercial companies from the oil fields, such as in Mexico, the result is a slow and painful decline in the oil fields' production, while costs spiral upward to uncompetitive levels.

One example of how the ISS operational structure forces companies to behave differently is Boeing. Boeing is the major American contractor for the ISS, and according to Boeing's web site, the company is the *"prime contractor, responsible for design, development, construction and integration of the ISS."* It also *'directs a national industry team comprising most major U.S. aerospace companies, hundreds of small contractors, and Boeing itself."*   http://www.boeing.com/defense-space/space/spacestation/

Few at NASA or in Congress would agree that Boeing was 'responsible for the design and development' of the ISS as this is seen in the government as NASA's responsibility.

Contrast that to the behavior of the same company in the civil aviation market, where Boeing is risking its future on the Boeing 787, also known as the Dreamliner.

Boeing's website states, *"The program has signed on 43 of the world's most capable top-tier supplier partners and together finalized the airplane's configuration in September 2005. Boeing has been working with its top tier suppliers since the early detailed design phase of the program and all are connected virtually at 135 sites around the world."* http://787flighttest.com/category/bg/

Do you see the difference between a low-competition, virtual monopoly and a diverse pool of subcontractors competing and innovating side by side to achieve higher performance at lower costs? A partial list of

Boeing subcontractors for the Dreamliner reveals that the plane's flaps are made at Boeing Australia and the fairings at Boeing Canada Technology. Mitsubishi Heavy Industries makes the unique carbon composite wings and in addition has a multi-billion dollar contract for the critical carbon fiber. The horizontal stabilizers are manufactured by Alenia Aeronautica of Italy, and the fuselage sections by Global Aeronautica and Boeing's facility in South Carolina. The airplane doors? Passenger doors are manufactured by Latecoere in France, and the cargo doors by Saab of Sweden. The French company Messier-Dowty builds the landing gear using titanium produced by the Russian company VSMPO-AVISMA.

The result has not been without delays and frustrations, but the end result allows Boeing to mass produce planes, sell them in every market, make a good profit, while all the time keeping customer ticket prices stable and allowing for market innovation.

Same company. Very different behavior with very different results.

It is hardly a coincidence that absent from the ISS program is the cutthroat competition seen in the aviation industry, personal computers, automobiles or the oil fields. Nor, does the space station enjoy the pace of innovation anywhere close to markets not controlled by a handful of government agencies.

Why is the ISS structured so uniquely? An international consortium of government agencies for manned space operations is often explained as a vision of a program firmly rooted in a Cold War mentality. In this explanation of events the United States has grown comfortable using space as an arm of national pride and branding. Having won the race to the moon we were unable to unshackle space operations from NASA and allow market forces to take over.

This explanation of space as a product of the Cold War falls away, however, when contrasted with the other great space program of the Cold War, international satellite communications. U.S. President John F. Kennedy in 1962 created the commercial company Comsat with a stroke of his pen, and even appointed its original board of directors. A year or so later, Comsat created Intelsat, which was made up of over 140 nation states. Unlike the ISS program, the United States opted for a multinational space effort to be a commercial company that could tap financial markets and move far more quickly and efficiently than a government organization.

Later, the Soviets created their own satellite consortium known as Intersputnik, and it is telling that today both Intelsat and Intersputnik are successful commercial organizations, and the satellite industry enjoys robust competition, fast paced innovation and yet, critically, the United States government is a huge customer for satellite bandwidth. By acting as a commercial customer, the Pentagon and all branches of the Federal government allow for market innovation and cost-efficiencies.

How different it is with the ISS. NASA, with the backing of Congress and the White House, was designated as the lead American agency to design, develop and eventually operate the facility. Other ISS nations, emulated the closed and nationalistic American example with varying degrees of enthusiasm.

Ironically (and I write this as someone who represented the Russian company RKK Energia in Washington DC for much of the 1990s), it was the Russians who pushed back against this consortium of centralized government space agencies and sought to have more non-governmental organizations in control of the design and operation of the space station, including the Russian firms Khrunichev and the company Energia. Many Russian space officials felt at that time that their space agency should have been more of a coordinating body, not a designer, developer and operator of programs, and this model of the space agency as a coordinating body is now being used by India and China, and to some degree in Russia.

The relevance of all this is that now the United States is no longer willing to keep the financial spigot open for space exploration, which results in a clear need to introduce market reform.

And there is a programmatic reason as well, since the year 2010 may be remembered as the opening of a new chapter in humanity's utilization of space, for at long last there is a stable, permanently occupied outpost in low Earth orbit, the ISS, for use by the majority of industrial nations. With the planned retirement of the NASA space shuttle fleet, the United States is forced into operational reliance on other nations and the commercial sector for access to the station, and there are many operational launch vehicles that can access the ISS, with more in development.

Given these and other political and budgetary realities, it is apparent that most of the G20 nations will have access to space station facilities in the years to come.

2010 will also be remembered, no matter the final outcome with ISS, as the year when the traditional orthodoxy of American space programs was up-ended by a new U.S. administration that decreed that 'Returning to the Moon' is not enough of a rallying cry to spend billions. Required from this point onwards is a re-examination of not just where we should go as a nation, but how we should go.

Taken all together it seems clear that the operational phase of the ISS must function within the established realm of Earthly market practices and proven business models. No longer can ISS member states operate in a manner at odds with business as if somehow space was different. As a permanent facility that is operated by five space agencies representing fourteen nations, all of which support the principles of market economics, it is high time that the outer space outpost of the European Union, the United States, Canada, Japan and the Russian Federation should be managed as if it was located not two hundred miles up but simply just a short distance away from Brussels, Washington, Ottawa, Tokyo, or Moscow.

THREE RECOMMENDATIONS FOR REALIZING A COST-EFFICIENT SPACE STATION AND CREATING A LEO MARKETPLACE

To achieve a more robust and cost-efficient ISS, three key actions would enable a fundamental shift to a more effective method of operation:

1. FREE AND OPEN COMPETITION FOR ALL SPACE STATION GOODS AND SERVICES.

Protectionism has long been recognized as an insidious killer of economic growth, so if the space station is to be viewed as more than a jobs program, then there is no reason on Earth, or above it, that the best manufacturer from any ISS member state should be barred from bidding on a required product or service.

Over the past several decades, every major American and Western manufacturer in consumer and technology markets has faced cutthroat international competition. Some companies and markets have emerged as winners, while others have lost and disappeared, but not so the civil space contractor. Almost alone among industrialized companies, they have been immune from true international competition, and it shows in rampant inefficiencies from top to bottom.

On March 12, 2010 French premier Nicolas Sarkozy publicly chastised the United States over protectionism after a European-led consortium pulled out of bidding for the Pentagon's mid-air refueling aircraft. *"This is not the right way for the United States to treat its European allies,"* Sarkozy said. *"If they want to be spearheading the fight against protectionism, they shouldn't be setting the wrong example of protectionism. In life there is what you say and then there is what you do."*

The prime minister of the United Kingdom echoed those sentiments. *"We believe in free trade, we believe in open markets, we believe in open competition,"* George Brown said.

http://politifi.com/news/Not-the-Right-Way-to-Behave-Sarkozy-Scolds-US-on-Protectionism-374828.html

According to the UPI, *"The European Union has warned the United States about possible protectionism, saying it 'would be extremely concerned if it were to emerge that the terms of tender were such as to inhibit open competition for the contract."*

An open market for space station goods and services would end the paralyzing protectionism that has stymied space station innovation and caused development and operational costs to skyrocket. Hence, if NASA seeks a station telescope and Italy allows U.S. firms to bid on its national space hardware, than Italian firms should bid on ISS equipment as well. NASA should be tasked by the White House to create procurement rules and regulations that open the door to international competition for supply of space station goods and services, making reciprocal open trade a fundamental requirement, as the goal should be to establish a single, free-trade zone for all our low-Earth activities.

Making NASA, ESA, RSA, CNES, DLR and others behave as commercial customers would create, finally, a commercial marketplace with companies competing to win government and commercial contracts, just as in the satellite industry, and in all other civilian markets.

One result can be predicted based on other markets where protectionism has been removed: space companies in business a decade after trade reforms would be smarter, leaner and more capable than those today. Encouraging open competition among the ISS trading partners would also have a profound impact on the national space programs. If Russia opened its market for ISS goods and services to America, Boeing, Lockheed and innovative smaller space companies could bid on Russian programs, and Russia's Energia and Khrunichev could bid on NASA programs. Similarly, Mitsubishi and Astrium could compete and contribute hardware and services to the formerly national space programs.

While the barriers of protectionism cannot be dropped too fast or too far, the developing status of space operations at ISS and in LEO calls for an open-trade zone implemented in stages, beginning with smaller projects and a progressing to operational openness. This would allow American and European governments and companies to target their chosen areas of market expertise in which to seek out their own market niches. Just as in any other industry, each ISS member would gear up for a more commercial effort using their own preferred government-industry relationships.

For the American market, lowering existing ISS protectionist barriers would force American industry to compete on space transportation and on-orbit manned operations, just as they have been in satellite communications, thereby enhancing our national security by enabling innovation at far lower cost.

2. CROSS OWNERSHIP OF NATIONAL SPACE COMPANIES

Once trade barriers start to come down, the next step would be to allow for cross ownership on commercial terms among space companies. To bid in Russia and win, Boeing might take shares in Energia; to win Japanese business, Energia might team with Mitsubishi, and so on. This would provide a huge pool of liquidity and financing currently unavailable for space programs, making new commercial projects far more viable (fuel depots for example), with governments acting as commercial customers enjoying competing proposals.

Also benefiting from the change would be innovative smaller space companies, which would now have a larger pool of strategic partners for growth and acquisition.

Certainly there is no suggestion for a purely open commercial space exploration marketplace, given the sensitivities of duel use technologies. As in the defense industry, regulations and firewalls would be implemented, but after a decade of working together under the umbrella of ISS, suggestions from the contractors themselves would help frame a regulatory regime to the satisfaction of ISS governments.

What is puzzling about the status quo is that the ISS has already benefited from the path taken by the Russian Federation, whose commercial practices have served the space station well. Russia's Mir space station received the majority of its funding from non-government sources, which included payments from European governments for crew transportation to and from the Mir, payment from NASA for their multi-month stays onboard the Mir, and even on-space advertisements and non-professional space travelers. These commercial funds kept open the Russian production lines for Progress and Soyuz.

MirCorp, the partnership of American investors with RKK Energia, of which I served as CEO, injected almost $30M in cash into the Russian space infrastructure, and would have contributed far more if the space station had not been de-orbited. From a financial and operational perspective, RKK Energia's control of Mir was a success, a fact not lost on other nations as they embark on their own manned space era.

India's space agency ISRO uses the Antrix organization to buy and sell space goods and services, and the China Space Agency has CASC, a huge state organization which operates over 70 Chinese space organizations and corporations, including China's Great Wall Launch Company. Among ISS members, Japan's JAXA is now speaking of focusing far more on operations and space utilization than technology development, precisely as a means of lowering costs.

Many companies have already experienced the benefits of cross ownership. In the 1990s, a minor stock swap between Energia and Boeing was discussed on a senior level, and during the same period the American company Spacehab included Energia's chairman on its corporate board. But further integration was deemed politically unacceptable, and the two major U.S.-Russian commercial space projects of that decade suffered because of the inability of the major contractors to behave more commercially. Both the International Launch Services (ILS) (a venture between Lockheed, Energia and Khrunichev) and Sea Launch (which involved Boeing, Energia and Yuzhnoye of Ukraine) ran into market structural limitations that impeded growth.

A new generation of space companies truly integrated with one another and with access to international capital markets and government customers, would provide a welcome addition to our low-Earth orbit capabilities. This was certainly the situation with the automobile industry, where Japanese and German and American manufacturers two decades ago opened plants and hired workers worldwide, reducing the political sensitivity of 'foreign' products.

Given national strategic concerns, true cross ownership would be more likely to take place on the subcontractor level than on the prime contractor level, but over time this market evolution could nevertheless blur the nationalistic attitudes of current ISS member states.

A commercial company with ownership from, say, Astrium, and a smaller Chinese CASC-owned company could reduce the political sensitivities of having China as a member of ISS.

Or, to consider examples, Long March rockets carrying satellites and cargo into orbit from Space Florida could provide a commercial path acceptable to the American government, or a future XCOR launching from South Korea into near-Earth orbit via an Asian subsidiary.

Free and open competition among ISS member agencies and cross-ownership of space companies would transform the ISS into a marketplace for goods and services, and as a result operational costs would be lowered while capabilities would be increased.

In the United States there is also movement away from the Cold War space agency mentality. Congress has declared the U.S. section of the ISS to be a National Laboratory, and under existing Congressional language, the next step should see the transfer of operational control of the U.S. National Laboratory in space to a private operator. Currently, other U.S. national laboratories are run by limited liability companies or non-profits, but none are operated by any agency of the United States government.

Whatever the structure of the laboratory operator, one must hope that the era of barter deals and protectionist acquisition practices would come to an end and this latest U.S. National Laboratory would be run like any other research facility.

If implemented correctly, the space community would finally have a success story for the White House: We can predict costs, we can keep operational expenses low, and we can create jobs, as the result of a program that has dozens of cutthroat competitors.

Notwithstanding the title of this article, it is hard to imagine that if successfully implemented, the evolution of space into a commercial marketplace should, could or would be stopped at low-Earth orbit. As such, the final and most exciting step required would be to:

3. TRANSITION TO OPEN COMPETITION FOR PROGRAMS BEYOND LOW EARTH ORBIT

Nothing is more dangerous in the current U.S. policy discussions than drawing an artificial line between low Earth orbit and deep space exploration, expecting an open competitive economic business model for one and a static government monopolistic structure for the other. Yet this is precisely the position of the Obama Administration, as it (correctly) argues that LEO is open to commercial business, however NASA programs beyond LEO are not. Once it is demonstrated that capitalism can thrive in the hazardous environment of space, why then should a line be drawn blocking market forces beyond 200 miles above the Earth's surface?

As noted, the United States has shown itself capable of behaving as a commercial customer for services in the geostationary orbit, located some 36,000 km from earth, and private markets have indeed thrived at 36,000 km, including banks, manufacturers, insurance underwriters and stock markets, not to mention launch providers.

If government as a commercial customer works at 22,000 miles and soon will work on the ISS at 200 miles, then there can be no doubt that it will also work for asteroid and Mars missions. Yet government agencies designing future Mars landers have barred foreign bidders, and they have divvied up asteroid mining missions along the current protectionist lines, thus assuring the same astronomical costs as the ISS.

The artificial boundary currently being discussed in Washington makes no sense. If market reforms are enacted in LEO but not beyond for deep space efforts, the result will be industrial chaos, and embarrassment for those national space agencies that cling to the current model for programs beyond LEO.

The steps suggested here will prod all sorts of mashups between entrepreneurial companies worldwide and governments behaving as commercial customers, and not as operators and competitors.

CONCLUSION

Two decades ago, the United States enjoyed open market satellite commerce only within its borders. International satellite communications was controlled by Intelsat, which finally crumbled in the face of commercial pioneer PanAmSat. I was privileged to work with the chairman of PanAmSat, and heard first hand the fears of those clinging to the Kennedy era model of government control.

West Germany was first to allow PanAmSat to operate, and then came the United Kingdom. America was third, and what followed was the explosion in growth in the international communication marketplace, with low cost phone calls and live news feeds from every corner of the globe soon becoming commonplace.

Examples such as this give us cause for optimism. More and more space agencies recognize that the status quo is no longer acceptable, and within the decade the ISS will be far more market driven than today. Soon enough, low-Earth orbit will be filled with competing orbiting platforms, and launch vehicle services, and swarms of nanosatellites competing with geo big-birds whose secondary robotic laboratory payloads will be competing with manned orbiting space laboratories, and all will be competing with way stations, fuel depots and unmanned astronomical observatories. Competition will be the norm not the exception, and governments will buy exploration services just as they now do communication capabilities.

And it all must start now with the ISS.

•••

JEFFREY MANBER

Jeffrey Manber is a recognized pioneer in the development of a commercial space marketplace. With Shearson-Lehman he helped create the first Wall Street fund devoted to commercial space. Later, he served in the Reagan Administration and was part of the new Office of Space Commerce within the Department of Commerce.

During the 1990s, Mr. Manber was Managing Director of Energia Ltd., the Washington arm of the Russian space company. In 1999 he became CEO of MirCorp, the Dutch venture that leased the Russian space station Mir and opened the door to commercial space travel.

Today, Mr. Manber is Managing Director of NanoRacks LLC, a commercial space venture providing standardized research platforms on the ISS, and also is senior adviser for SPI, a risk mitigation and financial services firm for space ventures. He is also the author of *Selling Peace*, published by Apogee Books.

CHAPTER 15

HARNESSING THE SUN
A PERMANENT SOLUTION TO GLOBAL CRISIS

FENG HSU, PH.D.
SENIOR VICE PRESIDENT, SYSTEMS ENGINEERING & RISK MANAGEMENT,
THE SPACE ENERGY GROUP

A previous version of this chapter was published in the book *Living in Space* published by the Aerospace Technology Working Group, 2009.

About 200 years has passed since the start of the industrial revolution, and humanity has now arrived at a major crisis related to its energy supply. In recent years there has been extensive debate and media coverage about clean energy, sustainable development, and global climate change, but what has largely been missing in the mainstream media is genuine knowledge about the point of view of scientists and engineers concerning viable and permanent solutions to many of these challenges. This chapter will elaborate on the prospects of mankind's technological capability focusing specifically on taming the energy of our Sun, especially on the great potential of harvesting solar energy directly from space before it enters our atmosphere (or SBSP, space based solar power), and explore the imperative to invest in the development of this critical human endeavor not only to resolve our crisis in energy supply, but also to address major crises including anthropogenic (human-caused) climate change, war, terrorism and sustainable and peaceful human development on this planet and beyond.

As you read this chapter, please keep in mind that I approach these questions from my professional viewpoint as an expert in risk management. Assessing risks and devising methods to address them has been my professional focus for more than two decades.

I. WHY FOSSIL BASED WORLD CIVILIZATION MUST BE REPLACED WITH A SOLAR CIVILIZATION

The debate about clean energy, fossil fuel energy, and the combustion economy inevitably raises the issue of greenhouse gas (GHG) emissions and their adverse impact on the Earth's climate. Most scientists hope that the climate debate is over, as they believe that the scientific evidence of anthropogenic global warming is overwhelming.

The potential negative consequences of anthropogenic climate changing are simply too significant to ignore – after all, what could be more significant (to us) than the extinction of our species? There is simply no reason for us to carry on with 'business as usual' and to continue marching down the path of a combustion-based world economy when it is no longer necessary for us to do so.

The historical and political view leads us to the same conclusion. Humanity's track record in regards to competition for local fossil fuel-based resources has not been very encouraging, inasmuch as geopolitical conflict arising from the ownership and operation of oil fields has had a profoundly destabilizing impact on world politics for more than a century. As we enter the era of so-called 'peak oil,' during which demand for energy will continue to increase while the supply of oil will progressively decrease, the search for alternatives will accelerate even while disputes over the remaining supplies of oil will also likely increase in severity. A reliable and abundant alternative to oil is highly desirable in this scenario as well.

An additional benefit that we may anticipate from going into space to harvest energy is the great potential to fundamentally change our way of thinking about Earth. Professor Frank White calls this the *Overview Effect*, and notes in his writings that it occurs when astronauts see the blue Earth from the depths of space. They report that the sight of Earth floating in the blackness of space fundamentally alters their perspective on humanity. If, through the pursuit and development of space based solar power, we can bring many more people to this profound realization of the oneness of all humans, then the positive consequences could be as profound as the political and economic ones.

II. SOLAR POWER FROM A HISTORIC PERSPECTIVE OF HUMAN EVOLUTION

Solar Energy, including both terrestrial-based and space-based solar power, is starting to be viewed by many scientists and visionaries as one of the most promising and feasible ways to completely overcome human dependence on fossil fuels.

At the 2007 Foundation For the Future International Energy Conference in Seattle, my presentation took a look back at energy use throughout human history, and here I would also like to offer a brief summary of the stages humanity has passed through in our quest for energy. In order to understand and fully appreciate the profound idea of harnessing solar energy, there are no better lessons to help us foresee what may be ahead than those we can learn by looking back at the path of our ancestors.

There have been three fundamental eras of energy supply and consumption in human prehistory and history. After the first fire was lit by mankind, humanity's energy economy was based on plants. We burned firewood, tree branches and the remains of crops from agricultural harvests. Around year 1600 we found coal, and entered into the 2nd era of energy uses with the first fossil-based energy supplies. The Romans used flaming oil containers to destroy the Saracen fleet in 670, and, in the same century, the Japanese were digging wells with picks and shovels in search of oil, to a depth approaching 900 feet. By 1100, the Chinese had reached depths of more than 3000 feet searching for energy, all many centuries before the West sunk its first commercial oil well in 1859 in Titusville, Pennsylvania. Demand for kerosene led to the commercial use of oil and gas, and the development of the internal combustion engine became the basis of the entire modern industrial economy. Oil and gas energy sources; being fossil-based, still belong to the 2nd era. Near the middle of the 20th century, propelled by atomic energy, came the dawn of the Techno-era of energy use and production.

As the world demand for energy continues to soar, we are running into profound energy and environmental crises, and there is great uncertainty about the world's future energy supply. If you plot the energy demand through the history of human civilization on a terawatt scale, you will see a huge increase beginning barely a hundred years ago. With oil supplies dwindling and coal highly polluting, it's evident to nearly everyone that we must now embark the next era of energy supply, and it's also clear that we can do this by rediscovering the mighty energy resource of our Sun. The era of taming solar energy through technology breakthroughs may well trigger the next giant leap of our civilization, elevating our species by transforming our combustion world economy into a forever sustainable Solar-electric world economy.

III. SOLAR ENERGY:
THE ULTIMATE ANSWER TO ANTHROPOGENIC CLIMATE CHANGE

The evidence of global warming is increasing and increasingly alarming. As a scientist at NASA's Goddard Space Flight Center, for many years, I received first-hand scientific information relating to global warming issues, especially on the latest of ice cap melting dynamics or changes on both poles of our planet. Whether this is due to human interference or cosmic cycling of our solar system dynamics, two basic facts are crystal clear:

1. There is overwhelming scientific evidence showing direct correlation between the level of CO_2 concentration in the Earth's atmosphere and historical fluctuation of global climate and temperature.

2. The overwhelming majority of the world's scientific community have reached consensus that catastrophic global climate change is highly likely if humans continue to ignore this problem, and continue dumping huge quantities of greenhouse gases into the atmosphere.

In my view as a risk assessment expert, from a probabilistic perspective it is orders of magnitude *more* risky for humans to do nothing to curb our fossil-based energy needs, and significantly less risky to shift our primary sources of energy supply. This underlying reason is simply that the risks of a catastrophic anthropogenic climate change could lead to the extinction of the human species.

From this perspective it is absurd to hear the argument made by some of our politicians, that humans should not worry about 'global warming' because if we restrict the burning of fossil energies there will be economic consequences. Those who make such arguments are clearly ignorant of the concepts of risk, uncertainty, and risk mitigation.

What we are really talking about is choosing between risks. Every human activity involves risk taking, and in matters of this scope we cannot avoid risk entirely. We must therefore choose between them, making science-based policy trade-offs, and hopefully selecting wisely.

Therefore, there must be a risk-based, probabilistic analysis underlying national and international policies that address all global warming and energy issues. As the measure of Risk is a product of event Likelihood and Consequence, I believe the choice is clear. When the consequence or risk of a potential human extinction due to catastrophic climate change is compared with the potential consequence or risk of loss of jobs or slowing down the economy due to restriction of fossil-based energy consumption, we must choose for the survival of humanity and accept the much smaller risk of negative economic consequences, which, in any case, are most likely short term and limited in scope. Furthermore, by making a paradigm shift of the world's energy supply through extensive

R&D and technology innovation on renewable energy production we may well create countless new jobs, and end up triggering enormous economic development and a new industrial revolution beyond what we have ever seen.

IV. SOLAR POWER:
THE BEST RENEWABLE ENERGY SOURCE FOR THE FUTURE

It took about 3.5 billion years of rare geologic events to sequester hydrocarbons and build up fossil deposits beneath Earth's surface. Humanity is now at an energy crossroads, and we have two distinctive and fundamental directions to choose between:

1. Either we look for energy based on cosmic-based, open, and unlimited original resources, which means everything that comes from the stars, including our Sun, or,

2. We follow the direction of using Earth-based, local, and confined secondary energy resources.

Using direct solar energy could be, in theory, about 1,200,000,000,000 times more efficient than using the secondary solar energy captured in oil, gas and coal, and going forward we can anticipate that humans will learn to bypass the solar-to-fossil inefficiency.

Some will argue that nuclear power offers an effective alternative, but of course there are significant risks with this as well.

In any case, there can be little doubt that the best place for a nuclear fusion reactor (which is what our Sun is) is about 149 million km away from Earth, where it operates on our behalf safely and free of charge. The Sun's energy takes only 8 minutes to arrive here, leaves no radioactive waste, and is terrorist proof. It puts out about 3.8E11 terawatts of energy per hour, and Earth receives about 174,000 terawatt each second. In fact, in every hour the Earth's surface receives more solar power than all humans use in a year.

V. SOLAR ENERGY COMPARED WITH OTHER SOURCES

Projected world energy use by fuel type in the next 30 years suggests that we are going to have an explosive increase in demand. According to recent U.S. DOE data, renewable energies including biomass, hydropower, geothermal, wind, solar, and others totaled about 6 percent of total energy production in the U.S., while nonrenewable fossil energies made up the rest.

To identify the best energy options for the future, we have to first understand our energy requirements and decide how to evaluate and compare the alternatives. Let us postulate that energy should be affordable for all human beings, inexhaustible in terms of the livable planetary lifetime, cause no harm to the environment of humans, and be easily available and evenly accessible to everyone around the globe. It has to be distributed in usable, flexible, decentralized, scalable forms, and there must be low risk of potential misuse for mass destruction. Energy has to help retain and improve human values and global collaborations, must help expand human presence and survival within our solar system, and has to be consistent in elevating human culture, quality of life, and civilization.

So what are our options? All fossil fuels are harmful to Earth's biosphere, while nuclear power poses major concerns concerning waste deposit and the risks of proliferation and misuse. Hydro power is limited and unstable, and liquid biomass competes for land with food production. (You may have heard that in Mexico tortilla prices have gone up about 60 percent in the last two years.) Hydrogen (fuel cell) carries high storage and transportation risks, and it is not a source of energy but rather a form of energy storage. Wind, geothermal, and tidal sources are intermittent, unstable, and presently costly. Nuclear fusion has been studied using government funds for more than half a century, and seems unlikely to be achieved any time soon; in any case it has high potential for misuse.

When you carefully compare and evaluate each available option of nonrenewable and renewable energy sources against these requirements and criteria, it is evident that solar power is the most viable source of renewable energy for sustainable human development into the future.

VI. THE PROSPECT OF SOLAR ENERGY DEVELOPMENT FROM SPACE

It would be reasonable to ask, Why solar energy from space instead of on Earth? Is it a technologically feasible or commercially viable human endeavor? My answer is positively and absolutely: 'Yes.'

One of the major challenges of terrestrial solar power is the high cost of photovoltaic (PV) cells, and the inefficiency of converting the Sun light energy into electricity. Depending on the location on Earth, there is roughly 7 to 20 times less energy per square meter on Earth than in space. Based on existing solar technology and PV materials, it would require a field of solar panels the size of the state of Vermont to provide U.S. electricity needs. Unless there are significant breakthroughs in the conversion efficiency of PV cells, to satisfy world demand would require about one percent of the land that is currently used for agriculture worldwide.

Space Based Solar Power has been systematically studied since the middle 1970s, and long before that, Nikola Tesla, the pioneer of modern electromagnetism and inventor of wireless communication dreamed of finding the means to broadcast electrical power without wires. Early in the 20th century Tesla addressed the American Institute of Electrical Engineers to explain his attempts to demonstrate long-distance wireless power transmission over the surface of the Earth. He said, *"Throughout space there is energy. If static, then our hopes are in vain; if kinetic – and this we know it is for certain – then it is a mere question of time when men will succeed in attaching their machinery to the very wheelwork of nature."*

The SBSP concept in its present form was originated in 1968 when Dr. Peter Glaser first developed the idea of SBSP as a source for continuous power generation for the Earth's future energy needs. Glaser's basic idea was that satellites in geosynchronous orbit would collect energy from the Sun, the energy would be converted to radio waves and beamed to receiving sites on the ground, and the ground antenna would then reconvert the radio waves to electricity.

In our current, more refined version of the SBSP system, solar energy is collected in space by satellites in a geostationary orbit. It is then converted to direct current by solar cells, which power microwave generators in the gigahertz frequency range. The generators feed a highly directive satellite-borne antenna, which beams the energy to the Earth. On the ground, a rectifying antenna (rectenna) converts the microwave energy to direct current, which, after suitable processing, is fed into the terrestrial power grid. A typical Solar Power Satellite unit, with a solar panel area of about 10 square km, a transmitting antenna of about 2 km in diameter, and a rectenna about 4 km in diameter is expected to yield about 1 GW of electric power, the equivalent of a large scale nuclear power station.

VII. THE TECHNOLOGICAL AND COMMERCIAL VIABILITY OF SPACE SOLAR POWER

Is SSP a viable option? Among the key technologies involved in SBSP are microwave generation and transmission techniques, wave propagation, antennas, measurement, beam control and calibration techniques. Key issues include potential effects on humans and the potential interference with communications, remote sensing, and radio-astronomy observations.

Current analysis suggests that it can be a viable energy option for base-load electricity generation to power the needs of our future. Further, SBSP satisfies every major criterion of a viable energy option listed above, with the exception of the cost based on current space launch and propulsion technology: space transportation cost is one of the major hurtles for SBSP, as solar power satellites will only become economically feasible if there is low cost space transportation.

To overcome the high launch cost, the development of a Reusable Launch Vehicle (RLV) and autonomous robotic technology for in-orbit assembly of large solar structures is needed, along with systems to assure safety and reliability for these large and complex orbital structures. Nevertheless, there are no breakthrough technologies that need to be invented, nor any theoretical obstacles that need to be overcome for an SBSP project to be carried out.

The U.S. government provided about $20M to study SSP in the late 1970s, but then abandoned this project with almost nothing additional spent up to the present day. The excellent book *Sun Power: The Global Solution for the Coming Energy Crisis* by my friend, Ralph Nansen, offers a detailed history on the subject. Ralph was the Boeing manager of the DOE-NASA funded SBSP proof of concept study, and published *Sun Power* in 1995, accurately predicting our current situation. Dr. Peter Glaser's book *Solar Power Satellites: A Space Energy System for Earth* also offers superb reading on this topic.

We can solve the cost issue to make SBSP a commercially viable energy option through human creativity and innovation on both technological and economic fronts. Besides the continuing quest for a low-cost reusable launch vehicle (RLV), there are other possibilities for ingenious commercial or business models that could overcome the SBSP cost issues.

One model now being pursued by the Space Island Group, an American private aerospace entrepreneurial company based in California, is to use modified Space Shuttles by turning the huge volumes of the external tanks into commercial assets for space-based research and orbital tourism. A huge demand in space tourism would bring about a higher launch rate, and that will in turn drive down the space transportation cost, thereby helping to make SBSP more viable. If we compare this possibility with the commercial aviation industry, who would have thought that ordinary people could afford air travel just several decades after the Wright Brothers had succeeded in their first aircraft test?

In addition, we do not need to restrict our vision to choosing between terrestrial solar and SBSP. In fact, the dream of SBSP can be realized much sooner through the use of terrestrial solar energy and engaging in the pertinent R&D on a grand global scale. The advancement of major terrestrial solar technologies including the nano-particle based ultra high efficiency and low weight, low cost PV cells, along with super capacity and low cost energy storage systems will also support affordable terrestrial and SBSP development, and many companies are now engaged in this work. With rapid advances in nanotech-based PV solar cell material, now reaching over 50% efficiency, and which can be cheaply produced (along with revolutionary battery technologies), it is possible that one day we won't have to launch huge PV structures into Earth orbit to satisfy the base-load electricity consumption requirements of the entire planet.

Hence, it is thrilling to see the rapid advances in the PV cells research and annual growth in solar energy production of more than 30%, even without government policy support from major countries such as the U.S. and Russia. Indeed, if every house in the future were built with cheap and highly efficient solar cell materials on the roofs and sidings, and every shaded parking lot in shopping malls and office buildings was built and equipped with solar powered charging plugs for electric cars, then how different our energy picture would be.

VIII. ACHIEVING ENERGY FROM SPACE: A ROADMAP AHEAD

The realistic hope of a commercially viable SBSP system lies in a collaborative effort between the emerging private, entrepreneurial space businesses, government, and venture capital. I am not optimistic about government involvement in this great human engineering and technological endeavor, especially concerning the much needed support of the U.S. government. But I am happy to see that great private sector visionaries see the significance of future energy systems as part of their vision for space commerce.

One such visionary is the recently retired president of India, Dr. Kalam Abdul. Dr. Abdul had the great courage to speak publicly on SBSP while addressing the Symposium on *'The Future of Space Exploration"* organized by Boston University in January 2007. Dr. Abdul noted that space research is truly inter-disciplinary, and has enabled innovations at the intersection of multiple areas of science and engineering.

He also noted that, *"Civilization will run out of fossil fuels in this century. However, solar energy is clean and inexhaustible. And while solar flux on Earth is available for just 6-8 hours every day, incident radiation on a space solar power station would be 24 hours every day. What better vision can there be for the future of space exploration, than participating in a global mission for perennial supply of renewable energy from space?"*

Government support for policies and financial resources for R&D and the related technology demonstrations are crucial to the success of such giant effort, and to date nations other than the US have taken a leading role. The Japanese government became interested in the concept in the late 1970s, and updated the reference system design developed in the System Definition Studies, conducted some limited testing, and proposed a low orbit 10 megawatt demonstration satellite. Their effort has been curtailed by their economic problems and by their lack of manned space capability. SBSP interest by other nations has persisted, but only at low levels.

Therefore, for SBSP to be successful we need an organized consortium consisting of private businesses, venture capitalists from major international partners, along with government support of major industrial nations to bring down associated project and technology risks concerning safety, reliability, and technology maturity. A consortium-based Comsat model (as was used for successful launch and commercialization of communications by the satellite industry) should be a viable approach. A major Apollo-like effort with participation from the broad international community may the best way to successfully create, implement and operate a commercial-scale SBSP system.

IX. AN APOLLO-LIKE PROJECT OF SPACE SOLAR POWER

An inherent feature of solar power satellites is their location outside the borders of any individual nation. Energy is delivered to the Earth by way of wireless power transmission (WPT), but the use of WPT must be compatible with other uses of the radio frequency spectrum in the affected orbital space. Therefore, it is vital for international governmental involvement in coordinating global treaties and agreements covering frequency assignments, satellite locations, space traffic control and many other aspects of space operations.

A multi-governmental organization or entity should be put in place for a major SBSP project, as it would be extremely difficult, if not inconceivable, for any other single nation to do this alone at any useful or significant power scale. Space solar power is going to be a huge technology and engineering endeavor, similar to going to the Moon and splitting the atom.

Private enterprises will also play key roles in this process. The company I work for, the Space Energy Group (SE), is pioneering a fundamental SBSP energy solution, and our goal is to transform the US from an energy dependent nation to a net energy exporter by launching huge satellites into space to harvest energy from the sun and send it wirelessly to Earth. If large consortia including the Space Energy Group and competing firms such as Solaren are successful then humanity will have a vast source of extremely clean power for the next few ... billion years.

The Space Energy Group recently signed a preliminary agreement with a provincial government in China to provide 10 gigawatts of electrical power in incremental delivery over 10 years, starting around the middle of this decade. Overall, energy exports to China could grow to be worth more than $100B, thus reversing the balance of trade with America's biggest creditor.

As noted, to make SBSP a reality, companies such as SE and Solaren will require a great many launches to get the necessary hardware into space to meet their energy sale contracts. Hence, the number one problem that SE and others face is the high cost of launch.

X. LOOKING FORWARD TO AN EVER BRIGHT FUTURE

It is time for humanity to look to the Sun for answers to our ever-increasing energy needs, and to solve our environmental and economic fossil fuel crises.

I suggest that 'harnessing the Sun' will be the 3rd giant leap in the process of human evolution. The first, when human beings came down from the trees and started to use fire, led to tool-making, agriculture, and ancient civilizations. Then humans invented machinery and discovered electricity, which enabled the 2nd giant leap forward to modern industrialization. Now humans are running into profound energy and environmental crises, and we must embark on the next giant leap. By harnessing the Sun to transform combustion civilization, we can evolve into a solar-electric civilization fueled by the inexhaustible and direct energy source from the stars.

Can humanity achieve the third giant leap into the solar-electric civilization? My answer is positively YES. Humans are capable of profound achievements, and we can certainly succeed in taming the mighty power of our star.

Indeed, it is a policy issue more than a technology or economic issue. As Dr. Robert Goddard liked to say, *"It is difficult to say what is impossible, for the dream of yesterday is the hope of today and the reality of tomorrow."* As I noted in my talk at the Seattle energy conference, *"As intelligent creatures rooted in the cosmic origin of the universe, humanity was meant to survive and spread its presence all over the universe by milking the energy of the stars!"*

•••

FENG HSU, PH.D.

Dr. Feng Hsu is a world expert on risk and risk assessment. He is Senior Vice President, Systems Engineering & Risk Management with The Space Energy Group. He was formerly a research fellow of Brookhaven National Laboratory in the fields of risk assessment, risk-based decision making, safety & reliability and mission assurances for nuclear power, space launch, energy infrastructure and other high integrity social and engineering systems.

He also headed the NASA Goddard Space Flight Center risk management function, and was the GSFC lead on the NASA-MIT joint project for risk-informed decision-making support on key NASA programs, such as the GPM (Global Precipitation Measurement), LSS (Lunar Surface Systems) and the CxP (Constellation) etc. He was a leading engineer/scientist in the Shuttle and Exploration Analysis Department at Johnson Space Center, SLEP and Shuttle upgrade trade studies.

Dr. Hsu served on many agency and center expert panels supporting challenging SMA issues, and was co-chair of several international technical committees. He played key roles in the: (1) STS-107 (Space Shuttle Columbia) investigation team, (2) the RTF (Return to Flight) team, and (3) the ECO (Engine Cut-Off) expert team for the Discovery mission. Dr. Hsu has over 90 publications and is co-author of two books. He is frequently invited to be the keynote speaker in many international forums. His recent interests span from challenges to human space exploration to solar energy; and include global collective intelligence and risk based policy-making on emerging environmental and energy security issues.

Dr. Hsu holds a Bachelors degree in Applied Math, a Masters degree in Operations Research and Statistics and a Doctoral degree in Engineering Science. As a senior advisory member of the Aerospace Technology Working Group (ATWG) and a co-founder of Space Development Steering Committee, Dr. Hsu has been a strong advocate for Space Based Solar Power (SBSP) for years, and was instrumental in instigating the 2007 NSSO study on SBSP. Dr. Hsu has contributed whole-heartedly to the great human endeavor of harnessing solar energy for sustainable human development.

CHAPTER 16

A SPACE COMMERCIALIZATION MODEL
OCEAN PORTS AND INTER-MODAL TRANSPORTATION

THOMAS E. DIEGELMAN
NASA

AND

KENNETH J COX, PH.D.
ATWG LEADER

INTRODUCTION

Extensive literature published over the last 25 years has explored the concept of the commercialization of space, particularly in low-Earth orbit. A significant amount of this literature focuses on content that presents options on the approach – how to do it. Yet another significant segment concentrates on the vehicular aspect – how to get there. Still others center around the 'favorite idea,' where commercialization is the stage upon which to display this 'great idea.'

This chapter will present an alternative to the prescriptive space commercialization approach by focusing on questions instead of the answers – a pathfinder for developing the 'how to' answers and the 'propelled by' questions.

We begin the exploration of 'how to explore the commercialization of space' by a walk-through of a parallel universe, a terrestrial inter-modal transportations system centered upon the ocean port.

DO WE HAVE A MODEL FOR THE COMMERCIALIZATION OF SPACE?

The simple answer is no. While there is significant literature on terrestrial commercialization, there appears to be a void in the correlation of space development to the terrestrial successes well documented over the last 300-400 years.

Behind all of this we can postulate a mechanism that links the identified needs of humanity to the capacity to find or create solutions to meeting those needs. It would be speculative and perhaps even specious to call this a 'model' in a rigorously academic sense. But if we expand the definition of 'model' to embrace the concept that a chain of events in an environment, driven by needs being met, constitutes a 'model,' then we have a sufficiently broad definition to explore a model for space commercialization. By linking it to the still-evolving model of ocean based inter-modal shipping, and to commerce through a set of guidelines referred to here as axioms, we can develop a structured 'how to do' instead of a classic 'what to do' model.

Note that 'technology,' which is usually the focus of the literature on the topic of space commercialization, is relegated to a footnote in this approach. That is, it is not technology that drives this model, but rather the needs of humans and the ability to pay an affordable price for the service or goods rendered. Moreover, even the geopolitical events are footnotes. These are attendant conditions, boundary values if you will, in the model. The focus is completely upon the ability to supply goods or services to a market at a price the market will bear. And that certainly includes developing a market for those good or services.

Limits imposed upon the model by the amount of detail to be considered, and where connections to other systems are non-dynamic – sometimes referred to as 'model stubs', are always arbitrary. In this first level of investigation and concept exploration, these stubs will be identified but not explored in detail. The approach will be to draw upon a terrestrial 'parallel universe' and ask open ended questions to promote not only the definition of the model, but also to explore the boundaries of the model.

SOLVING EARTH'S PROBLEMS – THINKING THROUGH SOLUTIONS ABOVE EARTH

"You can never solve a problem on the level
on which it was created."

- Albert Einstein

Albert Einstein's thoughts spanned not only the realm of physics and our universe, but also the politics of his day. The approach that this comment addresses is precisely what is needed to successfully commercialize space: we must think beyond what it took to commercialize any corner of the Earth from the Earth, and think instead of solutions for space commerce that come from a confluence of physics, commerce, and politics, and be created by a broad consortium of people.

On Earth, risks are bounded by the terrestrial life supportive environment; distances are finite and definable; topology and cartography are manageable; and the relevant physics are clearly understood. Economics are more difficult to define – witness the failures of colonies, expeditions, etc., as well as entire financial systems (e.g., the financial collapse of 2008-2009) but in comparison to space, we live in a benign economic environment.

When we venture into space with the intent to commercialize, we will encounter the same difficulties as history's great explorers, including Columbus, De Gama, Hudson and others. We will also encounter the physics of gravity wells, LaGrange points, closed systems, and a threatening environment incapable of supporting human life, orbital debris and orbit decay, and the fragile physique of the human species in the absence of gravity of exactly 1 g. This set of conditions represents huge risks that are not present on Earth.

We know about these issues; this is not breaking news. What is perhaps a new thought is how this coalesces into an increased level of risk, and what can be done to mitigate it for the sake of economic development. This is where the classic approach to commercialization of space loses traction – to talk about better craft and better rockets, which while needed, is not the central issue. Risk is the central issue. More specifically, the total risk is the barrier to commercial viability.

When the problem is framed as a total risk posture, and is added to the 'exploration' risks, and the financial risks associated with any commercial venture, you have the totality of the problem, the mission, and the business case.

It sometimes seems to be an insurmountable level of risk. It is certainly formidable, and more than 50 years after the first successful orbital flights, commercial space is limited primarily to satellites, while in comparison, aviation progressed from Kitty Hawk and fabric wings to budding commercial applications less than 20 years, and to a global industry in 30.

It is not an insurmountable problem if, and only if, the risk is quantified in terms of the executability, sustainability, and logistical supportability. In this chapter, these measures are explored in comparison to an ocean port, which will be shown to be a fitting analog of a spaceport.

PROPOSING A MODEL FOR SPACE COMMERCIALIZATION: THE OCEAN PORT

The model of an ocean port will be explored to identify its driving functions, and we will see that the issues and forcing functions are similar for space based commerce, with additional constraints such as the physics of zero gravity, solar effects, and complete vacuum.

WHAT IS A PORT?

A port is a place where the mechanical infrastructure needed for large scale exchange of goods, traded for financial gain and to achieve a desired quality of life, is installed. Typically, as shown in Figure 1, the port infrastructure uses technology that is cost effective and robust, not leading edge or risk intensive. It is inter-modal, linking ocean, rail, and vehicular transport. It provides goods that are typically not available locally.[1]

The necessary capital investment is non-trivial, and often is financed either by bonds or a combination of governmental and quasi-governmental agency funding. While a terrestrial port, once built, is used where it is, the space based port is moveable, but moving incurs penalties called delta velocity ('delta V'), or energy to change orbit. This will be touched upon later.

Inter-modal transportation is inherent in the concept of the terrestrially based space port, as shown in Figure 1, and the containers are indistinguishable, uniform and easily handled, translating to lower delivered cost.

Figure 2 illustrates the concept of a terrestrial spaceport and ocean port handling the bulk bundling of commodities in the interest of cost avoidance. This also reflects the need for distribution to occur, although the port is itself not the destination, but merely a stop along the way.

Note that amenities, necessary for people, are absent; they are supplied by the surrounding support infrastructure. Terrestrially this occurs in cities, while in space it is habitat vehicles and modules, with infrastructure that has been bought along for the journey.

If we consider the International Space Station as a rudimentary spaceport, clearly the ability to dock Soyuz, shuttles, and Orion Capsules is a necessary attribute. The 'dock cranes' or Remote Manipulator System (RMS) / docking ports must be equally able to accommodate all of them.

Figure 1
Terrestrial Space Port (above) and Ocean Port (below) share a
common heritage, commerce, and technology.

Figure 2
Inter-modal transportation is a common theme for all port infrastructures,
whether for space transport (above) or on ocean (below).

WHO OWNS A PORT?

As an initial ownership model for space commercialization, large terrestrial ocean ports have been demonstrated capable of raising enormous amounts of required capital. Traditionally space is a governmental area of expenditure, but to fully expand commercialization into space this must gravitate towards the ocean port model. If we use as an example the Port of Houston and its governing body, The Port of Houston Authority[2] (POHA), we see that port operation and ownership is not an inherently governmental function. This is quasi-governmental agency, with certain powers of a government agency, but since it was funded by public bonds, solvency and profitability must be successfully demonstrated. It simply is not acceptable to lose money 'going frequently where everyone has gone before.' So it appears that a fundamental question to be addressed by the model for space commerce infrastructure is, Can a space-based port commercially interact and integrate with terrestrial commerce, or will it require forever its own niche for standards, processes and cost / risk success criteria?

Nowhere does the size of the rocket ships or the exact product mix going up and coming down from space or across oceans enter the discussion. Whatever is put into space is sent there to produce whatever is sent back, but if it does not provide a profit margin at a risk level that is acceptable, the only way to have even the beginnings of space commerce is government subsidy or government ownership.

Funding for a space commercialization initiative would logically follow the approach used for large terrestrial port construction, involving a complex set of stakeholders. The reader may refer to the Panama Canal as an example of the enormous complexity of such an endeavor [please see the bibliography].

Figure 3 hints at this dilemma. Terrestrial ship traffic is work-a-day dull, while the ground segment of the analog, the launch and processing spaceport, is envisioned as elegant, modern and futuristic.[3] There is clearly a disconnect between the likely reality, and the popular imagery.

In the commercial arena, the port concept is developed into a business case. Let's look at a few historical examples. The Erie Canal, the Pony Express and Air Mail all were innovative ideas in their time, and were in fact operated at a loss for a period. Some eventually made short term profits, but all eventually (and predictably) failed.

HOW WOULD A SPACE BASED PORT BE FINANCED?

We assume in this discussion that either a private or public approach can garner adequate financial resources, but there is a decision point here: recognizing the importance of market forces, as we just discussed, and bringing in ROI as a decision making criterion, places this project almost uniformly into the private sector. While governmental policy is frequently consistent, governmental funding rarely is.

Governmental will derived from the electoral process in the United States does not foster unlimited support for indefinite expenditures with undefined benefits, and thus consistent public funding of a concerted space commercialization initiative is not a likely scenario, as it would never enjoy the enduring public support of social programs. The total dollars that NASA received for space activities from its inception in 1958 to the end of FY2008 is $416B. Adjusted for inflation it comes to $807B[4]

Figure 3
Can space commerce systems function in synergy with terrestrial commerce systems? We believe so.

The total cost of successful space commercialization will be tallied in the hundreds of billions, and maybe trillions, and therefore it is safe to say that space commercialization must be privately funded to avoid the risk of shifting political winds. To commercialize space, it is mandatory that it is profitable to attract private capital, and public sector monies will only peripherally fund it.

As NASA and the space industry press forward towards the era of space commercialization, clear business case solvency must be demonstrated, and the total system must be built upon private funding.

A truly successful commercialization effort will have lots of financial performance, but not necessarily the 'glamour' that has been associated with the last 40 years of human spaceflight. The day that the vehicles as shown in Figure 5 are beasts of burden on a commercial endeavor, rather than a technology demonstration, is the day that one could legitimately feel that the commercialization of space is succeeding.

Just as these ocean vessels answered commercial needs without government financing to design and build, we must replicate that in space commercialization.

WHAT IS THE NASA ROLE IN THE COMMERCIALIZATION OF SPACE?

This leads to the question, 'What should NASA's role in space commercialization be?' Despite being a government agency, there is indeed a key role for NASA to play in this scenario. We suggest that it could and should be a significant source of very high risk, 'game-changing' technologies, as well as the interface between the private sector commercial players and whatever government participation there will be in the commercialization of space.

NASA should develop the capacity to work across contracts, across programs, and even in multiple destinations seamlessly, and of course without regard for profit, to share with the private sector its great depth of experience concerning the physics of space and its highly developed capacity for risk management. The public sector can, in turn, bring forward its best practices across many areas of commercial expertise.

NASA has the unique tool of the Space Act Agreement (SAA), which provides a legislatively-granted mechanism through which to enter into mutually beneficial agreements with companies, universities, start-ups and established firms, and even individuals, whereby NASA receives the right to use a technology while the developer retains full market rights. This mechanism is a key tool in the establishment and maintenance of space commerce through technology development and exploitation by allowing industry, and not the government, to focus on the market.

> *(Editor's note:* Please see Chapter 10, *The Emerging Organizational Framework for the Space Commerce Enterprise* for a more detailed discussion of the Space Act Agreement.)

Another area in which NASA must perform a vital role is the integration of robotics and human elements. Currently, robotic mission technology, operations concepts, mission profiles and destinations share little more in common than being developed under the NASA logo umbrella. Currently there are no 'best practices' defined for human / robotic missions since there have not yet been these types of missions. While tools and techniques vary widely in the mission types, NASA alone has the human, near Earth and deep space experience, tools and corporate knowledge for all these endeavors.

And while there are satellite operators even today that manage constellations of satellites, these are quite limited and do not involve missions requiring humans to venture off the surface of the Earth. The planned transfer of these operations to the commercial sector is a key element that will assure the emergence of space commerce: a keen knowledge of space physics and the knowledge of how to profitably and safely operate complex space systems is absolutely essential.

But NASA should no longer be the exclusive operator of space vehicles, particularly in the realm of space commerce. NASA should continue to conduct the developmental and experimental programs, which are of little commercial value until they are more mature.

WHERE ARE THE SPACE COMMERCE COMPONENTS LOCATED – LIKE TERRESTRIAL COMMERCE?

Site selection for terrestrial ports certainly favors locations that connect people and markets, especially when the port has inter-modal connections for rail and highway. A deep, protected harbor without railheads, pipelines or interstates highways will never become a dominant ocean port.

Figure 6[6] shows the major ocean ports across the United States. There is a predominance of ports on the east coast, some on the west coast, and a small cluster on the Gulf coast.

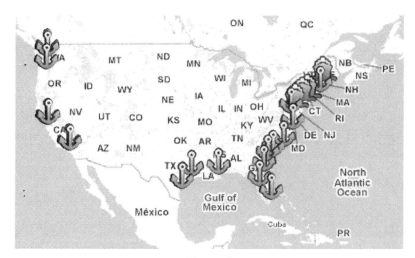

Figure 4
The Major Coastal Ports in the United States.
(Note that Huntington, WV is the 8th largest port at its inland location on the Ohio River.)

While some of this is due to historical roots and interrelationships between the expansion of the United States and the ports, the predominant theme is rooted in the 'connect to the people' concept. The tonnage capacity of the ports, shown in Figure 7 in order of throughput volume[7], shows that seven of the top ten ports, which handled 42% of the total tonnage of all of the ports in the United States in 2008, are located on the Gulf Coast, with one on the east coast and two on the west coast.

This can be simply explained by the conjunction of 'connect to the people' (the need) concept and the 'distance is not a difficulty' axiom. Both east and west coasts and the Midwest heartland is easily reachable from the ports on the Gulf Coast, so it's not surprising then that 72% of the tonnage enters through the Gulf Coast, while the east and west coast share the rest at only 15% and 13% respectively.

A similar pattern will be necessary for space commerce to flourish: space ports must be located on Earth where there is ready access to other means of affordable transport, and in space where there is the need for large volume transportation. Cost in space is also affected by another variable, the relative depth of the gravity well. The shallower the gravity well, the less expensive the transport because less energy is required to leave orbit and transect to another celestial body (or space station).

Leaving Earth to get to the moon requires leaving Earth's deep gravity well at a high cost in fuel, while transiting from LEO to the moon requires departing from a shallower gravity well and is therefore less expensive.

Rank	Port Name	Total	Domestic	Foreign	Import	Export	Coast
1	South Louisiana, LA, Port of	223	112	111	47	64	Gulf
2	Houston, TX	212	65	146	92	54	Gulf
3	New York, NY and NJ	153	62	91	71	19	East
4	Long Beach, CA	80	12	67	45	22	West
5	Corpus Christi, TX	76	21	55	43	11	Gulf
6	New Orleans, LA	73	36	36	19	16	Gulf
7	Beaumont, TX	69	22	46	41	5	Gulf
8	Huntington – Tri-state, WV	69	69	0	0	0	Inland (Ohio River)
9	Mobile, AL	67	29	38	23	14	Gulf
10	Plaquemines, LA, Port of	63	35	27	8	19	Gulf

Figure 5
2008 Top 10 United States ports by Tonnage
(figures shown in millions of tons)

The most obvious connectivity and accessibility points would be places in the Earth-moon system such as the LaGrange points, gravity neutral points in space that take the least energy to navigate to and from.

The concept of 'support capabilities' versus 'infrastructure capabilities' comes into play here as well. Whether a given operation is performed terrestrially at a port or at another adjacent but removed location is determined by risk, practicality, safety, security, and cost. Crude oil transport is relatively inexpensive via pipeline or ship, so refineries can be located anywhere. But in space, refining the moon's regolith will likely occur on the moon's surface near its sources because it will be much more expensive to transport the raw ore, and much less expensive to transport the refined (and lower mass) products.

While there are other considerations such as disposal of slag, the cost to transport a mass of goods on the surface and in space dominates the business decision.

Hence, a design that seems to work well but requires massive Earth moving (or regolith moving) equipment, equipment weighing several tons and requiring enormous power to transport and operate is a fantasy not a design. Getting the equipment there and fueling it once it arrived would require enormous 'up mass' of cargo to be carried to the destination, and the end product would have to be highly valuable for the economics to work.

The same logic applies on Earth. Where orbital energy is a huge penalty in space since mass is the metric of concern, terrestrially volume is the key metric, and therefore for example, remote refining is terrestrially quite practical because movement of mass is relatively easy. Stated as an axiom, then you must satisfy the laws of physics and the laws of markets and commerce simultaneously.

The key points to be made are that a design for any space-based commercialization strategy must include a defined mission, a risk assessment, a forecast positive return on investment (or profit), a life cycle, a maintenance plan, and demonstration of all this through simulation modeling of the entire system.

The robust model will have executibility, sustainability and the logistical supportability necessary to create profit at a level that will attract investment and will result in positive economic impact.

In addition, it must be part of a larger economic ecosystem consisting of elements that all fit together into an economic engine that will very crisply define the constraints, the vehicles, and ultimately the feasibility of the total system.

Figure 8 shows a very small constellation of space-based destinations. Axiomatic design and operations rules concerning the relative merits of these destinations leap off the page.

EXAMPLE 1

The farther out an asset is, the more difficult and expensive it is to maintain. Therefore, mass should be kept small and design complexity as simple as possible.

EXAMPLE 2

Little of the 'local' in-space (or space-to-space) communication is likely to be hubbed through the Earth. That would be excessively costly and difficult, pointing toward an alternate approach, managing the 'space frontier' communication through space-based assets.

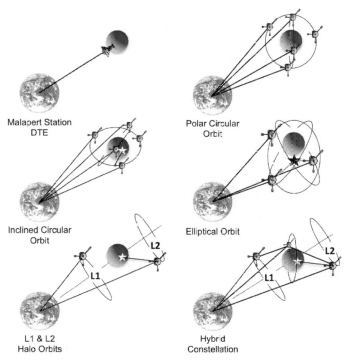

Figure 6
Examples of Possible Asset Locations In Lunar and Near Earth Orbits.

The communication system presented in Figure 9 shows how the total system design could affect the culture of the space community. All control assets today for space communication are located on Earth. As no nation has conducted a manned space venture beyond 400 NM from Earth since Apollo, Earth connected (hubbed) communication is logical. But from a cultural perspective this may be difficult to achieve since 'it's always been done this way,' (i.e., controlled from Earth) although the commercialization of space demands that assets are treated like the super tankers on the ocean: 'Call when you need help, or we'll see you in the next port of call.'

There is nothing radical in this thinking from a technology perspective, but as a side note, having control and communications not tied to an Earth-based management system may present a significant cultural challenge, and thus a cultural aspect of space commercialization may be needed as an axiom of the space commercialization model since commerce itself is about people and their real and perceived needs.

(*Editor's note:* Please see Chapters 5 and 6 for a discussion of the Cisco IRIS system, a space-based internet router that enables space-to-space communication, and eliminates the need for communication to be hubbed through Earth stations.)

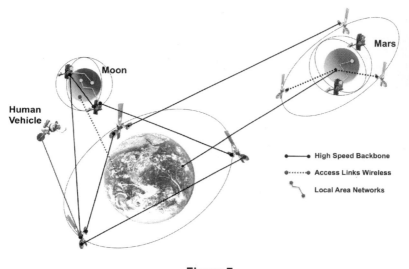

Figure 7
Space Commerce Communication Network
Potential asset-centric space communication system,
rather than an Earth-centric system.

While data on the sustainability of the active ports in the United States is available, perhaps the most convincing argument that sustainability is vital is shown in Figure 10[8]. The business case for the Panama Canal era exemplifies the concept of sustainable operations. If the Canal were to operate at a loss, and then look to expand, financial backers would be few. The canal is currently undergoing an upgrade to enable larger ships to pass through, and as it happened, the profit of the current system enables capital to be available for the design and construction of the upgrade.

Any space-based commercial system that succeeds will have to pass this type of litmus test for solvency: that is, it will have to operate profitably at a base level before expansion can be considered.

TOTAL SYSTEM EVOLUTION OF BOTH TERRESTRIAL AND SPACE-BASED ASSETS

Hence, the total system will evolve piece by piece, and in a somewhat predictable way, analogous to a terrestrial ocean port. A contemporary example will be used to illustrate this facet of the model: the migration from the Panamax ship to the Post-Panamax ship.

The Panama Canal is currently undergoing a major upgrade to the lock system to relieve the constraint on size of an ocean going ship that can pass through the canal. The current lock system is based on a 1900 design and was constructed 1903-1914. Shipbuilding and ocean freight economics have been growing into the current Panamax size. ('Panamax' is the term for the maximum size a ship can be to transit the canal. 'Post-Panamax' refers to any ship larger than that, which includes many of today's largest cargo and tanker ships. Figure 11[12] gives the definition of both configurations.)

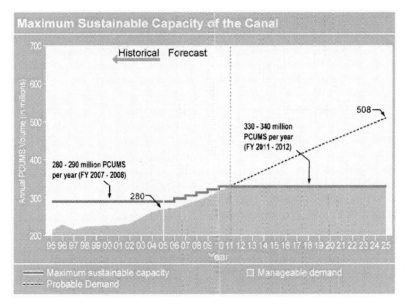

Figure 8
Historically Based Future Projection of Post Panamax TEU Performance.

Currently, the Panama Canal can accommodate a vessel 1000 ft long by 100 ft beam. This is roughly 50% more length and beam than any ship of the 1900 era. As an example, the Pruessen (The 'Prussian') sailing ship launched in 1902 was roughly 450 by 50 ft, and the 1918 'Carolinian' launched in Britain was roughly 360 by 50 ft.[10,11] Hence, there was considerable accommodation built into the canal for future expansion of ship size in the original design.

But current ship capacity exceeds what the canal designers envisioned. The technology that enabled growth in ship size includes arc welding (which replaced plates and rivets), metallurgy (yielding stronger and lighter metals), power systems (significant increases in horsepower performance), and control systems, none of which could have been anticipated or planned for. Nor could the coupled and multiplicative effects of these technologies be estimated, and in addition, computers and software tools for simulation and system engineering had not yet become a part of the ship designer's toolset. Finally, the advent of containerization, a profound innovation-revolution, has fundamentally changed both the economics of ocean freight operations, and the design of the ships themselves, as well as the process of port operations and in fact all intermodal transportation.

The current project to expand the capacity of the canal, scheduled for completion in 2014, constitutes a design upgrade to a system that is now 100 years old. 100 years of effective working life is an outstanding achievement for any technical or technological system, and this was achieved largely because the original designers sized the canal to accommodate ships that were double the size of those in operation at the time.

Based upon containerized shipping format, the Panamax vessel is no longer the optimum vessel configuration from an economics perspective. And it is the economic considerations that lead to the need for a canal expansion, that is, the need to accommodate extremely large vessels. But in the commercial world, the key factor is not size per se, but unit cost per unit shipped.

The standard measure of terrestrial cargo capacity is a function of volume, designated as the 'TEU', the 'twenty-foot equivalent unit,' 20x8x8 feet. A standard 40 ft container unit is two TEUs.

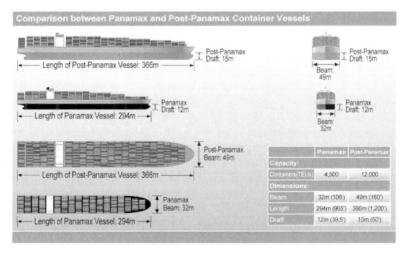

Figure 9
Comparison of Panamax to Post-Panamax ship dimensions.

For a spaceport, the TEU equivalent will not be a volume measurement, but rather a measurement of mass, likely notated as 'MT to

LEO,' or metric ton to low Earth orbit. (A metric ton is 1,000 kg (2,204.62262 lb), or approximately the mass of one cubic meter of water at four degrees Celsius. The nominal LEO orbit is defined here as 120 nautical miles (NM) or 222 km above the Earth's surface.)

How important is this change for the Panama Canal, and what is the effect on shipping cost, and therefore for delivered goods? Figures 12[13] and 15[13] show that the Post-Panamax system drives the shipping cost down for transport between existing ports (fuel and labor costs on operations are considered constant for the exercise), and the subsequent rise in total shipping volume is significant.

Comparison of Tonnage Growth per Segment			
PCUMS Tons Per Market Segment*	Year 2005	Year 2025	
		Canal without an expansion	Canal with an expansion
Containers	98	185	296
Dry Bulk	55	49	73
Liquid Bulk	34	19	28
Passenger	10	13	19
Car Carrier	36	40	58
Refrigerated Cargo	19	15	22
General Cargo	7	3	4
Others	20	6	8
Total PCUMS Tons	279	330	508
*Millions of PCUMS tons			

Figure 10
Panama Canal Growth Projections, 2010 – 2025.

Perhaps the most striking projection is that the importance of the canal to shipping, expressed in TEU / year, is relatively flat without the canal expansion (growth through 2025 is only 18%), while it is 82% (nearly doubled) with the expansion. With the venture into space commercialization, one could reasonably expect to see this kind of growth in commerce, and in wealth creation, if the lessors from terrestrial commerce are reframed by the laws of space physics.

For any transport system undergoing a change, the shift to Post-Panamax is not instantaneous, nor does it need to be completed quickly. The old canal assets will not soon fall into disuse, and the smaller ships will not disappear from service, as shown in Figure 13[14]. Based upon projections, the old locks will be as busy for the near future as they are today, because not all routes or commodity needs require a Post-Panamax ship configuration.

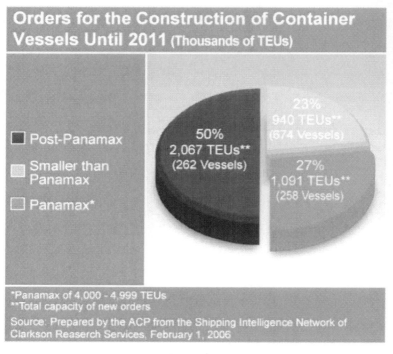

Figure 11
Shipbuilding Orders: Mixed Fleet Is Best For Profit Margin.

Since commercial space systems must obey the laws of physics and the laws of economics simultaneously, we can anticipate many different kinds of transport needs. We should expect to fly a mixed fleet of booster and cargo vehicles, including a Saturn V-like booster, a shuttle-like transport, a Delta IV Heavy-like system, and an Atlas V-like system, even while experimenting with the Single Stage to Orbit (SSTO) technology[15] and even the Space Elevator.[16] We expect NASA to be closely involved in designing and building the prototypes of the 'next gen' vehicles to assure a cost effective 'mixed fleet' of booster and cargo system vehicles.

No single government agency has control over the production of this vast an array of launch and vehicle equipment, nor does any entity in the private sector. Therefore, it is clear that only the private sector, and many pieces of it working together, could attempt the grand scale of enterprise that the commercialization of space will require, while the public sector must participate heavily in technology development.

An interesting parallel on the units of measure of the vehicles arises out of Figure 14.[17] The lift capability of the arsenal of lift systems shown is but a sample of what is available or might be available internationally. To get large masses out of Earth's gravity well to LEO requires a large system. The shuttle and Ares I are both roughly 25MT to LEO, Ares V is 180MT, and Saturn V is 120MT.

There is ample evidence as seen in Figure 15[17] to show that the 'flex' in the port / ship system has a very profitable future planned by size tailoring of vessels and missions, or needs. Non-canal ships like the *Eugen Maersk*, the world's longest ocean freighter at 1,300 feet. are already at sea, so technology is not a limiting consideration in size determination, nor is government funding. Economics surely is. It is clear that an armada of tools, and mass transfer (lift systems) will be necessary for the commercialization of space.

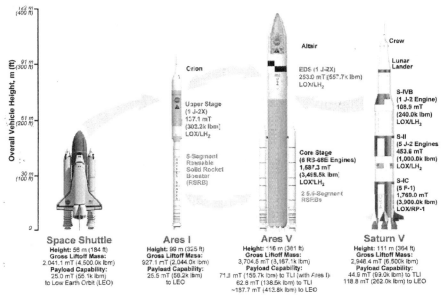

Figure 12
Booster Systems: Mass-To-LEO Baseline Today.

Available records over the history of the Panama Canal are also required to anchor the future estimates in the reality of actual performance and to manage the risks, but this is a problematic area for the space-based commercialization argument. We have only had government-funded, institutionally-controlled human space flight projects to date, and therefore much of the available literature and 'data' are wildly suspect.

The 50 shuttle launches per year, the 10 year shuttle program, the Space Station Freedom, the X-33, the X-34, the Single Stage to Orbit (SSTO) and the latest, the Constellation Program, have no collective success history with which to form the basis of a projection for the succeeding step. This may be the largest impediment in the successful modeling and the actual commercialization of space – accurate cost projections and therefore Return on Investment (ROI) that are needed to secure the necessary capital for such large undertakings.

This is why developing a successful commercialization model is so critical. If you cannot model it and show success, you can be assured that it will be even worse in the physical entity because of all the factors that you omitted in your model.

Note that to date, this has been the quintessential argument for government alone engaging in space-based forays – no one else has the resources available or is willing to commit these resources given the extreme uncertainties. But this is no longer true. Henceforth, space commercialization belongs to the private sector, with assistance in limited areas from the government.

The shipping industry has hundreds of years of data and many years of the current technology upon which to develop new models. Commercial shipping cost changes, assuming fuel and labor are relatively similar, show why it is an attractive option to build a larger canal and sail larger ships hauling identical cargo.

The Post-Panamax era also has other impacts on ocean commerce, which are potentially larger than the cost savings growth factor shown in Figure 15, particularly on the ports of call. Let's examine an example. Focusing the discussion on just ports in the United States, several trends emerge. First, tonnage is expected to increase by 60% (close to the 82% of the canal itself), and the bulk of that will be through the Gulf Coast, particularly the Port of Houston. Why? In Figure 6 we saw that the Gulf Coast services the central states and can nearly equidistantly reach either coast. If a planner for the Port of Houston Authority were looking at just local data and events, this huge positive impact would be obscured from sight, and the resulting business decisions would be poor. The confluence of the cost decrease from post-Panamax ship size, the upward growth of tonnage independent of the expanded Canal, the reduced shipping time due to the expanded canal, and the pre-planned expansion of the inter-modal transportation links and pipelines at the Port of Houston all converge to decisively impact future tonnage traffic into Houston.

The resulting axiom is: Change impacts to facilities and destinations are not limited to just first order effects on commerce in an immediate area; they include second and even third order effects that include reduced time, favorable unit of measure / unit economics and even global geopolitical considerations.

One additional axiom must be stated regarding estimating the impacts. Continuous and rigorous planning is required for space commerce to succeed, and such planning must be at a far greater depth and scope than is currently done for ocean ports.

Percentage Cost Savings per TEU per Voyage - Post-Panamax Vessels (Compared with a Weekly 4,000 TEU Panamax Vessel Service)		
Route	6,000 TEU Vessel	8,000 TEU Vessel
Asia - U.S. East Coast	8%	16%
Asia - U.S. West Coast	8%	17%
Asia - U.S. East Coast through Suez	7%	17%
Source: Transpacific Vessel Deployment Options with an Expanded Panama Canal, R.K. Johns & Associates Inc. 2004		

Figure 13
Comparison of Panamax and Post-Panamax ships.
Cost of Operations as a Function of TEUs.

In space, the divergent nature of destinations, product mixes, the high risks, and the extremely capital intensive nature of space commerce demands this degree of planning. This planning, like that for the terrestrial ports, must recognize a limited span of control, and interfaces to geopolitical stimuli, as well as evolving technology and other important parameters. Here is yet another example of executibility, sustainability and logistical supportability being the interrelated criteria, not just technology or simply the cost.

SECURITY: DIFFICULT ON EARTH – IMPOSSIBLE IN SPACE?

What better place to engage in terrorism than where there are very high valued assets and absolutely no law enforcement capability within 250,000 miles? This is the reality for space commerce. It potentially admits outright terrorism, pirate hi-jack of both assets and vehicles, and theft of high value commodities. Moreover, the assets that are infrastructure, the processing bases, the fueling stations, etc, are all vulnerable as well. To date, there have been no human spaceflight incidents of this nature in LEO or in the moon missions that are verifiable. (This excludes 'test' destruction of satellites.)

However, while the Cold War is over, it is but a reminder that conflict can readily grip competing power structures. Extraterrestrial Terrorism (the new 'E.T.') might well be the cause of 'Cold War Part II,' or World War III, because of the enormity of the stakes, the risks, and the sheer amount of capital required to undertake this adventure. Whether such exposure is a stabilizing influence (an unthinkable act), or is in fact vulnerability with apocalyptic consequences, presents an interesting sidebar discussion that is not pursued here. At a minimum, though, space commercialization must prepare some contingency and recovery plan for addressing this issue. Without a rigorous enforcement capability, terrorism cannot be outlawed in practice, and it will not go away of its own accord.

It is unclear that the mission scope of the United States Air Force, which has the Missile Command and stewardship for the GPS system among other space assets, would extend itself or be authorized to extend into 'outer space,' which would include LEO, lunar, geosynchronous, and eventually beyond. Perhaps this might be yet another inherently governmental function, protecting the commerce lanes as the Coast Guard does on the high seas and ports.

Recall the timid beginnings of the American Navy. Only after pirates raided ships and were strangling commerce, did the Congress of 1794 decide to build the United States, the Constellation, the Constitution, the President, the Congress and the Chesapeake.[26] In that era, the US was a self sufficient nation, unlike today, as we could not now sustain our standard of living without strong, secure commercial operations extending globally. But even when the six ships were approved, waffling occurred in the funding the last three. As there were no other warships in the ocean flying the colors of the United States of America, the concept of privateering was born, and was supported by, among others, Thomas Jefferson:

> "...every possible encouragement should be given to privateering in time of war with a commercial nation... Our national ships are too few in number...to retaliate the acts of the enemy. ...by licensing private armed vessels, the whole naval force of the nation is truly brought to bear on the foe."[27]

Space security might therefore be yet another industry spawned by the commercialization of space: policing the commerce routes in and beyond LEO. This is a germane topic to address because it is a required support function that has no placeholder in a terrestrial ocean port plan, yet without it there may be a fatal risk flaw in spaceport commercialization. The recent adventures of Somali pirates attacking international shipping lanes, and the solutions found therein, should be watched and analyzed carefully.

(Editor's note: Please see Chapter 20, The US Space Guard: Institutional Support to Space Commerce, for a more detailed discussion of this issue.)

JURISDICTION: IT IS AN ISSUE TERRESTRIALLY — WHAT ABOUT IN SPACE?

NASA has standard agreements with the FAA[20] and STRATCOMM[21] to allocate US airspace on ascents and entries of space vehicles, and to do collision analysis for avoidance of space debris in the on-orbit phase. While these pertain neither to laws of physics nor to laws of commerce, they are real constraints and must be addressed by any space commercialization initiative. This set of functions would fall under the category of support infrastructure.

This function set has analogs in the ocean port model too, as traffic control may be rather pedestrian, but is nevertheless a critical issue. In fact, it is not an option to not have this support, but as yet there are no commercial services companies that perform it. That might be a business opportunity at some future date, but for the immediate discussion of space commercialization there are no non-governmental service providers.

One option would be to negotiate an arrangement with the military regarding airspace. For the near future, the FAA has jurisdiction in the civilian arena for the United States airspace below 400,000 feet altitude.

Perhaps more interesting is the concept of international partners in the space commercialization team that perhaps brought an exo-atmospheric vehicle to operational status, such as the atmospheric skimmer, or the SSTO like Skylon[22] shown in Figure 14

A Skylon is a conceptual, hydrogen-powered aircraft that would take off from a conventional runway, accelerate to Mach 5.4 using atmospheric air, and switch the engines to use the internal liquid oxygen supply to take it to orbit. The British company Reaction Engines developed this concept.

The point for us is that a definition of the infrastructure must encompass functions that might not be readily apparent. This forms then, a corollary to the existing axiom regarding fully identifying the costs for support infrastructure required for space commercialization success: forecast the future through planning.

One parenthetic thought on the Skylon type vehicle: If this were to be developed for cargo and expanded to handle human passengers it would be an entirely disruptive technology that would be a forcing function in the commercialization planning. The basic cost of mass to LEO might be reduced by a factor of 5 or 10, and as was seen as a result of the completion of the Panama Canal, breakthroughs in transportation costs completely change the commerce game. Carrier sizes change, times to port change, and most importantly, what was not feasible often becomes commercially feasible.

To frame this problem with numbers of vehicles and destinations, the Port of Houston receives more than 8000 ships per year making port, or roughly 25 per day.[23] The number, size, and requirements for this mixed fleet of 'visiting vehicles' dictate dock space, traffic control, and on-shore TEU handling capacity.

Figure 14
Deployment and flight configuration for Skylon SSTO vehicle concept.

The same situation, substituting mass for volume, would hold true for a space commerce infrastructure.

The payload mass capability of a booster system is more like an airliner than an ocean vessel. Out of the major airport adjacent to the Port of Houston, Houston Intercontinental, there are 1400 arrivals and departures per day,[24] and roughly 156,000 per day across the entire United States.[25] While the number of launches from and entries to the Earth is not likely to ever reach this level, the Skylon or a similar hypersonic, exo-atmospheric craft might not 'launch' like a rocket, but rather 'depart' like an airplane. Or perhaps they will blend into events called 'laun-parture' or an 'ent-rival' numbering more in the airport realm of events than ships docking at port.

This would hasten the infrastructure to change radically, requiring the axiomatic concept of space-based communications and control. This is also an excellent example why there must be system of system simulations in the business model, as non-connected elements may have first order effects on each other, in addition to more subtle but far-reaching second and third order effects on the system as a whole. Engaging in this type of simulation is a necessary part of the planning process.

DO WE HAVE ENOUGH INFORMATION AND UNDERSTANDING TO INITIATE THE COMMERCIALIZATION OF SPACE?

The short answer is no. But then, we never will if certainty or near certainty is required. This is and always will be a risk intensive business, even with superior planning. If the level of risk is commensurate with the potential ROI, then let the commercialization of space begin.

But how much of the cost of space operations has to do with providing a human habitat off the planet? Consider, then, the potential 'game changing' nature of robots. Newer robots have both dexterity and strength, and we must ask, 'At what point do we outfit a station or a waypoint with robotic 'inhabitants'?

In such case, what is the role of a human, and when is the human too costly or the risk of loss of life too great? Here is a potentially multiplicative technology confluence, where the technologies together offer leverage much beyond than their additive sum.

There are no clear answers to this conundrum, which is why the need for continuous planning and assessment is not only cost effective, but is in fact the only strategy suited to preventing being overcome by events, particularly technology driven changes.

This example also nicely demonstrates need for continuous planning to be the final axiom of the model. We won't get 100 years of use out of the access portal to space like we have from the Panama Canal. The technology that kept the Panama Canal on the cutting edge of technology for so many years, useful and cost effective until the present day, was a very slow to change, an open system that has been in use for centuries: water lift.

The dawning era of space commercialization begs the question of when and how emerging technologies will either be incorporated, or will entirely disrupt things, such that it effectively resets to a 'start again mode,' requiring an entirely restructured initiative. We recall that Ferdinand De Lesseps tried but utterly failed to build a lock-less canal system in Panama for 10 years, from 1879 to 1889. It took breakthroughs in medicine to overcome malaria, and in technology (in the form of steam shovels), and ten additional long years of work to realize the vision.[19]

If this seems bold, recall that the 'Space Age' was ushered in back in 1957, and by about 1992 it was universally declared that we are living in the 'Information Age.' Over 35 years, we went from dreaming of inhabiting Mars to watching Mars movies on 3D TV. The 'half-life' of the Information Age will no doubt be shorter than the Space Age, and maybe we are already into another age after just 20 years, the cusp of the 'Age of Space Commercialization'?

CONCLUSION

We have explored the laws of physics and the laws of commerce to derive a set of axioms that we believe will be useful as for evaluation of the 'readiness' of a space commercialization proposal.

Such axioms include the need to define the total system, model and simulate the system of systems, and carefully examine all associated assumptions. From that body of work will come the defining technologies, the cost estimates for infrastructure, and most importantly the evaluation of executibility, sustainability and logistical supportability of the entire system of systems. Once this is completed, a concept can also be assessed against a very successful and applicable reference system, the ocean port and container ship commerce model.

Our set of axioms, given below, will no doubt require further tuning and refinement as we incrementally move toward that next great adventure of the Commercialization of Space. These are the criterion cornerstones against which any proposed approach to space commercialization could be judged at a system level, particularly in the absence of any prior history of a successful space commercialization initiative.

AXIOMS OF THE SPACE COMMERCIALIZATION MODEL

1. To commercialize space, it is mandatory that a plan has long-term profitability that is demonstrable through system modeling.

2. Only the private sector has the resources, potential to obtain financial backing, and the experience available on the grand

scale required to plan space commercialization and execute that plan. A 'plan' is defined as including defined mission, risk, return on investment, life cycle, and maintenance plan, and these can be demonstrated through simulation modeling of the entire system.

3. Space based commercialization must address viable missions, managed risks, adequate return on investment, life cycle design, thorough maintenance plans, all through effective simulation and modeling that demonstrates the executibility, the sustainability and logistical supportability of the system of systems.

4. Space vehicles are just beasts of burden, not technology 'wunderkind.' Terrestrial shipping and space shipping have analogous attributes that can inform plans for space commercialization.

5. NASA must be a catalyst, but not in the prime operations manager. The 'heavy lifting' of operations must shift to the commercial sector.

6. The location of space-based assets is not defined by a mission, an adventure, or a need to explore, but by the imperative to connect supply to the need, as in any free market.

7. Clear understanding of the significance of 'distance from Earth' must be demonstrated for a concept to be proven executable, sustainable and logistically supportable. When is distance from Earth a critical factor, and when is it inconsequential?

8. Compliance with the laws of physics simultaneously with the laws of capital generation, investment and ROI are non-negotiable.

9. The application of new technology cannot disrupt a commercial revenue stream. Technology is only attractive to solve a need, not for its own sake inserted into space commercialization. Technology also cannot add substantial risk; rather, it must be applied to decrease risk.

10. Mass to space commerce is as volume is to terrestrial commerce. This will drive design considerations for the artifacts and the business cases for space commercialization.

11. Research, development and art in and of themselves have no commercial value to operations in space commerce.

12. Only the private sector has experience, the relevant historical data and culture to create, manage, and operate a functional commercialization system.

13. Success builds upon success. Since there is very limited history and certainly only a weak pattern as yet of commerce and human manufacturing in space, incipient efforts at space commerce must be managed with the expectation and preparation for significant degrees of failure for the near future. Contingency plans are consequently mandatory.

14. Due to the sheer size and complexity of the total system model for any space commercialization concept, the second and third event order effects must be understood, and incorporated into the system model, and into the physical system when it is built.

15. Continuous, rigorous, and inter-disciplinary planning is required for space commercialization to succeed and continue. This planning must be more robust, integrated and in depth than is routinely done for terrestrial initiatives.

•••

TOM DIEGELMAN

Tom Diegelman has been in the aerospace community for over 35 years, involved in the research, development and operation of training simulators, ground based flight control installations and facility operations. Tom started his career with Cornell Aeronautical Laboratory as a research engineer, working on early versions of shuttle handling quality study simulations and shuttle shock tunnel testing.

Tom moved to Houston in the late 70's to join Singer / Link Flight Simulation and worked in the Shuttle Mission Training Facility (SMTF) as a model developer, and later a manager of simulation projects. In 1988, Tom joined NASA to lead the $170M redesign of the SMTF. Assignments at NASA / JSC include projects in advanced mission control technology, technology development, and facility operations control. He served as Facility Manager for Mission Control for 3 years before accepting an account manager position in the Technology Transfer Office, developing partnerships and Space Act Agreements.

The design of the training facility for the Constellation Program culminated his nearly 30 years of experience at JSC in Jake Garn astronaut training facility. Tom was elected to Seabrook City Council in 2006, and served two terms, during which he worked closely with the Port of Houston Authority on the Seabrook / Bayport Terminal Facility issues. Tom is a member of Baytran, a non-profit organization promoting inter-modal transportation solutions in the Houston / Bay Area, and continues to be involved in local, state and federal government on behalf of the space technology community.

He is also coauthor of Chapter 12, *Heavy Lift Launch: How Boosters Work, Their History, and the Role of Heavy Lift in Space Commercialization.*

KENNETH J. COX, PH.D.

Dr. Kenneth J. Cox earned his bachelor's degree in 1953 and his master's degree in 1956 in electrical engineering from the University of Texas/Austin, and his PhD at Rice University in 1966.

In 1963 he joined NASA to develop the flight control system for the Little Joe II Booster Vehicle. Later, Dr. Cox became the Technical Manager for the Apollo Digital Control Systems, which included the Lunar Module, the Command Module and the Command/Service Module, the first spacecraft to fly with a digital flight control system.

Ken is coeditor of this volume, and also coauthor of Chapters 1 and 24. He has been the leader of ATWG since it was established in 1990.

REFERENCES

1. "Vision Space Port: renewing America's Space launch Infrastructure & Operations", Carey McCleskey, et all, April 2001. All art in this chapter was provided courtesy of Pat Rawlings, SAIC, Art Director
2. Port of Houston Authority, 111 East Loop North, Houston, Texas USA 77029, Phone: 713-670-2400, www.portofhouston.com
3. Xxxx http://en.wikipedia.org/wiki/Tomorrowland
4. "Putting NASA's Budget in Perspective"(Unless otherwise indicated, the dollar figures cited in this webpage were obtained from The World Almanac and Book of Facts 2000, World Almanac Books, PRIMEDIA Reference Inc., 1999, ISBN 0-88687-847-0.) and NASA budget submission: http://www.nasa.gov/pdf/142458main_FY07_budget_full.pdf
5. "Means Tested Welfare Spending: Past and Future Growth", Robert E. Rector, Testimony, March 7, 2001.
6. "Tonnage by Ports", Army Corps of Engineers, Navigation Data Center, http://www.iwr.usace.army.mil/ndc/wcsc/portton08.htm, 2008
7. Ibid ref 8
8. "The Proposed Expansion of the Panama Canal", Panama Canal Authority, April 24, 2006, Autordad Del Canal De Panama
9. Charles Duell, http://www.ideafinder.com/guest/archives/wow-duell.htm
10. http://werften.fischtown.de/archiv/preussen1.htm
11. http://www.ibiblio.org/hyperwar/OnlineLibrary/photos/usnshtp/ak/w1ak126a.htm
12. ibid ref. 8
13. ibid, ref. 8
14. Ibid ref 8
15. Single Stage to Orbit – Skylon; http://nextbigfuture.com/2009/01/progress-to-skylon-single-stage-to.html
16. Space Elevator: http://www.spaceelevator.com/
17. ibid, ref 8
18. NASA "Tech Briefs", March 2010
       http://en.wikipedia.org/wiki/Ferdinand_de_Lesseps
       http://www.faa.gov/
       http://www.stratcom.mil/about/
19. Skylon ibid
    Ibid , ref. 2
       http://askville.amazon.com/flights-day-IAH
           airport/AnswerViewer.do?requestId=16096112
    Flights per day.http://www.answerbag.com/q_view/34532
       http://en.wikipedia.org/wiki/Original_six_frigates_of_the_United_States_Navy
20. Outfitting The Early American Privateers: Privateering In The Early US: What It Was, And What It Cost
    http://americanhistory.suite101.com/article.cfm/the_business_cost_of_american_privateers#ixzz0j3nBMZoI

CHAPTER 17

COMMERCIAL SPACEPORTS IN THE AMERICAS

THOMAS L. MATULA, PH.D.

INTRODUCTION

Commercial spaceports are launch facilities dedicated to serving the needs of the commercial launch industry. The need to move beyond the restrictions and costs of using government facilities was the key driver in the emergence of the industry, and it came about as a result of the gradual commercialization of space launch starting in the 1980s. Today, commercial spaceports serve a key function in the expanding space commerce industry.

This chapter will start with a brief history of the emergence of commercial spaceports and show how their development has paralleled the developing of the space commerce industry, followed by a proposed model for classifying commercial spaceports based on their history and target markets. Finally, the economics of spaceport development will be discussed.

HISTORY

The history of commercial spaceports is most easily divided into three eras. The Comsat Spaceport Era, the SSTO Spaceport Era and the Suborbital Spaceport Era. Each era is marked by a different perception of the needs and requirements of the commercial launch industry. The Comsat Spaceport Era spans 1979 to 1995 and marks the need for facilities to launch commercial communication satellites. It was followed by the optimism of the SSTO Spaceport Era of 1996 to 2002. The Single Stage to Orbit (SSTO) Spaceport Era started with the proposal for Lockheed's proposed SSTO called VentureStar. As part of the VentureStar Project, Lockheed requested proposals for launch sites, and eighteen states responded. The third and current era, the Suborbital Spaceport Era, started with the end of the VentureStar and with it plans for developing SSTO. Following the end of the SSTO Era, many spaceports refocused their efforts on the previously ignored suborbital market, stimulated by the growing interest in suborbital tourism resulting from the X-Prize. This is the current era and is driving many of the spaceport efforts today.

THE COMSAT SPACEPORT ERA: 1979-1995

The demand for commercial satellites, especially communication satellites, created the demand for commercial launch vehicles (Matula and Mitry, 2000). Prior to the 1980s commercial satellites were launched by national space agencies with a cost reimbursement arrangement (Johnson-Freese and Handberg 1997). In 1979, the first successful launch of the Ariane launch system from Guiana Space Centre in French Guiana marked the beginning of the commercial launch industry. The Ariane was designed specifically to serve the needs of the commercial satellite industry, which is why it's considered the first commercial launch system. This makes the Guiana Space Centre in French Guiana the first commercial spaceport.

In the United States, commercial satellites continued to be launched on both expendable launch vehicles like the Delta and Atlas under a cost reimbursement agreement with NASA. The Space Shuttle was also used for launching commercial satellites under the same cost reimbursement arrangement. Following the Challenger accident, commercial payloads were banned from the Space Shuttle by Executive Order, laying the foundation for the commercial launch industry in the United States. In order to accommodate the emerging commercial space launch operations, several commercial space launch facilities, commonly known as commercial spaceports, emerged in the 1990s (Johnson-Freese and Handberg 1997).

In 1989, Spaceport Florida was the first commercial spaceport in the United States, and was created to serve existing Expendable Launch

Vehicles (ELVs) like the Delta and Atlas that were pressed into service for the launching of Comsats following the banning of commercial satellite launches from the Space Shuttle. Spaceport Florida was closely followed by California Spaceport and the Kodiak Launch Complex in Alaska. The Spaceports in both California and Alaska were developed to support the proposed constellations of communication satellites for the satellite mobile phone markets, but demand failed to meet expectations. Spaceport Florida, by contrast, was created to serve the market for Geosynchronous Communication Satellites.

SSTO SPACEPORT ERA: 1996-2002

The Comsat Spaceport Era of commercial spaceports was superseded by the SSTO Era. It was initiated by the flight tests of the DC-X launch system in the early 1990s. The DC-X was a sub-scaled prototype of a Single Stage to Orbit launch system proposed by McDonnell-Douglas. Although it made only a dozen flights, it stimulated the quest for development of a SSTO launch system. This resulted in NASA's X-33 and X-34 Demonstrator Programs. Lockheed Martin won the competition for the X-33 Demonstrator with a lifting body SSTO that was intended to be a sub-scale demonstrator for the VentureStar, a commercial SSTO.

As part of the VentureStar program, Lockheed solicited proposals for launch sites for the system. Eighteen states responded with plans for commercial spaceports designed to meet Lockheed's needs (Matula and Mitry 2000). Since the VentureStar was a SSTO system, it did not need a coastal location such as expandable launch vehicles required, but could actually overfly land areas safely (Matula and Mitry, 2000). As a result, spaceport proposals were submitted from both existing commercial spaceports like Spaceport Florida and California Spaceport, and from inland states including Nevada and Oklahoma, which had no existing facilities or previous history of space launch.

The most serious efforts were from Montana, Oklahoma and Washington, which had existing facilities in the form of closed military bases that would be converted to serve the needs of VentureStar. Some states went as far as creating state spaceport authorities and funding detailed business plans. However the failure to complete the X-33 demonstrator vehicle and changes in market demand for space launch resulted in the VentureStar program being cancelled. This in turn led to most of the proposed commercial spaceport projects lapsing into inactivity and being abandoned due to the lack of any market drivers. However a few did survive to be reorganized into the next Era, the Suborbital Spaceport Era.

SUB-ORBITAL SPACEPORT ERA: 2002 - PRESENT

The end of the SSTO Spaceport Era resulted in a refocus of the surviving commercial spaceports into a new direction, servicing the emerging demand for suborbital launch systems. The redirection was most apparent in the newly proposed spaceports, while the existing ones, Spaceport Florida, California Spaceport, and Mid-Atlantic Regional Spaceport, continued their focus on the commercial Expendable Launch Vehicles (ELVs) that were already using their facilities.

The stimulus for the new direction of commercial spaceports was the Ansari X Prize (NASA, 2010). The Ansari X Prize was created to stimulate the development of suborbital space tourism. The result was an explosion of proposed suborbital launch systems, which created a demand for commercial spaceports to serve their needs. Spaceports previously proposed for the VentureStar system were refocused towards the needs of suborbital systems, the most prominent among them being New Mexico's proposed Southwest Regional Spaceport, the Oklahoma Spaceport, the proposed Gulf Coast Regional Spaceport, and the Mojave Air and Space Port.

Burt Rutan and Paul Allen won the Ansari X Prize in 2004 (NASA, 2010). Following their victory, Richard Branson announced that he was licensing their system for a suborbital tourism spaceline called Virgin Galactic. (*Editor's note*: Please see Chapter 7, *A Tourist's Perspective on Space*.) Shortly after its creation, Virgin Galactic selected New Mexico's Southwest Regional Spaceport as the base for its launch operations (Gomez, et al, 2007). Other suborbital tourism ventures selected other commercial spaceports. Rocket Plane Kistler selected Oklahoma Spaceport for its base of operations, although later the venture failed to secure the financing needed. Blue Origins, another suborbital tourism venture, made a different choice, and is building its own private spaceport in West Texas. Although not selected for its operations, Mojave Air and Space Port has positioned itself well as a research and test facility. Another facility considered for VentureStar, Cecil Field in Northern Florida has also gone ahead with licensing as a commercial spaceport.

SPACEPORT CLASSIFICATION

One challenge when discussing spaceports is the wide range of facilities that call themselves spaceports, from major existing facilities like Spaceport Florida to the proposed Spaceport Wisconsin. In this chapter, a classification system is proposed that is based on the history and capabilities of the different facilities. The proposed classification system is based on a two by two matrix, with the horizontal axis based on capability to support suborbital and/or orbital launches. The vertical axis is based on the facility's history: Is it an existing facility that has been converted to commercial needs, or is it a clear sheet development? The result is a simple but practical classification system shown in Figure 1. Examples of different commercial spaceports are provided in each element of the matrix. It is not intended to be a comprehensive survey of commercial spaceports either globally or in the United States.

	Suborbital	Orbital
Converted Facilities	Mojave Air and Space Port Oklahoma Spaceport Cecil Field Spaceport	Spaceport Florida Mid-Atlantic Regional Spaceport California Spaceport
New Start Facilities	Spaceport America Blue Origin Spaceport Spaceport Sheboygan	Guiana Space Centre Kodiak Launch Complex

Figure 1
Classification of Commercial Spaceports

CONVERTED SUBORBITAL

Converted Suborbital Spaceports are commercial spaceports limited by location to only suborbital launches. All existing converted suborbital spaceports started as airfields, either commercial or military, in locations that enabled them to provide the airspace and facilities needed for suborbital launch operations. Converted Suborbital commercial spaceports have the advantage of lower start-up costs since they have existing infrastructure to use, especially expensive facilities like long runways, hangers, and associated support buildings. Three examples are highlighted below.

MOJAVE AIR AND SPACE PORT
(http://www.mojaveairport.com/)

Mojave Air and Space Port is located in southern California near Edwards Air Force Base. The home to Burt Rutan's Scaled Composite Corporation, it was the site of the successful test program for SpaceShipOne, the vehicle that won the Ansari X Prize. It is currently home to a flight test program for Virgin Galactic's SpaceShipTwo, as well as other entrepreneurial suborbital space ventures. Mojave Air and Space Port was already an existing commercial airport with an emphasis on pilot training and flight test operations, and the conversion into a suborbital facility was a logical extension of those existing aviation activities.

CECIL FIELD SPACEPORT

(http://www.cecilfieldspaceport.com/)

Cecil Field Spaceport in located in Jacksonville, Florida at the former Naval Air Station Cecil Field. Vacated by the U.S. Navy in 1999, Cecil Field pursued licensing to serve the needs of air launch suborbital systems. In 2010 it became an FAA licensed spaceport for air launched suborbital vehicles. Its main advantage is its proximity to the Atlantic Ocean, which makes it ideal for testing of air-launched suborbital systems.

SPACEPORT OKLAHOMA

(http://www.okspaceport.state.ok.us/)

Spaceport Oklahoma, located in Burns, Oklahoma, was originally Clinton-Sherman Air Force Base, a former U.S. Air Force Strategic Air Command base. When it was closed in 1969 it was converted into an industrial park. Its remote location and large runways stimulated interest in the facility as a site for Lockheed's VentureStar. After the VentureStar project was cancelled, the decision was made to use it as a suborbital launch facility. Rocket Plane Kistler, a suborbital launch venture located there with the intention to use it as its base of operations. Although Rocket Plane Kistler went bankrupt in 2010, the field continues to be used by other suborbital launch ventures.

NEW SUBORBITAL

New Suborbital spaceports are facilities that are being built from the ground up at locations with no space launch history. Limited by their geographic location to suborbital launches, they are focused on the emerging demand for suborbital launch facilities. New suborbital commercial spaceports are much more expensive to develop then Converted Suborbital commercial spaceports because they start with bare land and few, if any, improvements. This means that all of the necessary infrastructure, from runways to hangers, must be built new, often an expensive proposition. This of course creates a much higher barrier to their development, and has significant consequences for their eventual economic success.

SPACEPORT AMERICA

(http://www.spaceportamerica.com/)

Spaceport America is located in Upham, New Mexico near the White Sands Missile Range. Spaceport America originally was started in the early 1990s as the Southwest Regional Spaceport. The stimulus to its development was the military's DC-X program, a subscale prototype of a Single Stage to Orbital system that was being tested at nearby White Sands Missile Range. McDonnell Douglas had plans to develop it into a commercial launch system, and the valley of ranches that Upham, New Mexico was located in was considered an ideal site.

Following the failure of McDonnell Douglas to win the NASA X-33 competition, the focus of the Southwest Regional Spaceport shifted towards attracting the winner, Lockheed's VentureStar. But then with the cancellation of the VentureStar. Southwest Regional Spaceport shifted its focus again, this time to the emerging suborbital tourist industry. In 2006 it was selected as the launch site for Virgin Galactic Space Lines, and actual construction began. Its name was also changed from the Southwest Regional Spaceport to Spaceport America. Current plans are to finish the spaceport in 2010 to support Virgin Galactic launch operations beginning in 2012.

Figure 1
Illustration showing Spaceport America
Image courtesy of Ad Astra Rocket Company

BLUE ORIGIN SPACEPORT
(http://www.blueorigin.com/)

Blue Origin is a Seattle, Washington based firm that is develop a private Single Stage to Orbit system based on the original DC-X design. As part of its program, it has developed its own private spaceport in west Texas on a cattle ranch just north of the town of Van Horn. Currently the company is conducting its space launch test program at the site.

SPACEPORT SHEBOYGAN

(http://www.spaceportsheboygan.org/)

Spaceport Sheboygan is located near Sheboygan Wisconsin on the shore of Lake Michigan. A number of NASA sounding rockets have been launched from the site, and the proposed spaceport is being designed to serve the space educational needs of the Great Lakes region.

CONVERTED ORBITAL

Convert Orbital commercial spaceports generally have the fewest barriers to development since they are located at facilities that have already been launching satellites into orbit for many years. It should be noted that although these are designated as orbital commercial spaceports, they are also able to serve the suborbital market as well, which gives them a competitive advantage in attracting customers. The infrastructure required for launch operations, from launch pads and runways to tracking and payload integration facilities, is already in existence, and as a result, the conversion is largely administrative, with specific pads and facilities turned over to commercial spaceport for its use. As a result, expenses beyond administrative and operation costs are usually limited to modifications and upgrading of the launch pads and payload integration facilities, usually to meet the needs of specific customers.

SPACEPORT FLORIDA

(http://www.spaceportflorida.com/)

The oldest commercial spaceport in the United States is located on the Cape Canaveral Air Force Station, and uses launch pads originally built for U.S. Air Force needs. Created in 1989 to meet the demand for a commercial facility to launch payloads on existing systems like Delta and Atlas, it has developed into the premier spaceport in the United States. The majority of commercial launches to orbit from the United States are from Spaceport Florida.

CALIFORNIA SPACEPORT

(http://www.calspace.com/SSI/Welcome.html)

Like Spaceport Florida, California Spaceport is located at an existing facility for launching orbital vehicles, Vandenberg Air Force Base. It was created in 1990 to provide a launch site for Expendable Launch Systems like Atlas and Delta following the banning of commercial payloads on the Space Shuttle. It is currently the premier location in the United States for launching commercial satellites into polar and high inclination orbits.

MID-ATLANTIC REGIONAL SPACEPORT
(http://www.marsspaceport.com/)

Developed from NASA Wallops Island launch facility on the coast of Virginia, the Mid-Atlantic Regional Spaceport, nicknamed MARS due to its initials, was created to serve the needs of small and medium size launch vehicles. Since the NASA Wallops Island facility is home to NASA's suborbital research program, MARS is also a major player in the suborbital launch market.

NEW ORBITAL

New Orbital commercial spaceports have the biggest barriers to overcome. Because orbital launches require a large safety area under the launch track, orbital facilities are usually located on coastal land that is usually highly desirable for other uses. This usually brings them into conflict with other potential users, driving up the cost of land. Orbital launch facilities also require the most infrastructure, from launch pads to extensive launch tracking systems, and this also increases the cost of their development.

GUIANA SPACE CENTRE
(http://www.esa.int/esaMI/Launchers_Europe_s_Spaceport/)

The Guiana Space Centre is located near Kourou in French Guiana in South America. It was constructed in the late 1970's by the European Space Agency (ESA) specifically to serve the needs of the Ariane launch system. Since the Ariane launch family was designed to meet the needs of the commercial communications satellite industry it has a strong claim to being the first commercial spaceport, although it is still owned by the European Space Agency.

KODIAK LAUNCH COMPLEX
(http://www.akaerospace.com/)

The Kodiak Launch Complex is located on Kodiak Island in the Gulf of Alaska. It is owned and operated by the Alaska Aerospace Corporation, which is in turn owned by the state of Alaska. It was developed in the 1990s to serve the needs of the emerging satellite mobile phone market. Satellites for these mobile phone systems required high inclination and polar orbits, making a high latitude site like Kodiak Island ideal for launching them. However the collapse of the satellite mobile phone industry eliminated the original target market for the Kodiak Launch Complex. Since then it has only served a limited number of suborbital launches for the Department of Defense related to testing systems for missile defense.

COMMERCIAL SPACEPORTS AND ECONOMIC DEVELOPMENT

There are two major differences between commercial spaceports and traditional government and military spaceports. The first is that like seaports and airports, spaceports are seen as a tool to attract economic activity to a region, and thus the driving factor behind most commercial spaceports is the desire to stimulate local economic development. By contrast, traditional government launch facilities are focused on simply meeting the need for access to space for the programs that fund them.

The second major difference is funding. Traditional government spaceports are funded as part of the programs they serve, while commercial spaceports are expected to be self-funding from the revenue streams they create. The underlying problem is that the revenue models generally used for airports and seaports will not work for commercial spaceports (Matula and Mitry, 2002).

The revenue streams from commercial airports and seaports are a result of the high volume of traffic that moves through them on daily basis. The typical commercial airport will see many flights a day, with thousands or even millions of passengers a year, not to mention hundreds of thousands of pounds of airfreight. Similarly, active seaports see hundreds of thousand of tons of cargo in a typical year.

(*Editor's note*: See Chapter 16, *A Space Commercialization Model: Ocean Ports and Inter-Modal Transportation*.)

In contrast, a commercial spaceport is considered busy if there are more then a dozen launches a year.

These key differences have had a major impact on the commercial spaceport industry. Although commercial spaceports have been around for many years, few have achieved the desired level of economic success. Like the commercial launch industry, the commercial spaceport industry has left a trail of failed projects and failed ventures, and a key factor has been that the projected drivers of demand, often used in the business plans of commercial spaceports, and typically high volumes of satellite launches or high volumes of suborbital tourism, have failed to develop on the timelines expected by the developers of the spaceports.

Another factor is the relatively small size of the launch industry, with few firms or launch systems. The long lead times and high development costs for new systems, combined with a lack of demand, have created major barriers to profitability, in fact even breaking even is a challenge for commercial spaceports.

This is why Matula and Mitry (2002) have argued that a new business model is needed for commercial spaceports, a model designed around their economic assets and less dependent on demand for launch services.

We suggest that the key economic assets of a spaceport are:

- Large land area for use as a safety zone.
- Advanced telecommunication infrastructure.
- Storage and handling facilities for cryogenic gases and other chemicals used in launch operations.
- A runway capable of handling commercial jets and controlled airspace.
- A skilled technical workforce.
- Access to educational and research institutions.

The key to developing commercial spaceports is therefore to leverage these assets to attract complementary business activities, which then create additional revenue streams (Matula and Mitry, 2002). Examples include alternative energy research, explosives research, rocket engine research, security training, flight testing, ecotourism, biotech research, manufacturing, agricultural research, and educational activities.

All would have the potential to generate significant revenues in the near term while the launch traffic models develop as space commerce industry itself matures and demand increases. In addition, activities such as biotech, rocket engine development and education have the potential to add to the launch traffic for the facility. The key point that Matula and Mitry (2002) make is that developers of commercial spaceports must cast a wide net to attract complementary business and economic activities to drive the development of any spaceport facility.

SUMMARY

Commercial spaceports emerged with the demand for commercial launch services, with the first facilities appearing in the 1980s. Since then, many of commercial spaceports have been developed. The most successful have been facilities like Spaceport Florida and California Spaceport, which were based on existing launch infrastructure and demand. New start commercial spaceports have had a much more difficult challenge due both to higher costs of development and the need to create new demand. Although some, like the Guiana Space Centre and Spaceport America, have overcome these difficulties through the strong government support, ultimately the long term success of the commercial spaceport industry will be dependent on the creation of new demand for commercial launch services.

•••

THOMAS L. MATULA, PH.D.

Dr. Matula has a Bachelors degree from the New Mexico Institute of Mining and Technology (1983) and both an MBA degree (1984) and Ph.D. in Business Administration from New Mexico State University (1994). His dissertation focused on development of a model designed to identify factors that would influence public support for commercial spaceports. He since has published numerous articles on space policy and economic development strategies for the space industry. Dr. Matula has served on the American Society of Civil Engineer's Space Engineering and Construction Committee and its Subcommittee on Space Education Initiatives. His academic career includes over twenty years of teaching and research on business strategy and marketing.

REFERENCES

Johnson-Freese, J., and Handberg, R. (1997), *Space: The Dormant Frontier: Changing the Paradigm for the 21st century*, Praeger.

Cecil Field Spaceport (2010). "Cecil Field Spaceport", Retrieved from http://www.cecilfieldspaceport.com/ on July 31, 2010.

Gomez, Lou, Bill Gutman, Burton Lee, Bernie McCune. (2007). "History of Spaceport America", Retrieved from http://spacegrant.nmsu.edu/isps/presentation/history.pdf on July 31, 2010.

Matula, Thomas L., and Darryl J. Mitry (2000), "Public Attitudes Toward Overland Rocket Flight," in the *Proceedings of Space 2000: The 7th International Conference on Engineering, Construction, and Operations in Space*, Albuquerque, NM, Feb. 27 - March 2, 2000. 160-166

Matula, Thomas L and Darryl J. Mitry (2002), "Spaceports as Multi-use Industrial Facilities – A Marketing Approach," in the *Proceedings of Space 2002: The 8th International Conference on Engineering, Construction, and Operations in Space*, Albuquerque, NM, March 14-17, 2002. 135-141

NASA, (2010). "Ansari X Prize : A Brief History and Background." Retrieved from http://history.nasa.gov/x-prize.htm on July 31, 2010.

(Editor's note: Please see the following Chapter 18, *A New European Spaceport: Law and Politics in Spain* for a discussion of a European perspective, with a focus on the underlying legal issues.)

CHAPTER 18

A NEW EUROPEAN SPACEPORT
LAW AND POLITICS IN SPAIN

GARRETT SMITH, PRINCIPAL AUTHOR
FOUNDER & PRESIDENT, COSMICA SPACELINES

AND

DR. VASILIS ZERVOS, CONTRIBUTING AUTHOR
PROFESSOR OF ECONOMICS AND SPACE POLICY,
THE INTERNATIONAL SPACE UNIVERSITY

INTRODUCTION

The development and expansion of commercial human spaceflight requires legal and regulatory mechanisms to provide a robust framework under which commercial operators can fly paying participants. The term 'participant' is specifically chosen as opposed to 'customer,' as it is the term used in FAA regulation in order to distinguish them from 'passengers.' FAA documents state, *"Space flight participant means an individual, who is not crew, carried aboard a launch vehicle or reentry vehicle."*

Currently, only the United States has specific national legislation to govern this new activity with the mandate to promote the industry. Spain, to the contrary, has neither a national space law nor a clear legal framework under which commercial space launch services could be regulated. This chapter investigates under which legal basis a suborbital spaceflight operator might proceed to obtain a launch license to operate from the airport in Saragossa, Spain.

Following a brief technical overview of the Saragossa airport, this chapter analyzes the potential regulation of this industry and presents reasons why Spain, and not Europe, holds the competence to legislate in this domain.

The creation and development of a new high-technology industry needs a clear regulatory framework and market rules in order to develop. The legal framework necessary for suborbital flight operations will facilitate regional and industry-wide economic development for a dynamic and infant industry that commercializes technologies largely developed under public funding similar to recent examples such as the Internet and radio-navigation.

Three legal frameworks are suggested for how to operate a commercial spaceflight service under the supervision of the Spanish government. These are:

1. Operate under a yet to be defined national legislation;
2. Operate under a yet to be defined bi-lateral agreement between the U.S. and Spain which gives the FAA Office of Commercial Space Transportation jurisdiction over commercial space launches on Spanish territory; and
3. Operate under the existing Spanish aviation law with interpretations and additional rule making.

In addition to a literature review, I conducted semi-structured interviews with experts in the field to understand the feasibility of each approach, and to gain additional knowledge and breadth surrounding the topic. The results of the interviews were analyzed in concert with the literature to identify the strengths and weaknesses of each legal approach.

The role to be played by the autonomous community of Aragón, and other competent government organizations, is also briefly explored. The chapter concludes with a discussion of the probable means to implement the legal framework, and presents recommendations for additional research towards enabling commercial human suborbital spaceflights from Saragossa.

THE EMERGENCE OF SPACE COMMERCE

Space tourism is an emerging segment of the adventure travel industry aiming to open space flight to civilian participants as a commercial service. These new space launch services cater to a wealthy subset of the general public but are intended to eventually serve the middle class tourist when launch costs drop as a result of expected operational efficiencies and economies of scale. Many high technology entrepreneurial companies are moving to exploit this emerging market by developing rocket powered vehicles to take participants on an out-of-this-world experience to the edge of space. In addition to participants, there is also significant potential to fly research payloads on these same vehicles.

The development of security benefits and spin-offs are expected, following significant private investments under expectations of a promising and dynamic market. Quantifying direct and indirect benefits for such an infant industry is a challenging task at this stage, but it is clear that they may be significant. Market studies predict that by 2010 suborbital tourism could achieve between less than $700M and over $1.1B, depending on passenger 'fitness' requirements and restrictions.[35]

The commercialization of technologies with public heritage has created flourishing new industries and value added applications such as the Internet and radio-navigation, and health, safety and operations regulations of a clear and unambiguous nature have done much to benefit the development of the now global aviation industry. Hence, it is our view that market growth for the commercial space industry is to a significant degree dependent upon the capacity and willingness of states and nations to provide an unambiguous legal and regulatory framework for operations.

These are challenging times for economies and regulators alike, and novel arrangements are needed to assist novel industries and the diffusion and applications of innovation. Despite the challenges associated with estimates of the future market, it is clear that this is a strong indication of how important it is for the state to analyze and act in its role as the facilitator of sustainable economic development. A clearly defined and safe operations framework benefits the industry as a whole and is an obligation that the state must fulfill.

Indeed, space commerce is experiencing significant development in the United States and throughout the world, facilitated to various degrees by legal initiatives. In the United States the Federal Aviation Administration (FAA) holds the authority to regulate commercial spaceflight through the Office of Commercial Space Transportation (AST). The U.S. Congress, via The Commercial Space Launch Amendments Act of 2004, furthered the AST's regulatory authority with the specific intention *"to promote the development of the emerging commercial human spaceflight industry."*[1]

In addition to the U.S. federal government, various state and local governments are passing laws to provide tax relief, implement liability limitations, and develop spaceport facilities for the benefit of commercial launch providers and as incentives to locate in their jurisdiction. These governments intend to benefit from economic development through high paying aerospace jobs, tourism visits, and ancillary services. The principal commercial spaceports actively courting spaceflight operators include:

Spaceport America, New Mexico; the Mid-Atlantic Regional Spaceport, Virginia; Space Florida for Cape Canaveral and Jacksonville; Mojave Air & Space Port, California; and Spaceport Sweden, in Kiruna. Numerous other spaceports are conducting preliminary investigations to establish the economic and technical feasibility of their facilities.

Although seven European nations have enacted national space legislation,[2] these are not as comprehensive nor as pro commercial as the space legislation found in the U.S. European governments are taking a more cautious approach while awaiting the development of a viable participant spaceflight market. There are, however, positive developments designed to promote operations under existing legislation with appropriate interpretations. An example is Spaceport Sweden, in Kiruna, Sweden. While the Swedish government has no new regulations to allow commercial participant spaceflight, it has an established sounding rocket legislation under which Virgin Galactic hopes to operate suborbital participant spacecraft.[3] Another effort concerns the analysis by Marciacq et al. to *"accommodate sub-orbital spaceflights into the European Aviation Safety Agency (EASA) regulatory system, from the perspectives of aircraft certification and operation."*[4] The regulations would apply to all European states, and non-European EASA affiliated states, and would be enacted by the national airworthiness authorities.

Spain, the country of interest for this chapter, does not have a national space law or any other specific legislation regulating suborbital spaceflight. Suborbital spaceflight operators wishing to operate there would thus be assuming a higher business risk due to the legal uncertainty surrounding their activities. The purpose of this chapter is to identify the best legal approach through which to obtain regulatory approval to operate commercial human suborbital spaceflights from Spain, with a case study based on the Saragossa airport. This narrow scope will provide concrete recommendations, although the analysis and conclusions will generally apply to the entire nation with adaptations specific to the different regional autonomous communities.

The choice of Saragossa has been influenced by the fact that Saragossa has a sufficiently long runway to accommodate proposed suborbital vehicles, and is currently a Space Shuttle Transoceanic Abort Landing (TAL) site. It has also been chosen due to its proximity to the airport of Lleida-Alguaire, an alternative spaceport location, which was used as a case study by students attending the International Space University's Space Studies Program in Barcelona in summer 2008.[5] Spain has been chosen more globally as a departure point for space tourism due to its favorable Mediterranean weather, low density population in the arid interior, and its ranking as the 3rd country in the world for tourism.[6]

TECHNICAL SCOPE

It is important to stress that this chapter only addresses suborbital, and not orbital, spaceflight. Although suborbital spaceflights reach an extremely high altitude, only a small portion of the flight path enters the realm of outer space. In the ballistic flight phase, vehicles will reach an altitude above 100km, the unofficial boundary of outer space, for 30-90 seconds, or less than 10% of the total flight time. This altitude is much less than the minimum required orbital altitude of 200-300km where a satellite can remain in a stable orbit for an extended duration without significant atmospheric drag, yet higher than the approximately 20-30 km maximum operating altitude for high altitude balloons and special purpose aircraft.

As a further limitation of scope, this chapter only deals with those vehicles that depart from, and return to a runway in horizontal, aerodynamically supported flight. This has been chosen in order to enable a legal analysis based upon current aviation law and practice as an alternative to the analysis using space law. This dual analysis is not appropriate for the new generation of human-rated vertical launch and vertical landing vehicles, which remain squarely in the domain of rocketry and have few similarities with aircraft.

In order to clarify the scope, Table 1 on the following page summarizes numerous suborbital vehicle projects to clearly identify which fall within the argument of this chapter. The list emphasizes European initiatives, but is non-exhaustive and does not attempt to predict those which will be commercially and technically successful.

SARAGOSSA AIRPORT AS A SPACEPORT

Saragossa Airport is a commercial and military airport located on the northwestern outskirts of the city of Saragossa. The airport has a space legacy since its selection as a Space Shuttle TAL site, but the link to the space industry will likely be severed with the planned retirement of the Space Shuttle in 2011. Thus the opportunity presented by commercial human spaceflight should be seriously considered as a means to preserve and further develop the presence of the space industry in Aragón.

There are several issues that any spaceport must successfully manage in order to receive approval before use as a base of operations for spaceflights. These include but are not limited to:

1. Runway length
2. Noise
3. Propellant handling
4. Flight corridor
5. Air traffic integration

Suborbital Vehicle	Company	Country	Architecture (see note below)	Within Scope
Six-Pack (Fishbowl Cabin)	Armadillo Aerospace	United States	Single-Stage, Vertical Launch & Rocket Landing	No
VSH	Astronaut Club Européen	France	Two-Stage, Air Launch & Jet Landing	Yes
New Shepard	Blue Origin	United States	Single-Stage, Vertical Launch & Rocket Landing	No
Ascender	Bristol Spaceplanes	United Kingdom	Single-Stage Bi-Modal, Horizontal Take-Off & Jet Landing	Yes
TBN	EADS Astrium	France / Germany	Single-Stage Bi-Modal, Horizontal Take-Off & Jet Landing	Yes
Thunderstar	Starchaser Industries	United Kingdom	Two-Stage, Vertical Launch & Parachute Landing	No
Project Enterprise	Talis Enterprise	Switz / Germany	Single-Stage, Horizontal Launch & Glide Landing	Yes
SpaceShipTwo / WhiteKnightTwo	Virgin Galactic / Scaled Composites	United States	Two-Stage, Air Launch & Glide Landing	Yes
Lynx (Mark I & Mark II)	Xcor	United States	Single-Stage, Horizontal Launch & Glide Landing	Yes

Table 1
Suborbital Vehicle Architectures and Scoping for Legal Analysis
Architecture Note: 'Launch' means under rocket power. 'Take-Off' means under
jet engine power.

It is assumed, for the reasons shown below, that these issues are manageable at Saragossa airport even though a thorough technical analysis has not been performed. Further studies, in the context of a potential spaceport license application, will be necessary to mitigate the risk associated with these technical issues.

RUNWAY LENGTH

The Saragossa airport has sufficient infrastructure to permit suborbital spaceflights with minimal additional development. The WhiteKnightTwo, SpaceShipTwo launch stack needs a runway approximately 2600m long for take-off and landing[7]. The Xcor Lynx space plane needs 2400m[8]. The author is unaware of the needs for the other vehicles but assumes that runways of 2500-3000m are sufficient for the majority. Saragossa has two runways, 12R/30L at 3718m long and 12L/30R at 3000m long, permitting take-off and landing from either, which allows additional operational flexibility. The wind conditions have not been evaluated, but could play a role in the selection of Saragossa since the airport does not have a crosswind runway. In the event of adverse wind conditions, the vehicles may not be able to fly on schedule, leading to unsatisfied participants.

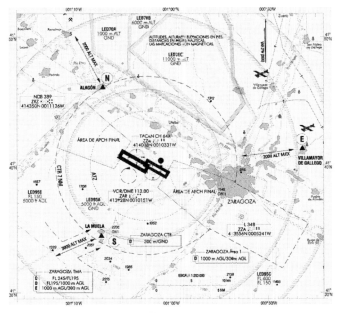

Figure 1
Saragossa Airport Visual Approach Chart (Source: AENA)

NOISE

Noise is also of concern, but should be manageable since the airport is home to fighter jets and to large commercial aircraft. The author assumes that rocket vehicle noise will not be more severe than existing commercial and military aircraft movements and will not adversely impact the surrounding population. Noise from launches could generate concern, however, if the flight frequency increases as the market develops.

PROPELLANT HANDLING

An industrial safety concern includes explosive propellant combinations, and perhaps hazardous or toxic substances, which may be necessary to provide the performance for a space vehicle to reach and maneuver in outer space. Storing these substances is thus necessary within the perimeter of the airport. Appropriate storage and handling procedures must be implemented to limit the consequences in case of an accident. Fortunately, the airport has sufficient terrain and a suitable location is likely to be identified. If the military stores explosive substances, in the form of bombs and other munitions, on-site isolation from the existing depots is also necessary.

FLIGHT CORRIDOR

The FAA has identified flight corridor requirements in the licensing procedures for launch sites[9] to ensure that the uninvolved public remains safe in the case of a launch accident. Similar provisions will be necessary in Spain. At Saragossa, as illustrated in Figure 1, the area to the northwest of the airport has very little habitation and development. However to the east and southeast there are industrial areas and residential buildings. The spaceport application will need to demonstrate through a compelling risk analysis that there is minimal potential for loss of life in these areas in case of an accident. On the positive side, once away from the city of Saragossa, the population density is low due to the arid environment, and thus the risk of endangering the population is reduced.

AIR TRAFFIC INTEGRATION

Integration of commercial spaceflights with the existing air traffic will depend greatly on the type of vehicle. Air launched or bi-modal vehicles will operate as traditional aircraft until they achieve an altitude above commercial air traffic. Vehicles launched from the ground however will have a much greater climb rate and will need the equivalent of a vertical corridor to safely pass. An analysis by Marciacq et al. supports the feasibility of integration when it states that *"the basic procedures to cater for special needs (e.g., air shows, large military exercises, climb of weather observation balloons, etc.) are already in place today and could easily be adapted to the needs of [sub-orbital aeroplanes].*[10]*"*

Assuming these technical issues could be resolved, the economic development potential of a spaceport is significant. Business plans and economic impact reports exist for Spaceport America, in New Mexico, and Spaceport Florida which show that commercial spaceflight could have a very positive impact on the local economy.[36, 37]

The key reasons are impact on local employment and value added activities created by the necessary investments. It must be noted though, that they tend to focus more on potential benefits at large, stopping short of developing a more balanced cost-benefit analysis that would also consider assessment of risks and other 'hidden costs' inherent in such type of investments, or opportunity costs. A similar analysis would be necessary for Saragossa to identify the drivers, comparative economic potential, and also assess the strategic competitive environment and its implications on the results.

LEGAL CONTEXT

A very complete analysis of the legal environment in Europe, with an aviation law viewpoint, is presented by Marciacq et. al.[4] with an emphasis on demonstrating the EASA competence for regulation of sub-orbital aeroplanes. This paper is recommended reading to better understand the legal issues surrounding suborbital spaceflight and to fully grasp the various arguments and rationales presented herein. Marciacq et al. are also well aware of the legal limitations of the approach, as they clearly identify that EASA does not have competence for the portion of the activity occurring in outer space.

Another thorough discussion, this time from a space law viewpoint, is presented by Sánchez Aranzamendi[2], a Resident Fellow at the European Space Policy Institute evaluates the national space legislation in European and other countries, and explores the impact of this legislation on the commercial space sector and makes policy recommendations for Europe.

The challenge lies in determining which legal framework, or multiple frameworks, applies, since suborbital flights operate in both the aviation and space environments. There are two schools of thought on this issue: spatial and functional. In the spatial approach, a suborbital flight remains an aviation activity until it passes the boundary from the atmosphere into space. Since this boundary is not absolutely defined, either technically or legally, the spatial approach does not definitively resolve the problem. Practically, the spatial approach would oblige an operator to conform to both aviation and space regulations, which could double the regulatory burden.

The functional approach qualifies the activity based upon the vehicle purpose or capability. The purpose of suborbital vehicles is clearly to give the participant a space experience by entering outer space, thus leading to the likely conclusion that it is a space activity. The U.S. has used the functional approach by providing a clear definition of the vehicles regulated by the AST based upon performance criteria. According to the AST, *"Suborbital rocket means a vehicle, rocket-propelled in whole or in part, intended for flight on a suborbital trajectory, and the thrust of which is greater than its lift for the majority of the rocket-powered portion of its ascent."*[11] This definition simplifies the issue by ensuring there is only one set of applicable regulations independent of the flight phase or altitude.

Spain, due to the lack of relevant legislation and with no historical precedence, has yet to confront the issue.

ARGUMENTS FOR SPANISH COMPETENCE

Although a pan-European approach would be preferred, as it would allow operators a consistent regulatory environment in all European Union Member States, arguments are presented in this section to demonstrate Spanish competence to regulate suborbital spaceflights.

According to the text of the European regulation establishing EASA, *"It would not be appropriate to subject all aircraft to common rules, in particular aircraft that are of simple design or operate mainly on a local basis, and those that are home-built or particularly rare or only exist in a small number; such aircraft should therefore remain under the regulatory control of the Member States, without any obligation under this Regulation on other Member States to recognize such national arrangements[12]."* With clear guidelines for aircraft that "operate mainly on a local basis," are 'particularly rare,' or 'only exist in small number,' we see that all three conditions will be met by suborbital airplanes until such time as the industry has grown to the point of providing point-to-point suborbital flights, or until demand rises dramatically to justify production of fleets of multiple spacecraft by any one manufacturer. Thus from an aviation perspective, Spanish airworthiness authorities are the competent regulatory body for the immediate future.

If we approach the issue from a space law perspective, one needs to consider international obligations. The Outer Space Treaty[14] requires signatory states, including Spain, to provide national supervision of their space activities, which also justifies the argument of national sovereignty for regulating space activities.

Regarding international law, one must also review the treaties delegating powers to the supranational European Union. In reviewing the Treaty on the Functioning of the European Union[34,] nowhere does it appear that the competence for suborbital spaceflight should be delegated to Europe; thus it must remain with the member state. Some may argue that the European Union and the Member States share the competence for commercial spaceflight. But, according to Sánchez Aranzamendi, Article 189 of the TFEU *"seems to exclude even the widest interpretation of the concept of harmonization,"[2]* thus leaving little doubt that Spain is competent to legislate on the matter.

In view of the above arguments, it is suggested that Spain clearly holds competence to regulate suborbital flight operations regardless of whether it is considered an aviation or space activity.

SPANISH REGULATORY REGIMES

Having determined that Spain is sufficiently competent to supervise
suborbital spaceflight, we will now consider three possible means that it
could pursue for regulating commercial spaceflight.

1. Implementation of a new national commercial space law
    specifically addressing suborbital rocket vehicles and assigning
    regulatory competence to a Spanish agency.
2. Establishment of a space cooperation treaty with the U.S. to
    operate under FAA regulations when controlled and operated by
    an American citizen or entity
3. Operation under existing aviation law with special conditions and
    equivalent safety findings, similar to the EASA approach, but
    addressed only at the national level.

1. NEW NATIONAL COMMERCIAL SPACE LAW

A new national law is sufficient to regulate commercial spaceflights
and to provide a clear definition for this activity. This law could be
modeled upon another country's law, or could be created anew by
considering the key aspects and interests of the Spanish air and space
industries.

Key reasons for implementing a national space law, according to
Riemann,[13] are to:

1. Meet international obligations for supervision of space activities
    under the Outer Space Treaty[14] Article VI.
2. Manage the risk of international liability under the Liability
    Convention.[15]
3. Ensure registration of space objects in accordance with the
    Registration Convention.[16]
4. Promote safety, and
5. Promote commercial development.

In order to reduce risk for suborbital operators, the Spanish
government must clarify which ministry is competent to provide the
approval and oversight. Obligations under the OST could be met through
the need of a suborbital operator to apply for flight approval through the
appropriate branch under the Ministry of Transport (Fomento), the Ministry
of Defense, or the Ministry of Foreign Affairs and Cooperation. A yet to
be defined application process plus a flight plan filing would provide the
appropriate opportunity for the required national supervision.

Although suborbital spaceflights will initially occur only within or
above the sovereign territory of Spain, foreign registered aircraft also
transit its territory, so any aerial collision between a Spanish suborbital
spacecraft and a foreign aircraft might give rise to the objective liability
regime under the Liability Convention. The government of Spain needs to

frame how they will share the liability with private operators in the case of such an accident. This is done in other nations, such as the U.S. and France,[17] by requiring a minimum level of third party liability insurance coverage, with the State assuming the responsibility above a certain limit. Spanish national responsibilities under the Registration Convention are already covered by Royal Decree 279/1995,[18] which establishes the Spanish Registry of Objects Launched into Outer Space. This will be useful to govern future space activities with orbital applications, but is not necessary for suborbital flights.[19]

Finally, it is in the interest of the Spanish government to promote safety of third parties within the Spanish territory, and to promote the commercial development of the industry. Both of these objectives can be assured by delegating the competence for regulation to a state agency. This would likely be the State Agency for Aviation Security (AESA) but could also include, to various degrees, input or oversight from the General Directorate for Civil Aviation (DGAC), the Spanish Airports and Air Navigation (AENA) and the National Institute for Aerospace Technology (INTA).

Two means are likely to be used to propose a new Spanish national law.[20] The first is via a bill prepared by the government, approved by the council of ministers and submitted to the congress and senate for approval. This method would likely be used if an operator interested in launching from Spain contacted the Ministry of Transport. The second method is via the legislative assembly of an autonomous community sending a request to the national government to adopt a bill, or by sending to the Board of Congress a proposal of law. The government of Aragón could pursue this second method in the event that they decided to promote commercial spaceflights from Saragossa as a strategic economic interest to the region.

2. SPACE COOPERATION TREATY BETWEEN SPAIN AND THE UNITED STATES

An innovative way to manage the regulation of commercial suborbital spaceflights would be to utilize the existing FAA framework and extend this framework via treaty to apply to operations from Spain. This learn-as-you-go approach would give Spain the necessary legal framework to immediately benefit from the commercial development potential while instituting the necessary regulations and laws. The DGAC would likely have final approval for any FAA issued launch license, which would presumably apply only to operations under the control of a U.S. citizen. This arrangement would allow Virgin Galactic and other U.S. operators to fly from Saragossa under familiar regulations.

A provision in U.S. national law[21] requires U.S. citizens to apply for a launch license in a foreign state and also requires foreign entities in which a U.S. citizen has a controlling interest to apply for an FAA launch license.

A *"controlling interest means ownership of an amount of equity in such entity sufficient to direct management of the entity or to void transactions entered into by management."*[22] Hence, the two conditions for operating from Saragossa under U.S. law are:

1. Existence of a treaty in force between the U.S. and Spain covering commercial spaceflight, and
2. Operation of commercial spaceflights by an American controlled entity.

The challenging aspect of this approach is to find an existing treaty or to negotiate a new treaty that will specifically cover commercial spaceflights. There are several existing space cooperation treaties in force. The Agreement on Space Cooperation signed at Madrid on 11 July 1991 and entered into force on 9 May 1994[23] concerns landing of the Space Shuttle in the event of a TAL event at the air bases of Moron, Rota, or Saragossa and at the airport of Las Palmas de Gran Canaria. This treaty, however, is not suited to supervise commercial spaceflight, as article 1 of the treaty clearly limits it to emergency situations.

The remaining provisions of this treaty could potentially be used because the term 'space shuttle' refers to any manned space vehicle as defined in the text. In the event that both U.S. and Spanish authorities wanted to cooperate on a suborbital spaceflight demonstration and were willing to overlook the non-emergency nature of the spaceflights, the notification procedure could be used to implement the remaining provisions of the treaty. This demonstration would have to be under the responsibility of the U.S. government in order to comply with the terms of the agreement. An operator fulfilling a research contract to perform high altitude atmospheric or microgravity studies would be an example, but again, this arrangement would be overly burdensome for regular commercial spaceflights.

The other treaty in force, Memorandum of Understanding between the Instituto Nacional de Técnica Aeroespacial (Representing the Comisión Nacional de Investigación del Espacio) and the U.S. National Aeronautics and Space Administration, entered into force 14 April 1966[24] concerns launching of sounding rockets for high altitude experiments. At first glance, this treaty could cover a demonstration flight, potentially within the framework of NASA's Commercial Reusable Suborbital Research program, since there is a provision for joint experiments using *"additional equipment as may be necessary in each case,"* but only for scientific purposes as stated in the treaty and here again under the supervision of NASA and INTA.

From a civil aviation perspective, the Nat-I-1363 Memorandum of Agreement between The United States of America Department of Transportation Federal Aviation Administration and the Government of

Spain Ministry of Transport, Tourism and Communications Subsecretariat of Civil Aviation, entered into force 22 July 1982[25] could be a starting point for a further agreement for collaboration on commercial space transportation. Article VI of this treaty provides for an amendment procedure *"to provide for expansion of requirements and continuation of the program."* It would thus suffice for the DGAC to negotiate with the FAA for an annex expanding the scope to include commercial space transportation and then having both States ratify the annex as a new treaty document.

Based upon the authors' understanding of the competence granted to the DGAC[26], this organization has the authority to negotiate a treaty with the FAA (or other foreign aviation authorities) to promote cooperation related to civil aviation, which would of course require approval in accordance with the process defined in the Spanish constitution[27] and as practiced by the U.S. government[28]. It is unclear under which process this treaty would be approved by Spain, as it could be by:

1. Organic law;
2. Parliamentary authorization; or
3. Signature by the government.

In the U.S., the treaty could enter into force after executive agreement or senate approval. If the need were recognized to elaborate a comprehensive treaty arrangement, Spain and the U.S. should build on the past tradition of aviation and space cooperation. The major changes in space cooperation to enable commercial spaceflight would entail a change in implementing agencies. While current agreements are primarily between NASA and INTA, future commercial space agreements will probably involve the FAA and the DGAC. This change in implementing agency is an additional reason that existing space cooperation treaties are not likely to work from a practical standpoint.

3. EXISTING AVIATION LAW WITH SPECIAL CONDITIONS AND EQUIVALENT SAFETY FINDINGS

The final method to examine for governing commercial human spaceflight is to utilize the existing regulatory framework for aviation activities. As there is no internationally binding altitude limit for the boundary between sovereign air space and the domain of outer space, one could argue that space tourism occurs within the sovereign airspace of a State. The popularly accepted value for this boundary at or around 100km has no value in customary international law and is thus not enforceable. Spain could reasonably claim sovereignty of its airspace up to an altitude of approximately 120-200km, or make a domestic legal distinction for aviation activities, without extending its airspace to the lowest orbits currently in use. Australia, in 2002, made a practical clarification to separate air and space activities by amending its domestic space law to apply to space activities that occur above 100km altitude, although without intending to set an international standard for this boundary.[29]

Qualifying the anticipated suborbital flight altitudes as sovereign airspace would thus allow application of aviation law and regulations. Since aviation activities are currently regulated by the AESA and the DGAC, these would be the appropriate organizations to approach for licensing approval. In order to qualify under the existing technical requirements, special conditions and equivalent safety findings would need to be granted by the national authority in the same way as described by Marciacq et al. for EASA approval.[30]

Should the DGAC or the AESA wish to further solidify their jurisdiction over commercial spaceflights, the government could issue new law through regulation (reglamento),[27] which could take the form of a decree (decreto) by the Council of Ministers, an order (orden) by the Minister of Transport, or an instruction (instruccion) or an order of regulation (circulares) from the DGAC or the AESA. This action would be a regulatory rather than a legislative action.

ADDITIONAL LEGAL ISSUES FOR CONSIDERATION

There are additional legal issues for a commercial spaceflight operator to consider that go beyond the scope of a simple licensing authorization. These include but are not limited to regional, national and supranational laws impacting participant liability, third party liability, contract law, advertising law, insurance law, environment law, private law, competition law, and consumer law.

In Spain, there are up to four competent jurisdictions regulating a space tourism operator. These are the municipality, the autonomous region, the State (Spain) and Europe. Each of these levels has competence in some aspect of the space tourism operation.

Spain is based upon a federal system with the autonomous regions keeping legal competence for many government affairs. The national level will only be responsible for the issues such as air and space law, while the autonomous regions will be responsible for tourism, contract and liability issues, and municipalities may be responsible for local issues.

An example of an additional legal issue at the national level is spaceport licensing. While this chapter has investigated licensing of a launch operator, the airport of Saragossa will most certainly also need to obtain an authorization to operate as a spaceport. This of course depends upon the legal regime under which space tourism activities fall. If it remains under the existing aviation law, then a simple extension may be all that is necessary to allow operation of rocket powered vehicles from the airport. If the treaty option is retained, then the airport will need to file for a spaceport license with the FAA, but this may only be allowed if the spaceport itself is under the control of an American citizen or entity, which is not the case in Saragossa. Thus a treaty might leave the spaceport licensing in limbo, which could prevent an operator from obtaining a permit or license. The creation of a privately operated air and spaceport could be envisaged under the current Spanish laws and could lead to spaceport licensing approval under the treaty if this facility is majority owned by American interests. The private airport of Ciudad Real was developed through private investments, and a private spaceport could also be envisaged.

Since the autonomous communities retain competence for most legal issues, they will be heavily involved in approving the legislation that will encourage development of this industry. This is directly comparable to the actions by states such as Virginia and Florida in the U.S. that limit participant liability and provide tax exemptions through 'zero-g, zero tax' laws. Virginia[31] exempts *"any gain recognized from the sale of launch services to spaceflight participants ... or launch services intended to provide individuals the training or experience of a launch, without performing an actual launch."*

Concerning participant liability, Virginia enacted the Space Flight Liability and Immunity Act,[32] to provide a clear and legally binding informed consent statement for participants. Both actions provide direct financial incentives to operate from Virginia by reducing the business risk assumed by a spaceflight operator. The autonomous region of Aragón could encourage spaceflight operators to operate from Saragossa by passing similar legislation. Other initiatives such as spaceport development subsidies and local tax districts for infrastructure improvements would go a long ways towards convincing operators to expand in or relocate to Saragossa.

Finally, some European laws would also apply. One example of this is the EC Package Holidays Council Directive 90/314/EEC as discussed by O'Brien.[33] In this case a space tourism operator could be subject to additional regulations if it were considered part of a travel package grouped with transportation, accommodation or other tourist services. Contractual agreements with the package organizer or appropriate corporate structuring could limit the responsibility of the spaceflight operator.

METHODOLOGY FOR EVALUATING THE LEGAL STRATEGIES

At the outset of the research for this chapter, the authors were unfamiliar with the applicable Spanish and international laws, and the chosen research approach was to conduct a series of semi-structured interviews with experts familiar with the legal and political environment in Spain and knowledgeable in the fields of space law and aviation law.

Interviews were conducted via a two step process. First contact was made by email for five of the seven interviewees, and followed up with a telephone interview. The other two interviewees were introduced to the questions and interviewed in person. One interview did not sufficiently address any of the prepared questions and thus has been eliminated from analysis.

The choice of a semi-structured interview process was to enable investigation of the specific questions while allowing the discussion to expand into other areas relevant to the subject of space tourism in Spain.

ANALYSIS AND SYNTHESIS OF THE INTERVIEWEE RESPONSES

The combination of interviews and literature research has made it possible to reach qualitative recommendations, but naturally it has not yielded any absolute legal strategies for obtaining authorization to conduct suborbital spaceflights from Saragossa airport. Table 2 shows the perceived strengths and weaknesses of each approach, followed by a summary that proposes a final recommendation.

EASA

Although the EASA framework was not specifically addressed during the interviews, the author felt it was essential to evaluate this approach. Oversight of commercial spaceflight by EASA would be an appropriate strategy, but first the activity would need to be legally defined as an aviation activity rather than a space activity, and included in the competence transferred to Europe. Since this classification is not yet resolved, it cannot be certain that EASA has competence, and further clarification of EASA's role, mandate and involvement will need to be provided within the framework of this newly emerging industry.

NEW NATIONAL LAW

A new national Spanish law specifically addressing the issue of human commercial spaceflight is a guaranteed method for adequately regulating the activity. Passage of a new national space law through the Spanish parliament would be sufficient to govern the activity, although the process might be time-consuming and could distract from the immediate issue, which is for an operator to be granted a launch license.

TREATY WITH THE U.S.

Establishment of a treaty with the U.S. was a very controversial subject during the interviews. The treaty process is seen as an imperialistic approach due to the envisioned application of FAA regulations on Spanish territory. The treaty would need to be negotiated under the supervision of the Ministry of Foreign Affairs and Cooperation and would directly involve the DGAC and the FAA, and its practicality depends directly on the quality of the relationship between the U.S. and Spain and on their willingness to work together. The lead time for this approach depends upon the process used for ratification, as approval through the legislative branches would be longer than an expedited executive agreement.

EXISTING AVIATION LAW

The use of existing aviation law is the most likely and most direct approach to obtaining launch authorization. The competence for this activity rests with the Ministry of Transport and is exercised by the DGAC and AESA. AENA should also be considered as a service provider due to its management of the Saragossa airport. INTA may have some competence since suborbital flights are also a space activity. Even if it were possible to initiate the activity under existing aviation law, additional interpretations, rules and regulations would need to be created.

SYNTHESIS

A clear result from the literature review and the interviews is that the DGAC should be the first organization approached to request regulatory action to support suborbital spaceflight launch authorizations. In addition to having relevant, though not comprehensive competences, the organization also has the authority to create additional regulations to supervise and manage suborbital flight operations. The DGAC will be able to coordinate internationally with the EASA and the FAA, and domestically with the AESA, the INTA and other Spanish Ministries to identify the most appropriate of the four alternative approaches to follow, or create a new approach.

A few key points about the political situation have also been noted. Firstly, political support will require demonstration of a clear economic interest in developing commercial spaceflight in Spain. As with the spaceports in the U.S., an economic impact statement and business plan will need to be created for the spaceport authority based in Saragossa, which must show that investments by the government will deliver a return in the form of local employment and future tax revenues.

The autonomous regional governments will need to show proactive efforts in order to attract operators. In addition to supporting the national regulatory activities through their political network, they will need to enact regional laws. This means passing legislation providing financial incentives to commercial operators to reduce liability and taxes, and codifying informed consent laws to specify what it means to be informed so that any operator would be less likely to be unfairly pursued, in case of an accident, by a participant who had previously agreed to assume the inherent risk involved in spaceflight. Additional investments in spaceport infrastructure at a regional level will also be needed to reduce the startup costs for an operator.

As the industry expands and commercial activity develops, a Spanish national law will be required to clarify the competence and to structure the legal environment. This law will clearly define who is responsible for approving flights within the Spanish government and how the responsibilities overlap with EASA, FAA or within the national ministries. This law is also necessary to address the issue of a combined air and space activity. Further reflection will be required to determine the most appropriate means of implementing the national law whether it comes from a rule-making effort within the Ministry of Transport or from a legislative effort.

EASA [European Aviation Safety Agency]	
Strengths	*Weaknesses*
• Provides clear legal basis for certification and operations of winged suborbital vehicles • Pan-European approach will facilitate expansion to other European States • Certification demonstrates compliance to necessary safety standards thereby reassuring participants and public • National aviation authorities could provide national supervision to comply with space treaty obligations	• Type certification may be costly and time consuming for vehicle manufacturers • Excludes vertical launch and vertical landing vehicles from the regulatory framework • Lack of defined liability sharing between operator, EASA and the State
New Spanish National Law	
Strengths	*Weaknesses*
• Clear legal basis for operations of any suborbital vehicle • Identification of national authority for approval of operations in outer space • Clarification of liability sharing between operator and State	• Time consuming legislative process may slow development of industry • Legislative process opens the discussion to a larger audience of interested individuals which may oppose the specific needs of suborbital operators

Table 2
Comparison of Legal Approaches to Obtain Suborbital Spaceflight Launch Authorization

Treaty with the U.S.	
Strengths	*Weaknesses*
• Existing FAA regulations can be utilized for timely licensing approval • Familiarity of launch operators with licensing procedure will reduce risk and lower cost of entry into new market • Potential extension to existing space and aviation cooperation treaties • Can be negotiated directly between the DGAC (Dirección General de Aviación Civil (General Directorate for Civil Aviation)) and the FAA	• May apply only to U.S. controlled operators • Unlikely to be able to use an existing treaty as the sole legal basis • Ratification of treaties can occur several years after the signature of the treaty • Spaceport licensing might not be provided for in agreement

Existing Aviation Law	
Strengths	*Weaknesses*
• No legislative changes required to the existing law • AESA, DGAC and Ministry of Transport can rely on existing aviation experience • Most rapid approach to spur commercial development of the industry	• Incomplete regulation burdens operator with additional risk • DGAC/AESA may decide they are not the competent authority • New interpretations and regulations to be created by the DGAC/AESA

Table 2, Continued
Comparison of Legal Approaches to Obtain Suborbital Spaceflight Launch Authorization

CONCLUSIONS AND RECOMMENDATIONS

There is certainly a need to structure the legal framework in Spain to permit suborbital spaceflight, but the alternatives for achieving that objective examined here show promise that a solution can be readily found. The current legal environment provides a starting point for further law making and regulation. Aviation law is well developed in Spain and can be extended through both executive and legislative action to provide a robust and straightforward process that permits licensing of commercial spaceflight operators while ensuring the safety of the public and participants.

Identification of the competent authority, most likely the DGAC, is the first step that is necessary to begin driving forward the discussion within the Spanish government. The authority must conduct an investigative dialog with the national, European and international counterparts in order to make an informed decision on the approach that will ensure success of the commercial spaceflight industry during the initial development but also during future expansion towards point-to-point suborbital travel or orbital transportation.

In order to bring space tourism to the airport of Saragossa, several further studies will need to be conducted. Most importantly, a thorough economic evaluation must be prepared to determine whether potential investments in infrastructure are justified. The study should identify benefits from participant spending, tourist visits to witness the spaceflights, high technology employment and any additional economic activity in support of the industry. A technical feasibility study will also be necessary. This study should evaluate whether concerns such as the safety, air traffic integration, environmental, noise and infrastructure can be satisfactorily resolved at the airport. If not, an alternative location would need to be found using an existing runway or by constructing a dedicated facility.

Spanish legal experts should conduct further research to expand upon the law making approaches presented herein. Familiarity with aviation and space law will be crucial to investigate the subtleties of the existing law and to construct a legal approach that considers the political environment. It is recommended that the DGAC should lead this further research so that the conclusions can be acted upon within the directorate.

Finally, political support by local and regional politicians should not be underestimated. The regions where spaceports are created will be the ones to benefit most from the resulting prestige and economic development. These politicians will be able to use their existing networks to bring enthusiastic and visionary leaders to such a challenging project ensuring success at all levels of government. At Saragossa airport, Aragón has a vested interest in keeping a link to the space industry once the Space Shuttle is retired. The opportunity of commercial spaceflight should be actively pursued to maintain and further develop this connection to outer space.

•••

Note: This chapter is based largely on Garrett Smith's prior unpublished work, under the guidance of Dr. Vasilis Zervos, in the context of the Masters of Science in Space Management program, Class of 2009, at the International Space University, Strasbourg, France. Both authors have further contributed to improve upon the original work.

ABBREVIATIONS AND ACRONYMS

AENA	Aeropuertos Españoles y Navegación Aérea (Spanish Airports and Air Navigation)
AESA	Agencia Estatal de Seguridad Aérea (State Agency for Aviation Security)
AST	Associate Administrator for Commercial Space Transportation, Office of Commercial Space Transportation, Federal Aviation Administration
COPUOS	United Nations Committee On Peaceful Uses of Outer Space
COTS	Commercial Orbital Transportation System
DGAC	Dirección General de Aviación Civil (General Directorate for Civil Aviation)
EADS	European Aeronautic Defense and Space Company
EASA	European Aviation Safety Agency
ECSL	European Center for Space Law
ESA	European Space Agency
FAA	Federal Aviation Administration
INTA	Instituto Nacional de Técnica Aeroespacial (National Institute for Aerospace Technology)
ISU	International Space University
NASA	National Aeronautics and Space Administration
OST	Outer Space Treaty
TAL	Transoceanic Abort Landing (site for NASA's Space Shuttle during emergency conditions)
TBN	Temporary name for EADS suborbital space tourism project
TFEU	Treaty on the Functioning of the European Union
VSH	Véhicule Suborbital Habité (Human Suborbital Vehicle proposed by the European Astronaut Club)

ACKNOWLEDGMENTS

The authors would like to thank all of the interviewees for their time spent during the interviews. This project could not have happened without their participation. As the interviews were conducted with an understanding of confidentiality, the authors have chosen to maintain the anonymity of the interviewees.

In addition, the following individuals contributed to this research by providing guidance, research material or review:

Timi Aganaba, Teaching Associate at ISU

Tanja Masson-Zwaan, Deputy Director, Int. Institute of Air and Space Law.

GARRETT SMITH

 Garrett Smith is the Founder & President of Cosmica Spacelines, a start-up based in Toulouse, France, which is addressing commercial space opportunities in Europe. Since 2005, he has developed extensive insight into the space tourism industry through research, networking and as an investor in Benson Space Company. He is also the founder and past president of the Space Tourism Working Group within the Toulouse-Midi-Pyrénées branch of the 3AF (Aeronautics and Astronautics Association of France).

As an aircraft cabin interiors expert, Garrett applies a customer centric approach to all aspects of his work. He managed the Airbus A380 cabin customization, working directly with the management at major airlines such as Air France, Lufthansa, Singapore Airlines, and Virgin Atlantic Airways Ltd.

Garrett has an expert understanding of aerospace vehicles, developed in multiple positions within Airbus and Boeing. He has worked in technical engineering positions and managed both people and projects since beginning his career in 1997.

Garrett holds a Master of Science in Space Management from the International Space University and a Bachelor of Science in Aerospace Engineering from Boston University. He pursued post-graduate engineering courses at the University of Idaho.

When not working on aerospace projects, Garrett greatly enjoys spending time with his family. He can often be found in the Great Outdoors mountain biking, whitewater kayaking, snowboarding or hiking.

VASILIS ZERVOS

Vasilis Zervos is currently resident faculty at the International Space University (ISU), in Strasbourg, France since 2006, where he holds the position of associate professor in Economics and Policy and ISU's Executive MBA program leader. He is actively involved in teaching areas such as Industrial Economics and Economics of Procurement, Strategic Partnerships, Strategic Trade and various other Business and Economics courses applied to the space industry and economy. Formerly, he has taught topics in the area of Economics and Business at the University of York from 1996 to 1999 and Nottingham University Business School from 1999 to 2007.

His research interests are in the area of Industrial Economics, primarily focused on Space, Aerospace and Defense Industries, as well as, Economics of Innovation and Foreign Direct Investment, where he has published numerous peer-reviewed papers and book-chapters. He has supervised numerous MBA, MSc and MA dissertations in various Business and Economics areas, has participated in European-funded projects in financing and space industrial assessments and actively referees for economics and innovation journals. He holds a DPhil in Economics (European Space Industry) from the University of York, an MSc in Economics (Macroeconomic Policy and the European Central Bank) from the University of Birmingham and BAs in Economics from the American College of Greece (Athens) and University of Thessaly (Volos-Greece).

REFERENCES

1. The Commercial Space Launch Amendments Act of 2004, Public Law 108–492 - Dec. 23, 2004
2. Sánchez Aranzamendi M., ESPI Report 21, September 2009, accessed on 18/05/2010 from http://www.espi.or.at/images/stories/dokumente/studies/espi%20report%2021.pdf
3. Coppinger R., Spaceport Sweden could class SpaceShipTwo as sounding rocket, July 10, 2008, accessed 18/05/2010 from http://www.flightglobal.com/blogs/hyperbola/2008/07/spaceport-sweden.html
4. Marciacq et al., Accommodating Sub-Orbital Flights into the EASA Regulatory System, Presented at the 3rd IAASS Conference, 21-23 October 2008 Rome, Italy, accessed 18/05/2010 from http://www.congrex.nl/08a11/presentations/day1_S09/S09_05_Marciacq.p

df
5. International Space University, Space Studies Program Student Report, FuturIST: Future Infrastructure for Space Transportation, August 2008
6. World Tourism Rankings, accessed on 18/05/2010 from http://en.wikipedia.org/wiki/World_Tourism_Rankings based upon data from the UNTWO World Tourism Barometer.
7. David Mackay, Test Pilot, Virgin Galactic, personal conversation 12 March 2008, Blagnac, France
8. Hobby Space, accessed 18/05/2010 from http://www.hobbyspace.com/nucleus/index.php?itemid=5841
9. Title 14 CFR, Part 420.23.d
10. Marciacq et al., in section 6.1 (p. 13)
11. Title 14 CFR, Part 401.5
12. Regulation (EC) No 216/2006 of 20 February 2008 on common rules in the field of civil aviation and establishing a European Aviation Safety Agency, and repealing Council Directive 91/670/EEC, Regulation (EC) No 1592/2002 and Directive 2004/36/EC (Official Journal 79 L 1, 19.3.2008)
13. Riemann F., lecture notes, National Space Legislation - Regulatory Rationale and Approach, 12 December 2008, International Space University
14. Treaty on Principles governing the activities of States in the exploration and use of outer space, including the moon and other celestial bodies, 1967 (610 UNTS 205).
15. Convention on International Liability for damage caused by space objects 1972 (961 UNTS 187)
16. Convention on Registration of Objects launched into Outer Space, 1976 (1023 UNTS 15)
17. Aganaba T., lecture notes, Third Party Liability – A Public Law Perspective, 30 January 2009, International Space University
18. Royal Decree 278/1995, dated 24th February 1995, Official Gazette n° 53, 9th March 1995, accessed 18/05/2010 from http://www.oosa.unvienna.org/pdf/spacelaw/national/royal_decree_278_1 995E.pdf
19. Marciacq et al., in section 5.2 (p. 12)
20. Cabrero O., section 3.2.2 Legislative Process from Features - A Guide to the Spanish Legal System, 15 January 2002, accessed 18/05/2010 from http://www.llrx.com/features/spain.htm
21. Title 14 CFR, Part 413.3
22. Title 14 CFR, Part 401.5
23. Agreement on Space Cooperation, 11 July 1991 (1785 UNTS 393)
24. Agreement providing for a project in Spain to measure winds and temp. at high altitudes and for continuing other cooperative space research projects (17 UST 493; TIAS 5992; 586 UNTS 79)
25. Nat-I-1363 Memorandum of Agreement between The United States of America Department of Transportation Federal Aviation Administration

and the Government of Spain Ministry of Transport, Tourism and
Communications Subsecretariat of Civil Aviation, entered into force 22
July 1982, (TIAS 10547)

26. Article 10.1.g, Sec. I. Page 42716, Official Gazette n° 119, 15th May 2010
accessed 18/05/2010 from
http://www.fomento.es/NR/rdonlyres/609D1F05-AB64-4C00-A29F-
D891077D9C4E/73598/BOEA20107797.pdf

27. Cabrero O., section 3.2.1 Types of Law from Features - A Guide to the
Spanish Legal System, 15 January 2002, accessed 18/05/2010 from
http://www.llrx.com/features/spain.htm

28. COPUOS, National legislation and practice relating to definition and
delimitation of outer space, A/AC.105/865/Add.1, 20 March 2006

29. Berkey I., United States Treaty Research, lecture notes for Advanced
Legal Research Class, February 15 & 17, 2010., section Treaties vs.
'Executive Agreements', accessed 18/05/2010 from
https://www.law.northwestern.edu/library/coursesupport/instructionalservi
ces/instructionalmaterials/treaties/

30. Marciacq et al., in section 3.2 (p. 6)

31. Virginia Senate bill 286, approved 2 March, 2008

32. Virginia House bill 3148, approved 4 April, 2007

33. O'Brien L., Duties and Liabilities of Space Tourist Operators, 2007, IAC-
07-E6.2.11

34. Consolidated Version of the Treaty on the Functioning of the European
Union, accessed 18/05/2010 from http://eur-
lex.europa.eu/LexUriServ/LexUriServ.do?uri=OJ:C:2008:115:0047:0199:
EN:PDF

35. "Suborbital Space Tourism Demand Revisited," 2006, Futron Corporation,
accessed 18/05/2010:
http://www.futron.com/upload/wysiwyg/Resources/Whitepapers/Suborbita
l_Space_Tourism_Revisited_0806.pdf

36. "Space Florida, Spaceport Master Plan 2010, 2009," Reynolds, Smith and
Hill inc. accessed 18/05/2010
fromhttp://www.spaceflorida.gov/images/stories/docs/Space%20Florida%
20-%20Spaceport%20Master%20Plan%202010.pdf

37. [Futron 2005] New Mexico Commercial Spaceport Economic Impact
Study, 2005, Futron Corporation, accessed 18/05/2010:
http://www.spaceportamerica.com/images/pdf/Futron_Report.pdf

CHAPTER 19

JURISDICTIONAL CHOICE AND ITS IMPACT UPON SPACE BUSINESSES
QUESTIONS AND CONSIDERATIONS

CHRISTOPHER STOTT
CHAIRMAN AND CHIEF EXECUTIVE OFFICER, MANSAT LIMITED

When you first consider starting a business, you might think about your product, prices, the market, potential customers, financing, and perhaps even the location of your factory, plant or offices, shipping and logistics routes. But do you also first think about your choice of jurisdiction? This can be one of the most important decisions a business can make yet it is little discussed and often quite misunderstood.

Every business, no matter if it is addressing the space market or any terrestrial market can consider the choices with a set of common decision-making parameters. However, as important as this issue is for most companies, it is especially important for space companies, as they must endeavor to put aside the intrinsic fascinations and distractions of the 'space' element of their ventures to focus on the business basics. Whether their business is satellite communications, remote sensing, navigational, mining asteroids, or sending tourists into space, they must first remember that their 'space' business is still first and foremost a business, and that as a business it must function as such irrespective of its 'space' cache.

It is also important to note that businesses involved in space activities must address an additional set of considerations concerning the regulation of space activities in their decision-making. Companies working in differing fields of the space marketplace face such considerations in different ways, but all to a greater or lesser degree, and always with issues of fundamental importance to the eventual success of the business at stake. These regulatory issues differ in their application from nation to nation, from jurisdiction to jurisdiction; so, the choice of business jurisdiction can dictate their application and thus the success or failure of your enterprise.

Imagine golden threads of regulation, revenue, and reputation tying a space company to its jurisdiction, which we would also identify as its place of incorporation, and these in turn effect profitability and the cost of business. Those who work to understand these considerations are most often successful, while those who do not almost always fail.

So, from the perspective of an executive or entrepreneur in the space industry how do you choose the optimal jurisdiction in which to establish your new company? What additional parameters are there that the space venture must consider, along side those in keeping with the normal course of business? This chapter cannot answer these questions for your specific enterprise, but it will instead seek to highlight certain key issues that every business should consider. By raising the issue of jurisdictional choice and its many considerations, the author is seeking to give decision makers the parameters through which to make an informed decision that is correct for their specific business needs.

The location considerations for space businesses can be summed up in three basic categories: those affecting regulation, reputation, and revenue.

TO SET THE SCENE
THE IMPORTANCE OF JURISDICTIONAL CHOICE FOR A COMPANY IN ANY MARKET

When you create your company or joint venture you must first choose a nation or state within a nation, a 'jurisdiction,' in which to legally form or 'incorporate' your venture. By so doing you give your new company life and legal personality under the law, and hence the ability to trade and to conduct business. To use an analogy, think of your company, your body corporate, as a person with a legal personality: what nationality do you want them to have or, more importantly, do you need them to have to succeed in business? In essence, what business passport will they be carrying and working under? When making this choice of jurisdiction you will thus be choosing the specific laws, regulations, and taxes that will apply to your business, and so of course you must strive to find the best a jurisdiction to match your particular business needs. Again the importance of this cannot be over stressed.

The question of jurisdiction, which refers to whose law (juris) speaks (diction), is a crucial decision, as these laws and regulations will apply to your business and will in turn drive the cost of your doing business, the ability to conduct business legally or not and under what sort of regulatory constraints, and will significantly impact your capacity to win business or not, to trade with customers and partners, to find finance and skilled labor, and a host of other issues in that nation or the countries of your customers. It is akin to choosing not just where to build your company, but upon what legal and cost foundation to build your company: build a strong foundation and you will have the route to success; build a poor foundation and no matter how successful your company may or may not be in the future, it will always struggle with inherent and predetermined constraints and costs that will more than likely lead to failure.

Hence, every aspect of a nation's laws, business regulations, and taxes must be assessed before making an informed decision.

You have the whole world to choose from in today's globalized economy, the choice of almost any nation, or sometimes even the states within a nation. Prior preparation and investigation of the choices is of paramount importance. Speak with legal and accounting experts. Take advice from your bankers. Take advice from your prospective customers too. Examine what others in your industry are doing: are they succeeding or failing in this regard? Why? What can you do differently to give your venture an advantage or a level playing field?

At present, according to the US State Department, there are 194 nations and 61 associated territories to choose from[1] in which to incorporate your venture. On the most macro of levels, incorporating your company in France versus China, purely for example, brings with it not just differences in language and access to regional markets, but differences also in terms of legal regimes, business regulations, taxation rates, intellectual property regimes, employment law, union law, vacation and national holiday entitlement, all of which in turn affects productivity, the ability to raise capital by taking a company to market, social provisions, and reputational issues in terms of visibility with your customer base.

General questions that can come from such considerations range across issues including these:

1. Can I hire the right people for my venture?
2. Can I attract the right capital and investors?
3. Can I manufacture and ship my products?
4. Can I protect my intellectual property?

---

[1] Source: US State Department.

5. Can I be price-competitive in the market under this tax regime?
6. Will I have an advantage over my competition or will they have an advantage working from a different jurisdiction than mine?
7. Are my customers able to buy from me if I trade from this nation?
8. Is it to my advantage to trade from here as a company?
9. What will it cost me to trade from this jurisdiction? What regulatory fees and taxes will I be paying? Are there hidden costs?

To the greatest business consideration of all: Will I make money for my shareholders and am I protecting their interests? An investor's money is a sacred trust and must be guarded at all times.

So, will you be more successful operating from one nation or jurisdiction versus another? The answer is quite often, Yes.

It is possible to break down the myriad of factors to consider into the three basic parameters of revenue, regulation, and reputation: How will incorporating here affect my revenues, the regulations under which I will conduct my business, and ultimately my reputation with my customers, investors, financiers, and international regulators?

While the businessperson is considering this choice, many jurisdictions on the world stage are at the same time competing for their business, working to attract new economic activity to their nation or state, and this can also affect the choice.

Many jurisdictions compete for economic development opportunities by offering a tailored regulatory and legal home for incorporation, providing policies and practices of competitive taxation, rule of law, specialized business courts, political stability, membership in internationally-recognized regulatory regimes that are backed by access to markets via networks of treaties, such as World Trade Organization (W.T.O.) membership for example. Jurisdictions such as the Isle of Man and Singapore compete on along side the United Kingdom, Switzerland, and the United States.

It is worth noting too, that within nations, states also compete for national and international business, and soon they will compete to be the terrestrial home for space-based enterprises. In the United States, the states of Delaware, Mississippi, and Nevada compete avidly for companies, while the economic powerhouses of California and New York offer less attractive tax regimes for businesses (or, from some perspectives, downright unattractive tax regimes) and tend to be more restrictive of their operations.

This is also the case with the Cantons of Switzerland or the Crown Dependencies and Overseas Territories of the British Isles.

The choice of incorporating your business in one state versus another may bring more subtle differences in profitability and shareholder value as well as differences in product liability, state income taxes, and even in the cost and distribution of capital and thus access to finance.

The Unique Factors for Space Companies

For space companies, the decision is still harder and has further reaching consequences than for those of a non-space business. Additional considerations amplify the parameters of regulation, reputation, and revenue, which in turn greatly narrow the choice of jurisdictions specifically driven by the company's choice of markets and customers.

The space marketplace is quite diverse in terms of the services and products that it offers, and the customer base it seeks to serve.

Activities in space are conducted under international treaties whose application and regulation differs in every nation. These regulatory considerations also differ in regards to each sector of the space industry.

For example, Satellite Operators must secure orbital spectrum via their national regulators through the orbital filing process at the International Telecommunications Union (ITU). They must also secure landing rights to legally offer services in the markets they serve from orbit.

Launch Providers must balance launch site location, liability and regulation with access to international markets. Please see the example of the Sea Launch Company discussed later in this chapter.

Remote Sensing Providers faces 'shutter control' on their imagery and its sale. For example, US companies must work under the Land Remote Sensing Policy Act of 1992 and Presidential Decision Directive-23 (PDD-23) that governs the export of remote sensing equipment, satellites, and services.

Those in manufacturing and in insurance face issues focused specifically on Export Control laws and regulations through to Government subsidies to competitors. This affects the ability to use specific technology in the construction of spacecraft through to the purchase and use of specific launch vehicles. For Insurance organizations it also affects and limits their ability to address technical concerns of specific systems and subsystems in space construction, launch, and operations. A space specific element of programmatic, cost, and market risk is introduced defined by the actions of those under a specific regulatory system.

For those that commercially operate satellites, spacecraft, or spaceships in orbit (which we refer to 'space assets'), regulation is often the first key parameter and question: do the necessary laws or regulations exist in this jurisdiction that will allow me to legally conduct my business in space? Specifically, is the jurisdiction a signatory to the larger set of international treaties and agreements that will allow me to conduct my space business?

While many nations have signed the United Nations Outer Space Treaty, Agreements and Conventions, far fewer have enacted national regulatory and licensing regimes to allow commercial activities in space. The first enquiry within a jurisdiction should be with a regulator or legal advisor to ascertain whether or not that nation has signed the required UN Space Treaties and in turn has in place the necessary legal and regulatory structure required under the Treaties to license and regulate your activities? Will they have to write new laws to allow you to conduct your space business? How long will this take and how much will it cost? Can you wait or take this risk?

According to the United Nations Office of Outer Space Affairs (UNOOSA) as of the time of going to print, only 20 of the 194 nations in the world currently have the necessary national space law in place to allow the launch and operation of a space object[2]. However, 33 nations and two International Non Governmental Organizations (INGOs) have filed spacecraft orbital ephemeris data with the Secretary General of the United Nations as required under the terms of the Outer Space Treaty and the Registration Convention.[3] Whereas 64 nations are on record at the ITU in Geneva holding active orbital spectrum filings for geostationary and other satellites.[4]

These figures, and the inclusion of the two INGOs in the UN Registry, is instructive as the reader should note that while many nations have activities in space via their own government agencies this does not equate to their having in place the necessary legislation to either allow

[2] Namely: Argentina, Australia, Belgium Brazil, Canada, Chile, China, France, Germany, Japan, Netherlands, Norway, Republic of Korea, Russian Federation, South Africa, Spain, Sweden, United Kingdom (including Isle of Man, Gibraltar, Cayman, Bermuda), Ukraine, and the United States of America. Source United Nations Office of Outer Space Affairs: http://www.oosa.unvienna.org/oosaddb/browse_all_js.jsp?dims=COUNTRY_CODE|DATE

[3] Namely Algeria, Argentina, Australia, Brazil, Canada, China, Chile, Czech Republic, Egypt, France, Germany, Greece, India, Israel, Italy, Japan, Kazakhstan, Luxembourg, Malaysia, Mexico, Nigeria, Pakistan, Republic of Korea, Russian Federation, Spain, Sweden, Thailand, Turkey, Ukraine, United Arab Emirates, United Kingdom, United States, Venezuela, European Space Agency (ESA), and the European Organization for the Exploitation of Meteorological Satellites (EUMETSAT). Source United Nations Office of Outer Space Affairs: http://www.oosa.unvienna.org/oosa/SORegister/index.html

[4] ITU Radiocommunication Bureau (BR) 2009 Annual Space Report to STS-10 on the use of the geostationary-satellite orbit (GSO) and other orbits to the Technical Sub-Committee of the United Nations Committee on the Peaceful Uses if Outer Space (COPUOUS). Source ITU: http://www.itu.int/ITU-R/space/snl/report/

commercial space activities via companies registered in that nation or such legislation in place to protect the legal rights of those companies.

Further of note is that some nations will allow commercial space activities, but choose to do so via their jurisdictions under national regulations as opposed to working from national law, for example Luxembourg and Papua New Guinea.

Without the necessary space regulation and licensing in place, a business cannot legally be conducted from that jurisdiction. Regulation is key, in turn affecting even the ability to earn revenues, thus affecting the business' reputation.

THINK OF SPACECRAFT LIKE SHIPS ON THE HIGH SEAS

The law applies to the activities of those operating space assets much as it does to those operating ships on the high seas, yet with the added focus of national security interests, space law, and international treaties binding their actions.

A ship is registered or 'flagged' to a particular nation, and the laws of that nation apply to the activities on that ship wherever it sails. Similarly for space assets, but with the additional issues that the jurisdiction of registration or 'flag' are impacted by the terms of the United Nations Outer Space Treaty and its associated Conventions, and by the International Telecommunications Union (ITU) as well. Both require the jurisdiction or state of registration to bear international liability[5] for the actions and activities of that object.[6] It does not matter where your assets are physically located in space; they are still legally and financially tied to their jurisdiction of registration. One hundred percent of the money 'spent in space' is in reality spent on the ground.

Inasmuch as one hundred percent of the money spent and earned in space is currently accounted, transferred, and useful only here on Earth, the 'golden threads' of regulation, reputation, and revenue attach each asset back to its terrestrial state of registration. When there is genuine space-based space commerce the situation will change, but for the time being, until the first bar opens for business in Low Earth Orbit and you wish to spend your space bucks on a rare single malt, space commerce and Earth commerce will always be consummated with some sort of exchange back on Earth And hence regulated, taxed, and controlled back on Earth.

The golden threads of commerce attach every object in space to its jurisdiction of incorporation, ownership, and hence regulation, taxes, costs, risk, and reputation.

---

[5] Article VII, United Nations Outer Space Treaty.
[6] Article VIII, United Nations Outer Space Treaty.

To launch and operate any asset in space, a series of international treaties, agreements, and licensing requirements must be met under national and international law, most notably the UN Outer Space Treaty, the Liability Convention, and the Registration Convention, and thus all national space laws are derived from a nation's ascension to the UN space treaties.

The connection of regulation and governmental liability to the activities of space assets and the companies that own them is unique in the business world and worthy of brief discussion as an example. Under the UN Outer Space Treaty and the Liability Convention and Registration Convention, all states signatory to the agreements are internationally liable without limit for the actions of their agencies and 'non governmental entities' (companies) in space and are required to regulate said activities. This does not happen with the aviation or shipping or even with the international arms industry. It only happens with the space industry.

Hence this national liability always translates into costs for the business in question: regulatory costs, licensing, spectrum fees, corporate taxation, and even in some cases specific taxes upon the cost of insuring the launch and operation of space assets, usually named as Insurance Premium Tax.

Liability consideration is not a factor that affects any other businesses or markets, its significance may not occur to the budding space entrepreneur until too late, and at a late stage prior to launch it can add literal millions to the cost of any project.

Hence, there is a 'golden thread' of regulation attached to each and every satellite and space craft, wherever in space it may be, that ties it back to the jurisdiction that licensed its launch and operation. For space companies, these golden threads embody all that is unique concerning regulation, reputation, and revenue. As per international treaties and associated national laws, the assets upon which a space business earns its revenues are subject to the laws and regulations from their jurisdiction of incorporation.

So again, the first consideration in choosing the jurisdiction in which to incorporate a space venture that launches or operates space assets is a series of simple questions focused around the three 'R's of revenue, regulation, and reputation.

Has this jurisdiction signed the relevant UN Space Treaties and Conventions? (Without ascension to the Treaties and Conventions the business will not be able to operate in space from that jurisdiction.)

Does this jurisdiction have in place national space law and regulations that will allow me to license the launch and operation of my space assets? (Without a national licensing regime and associated regulations in place, space operations will not be feasible.)

Have others successfully navigated this regulatory process before me in this jurisdiction, or will I be the first to do so? This element of regulatory risk in itself can be a crucial element of cost and potential delay to any venture.

Are there any space specific taxes or regulatory fees? (Often there are. For example, Insurance Premium Taxes, Launch Permits, Operations Permits, Export Control Licenses, Spectrum Usage License and Fees, etc.)

Are there other hidden costs? Requirements to place infrastructure in the jurisdiction (such as satellite control centers and associated employees), conditions on your use of the jurisdiction (such as access to your satellite footprint and coverage of the jurisdiction), hard or soft requirements to use national telecommunications providers or specific providers of spacecraft or launch services are some examples of questions that will need to be addressed.

THE EXAMPLE OF THE SEA LAUNCH COMPANY

An example of jurisdictional confusion is a key element of the story of the Sea Launch Company, and it had a direct impact upon the company and its profitability. Formed in 1995, Sea Launch developed its launch business based from an ocean-going platform. Its founding partners were Boeing, Kvaerner, Energia and Yuzhnoye. The partners chose to incorporate and headquarter the company in the Cayman Islands. The Caymans are British Overseas Territories and thus under British jurisdiction.

At that time the Cayman Islands did not have a licensing regime in place for the launch and operation of a space object, and had not passed into law the UK Outer Space Act. As such, it did not have the ability to issue a launch and operations license for the launch of Sea Launch's Zenit Rockets.

Sadly this only came to light only in late 1998, when after many years of work and investment the Boeing Company, on behalf of the Sea Launch Company, was denied a launch license from the US Government on the basis that Sea Launch was in fact a British company given that its stated headquarters were in the Cayman Islands and hence a British Overseas Territory. This triggered a series of events where Sea Launch was fined by the US State Department for Export Control (ITAR) violations, and US Customs and Excise impounded its launch vehicles.

In turn, the Sea Launch Company then sought to belatedly seek a launch license from the British Government, and according to the UN Outer Space Treaty a special agreement was reached between the UK and US Governments, through the intervention of the UN Secretary General, to allow the first test launch to proceed. This all required many months to resolve, at a significant cost to the Sea Launch Company, its customers, most especially its first customers, and its investors.

Eventually the Cayman Islands retroactively passed the UK Outer Space Act, but by then Sea Launch had endured the cost and disruption to move its headquarters, and hence its jurisdiction for licensing, to Long Beach in California, from which it then obtained US launch licenses. The US State Department publicly fined the Sea Launch Company $10M[7] for its breeches of the US Export Control legislation and regulations. Ironically, its launch vehicles were also briefly impounded at US Customs during the transfer of operations to California for having improper documentation.

INTERNATIONAL TELECOMMUNICATIONS UNION AND ACCESS TO ORBITAL SPECTRUM

A close second and equally important consideration in regard to ascension to international agreements and treaties is membership of that jurisdiction to the International Telecommunications Union (ITU).

Why? To operate in any object in Earth Orbit or beyond you must have access to the necessary radio frequencies with which to do so. You need to control your spacecraft and to use it for data collection, broadcasting, etc. Yet radio spectrum is a limited natural resource. The use of these frequencies, this resource, is decided by the ITU, a UN body, working in coordination with national governments.

The British Spectrum Regulator, OFCOM, in the United Kingdom puts it far more succinctly[8]:

> "Satellite services are important for business, social and scientific applications, offering a unique ability to deliver communications to many parts of the world not adequately served by other means. In order to operate a satellite network, it is necessary to obtain access to spectrum for the uplink (Earth to satellite) as well as the return path from the satellite to stations in the service area. It is also necessary to secure an orbital position in space for the satellite. A satellite's orbital position will influence the area of the globe that it can serve."

Spectrum and orbital positions are valuable and limited resources. Radio spectrum is in high demand as new mobile and broadband technologies develop and it becomes increasingly challenging to find frequencies to deliver new communications services. Orbital positions from which satellites can serve commercially attractive markets, such as the USA and Europe, are very popular and are becoming congested. If the

---

[7] US State Department: http://fpc.state.gov/documents/organization/17353.pdf
[8] OFCOM 2007, Procedures for the Management of Satellite Filings. Section One, section 1,1 to 1.3, page 1.

spectrum and orbital positions are not used efficiently, competition, innovation and growth in communications services will be hindered to the detriment of consumers and businesses.

"Spectrum and orbital positions have to be managed and planned in order to avoid interference and ensure that adequate separations are maintained between satellites. The international nature of satellite services means that coordination takes place within a framework of international rules administered by the International Telecommunication Union (ITU). . ."

To put it as simply as possible, no frequencies means no business.

To gain access and use of orbital frequencies companies must apply to their national governments, i.e. via the jurisdiction of their incorporation, to request the frequencies they need. In turn their national government then manages this application to the ITU. Every nation handles this in a different manner and with different costs. The one constant is that every nation charges for the use of spectrum, bar none, either through direct fees or indirect taxes.

All nations are ITU members. In fact there are more members of the ITU[9], a United Nations organization, than there are members of the United Nations[10] itself.

However, of key consideration for the space business, is that only a sub set of ITU member states submit orbital frequency filings,[11] and an even smaller sub set of these jurisdictions will allow their companies to make their orbital frequency applications (filings) to the ITU via their national regulators to obtain the necessary orbital frequencies from with which to conduct their business.

For example, in order to conduct a satellite communications business, a series of orbital frequencies are needed in various radio frequency bands, normally the C, Ku, Ka, or S bands, with assigned coverage of 'foot prints' over the target markets. To obtain these frequencies with the necessary antenna patterns or coverage of the Earth below (the satellite's 'footprint'),

---

[9] As of December 2009, the ITU has 191 Member states. Source, ITU: http://www.itu.int/members/index.html

[10] As of December 2009, the UN has 190 member nations. Source: http://www.un.org/en/members/index.shtml

[11] As of December 2009, 64 member states had active satellite spectrum filings at the ITU. ITU Radiocommunication Bureau (BR) 2009 Annual Space Report to STS-10 on the use of the geostationary-satellite orbit (GSO) and other orbits to the Technical Sub-Committee of the United Nations Committee on the Peaceful Uses if Outer Space (COPUOUS). Source ITU: http://www.itu.int/ITU-R/space/snl/report/

orbital spectrum applications are needed. These are commonly known as orbital filings. In addition, for the operation of any spacecraft, Tracking, Telemetry, and Command (TT&C) frequencies are needed to manage and to legally control the space assets themselves.

For remote sensing satellites, frequencies are needed for both data transmission and TT&C, while for space tourism, Earth-to-Space communications and TT&C are needed.

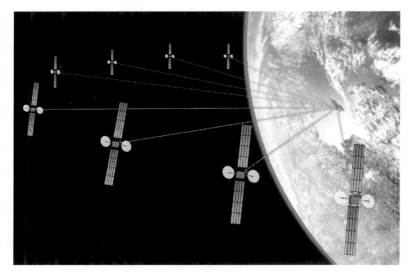

Figure 1
The golden threads of revenue, regulation, and reputation
tying the space business to its jurisdiction.

NO FREQUENCIES, NO FINANCING

The investor community has learned very clearly that confirmation of radio frequency licenses is a key pre-requisite to receiving financial backing for any space venture.

Hence, the entrepreneur must determine if the proposed home jurisdiction is a member of the ITU, has a track record in making orbital filings, and further will they allow your company to apply for the radio frequencies that you need and are the laws and regulations of that jurisdiction in place to allow you to legally use the frequencies?

IN SHORT

1. Can they make orbital filings?
2. Will they allow you to use them?

3. Is there a regulatory path in place to allow you to use them with some certainty under the rule of law?
4. Have others successfully used this process before you?
5. Not forgetting, and most importantly, how much will they charge you to use them? They will charge you.

Every nation charges companies for the use of radio spectrum, whether for cell phones or for satellites. This is administrated either through direct charges, licensing, or through indirect taxation, and there is absolutely no escaping this particular 'cost of doing business' in any jurisdiction.

The charges are always there, but sometimes they're cleverly hidden. For example, prior to allocating orbital spectrum, some nations will require that your satellite provide service coverage to a percentage of their nation, for example Brazil. Others can choose to require you to give them commercial access to a given number of the transponders on your satellite, for example Papua New Guinea, which they will then sell into your marketplace in competition with you.

Still others still require you to give their national post and telecom companies' preferential terms, or require you to use their national or regional satellite manufacturers or launch providers, or require that you build a Satellite Control Center in their jurisdiction, for example Gibraltar.

Many employ an Insurance Premium Tax charged upon the value of the insurance premium your company is paying to insure the cost of the launch and operations of the company's space assets, for example here the United Kingdom (note: not the Isle of Man), Luxembourg, Australia, and Papua New Guinea amongst others. Such charges can be in the many millions of Dollars.

Some auction your own spectrum to you, or simply charge a fee to use the spectrum. This, of course, is all in addition to any national corporate taxes, employment or social charter charges you are paying.

Often space companies find that the cost of doing business in one jurisdiction can lead to double if not triple forms of taxation on their business, revenue, exports or imports, and always upon their use of spectrum, so ascertaining the true and real cost of working in the space business and in choosing most practical and cost effective jurisdiction is not a trivial matter.

Satellite operators also have to consider the impact of international treaties outside of the immediate jurisdiction in which they operate. Membership in the World Trade Organization (W.T.O.) ensures market access for their services.

Having an orbital filing with the necessary orbital position, associated frequencies, and market footprint is only half of the regulatory equation: market access to land and use their signals to offer their service is also a consideration. An orbital filing might be available from a jurisdiction, but can it be used in the larger regulatory context?

The question of Landing Rights and Market access is also important. Permission must also be granted by the nations to which you are broadcasting or offering services to legally allow use of your signals on the ground and in your markets.

Many developing nations have sought to attract space businesses by offering access to their orbital filings and spectrum. Yet you would do well to consider other questions of regulation and reputational risk.

HOW POLITICALLY STABLE IS THE NATION IN QUESTION?

1. Can customers and employees visit that nation or work from that jurisdiction?
2. Is my investment safe from capricious changes of government or local laws and regulations?
3. What is the jurisdictions' reputation for international business and trade?
4. Will working from this jurisdiction help or hurt my reputation as a business?

This question of reputational risk also carries with it a monetary cost in terms of business risk in association of clients and customers. Political Risk Insurance (PRI) is increasingly required by financiers prior to potentially funding a venture, so you must determine if that insurance is available in the jurisdiction you propose to be based in, and at what comparative rate. Unfortunately, this cost of protecting an investment from political and reputational risk is often a consideration that arises only later on, after a jurisdiction has already been chosen and work has begun, and it's too late to change.

Reputational consideration is also reflected in the impact of United States Export Control laws and regulations. If your jurisdiction is a 'proscribed' nation for US Export Control, this will at minimum add cost, delay, and risk to your procurement of space assets, and at worst will deny you access to the assets thus preventing you entirely from doing business and all. The Sea Launch story is an excellent example of this.

Export Control also impacts your ability to sell from or into a nation, or to be part of a larger space procurement or program. Hence, US Export Controls have greatly impacted the ability of US Satellite Manufacturers and Launch Service providers to sell outside the US. In turn, those wishing to procure and purchase goods from US companies or to sell products or services to US companies from outside of the United States have also seen Export Control greatly reduce, if not entirely stop their ability to sell to US companies. For example, at present, US companies are prohibited from doing business with Chinese companies in regards to space technologies and services and hence are unable to purchase satellite launches on China's Long March launch vehicles. Correspondingly the Chinese firm, the China Great Wall Industry Corporation, is unable to sell launch services to US companies.

If your markets were focused on US space companies or customers, then given existing US Export Control laws it would behoove you to utilize a US jurisdiction for that part of your business.

Another political consideration for those working in the space business, and who are specifically selling to US or European Government buyers, is the impact of 'Buy American,' or European Space Agency's policy of 'Juste Retour.' Through these policies many nations and national blocks will restrict what their tax funds can be spent on in regards to space procurements, technology and services. Hence, to win this business your company must be incorporated in their jurisdiction, again generating jobs and also taxes (i.e. expenses) there for you.

If you are seeking to be a prime contractor or a sub contractor there are also considerations. In the United States you can choose to incorporate in a state that is pro business, or pro space program, or one that is not. Furthermore, all major US Government contracts set aside a portion of the procurement budget for minority, Native American, or Women-owned businesses, and you may also have an advantage if you choose to incorporate in a state that is in a HUB Zone for the Small Business Administration.

THE US HUBZONE EXAMPLE

For the new or small space company seeking specific contracts from US Government Agencies being incorporated in a HUBZone can prove an advantage in the bidding process.[12] For example incorporating your company in a HUBZone in the United States can bring two basic levels of benefit for space businesses. The first relates directly to US Government contracts, while the second involves specialized assistance from the US Government. US Government contracts can be set-aside for HUBZone competition when the contracting officer has a reasonable expectation that at least two qualified HUBZone small business concerns will submit offers and that the contract will be awarded at a fair market price. HUBZone contracts can also be awarded as 'sole source', i.e. without competitive bidding, under certain conditions. In terms of special assistance, eligible HUBZone firms can also qualify for higher US Small Business Administration (SBA) guaranteed surety bonds on construction and service contract bids. A full 3% of all Federal Contracts can be set aside for those

---

[12] http://www.sba.gov/hubzone/

companies bidding from HUBZones.[13] Further, companies working from similar 'Federal Empowerment Zones and Enterprise Communities' (EZ/EC) can also benefit from employer tax credits, tax-free facility bonds, and investment tax deductions.[14]

To be successful in winning business in Japan, on the other hand, experience suggests that it is recommended to partner with a well-established aerospace company, and take their advice as to which prefecture in which to incorporate your venture. For contracts with the European Space Agency seek a Member State that is working under its 'Juste Retour' or just return ratio. Many nations are oversubscribed on their ratios, like France, Germany, and Britain, so if you choose a nation that is currently undersubscribed in its ratio you will likely benefit. For example, many of the larger European Aerospace Contractors, such as EADS and its space group, EADS Astrium, hold multiple operating units and product lines in different European jurisdictions, and indeed in different jurisdictions throughout the world for just these reasons.

Tax Dollars, Pounds, and Euros are predominantly spent via contracts on companies in the nations that grant them. Yet, beware additional taxation and social costs that can affect your business from working in these jurisdictions.

If you are working in the field of Remote Sensing, your business is the provision of data services. The core of service is focused around the

---

[13] Source: Reperi LLC. The HUBZone Act requires that 3% of all federal contracting dollars go to HUBZones. HUBZone designation is determined by the Federal Census and is based upon unemployment compared to state and federal data. Unlike other preferences, HUBZone does not hue to race and gender metrics, but is instead based legitimately on economics data. Areas that are generally affluent are therefore not HUBZones, while areas that are economically challenged are HUBZones. 35% of the workforce of a firm claiming HUBZone status must live and work in the HUBZone. HUBZone certification is a federal certification by SBA. Federal government set-aside contracts, under recent GAO rulings, receive the first preference when a contracting officer wishes to make an SB set aside, and therefore comes before any other designated program. A contracting officer can also determine that only one HUBZone is qualified and "sole source" procurements to a HUBZone, although under current law most contracting officers will compete between two qualified HUBZones. For instance, the Army SMDC in Huntsville frequently uses the sole sourcing option. All federally designated Indian Lands are HUBZones. Unlike other social responsibility programs that are targeted at race and gender, but may do little to actually impact economically depressed areas in a geographic sense, HUBZone strikes directly at the root by pushing economic benefit straight into challenged areas, regardless of the race or gender of the area's inhabitants.

[14] Source US Government Small Business Administration: http://www.sba.gov/hubzone/section05d.htm

five basic principles of getting the right data to the right person in the right format at the right time and at the right price. How will the questions of regulation, reputation, and revenue affect your decision making?

In terms of regulation, does your jurisdiction have specific remote sensing, data act, or 'shutter control' regulations or legislation? In brief, shutter control is the ability of your national government to decide what your company can take pictures of and to whom you can or cannot sell them to: in essence a potential regulatory cap upon your business and hence your revenues.

1. Shutter Control can limit your access to markets and to customers. How could this impact your sales?
2. What is their approach to issues such as Shutter Control or even to data management and the sale of imagery?
3. If they will ban the sale of imagery to your biggest customer, should you be in that jurisdiction?
4. Is it now too late to leave given the legal and financial consequences of your active spectrum, launch, and operational licenses?

Here regulatory risk mixing with reputational risk and national and international policy issues determine the markets you may have access to, and hence your potential revenues.

Asset-based space businesses are capital intensive, with necessary investments often in the range of multiple hundreds of millions of dollars. For the most part, financing will come from institutional investors, and must be secured via the laws and according to the political stability of the jurisdiction in question, in addition to being tied to the framework of international financial regulations and markets.

JURISDICTIONAL REPUTATIONAL (POLITICAL) RISK AND SPACE COMPANIES

Space activities are closely linked to national security and national politics. Can the politics of a nation affect your business or a change of government? Absolutely. Is this linked to those only working in the market segment of government space agency contracts? Not at all.

The considerations here are a blend of Regulatory and Reputational risk affecting ultimately your business, its growth potential, and its revenues.

THE EXAMPLE NAHUELSAT S.A.

Nahuelsat S.A. was incorporated in 1992 in Argentina and became that nation's first commercial satellite operator. It was founded by

European companies Aerospatiale, Daimler-Chrysler and Alenia Spazio. US Satellite Operator SES Americom later also became a shareholder. It became operative in 1994 and launched its own satellite in 1997. However, following elections in 2007, a new Argentinean government, by law, created a company named Empresa Argentina de Soluciones Satelitales S.A. (ARSAT) giving this company exclusive rights to provide satellite services to this new company all of the spectrum licenses and operational assets of Nahuelsat S.A. effectively putting Nahuelsat S.A. out of business.

Here, political risk manifested itself through national regulation and arbitrarily deprived a business of its means of survival, and the shareholders and investors in that business their investment, due to a political decision.

There is no perfect solution, nor a perfect answer in regards to guarding against such risk. The reader must just acknowledge its existence and as much as possible to mitigate against it through jurisdictional choice.

ACCESS TO FINANCIAL MARKETS

Another key question in regards to the choice of jurisdiction for your company is keeping future growth in mind, and enabling it by ensuring access to finance and capital markets. You should always be thinking of the value exit path for your investors to realize the return on their investment. When thinking of the exit you must also think of their entrance: what will encourage an investor to invest in your company, providing access to the finances you need to grow your company? Your choice of jurisdiction can play a large role here.

To address is how your financiers and investors will seek a return on their investment you must think about potential paths to their realizing the return on their investment: will you sell the company via an industry sale or take the company 'public' via placing shares on one of the international stock exchanges? The world's primary financial markets for stock offerings and trading are in New York, London, Hong Kong, and Singapore. How does your jurisdiction work with these others in mind?

1. Do companies incorporated in your jurisdiction have the ability to access these key public markets? Do those markets recognize them? Are their regulatory barriers or enablers to access those markets?
2. Does your planned jurisdiction have the ability and the track record for taking companies to the world's leading equity markets? For example, Isle of Man companies have become one of the world's leading listings on the London AIM market[15].

---

[15] Source, London Stock Exchange: http://www.aim.co.im/~aimcoi/listings.php

3. Are you establishing your venture in a jurisdiction that will carry more or less risk for those financing you?
4. Will this help or hinder your ability to seek and to use capital?
5. Will your investors have a validated exit route to seek a return on their investment or your own venture to seek more necessary capital from the markets to grow and mature?

Here your revenues are affected by the financial regulations of your jurisdiction. Make the choice wisely.

CONCLUSION

You have a choice in jurisdictions for your company. Though you literally have the entire world to choose from, you must choose a jurisdiction whose regulations and reputation will allow you to maximize your revenues, profit, and the ultimate success of your space venture. Your choice of jurisdiction is also dictated as to the market segment in the space industry you're working in (or wish to work in). It is also dictated by your customer's needs and by the needs of your investors. The risks of regulation, reputation, and revenue must always be at the forefront of your decision making process.

•••

CHRISTOPHER STOTT

Mr. Christopher (Chris) Stott is Chairman and Chief Executive Officer of ManSat Limited. ManSat is one of the world's leading firms specializing in orbital spectrum.

Mr. Stott serves on the Main Board of the International Institute of Space Commerce as a Founding Member, and is a Trustee of the International Space University where he serves on faculty and has served as a Co-Chair of the School of Business and Management.

Mr. Stott also serves as a Main Board Director of the Society of Satellite Professionals International, the Satellite Industry's largest professional association.

In September 2003, Chris was appointed as the Honorary Representative of the Isle of Man to the Space Community by the Island's Chief Minister and Council of Ministers. He continues to serve in this position today.

Chris left his position as Director of International Commercialization & Sales with Lockheed Martin Space Operations' $3.4B Consolidated Space Operations Contract (CSOC) in Houston to found ManSat Limited. Chris came to Lockheed Martin from the Boeing Space & Communications Company in Huntington Beach, California, where he worked International Business Development for the Delta Launch Vehicle program.

Chris has also worked extensively in British and American politics as an Office Manager, Staff Aide, and Speech Writer in the British House of Commons and House of Lords, and as an Intern in the US Senate and as a Political Aide on two US Presidential Campaigns.

Educated at Millfield School in Somerset, England, Chris attended the University of Kent, Canterbury where he obtained a Bachelor of Arts Degree, with Honors, in American Studies Politics and Government. While at Canterbury, Chris also received a Diploma from the University of California, San Diego where he studied International Relations at the University of California and Marine Policy and at the Scripps Institute of Oceanography. Chris holds a Masters Degree in Space Studies (Msc) from the International Space University.

A published Fellow of the Royal Astronomical Society Chris is also an invited member of the International Institute of Space Law. Chris is the co-author of Britain and Europe's first work on space privatization and commercialization, *A Space For Enterprise; the aerospace industries after government monopoly,* Stott & Watson, Adam Smith Institute, London, 1994.

CHAPTER 20

THE US SPACE GUARD
INSTITUTIONAL SUPPORT
TO SPACE COMMERCE

BRENT D. ZIARNICK
CAPTAIN, U.S. AIR FORCE RESERVE

INTRODUCTION

This chapter discusses some methods and institutions that will bridge the gap between today's practical reality of space commerce as satellites and signals and future visions of commercial empires in an outer space populated by thousands of human beings and shared by space enthusiasts. It argues that the present and future of space commerce are not two isolated and foreign concepts, but merely two points on a continuous wave of human progress that already shares a common character and logic. By identifying the underlying structural similarity between the present and future of space commerce, we can envision a way to connect the two concepts in the mind of the public that will enhance the former and prepare the way to reach the latter. The ultimate purpose of establishing a continuum of space commerce in this paper is to argue for the logic and necessity of creating an institution that can act as the stewards of the space industry in any form – a military space service.

The service will be formed by merging some of today's military and civil space agencies, and would be immediately relevant and useful in today's space activities. At the same time, it will be inherently adaptable to any future direction of space commerce while maintaining a doctrine and culture that will be equally comfortable operating Global Positioning System satellites or rescuing stranded passengers on a punctured and decompressing space station.

It will be built from military personnel currently serving in uniform as well as civilian professionals, instructed by heroic deeds from the past, and possessing an unswerving belief in space's limitless potential for the future. It will be a guardian and protector first, but a warrior always. It will take its name and lineage from the guardians that protect Americans from the foreign environment of the sea, and seek to protect her charges as they conquer the vast reaches of outer space. It is the United States Space Guard.

IMPORTANCE OF INSTITUTIONS TO ECONOMIC DEVELOPMENT

Many chapters of this book appropriately focus on the private sector as the critical driver of space development, but there is a key role for governments to play as well. Visionaries, entrepreneurs, capital, and successful business plans are the most critical needs or the development of space commerce, but other necessary pieces of the puzzle include the institutions that provide critical infrastructure and guidance which encourage space commerce to flourish. One such institution may be the formation of a military space service modeled after the US Coast Guard and dedicated to supporting space commerce. To begin to understand how a Space Guard could assist the expansion of space commerce, we must first seek to understand the building blocks of space commerce.

THE SPACE COMMERCE DICHOTOMY

Space commerce is a wide and varied field of human endeavor. The possibilities span a range, from science fiction notions of galaxy-hopping passenger liners like the gargantuan *Hyperion* in E.E. 'Doc' Smith's space opera *Triplanetary*, to the hard financial reality of satellite-enabled entertainment and navigation firms like Sirius XM, DirecTV, and Garmin, companies whose stocks currently trade on major exchanges.

However, because the concept of space commerce is so varied, between space enthusiasts and current space commerce executives there exists a seemingly unbridgeable gulf in perspective. Space enthusiasts often think of space commerce as human colonies in space, mining for

Helium-3 on the moon, giant solar power generating satellites beaming clean power back to Earth, and tourists spending honeymoons in low Earth orbit. The CEOs in charge of 'real' space commerce operations often view it as haggling for better insurance rates on a new satellite launch, negotiating for more electromagnetic spectrum bandwidth, and finding ways to keep bad weather from degrading the picture on a satellite TV during Super Bowl parties. However real this separation feels, it belies the fact that both are intimately connected and share the same internal logic and building blocks, building blocks that can be identified through the exploration of a perhaps unlikely subject - military history.

A CONTINUUM OF SPACE COMMERCE

"In these three things – production, with the necessity of exchanging products, shipping, whereby the exchange is carried on, and colonies, which facilitate and enlarge the operations of shipping and tend to protect it by multiplying points of safety – is to be found the key to much of the history, as well as the policy, of nations bordering upon the sea."

Rear Admiral Alfred Thayer Mahan, US Navy, 1890[1]

Space commerce is much like sea commerce before it, and thus it should come as no surprise that the words of the prophet of sea power, Admiral Alfred Thayer Mahan, can again be pressed into service to explain the fundamental nature of space power as well. And space power, regardless of the popularity of the term in warfighting circles, is primarily space commerce.

Like sea commerce, space commerce (in the past, present, or even in the far future) is comprised of three essential elements: production, shipping, and colonies. These three concepts will always be paramount in space commerce, and the maturation of space commerce from the present to the visionary will only change these elements in their manifestation, not in their essence. As Mahan describes it above, space commerce production is goods and services that are derived from or created in space, are traded, and from which wealth is generated. Shipping is the total of services that transport space production to their respective markets, as well as the lines of communication that allow the transportation to take place. Colonies are the places which generate the production, and which constitute markets in and of themselves, and which advance the safety of shipping by offering places of 'safe haven' and protection.

---

1. Mahan, Alfred T. *The Influence of Sea Power Upon History*, 1660-1783. John Wilson & Sons. Cambridge. 1890. P 28.

These elements are easy to envision for sea commerce: production includes oil, marine products, and other raw materials and manufactured goods that are transported over the sea. Shipping includes the countless oil tankers and container ships seen throughout the world's ports and oceans. Colonies (also called bases) are the many ports around the world that offer shelter in storms as well as places for shipping to obtain and deliver loads of cargo.

For space commerce these elements are identical, even though the time frames under examination showcase very different forms of each element.

Mahanian Space Commerce Model

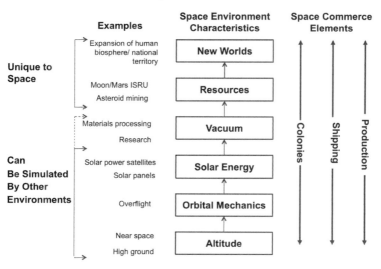

Figure 1
A Space Commerce Model
Elements of space commerce extend across the spectrum of present and future industrial opportunities. It is inspired by the writings of Admiral Alfred Thayer Mahan on sea commerce.

As Figure 1 shows, the space commerce elements are present no matter what sort of commerce is examined. Whether the aspect of space that is being exploited for commerce is relatively simple, such as high altitude or orbital dynamics using contemporary technology (as exploited by navigation, communication, and imagery satellites), or an opportunity requiring more advanced technology (such as extracting asteroid or lunar resources for economic use), the same elements are still present. Whether they are in use today or exist only in the lab or in a science fiction writer's imagination, all types and tools of space commerce can be described with these fundamental space commerce elements.

Production – Space commerce production is the total of goods and services, both drawn from and transported through space. As space commerce matures, types of production will be added, subtracted, and expanded over time, and it is also likely that the nature of the production will change dramatically from that which is prevalent today.

Current Form – Near-term space commerce production mostly includes information in the form of imagery and navigation data. Visual data such as satellite photos and weather data are produced by platforms in space using the unique space environment of high altitude, which cannot easily be obtained by other means. Though digital information does not equate with production in a classical 'goods and services' sense, it is in fact the primary product of today's space commerce.

Future Form – As space technology matures, future production may include spacecraft propellants from in-situ resources, industrial quantities of solar power, other natural resources including water, and microgravity-processed pharmaceuticals or structural materials.

Shipping – Shipping is the means of transporting space production from the place of its construction or extraction to its ultimate market, whether on Earth or another space destination.

Current Form – Most space 'shipping' today is conducted not by rockets and transports (though certainly some is), but rather by electromagnetic (EM) radiation in the form of signal waves that transport data from a satellite to its ground station on Earth. Satellite dishes, not space shuttles, are the prime tools of today's space shipping as they collect the transmissions that allow communication across the entire globe. As a proportion of total commerce, rockets are currently only minor players compared to antennas, although they will take will take a larger role in the future.

Future Form – Although electromagnetic transmissions will always play an important role in space commerce, the future will be the era of spacecraft that are truly analogous to the merchant marine of today. Near term examples include unmanned 'space tugs' that will transport spacecraft from low earth orbit to geosynchronous orbit, as well as manned spacecraft traversing the void between the Moon, Mars and Earth. Later, perhaps there will be great starships travelling between solar systems with cargoes of unimaginable wonders.

Colonies – Colonies are the places where many of the activities of space commerce originate and end. Colonies allow the production of space-based products, the consumption of those and other products, and facilitate the safe transportation of these goods.

Current Form – While the International Space Station may be the first to come to mind, the most common space colonies today are the satellites that provide platforms where production takes place. Although satellites aren't normally considered colonies, they perform the colony function in today's space commerce: they provide places where production can occur (often imagery or other data) and where goods can be shipped (through EM signals). Colonies certainly exist today in space commerce.

Future Form – Space colonies will advance to become 'traditional' inhabited colonies familiar to space enthusiasts - outpost communities that conduct scientific exploration, mining, manufacturing, tourism, spacecraft maintenance and repair for cruisers and merchant spacecraft of all types.

Although today's satellites and electromagnetic data transmissions look far different from future versions of commercial empires of mining bases and merchant transport spacecraft, space commerce today and tomorrow share a common logic and grammar, comprised of production, shipping, and colonies.

Similarly, planning to support and defend space commerce in any form can use this framework as a theoretical departure point. Since Admiral Mahan's model originated as an explanation of sea power, looking to the service whose modern mission is to support and defend sea commerce may provide a useful model for an equivalent space service. This service is the United States Coast Guard.

THE COAST GUARD MODEL

> " . . .the fundamental reasons for the two services are diametrically opposed. The Navy exists for the sole purpose of keeping itself prepared for . . . war. Its usefulness to the Government is therefore to a large degree potential. If it performs in peacetime any useful function not ultimately connected with the preparation for war, that is a by-product. On the other hand, the Coast Guard does not exist solely for the purpose of preparing for war. If it did there would be, of course, two navies--a large one and a small one, and that condition, I am sure you will agree, could not long exist. The Coast Guard exists for the particular and main purpose of performing duties which have no connection with a state of war, but which, on the contrary, are constantly necessary as peace functions. It is, of course, essentially an emergency service and it is organized along military lines because that sort of an organization best enables the Coast Guard to keep prepared as an emergency service, and by organization along military lines it is invaluable in time of war as an adjunct and auxiliary to the Navy. . . .while peace time usefulness is a by-product of the Navy, it is the war time usefulness that is a by-product of the Coast Guard."
>
> Captain Ellsworth Bertholf, first Commandant of the U.S. Coast Guard[2]

---

2.   As quoted in Robert Johnson, *Guardians of the Sea*, (Annapolis: Naval Institute Press, 1988), p. 59.

The United Sates Coast Guard has existed in some form since the earliest beginnings of the American Republic.   In 1790 the Congress commissioned the Revenue Marine (Cutter Service), and over time other federal agencies such as the Lifesaving Service, the Steamboat Inspection Service, Bureau of Navigation, and Lighthouse Service were added to form the modern Coast Guard – America's guardian on the ocean.[3]   It performs three broad missions: Maritime Safety, Maritime Security, and Maritime Stewardship.[4]

The Coast Guard is best known for Maritime Safety, which is defined as marine safety and search and rescue operations.[5]   Marine safety programs include developing standards, regulations, and compliance programs to enhance mishap prevention, and also include reviewing plans for ship construction, repair, and alteration.[6]

Perhaps the most visible Coast Guard operation is search and rescue, intervening in emergency situations where prevention has failed and mariners are threatened by an unforgiving sea.   The Coast Guard's presence makes sea travel safer, and enables insurance premiums to be far lower than they might otherwise be.

Maritime Security is the oldest of the Coast Guard's responsibilities, and the Coast Guard is the nation's primary law enforcement service on the water.[7]   The Coast Guard enforces both US Federal law in territorial waters as well as international treaties all over the world.   Maritime Security sub-missions include drug interdiction, migrant interdiction, defense readiness, and ports, waterways, and coastal security.[8]   As part of its role in defense readiness, the Coast Guard accomplishes military missions such as maritime interdiction and coastal sea control.

Maritime Stewardship is the final broad Coast Guard mission, which recognizes that the sea is one of the world's most important natural resources and must be protected.   Maritime Stewardship includes protection of living marine resources, maritime environmental protection, fishery law enforcement, aids to navigation, and ice operations sub-missions.[9]   Stewardship ranges from protecting sea life, the sea environment, and commerce from varied threats such as icebergs and or becoming lost.   Stewardship through education and prevention, law enforcement, emergency response and containment, and disaster recovery

---

3.   Coast Guard Publication 1, *U.S. Coast Guard: America's Maritime Guardian.* May 2009. Pg 24.
4.   Ibid, iv.
5.   Ibid, 5.
6.   Ibid, 6.
7.   Ibid, 8.
8.   Ibid.
9.   Ibid, 11.

addresses the gamut of possible scenarios the Coast Guard must confront.[10]

The Coast Guard accomplishes these three broad missions by being *"Military, Multi-Mission, and Maritime with a Humanitarian Reputation."*[11] The Coast Guard is military because its duties often place its guardsmen in harm's way, and military discipline is essential to performing dangerous duties with skill and bravery. Regardless of its military character, as Commandant Bertholf noted in the opening quote, the Coast Guard's primary mission is to perform peace time missions, and their war functions are secondary use and exist only in potential.

The Coast Guard's multi-mission nature requires it to be prepared as warrior, police officer, rescuer, businessman, and diplomat.

The Coast Guard facilitates sea commerce by interdicting to stop smuggling, while providing a safe haven for trade. The Coast Guard provides security at essential ports and waterways leading to them, and supports shipping by assisting in navigation, ensuring vessel integrity, and providing essential emergency services.

As with the sea, space commerce is in need of an organization dedicated to Space Safety, Space Security, and Space Stewardship.

THE SPACE GUARD: A FAMILIAR CONCEPT HIDDEN IN PLAIN SIGHT

The genesis of the Space Guard has often been associated with the concept of a Space Navy, a staple in science fiction. From the Interplanetary Patrol in Robert Heinlein's *Space Cadet* and the ubiquitous Starfleet of *Star Trek* fame (or the more insidious Imperial Fleet in *Star Wars*), the idea of a space navy is embedded in popular culture to the extent that writers have almost universally concluded that future space military forces will be modeled after the Navy rather than the Army or Air Force. Hence, almost no story featuring a space military includes a 'colonel' (an Army and Air Force term) instead; they typically reference a 'captain' (a Navy term) as the commanding officer.

However, many space futurists and science fiction writers prefer to envision a future that is not based on the military occupation of space. In doing so they, unfortunately, often make the mistake of conflating a warfighting organization with a military organization, when in fact these two concepts are not equivalent. The Navy, Army, Air Force, and Marine Corps exist primarily to fight and win wars, while the Coast Guard, with its primary roles of protecting and expanding commerce and protecting lives on the high seas, is also a military organization.

---

10. Ibid, 12.
11. Ibid, 63.

This same military misunderstanding encountered in science fiction plagues the contemporary space enthusiast community. When space enthusiasts view how government can help the space community, or when young people want to become government space leaders, they often look to the National Aeronautics and Space Administration (NASA) rather than Air Force Space Command. Space enthusiasts and proponents of space commerce often decry military space efforts as 'arming the heavens' or war hawks defiling the pristine environment of space, though most military space leaders worry about mitigating space debris and preventing conflict as much or more than the enthusiast community. NASA employees see themselves as the precursors to Starfleet, even though the average day of a US Navy submariner comes far closer to the life of a Starfleet officer than any engineer in Houston. Even when space enthusiasts look at history, they say NASA should play the role of 'Lewis and Clark' in space without realizing that both explorers were military officers operating under the US Army during their expedition. The Space Guard concept may allow space enthusiasts to be enthusiastic about the military again once they realize that supporting a space military service need not sanction aggression and 'war hawk' behavior in the space realm.

The Space Guard's role would be to support space commerce first, and its wartime role would be a byproduct of its peacetime role and not its sole, or even primary raison d'etre. By providing services such as commerce protection, astronaut search and rescue, and enforcing 'rules of the road,' the Space Guard would provide commercial space enterprises with stability and support options they may not otherwise have. Insurance rates may significantly decline if Space Guard cruisers were on call to respond to space ships or stations in distress to recover crew and passengers in an emergency.

FUTURE SPACE COMMERCE AND THE SPACE GUARD'S ROLE

Perhaps the most well-written and reasoned vision of a mature and futuristic Space Guard was described in *Space Tourism: Do You Want to Go?* by John Spencer. Spencer's vision of a robust human infrastructure in space circa 2040 sees thousands of humans living and working in space, based primarily on a space tourism industry modeled after the maritime cruise line.[12]

In Spencer's vision, space stations are fashioned as orbiting super yachts. Based initially off of inflatable modules similar to systems being

---

12. Spencer, John. *Space Tourism: Do You Want to Go?* Apogee Books. Ontario, Canada. 2004. P 43.

developed by Bigelow Aerospace, these yachts will serve tourists spending vacations in splendor and luxury as they 'cruise' through low Earth orbit. Beginning in earnest around 2020, orbital yachts will be among the largest space industry operation that serves thousands of customers per year with a robust infrastructure by 2040. Why cruise ships rather than space stations? As Spencer says, *"Onboard a modern cruise ship you are safe, cared for, entertained, fed, and kept the center of attention."*[13] A perfect way for a tourist to experience outer space!

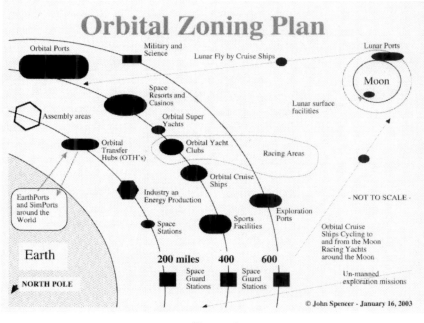

Figure 2
Orbital Zoning Plan in 2050 developed by John Spencer. Note that
all major developed orbits have a Space Guard Station.
(Courtesy of John Spencer)

But who will ensure passenger safety and patrol the increasingly crowded sky? The question of where transport ships would dock for services and loading and discharging passengers in this bustling space economy led Spencer to realize that the Space Guard Service (SGS) would be necessary for space commerce's health,[14] and he maintains that there could be *"over a dozen countries and hundreds of private corporations and institutes"* operating in orbit by 2050.

---

13. Ibid.
14. Ibid, 116.

Hence, a primary role of the SGS will be to manage and deconflict these multiple operations, in support of everyone's best interests.

Missions the SGS would perform include developing standards for construction and maintenance of space facilities, as well as inspection and monitoring of spacecraft and orbital platforms on a regular basis. In emergency situations, the SGS would provide rescue and Emergency Medical Services (EMS), and as the industry matures and expands the SGS can provide law enforcement as well as debris removal and the environmental management necessary to secure the safety of the space lanes.[15]

In time, the SGS may become the foremost uniformed presence in space, taking on additional roles of planetary defense against Earth-threatening asteroids (a logical extension of debris mitigation), potential first contact scenarios with extraterrestrial life, and deep space exploration, perhaps obviating the need of a more warfighting-centered military space service.

Spencer's orbital yacht scenario showcases a futuristic and mature expression of the space commerce model for production, shipping, and colonies in a time frame that many people alive today will not only see, but perhaps take leadership roles in creating.

Because the radical transformation of space commerce from electromagnetic waves to orbital yachts may take place over the span of a few short decades, space commerce leaders must confront this paradigm leap sooner rather than later and assess how an SGS can help develop space commerce.

SGS personnel will become industry leaders with experience and knowledge of the industry during and after their careers in uniform, adding to the breadth and depth of human capital available to the space industry and essential for the development of space commerce.[16]

Spencer suggests that the most important role the SGS can play in space commerce is to provide the safety needs critical for insurance companies to provide coverage for space activities, and for venture capital firms to release critical funds to build the space industry.[17]

Hence, the SGS will act as a security net both for travelers to be secure in their persons and businesses to be secure in their capital. Spencer envisions that the SGS will begin orbital operations to support the yachting industry in 2020, but ends his exploration of the SGS by insisting that the SGS must be created immediately to anticipate challenges and begin to develop solutions.[18] But is it premature and ill advised to propose the existence of a Space Guard now?

---

15. Ibid, 83.
16. Ibid, 129.
17. Ibid, 201.
18. Ibid, 202.

NO FUTURISTIC FANTASY, A PRESENT NEED!

Spencer's vision of a robust future space commerce seems in many ways like science fiction. However, a clear plan to build the Space Guard already exists in the form of a paper by Air Force Lieutenant Colonel (ret.) Cynthia McKinley, published in 1999 in the *Aerospace Power Journal*, the US Air Force's premier academic journal. Entitled *The Guardians of Space: Organizing America's Space Assets for the Twenty-First Century*, Colonel McKinley outlines the case for organizing a United States Space Guard (USSG) as soon as possible by utilizing present capabilities. Though McKinley's ideas match Spencer's almost exactly, she did not predicate or defend the existence of a Space Guard based on a futuristic vision, but instead from the cold hard military reality of ten years ago.

McKinley's USSG was born from a disconnect she identified between the Air Force's vision of an integrated 'Aerospace Force' and the functional differences between the roles of air and space forces.

While the Air Force leadership championed the idea of an aerospace force that merged air and space power into a seamless continuum of military power, McKinley argued that organizational, funding, and cultural tensions between air and space forces created an irreparable rift between the two.[19] While the Air Force had a 'fly and fight self-image' focused on fighting wars while USAF space forces already thought in terms of space services support through roles including operating space systems on a day-to-day basis, launching routine civilian and military rockets, and other activities not directly related to fighting.

"Like trying to mix oil and water, it is… unrealistic to expect the two to become one."[20]

In her model, the USSG addresses two key problems. First, it would allow the Air Force to focus on its primary mission of flying, fighting, and winning wars, without the cultural, organizational, and financial burdens of paying for and operating the space support equipment needed by space forces. Second, it enables the space forces to focus on supporting the effort to exploit space effectively, to include commercial as well as military and civil space efforts.[21]

The USSG would function as a fusion of civil, commercial, and military space personnel and missions in a uniformed service modeled after the Coast Guard. The USSG would need to strike a balance among competing civil, commercial, military space missions and interests. It would operate as a multi-mission service with responsibilities for space

---

19. McKinley, Cynthia, LtCol. "The Guardians of Space: Organizing America's Space Assets for the Twenty-First Century." *Aerospace Power Journal*. Spring, 2000. Maxwell AFB, Alabama. P 38.
20. Ibid, 39.
21. Ibid, 42.

operations, mission areas of space support (global positioning systems, government satellite communications. etc.), force enhancement (spacelift, infrastructure security), and space control (space surveillance, satellite jamming and defense) as well as providing space range management and debris mitigation.[22] It would merge separate mission requirements, core competencies, visions, and responsibilities to form a coherent federal response to the extension of the space enterprise and support the expansion of space commerce.[23]

The USSG would report to the Department of Transportation during routine peacetime operations, and serve as an adjunct to the Air Force during times of conflict, much like the Coast Guard's association with the US Navy.

McKinley did not provide an exhaustive list of agencies that would be merged to form the USSG, but we can guess which ones would be useful. The USSG would take over current non-military roles space missions, personnel, and funding from of the Air Force (Air Force Space Command), other Department of Defense agencies (sister service space commands), NASA (space flight operations), National Oceanic and Atmospheric Administration (space weather and meteorological satellite operations), and the Federal Aviation Administration (Office of Commercial Space Transportation), among others. Air Force space professionals and FAA and NOAA space experts would serve together as new USSG servicemen. They would continue to do the jobs they do today, except they would serve in a new organization dedicated to expanding the American space effort in all of its forms.

The USSG would be commanded by commissioned general officers (admirals?) trained and experienced in space specialties such as space launch, satellite tracking commanding, and on-orbit mission operations.[24] A few of the missions that America's corps of space guardsmen would accomplish include USSG members managing government space launches, operating 'global utility' satellites such as GPS, tracking the thousands of objects in orbit, supporting International Space Station operations, providing security for government space ranges, establishing regulations and safety practices for commercial spaceflight, and advocating for the space industry. Instead of a weak agency with no mandate and little to do, the USSG would have a clear and hugely important mission to safeguard America's efforts in space.

Like Spencer's SGS, McKinley's concept of USSG can provide necessary safety and security services for today's space commerce, whether it is electromagnetic spectrum defense against illegal satellite jamming or providing launch services to the commercial satellite or space tourist

---

22. Ibid, 44.
23. Ibid, 42.
24. Ibid.

industry. Whether space commerce operates in the present scheme of electromagnetic shipping or expands to rudimentary near-term space tourism, the USSG could provide unparalleled support.

LtCol McKinley believes that the USSG is the right organization for successful exploitation of space in the twenty-first century.[25] She pointed out that the USSG does not need to be a futuristic concept, but can be logically founded by only a reorganization of existing federal space agencies. A space guard was doable and desirable in 1999, and does not need to wait for 2040.

DEVELOPMENT OF HUMAN CAPITAL FOR SPACE COMMERCE

There is much to recommend that space enthusiasts embrace a military space service in the form of a Space Guard. A major reason is an often overlooked but critical function that the military has historically played in opening frontiers, and one that NASA cannot accomplish in like form for space. Historically, the military has been a key provider of skills and experience to servicemen and women with which they have been able to become leaders in their fields. Many leaders of the US maritime environment, especially in modern times, have gotten their start from stints in the navy. During World Wars I and II, the Army Air Corps gave essential skills to generations of pilots and mechanics who left the service and built commercial air transportation empires including companies such as Pan American Airways, Delta, Flying Tigers, and TWA. This added thousands of jobs, millions of dollars of infrastructure investments, and the essential services that the air travel industry provides today.

Similarly, today's Air Force Space Command trains hundreds of men and women to be spacecraft operators, satellite, rocket, and electronics technicians, and provides them with many other skills essential to space commerce.

Training and education are offered to officers and enlisted alike, but what is most important to space commerce is the human capital provided to enlisted troops. It is in this critical duty that the space enthusiast preference for NASA hampers space commerce. NASA does not take fresh young men and women out of high school and train them to be space professionals as the Air Force does. Instead, for most operational roles on the International Space Station or Space Shuttle NASA requires a bachelor's degree in the hard sciences or engineering fields, so very little 'new' human capital is developed in this way, as most NASA employees are among the population that was certainly college-bound anyway.

By contrast all a person must do to join the military space program is to enlist. For example, it is the youngest enlisted operators that directly

---

25. Ibid, 45.

communicate with GPS satellites on the Air Force operations floor, while officers only verify commands generated and transmitted by enlisted people. Enlisted people are also the primary maintainers of ground equipment and rockets used by the Air Force in the space mission. In this manner, people without advanced academic education nevertheless become highly skilled space technicians.

Also, due to the focus on leadership development that the military provides, enlisted people are often given the opportunity and even expected to lead large teams of people, which forms a wide and deep source of space expertise that can be used both by the government and by commercial space enterprises.

As the space enthusiast high school graduate is often barred from NASA, and often doesn't know about the opportunities available in space at Air Force Space Command, this loss of a 'blue collar' working pipeline of space professionals is a severe detriment to space commerce.

The Space Guard will change this paradigm. By being a military service with a primary focus on protecting lives and commerce, the space enthusiast can join without being forced into a militarist role. Space enthusiasts can feel assured that by enlisting they will work in an important role in the space field. The military historically opens all avenues of activity to enlisted forces, so by joining the Space Guard a high school graduate recruit can realistically expect to work on rockets or spacecraft, operate sensitive space missions, and when the time comes for mass human spaceflight, become an astronaut himself or herself.

Instead of being a pipe dream, a space enthusiast who for various reasons does not want to, or is not able to, attend college can still be a part of the space enterprise. This will be a profound improvement in the development of the human capital of the American space effort, as thousands of overlooked young adults will be given the opportunity to train as space professionals regardless of their academic standing or financial ability to pay for college. This direct investment of human capital into a now-overlooked and underserved segment of the population may well be the enduring contribution of the Space Guard to humanity's effort to conquer space.

COMMERCIAL RELEVANCE – A MISSION CASE STUDY

*"We propose that the lack of an independent Situation Response
capability is fundamentally responsible for the manned orbital space
flight industry's consistently excessive costs as it requires a zero-
tolerance engineering approach in Vehicle and Equipment
Manufacture. These high costs have deterred commercial businesses
from naturally pursuing the opportunities of manned, orbital space
flight, as has been promised throughout the last forty years."*

Alan Thompson & Gordon Smith[26]

Even if the Space Guard is a concept almost as old as the dream of
spaceflight, and regardless of the Space Guard's ability to fit in the worlds
of both present reality and future visions of space, how do we know if it is
really useful to space commerce? To more deeply explore how the Space
Guard can assist space commerce, we'll focus on one mission that both
McKinley and Spencer assign to their Space Guard concepts – space
emergency search and rescue. Alan Thompson and Gordon Smith make an
insightful analysis of the space industry and a compelling case for space
search-and-rescue in their 2009 study "Space Policy Development via
Macro-Economic Analysis."

Thompson and Smith attempt to understand the effectiveness of
space policy by looking at the economics of the space industry.[27] They
analyzed the human orbital space flight industry by examining how the
industry supports each of six critical industrial operations: refueling,
resupply, flight control, vehicle design, facility, and security.

They examine the hypothesis that the orbital manned space flight
industry can be modeled by the airline industry, but they then point out that
the airline industry's infrastructure is relatively low cost because of a deep
and mature commercial market and its associated competitive pricing. A
major cost advantage is available to commercial aviation because although
aircraft are isolated in flight, they *"enjoy a significant number of
established public and private airports should they need to land quickly"* in
an emergency, and on the ground they can be maintained and repaired
easily.[28] Therefore, airplanes need have relatively few emergency
redundant systems compared to orbital spacecraft, which must incorporate

---

26. Quoted in "Space Policy Development via Macro-Economic Analysis," by
    Alan D. Thompson and Gordon P. Smith, 2009. Page 27.
    http://www.nasa.gov/pdf/368983main_Applying%20a%20Macro-
    Economic%20Analysis%20to%20Space%20Policy%202009_06_09.pdf
27. Ibid, 3.
28. Ibid, 21.

nearly all of their emergency and maintenance capabilities on board due to their extended isolation. This drives vehicle design costs very high.[29]

A key difference, they argue, between the orbital manned space flight market and the airline market is therefore how much each relies on Damage Tolerant Design (DTD) methodologies.[30] Once on orbit, current manned and unmanned spacecraft are isolated and can tolerate almost no mishap without risking catastrophic mission failure. DTD methodologies require that multiple-redundant systems be included in the design of all spacecraft subsystems to allow a large amount of damage without losing the ability to function as intended.[31]

Attempting to mitigate economic risk by relying solely on DTD methodologies to build spacecraft capable of withstanding almost any type of problem over their mission life and still function dooms human spaceflight to economic unattractiveness.

After rejecting the comparison with commercial aviation, Thompson and Smith then turn to two additional industrial models, the cruise line industry (which was already introduced in this paper) and the automobile industry. Cruise lines and the auto industry share much in common with orbital spaceflight. All three are vehicle-based systems that depart from a particular location and operate for an extended period of time before reaching another destination.[32]

While a spacecraft must be completely self-sufficient through DTD, cruise lines have external emergency support in the form of the US Coast Guard and automobiles have an army of support from ambulances to tow trucks to the AAA. Hence, they point out that adding an emergency situation response capability to the industrial infrastructure of space flight would reduce vehicle design costs, since it would no longer be necessary for a spacecraft's emergency systems to cover every contingency, but simply to keep the crew safe until help arrives.[33] By analogy, could the average buyer afford a car if its design had to ensure that it could make the next town by itself with total engine failure or four flat tires?

The emergency response systems that serve cruise lines and autos directly contribute to low costs by specifically addressing the cost to drivers of safety and reliability, and these are the prime reasons for orbital manned spaceflight's commercially unaffordable costs.[34] Therefore, Thompson and Smith conclude that a space industry emergency response capability should be made a priority of space policy, and suggest that such

---

29. Ibid, 24.
30. Ibid.
31. Ibid, 15.
32. Ibid, 25.
33. Ibid 26.
34. Ibid, 27.

a policy will allow the long-promised commercial space sector finally begin to develop and mature.[35]

TANGIBLE BENEFITS

Specifically, Thompson and Smith see six tangible benefits for a government emergency response capability to space commerce and the United States:

1. An emergency response capability will add to national prestige by allowing the U.S., in times of emergency, to support any nation that is conducting space operations. It will also establish an authority responsible for defining industry standards and regulations.

2. Developing a rapid response capability will require technologies that can benefit the larger space industry by lowering costs and ensure timely space access.

3. Knowing that help is only a few hours away will assist in creating consumer confidence in the space industry, and will encourage private investment in orbital assets as well as consumer demand for space travel.

4. An effective and efficient way to repair satellites on orbit (a byproduct of rapid response) would reduce the manufacturing cost of satellites by eliminating the need for many system redundancies, as well as lowering insurance costs.

5. A stable and sustainable orbital human spaceflight industry made possible by emergency response may inspire younger generations to enter science and engineering, helping to strengthen the U.S. technical workforce.

6. Of all benefits, the strongest is that an emergency response capability will establish a space industry that is commercially based, affordable, and sustainable, that will generate tax revenue back into the economy through industrial growth.[36]

Thompson and Smith imply that this space emergency response service should be administered by NASA, but considering the history of the US Coast Guard and Spencer's and McKinley's visions, it seems much more fitting that space emergency services should be the province of a military-disciplined Space Guard.

---

35. Ibid.
36. Ibid, 29-30.

A WAY FORWARD

Figure 3 shows that both Mr. Spencer and LtCol McKinley are talking about the same organization. The missions assigned to the USCG, the USSG, and the SGS are remarkably consistent. As noted above, a powerful and logical US Space Guard could be formed immediately from elements of the US Air Force Space Command, NASA, FAA, NOAA, and other federal agencies. Mr. Spencer's future missions can be added to the Space Guard functions list as the needs of space commerce dictate.

Building the US Space Guard should therefore be a national space priority, and by identifying steps and actions that must be taken, we can determine a way forward to make the Space Guard a reality.

Figure 3
The present day Coast Guard, McKinley's near term US Space Guard, and Spencer's future Space Guard Service share a remarkable continuity of missions and roles.

1. CONTINUE TO DEVELOP THE IDEAS AND INFRASTRUCTURE TO EXPAND SPACE COMMERCE.

Space commerce will ultimately be the most important aspect of the human space enterprise. The Space Guard, regardless how interesting it is on its merits, must always be a secondary objective to space commerce. Hence, the Space Guard will exist to support and enhance contemporary space commerce, and must never become a goal unto itself.

The slow progress in developing human activity in space is largely due to the fact that governments are currently the primary movers in space operations, but space commerce will inspire a 'virtuous cycle' of government-private interaction in space.   By increasing the wealth generated by space activities, a larger pool of tax revenue will come from these activities, as well as an increasing need to support the safe execution of these activities.

Therefore, increasing space commerce provides for more government funds that can be devoted to the Space Guard, and also increases the need for a Guard presence.   And as the Space Guard grows, it can expand operations to provide support for more activities, giving private industry additional motivation to pioneer new avenues of space commerce.

2. CREATE A SPACE GUARD CONSTITUENCY IN THE SPACE ENTHUSIAST COMMUNITY, AND ACCEPT AS LEGITIMATE A MILITARY PRESENCE IN SPACE DEVELOPMENT.

For many years NASA has been the focus of the space enthusiast community, with good reason.   However, NASA is a historical anomaly. When looking at the other three environments that humankind has conquered in its history (land, sea, and air) the primary government agency that helped spur development has always been the military.   The space enthusiast community has often held Air Force Space Command at arm's distance, and has been hostile to military activities in space.   In order to expand space commerce and hasten the development of the Space Guard, the enthusiast community should recognize military presence in space as an ally rather than an enemy.

The military has historically been a key developer of human capital and have given many famous explorers and businessmen their start in their industries.   Some examples include the famous Louisiana Purchase explorers Meriwether Lewis and William Clark, who were both military officers, Lewis in the US Army and Clark in various militias.   America's westward expansion was accomplished under the protection of US Army cavalry and infantry units.   At sea, the US Navy and Coast Guard have undertaken important historical roles in supporting the merchant marine fleet and expanding seaborne commerce.   Aviation titans such as Pan-Am Airways founder Juan Trippe (US Navy bomber pilot) and Charles Lindbergh (US Army Air Service Reserve pilot) both became seasoned air experts through their military experiences.

To date, no such space industry titan has emerged.   The fact that the military avenue to space experience for aspiring space professionals has not been as equally accepted by the space enthusiast community or embraced by the industry (as evidenced by the relative lack of space entrepreneurial leaders with military experience) could be contributing to the lack of commercial leadership in space.

To correct this lack of human capital investment, the space community should begin to lobby for a Space Guard, which will open two fundamental and essential pathways to human capital development.   First, creating a Space Guard will give aspiring space leaders who lack the resources or inclination to go to college a place to gain experience. Second, by helping the space enthusiast community to be more aware of the importance of the military as a human capital pipeline, young space enthusiasts may decide to enter Air Force Space Command rather than abandoning their dreams of being space leaders.

Hence, by advocating for a Space Guard, the space community will assist in space commerce by enhancing the human capital development of future space leaders by opening a traditionally important avenue to experience: the military.

3.   INSTILL IN AIR FORCE SPACE COMMAND A SENSE OF STEWARDSHIP FOR SPACE COMMERCE AND RESIST AN ORBITAL COMBAT IMPULSE.

Finally, with an expansion of space commerce and a potentially new supply of young leaders entering the military for space experience, we must address perhaps the most important and dangerous consequence of the divide between military space and space enthusiasts, the Air Force focus on space warfare.

As many space enthusiasts have joined NASA, Air Force space officers generally tend not to be hard-core space enthusiasts, which means that they often see the future of military space from a historical rather than an environmental perspective. Instead of looking to the space industry to discover how the military can best advance space commerce and American space power, military space leaders often view the future of military space (including this author, at one time) as a replay of Air Force independence.

The Air Force has always been about 'flying, fighting, and winning' as LtCol McKinley explained in her paper, and it became an independent branch of the military not because it made a successful intellectual case that it should be an independent service, but because of its massive warfighting contribution to the American effort in World War II. In a sense, the Air Force became independent because of the B-17 bomber. The overwhelming ability of air power to inflict damage on an adversary, as proven by Dresden and Hiroshima, practically demanded that the Air Force be given co-equal status as a military service. The Air Force proved its worth in combat, and was recognized by being given independence for its combat effectiveness.

Many Air Force officers currently in service see a combat-oriented Space Force, not a commerce-oriented Space Guard, as the future of military space. Space enthusiasts who understand both the present and desirable future of the human space effort rightly see the focus on space combat as an impediment to the development of space commerce.

The history of the military's involvement in space suggests that the most effective role for a military space force would be as a support force rather than a combat force (as evidenced by the great successes of satellite navigation and communications programs versus the myriad of physical, philosophical, and economic problems encountered in failed space-based weapons efforts).   However, combat-centric military officers often myopically see space commerce as a potential danger to American space dominance because commercial technology with military potential will end up being used by prospective adversaries.

As space enthusiasts enter military service in space, the enthusiast vision of space expansion and development could begin to displace the zero-sum vision currently dominant in military space circles. The Space Force impulse could be transformed into a better theoretically-aligned Space Guard, protecting both space commerce and the nation.

This is not to say that space warriors have no place in space development. The Space Guard will always, by necessity, be militaristic (though by no means necessarily warlike), and must be prepared to use force in the defense of the country. Space war will always be a possibility, and the Air Force Space Command and the Space Guard must always be prepared for it. The critical philosophical change necessary is for military space leaders to no longer base the entire (or even primary) justification for its existence on the threat of space warfare. By embracing the Space Guard concept in the military, the human space effort can harness the necessary and valuable militaristic impulse and place it in service to space development, rather than at odds with it.

CONCLUSION

Through exploring present and future concepts of a Space Guard, we can now see how an institution dedicated to expanding and providing safety and security can support private space commerce both now and in the future.

Perhaps more importantly, we can see how a government military presence in space can support and enhance space commerce rather than hindering it. The creation of the United States Space Guard will be an important catalyst for the rapid development of space commerce and, by extension, the transformation of outer space into a vast and rich environment for humans and human commerce. Advocates of space commerce would do well to support the Space Guard.

•••

CAPTAIN BRENT D. ZIARNICK

Captain Brent D. Ziarnick is a U.S. Air Force Reserve space officer currently assigned to the 25th Space Range Squadron at Schriever AFB, Colorado. He has deployed as a space operations officer in support of Operations Enduring Freedom and Iraqi Freedom. As a civilian, he is a doctoral candidate studying economic development opportunities in the commercial space industry at New Mexico State University. He lives in Elephant Butte, New Mexico. The views expressed in this chapter are his own.

CHAPTER 21

A NEW PERSPECTIVE
ON 'HIGHER EDUCATION'
EDUCATIONAL INSTITUTIONS
IN LOW EARTH ORBIT

FRANK WHITE
THE OVERVIEW INSTITUTE

INTRODUCTION

In the early 1600s, Puritans in England began settling a 'New World' across the ocean from their homes in England. Less than a decade after establishing the Massachusetts Bay Colony, they turned their attention to the matter of education. In their own words:

> *"After God had carried us safe to New England, and wee had builded our houses, provided necessaries for our liveli-hood, rear'd convenient places for Gods worship, and setled the Civill Government: One of the next things we longed for, and looked after was to advance Learning and perpetuate it to Posterity; dreading to leave an illiterate Ministry to the Churches, when our present ministers shall lie in the Dust."*[1]

The result of the Puritans' 'longing' was the establishment of a small college in 1636 that eventually grew into Harvard University. As the description above indicates, the Puritans saw advancing learning as an important priority after building their homes and churches, establishing a government, and taking care of their livelihoods (commerce).

Today, we are witnessing a growing consensus that the next frontier for space commerce and space settlement is Low Earth Orbit (LEO).[2] While 'space' is usually envisioned as being at a great distance from the Earth, it is actually quite close. In fact, the distance from the Earth to LEO is far less than the distance the Puritans had to travel from England to New England. The challenge to space commerce and settlement has always been cost, not distance.

Satellites are already a LEO commercial success because of the return on investment (ROI). Lifting a satellite into orbit is far less expensive than putting a person there, and the financial return makes the investment worthwhile. The real payoff, however, will occur when the cost of access to LEO is low enough that it is profitable to send people there.

When observers talk about what is next, they most often mention space tourism, hotels, and similar translations of Earth-based activities to the space environment. Ultimately, to create a spacefaring civilization, we must assume that whatever human communities do on the surface of the Earth, they will do in LEO as well.

If this is so, then education, one of the most essential of human activities, will also take place in LEO.

Historically, higher education has, in particular, played a major role in commerce on the Earth. From private research universities to land grant colleges, these institutions have provided research and development, as well as training and education, to produce innovation and a talented, skilled workforce.

Given this historical symbiotic relationship between education and commerce, we might want to consider the role of 'higher education' (aptly named in the case of space!) in helping to grow orbital commerce.

CURRENT SITUATION

After a half-century of space exploration and development, the space environment is used for educational purposes, but not as extensively as we might expect. This does not mean that educational institutions are not interested. Many have space science departments or other levels of involvement in the space exploration enterprise. Others, like the International Space University (ISU), are wholly dedicated to matters related to the human expansion off of the Earth, into the solar system, and beyond. From the beginning (as the following chapter by Michael Simpson illustrates), ISU has envisioned itself as being located in orbit eventually.

The question remains, however, do any institutions of higher education imagine themselves having a presence in orbit? In most cases, it would of course be unrealistic for the entire college or university to be located in LEO, but it is not hard to imagine a unit of the institution in space and connected with the Earth-based campus. And just as some new organizations are located completely in cyberspace and never go through a bricks-and-mortar stage, so might future educational institutions skip the Earth-based stage and be located in orbit from the beginning.

This would certainly give new meaning to the term 'higher education.' It would also transform both space commerce and education at the same time.

CONSIDER THE POSSIBILITIES

1. Imagine a history lesson covering the Crusades. As students learn more about the invasion of the Holy Land by the European knights, they would be able to see the area under discussion rotating beneath them.
2. Picture a debate about immigration. As students discuss the issue of borders and migrations, they will do so with a perspective that shows how borders are mental constructs that are not visible from orbit. What does this mean for immigration policy?
3. Imagine a philosophy class, asking basic questions about the meaning of existence while looking at the Earth from space and in space.
4. Consider a physics class on the force of gravity, held in Zero-G.

The possibilities are endless, limited only by the imaginations of students and faculty. The question before us in 2010 is, 'How do we begin?'

Given that access to orbit for human beings remains quite expensive ($35M to place one person on the International Space Station for one week, for example), establishing LEO-based educational institutions is likely to take a phased approach. Moreover, the rise of online and distance learning suggests that what it means to have a 'presence in orbit' may require careful definition.

STAGES OF PLACING THE EDUCATIONAL ENTERPRISE INTO ORBIT

STAGE ONE: USING WHAT WE HAVE TODAY

The cost of establishing a large-scale physical presence in orbit today would be prohibitive for educational institutions even in good economic times. In the wake of the recent financial crisis, many (in the United States, at least) are struggling to maintain what they have and trying to avoid cutbacks.

Nevertheless, our vision of orbital education, making use of both a virtual and physical presence, can still begin to unfold. For example, an institution might be able to make an arrangement with the managers of the International Space Station to use views of the Earth from orbit at specific class times during the day or evening. As the previously mentioned class on the Crusades is being held, for example, the astronauts' view could be projected onto a screen in the Earth-based classroom. If it were relevant, some of the astronauts might participate in the class, commenting on what they are seeing from space.

Increasing numbers of courses today include online and distance components, and the distant students could also see the view from the space station on their home computer screens.

STAGE TWO: HAVING AN ORBITAL PRESENCE LINKED WITH AN EARTH-BASED PRESENCE

In Stage Two, the institution keeps most of its infrastructure on the Earth, while establishing an initial presence in orbit, perhaps with a professor and a few students.

This model mimics something that happens on Earth quite often: a group of students and professors goes abroad for a year to a pre-specified site that the college or University rents or owns.

Envisioning this stage moves beyond our current situation and raises two significant questions:

1. Where would the orbital group be housed?
2. How would the venture be financed?

These are real problems to be overcome. Still, we can see ways in which they might be managed. If, for example, the Bigelow structures being developed for space habitats prove successful, one of these might support a small educational presence. In addition, the financial challenges might be overcome if a consortium of institutions banded together and shared the costs.[3]

By having an off-world presence that can stand alone or be linked to the Earth-based facilities, such an institution would be able to differentiate itself from competitors and would also have the opportunity to begin supplying services to the burgeoning NewSpace industry. Through online connectivity, many other students could benefit as well. Donors, including the government, might find the opportunity to support such a pioneering venture interesting as well.

Even this modest step would require visionary leadership by the university or college, coupled with a willingness to innovate on the part of the government and/or private industry. Nevertheless, just as we can imagine modest beginnings for space tourism in the near future, we can imagine an initial orbital education presence of this kind.

STAGE THREE: CREATING AN ORBITAL UNIVERSITY

The ultimate vision of space-based education would be a much more significant orbital presence, up to a fully functional college or university. This facility would have most of the capabilities of an Earth-based institution, including living quarters and the ability to sustain a reasonably large population of students and teachers through an academic year. At the same time, the current distance education model would most likely be continued, with students on the Earth's surface participating online.

The growing importance of the cyberspace component makes a major difference in how an orbital facility would be structured. Today's Earth-based model has thousands of students physically present on campus and thousands more participating online. The orbital university might, at its most extensive, have no more than a few hundred people in orbit at any one time, with many more students and teachers being virtually present.

As is the case with some continuing education programs on Earth, the orbital university might require that distance students spend at least a semester 'in residence,' i.e., in orbit, while spending most of their time benefiting from the space perspective without leaving the surface of the Earth.

While this vision is unlikely to become a reality any time soon, it will become a necessity as space commerce and space settlement mature. Eventually, a spacefaring civilization is going to require a spacefaring educational system to be relevant to the needs of the new explorers and settlers.

THE OVERVIEW INSTITUTE AS AN EXAMPLE

It may be helpful to describe planning for one component of an orbital educational system with which I am quite familiar, The Overview Institute (TOI). This organization grew to a large extent out of my work in the book *The Overview Effect*, which examined the impact of seeing the Earth from space and in space on the astronauts.[4] The Overview Effect represents a cognitive shift experienced by space travelers, personified by Apollo 9 astronaut Russell L. ('Rusty') Schweickart's description:

> *"And that whole process of what you identify with begins to shift. When you go around the Earth in an hour and a half, you begin to recognize that your identity is with that whole thing."*[5]

Many of us who had been working on this issue separately gathered for the first conference on the Overview Effect in the summer of 2007, and a core group has been building the organization since that time (The institute is currently a project of the Space Frontier Foundation).[6]

In talking with David Beaver, one of the co-founders of the Institute and the prime mover behind the conference, it became clear to me that the institute ultimately had to be located in orbit.[7] How could we examine the long-term impact of the Overview Effect on the surface of the Earth when its most powerful manifestations occurred in LEO or on the moon?

Our vision of the Overview Institute's orbital facility is not that of an entire educational institution. Rather, it will be more like an institute for advanced study, or 'think tank.' One of the models that has inspired me in this regard is the Radcliffe Institute for Advanced Study at Harvard (RI). The Radcliffe Institute selects 'fellows' from a variety of fields, including academics, artists, and writers, to spend a year in Cambridge, Massachusetts, working on their own projects and interacting with the other fellows, faculty, students, and the public at large.[8]

A key ingredient of this model is that the fellows continue the work they have already begun elsewhere, with the expectation that being connected with Harvard for a year will enrich their work in ways that cannot be predicted in advance.

With an orbital facility in place, TOI will be able to offer the opportunity for thinkers from different fields to experience the Overview Effect and learn how 'overview thinking' might affect their work. We are interested in knowing, for example, how an economist would write about economics while viewing the Earth from orbit, or whether an artist would produce different work from that perspective.

We would expect the impact of the experience to continue when our fellows return to Earth, thereby spreading overview thinking even further. Some of the astronauts have also commented on the possibility of 'summit conferences in orbit,' believing that the decisions of political leaders would be fundamentally different if they discussed the world's problems with the orbital viewpoint in mind.

We would therefore design the orbital facility so that it could accommodate not only individuals pursuing their specific interests but also groups of people who might come together to talk about topics of common interest, with the Overview Effect as a backdrop.

Like many of the ideas discussed here, the Overview Institute's facility will remain in the planning stages until the cost of access to LEO becomes reasonable. However, we have already begun to explore prototypes of potential designs for our future home in a virtual world called Second Life.[9]

We plan to use our Second Life orbital facility for fundraising purposes, i.e., to show potential donors what we have in mind, and also to simulate the experience that we hope to create in the future. We also see this as an environment for communication, collaboration, seminars, and classes where participants can further explore the Overview Effect and its impact. We are currently working with Robin Snelson, who has been instrumental in creating a presence for the Space Frontier Foundation and Space Studies Institute in Second Life, and a talented designer, Motoko Karu, to develop our virtual facility.

Robin has also supported another group to create a presence for an 'orbital university' and Teachers in Space in Second Life.

Over time, we will look for opportunities to create even more immersive experiences on Earth, to give people an increasingly better idea of what we have in mind.[10, 11]

SUMMARY

As we saw in the case of the Massachusetts Bay Colony, when societies confront new frontiers, they tend to the most important priorities first. As they solve the problems of security and sustenance, they eventually turn to the need for education.

While educational institutions in orbit or on the moon are a matter of speculative planning today, there seems little doubt that they will eventually become a reality. The issue is not if but when, and the answer to that question depends on the extent to which costs are reduced and financial support is forthcoming.

As with many space-related issues, higher education in orbit is just a matter of time.

•••

FRANK WHITE

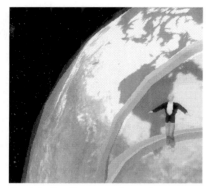

Frank White (Second Life avatar shown to the left) is the author of *The Overview Effect: Space Exploration and Human Evolution*, first published in 1987 and re-issued in 1998.   Based largely on interviews with astronauts, *The Overview Effect* documents the space flight experience, especially the impact on consciousness of seeing the Earth from orbit or the moon.

A member of the Harvard College Class of 1966, Frank concentrated in Social Studies, graduated magna cum laude, and was elected to Phi Beta Kappa. He attended Oxford University on a Rhodes Scholarship, earning an M.Phil. in 1969. He is the author or co-author of five additional books on space exploration and the future, including *The SETI Factor, Decision: Earth, Think About Space* and *March of the Millennia* (both with Isaac Asimov), and *The Ice Chronicles* (with Paul Mayewski). He also contributed chapters on the Overview Effect to three additional books on space exploration, *Return to the Moon, Beyond Earth*, and *Living in Space*.

Frank has also spoken at numerous space-related conferences. In 1988, he delivered the keynote address at the International Space Development Conference in Denver. In 1989 he spoke at George Washington University to mark the 20th anniversary of the Apollo 11 moon landing. In 2006 the Space Tourism Society awarded Frank a 'Certificate of Special Recognition.' In 2007 he delivered the keynote address at the first Overview Effect conference in Washington, D.C., and he was one of the main presenters on the occasion of the announcement of the Overview Institute's *"Declaration of Vision and Principles"* (also known as the *"Declaration of Interdependence")* at the 2008 ISDC conference in Washington, D.C.

Frank is now working with several associates to create the Overview Institute, which will conduct continuing research on the Overview Effect and share the findings as widely as possible.

He is married to Donna White. They have five children and five grandchildren.

REFERENCES

1. Excerpt from First Fruits, a fundraising pamphlet published in 1643 for potential donors to Harvard College (Sabin's Reprints, Quarto Series, No. VII, New York, 1865. Google Books online, 2010.)
2. Kenneth J. Cox, retired NASA engineer and the moving force behind ATWG (Advanced Technology Working Group), has been a strong advocate of this idea, and has urged me to explore the role of higher education in LEO. This chapter is, in part, a result of that.
3. An idea suggested to me by David Beaver (see footnote 7 below) when he reviewed this chapter.
4. *The Overview Effect: Space Exploration and Human Evolution*, Frank White, American Institute of Aeronautics and Astronautics (AIAA) Reston, VA, 1998.
5. Ibid, p. 11.
6. To learn more, go to the Overview Institute website: www.overviewinstitute.org
7. David is now working on a new project to bring the Overview Effect 'down to Earth' through a space-themed multimedia coffee house called Starport Café.
8. To learn more, go to www.harvard.edu and click on Radcliffe Institute under 'Schools.'
9. Second Life is a three-dimensional environment in which 'residents' are represented by avatars (www.secondlife.com). The residents create everything that happens in Second Life.
10. I've discussed this at some length with John Spencer, founder of the Space Tourism Society and developer of a fascinating immersive experience, Mars World ™. We agree that 'it's the experience that counts,' and there may be a number of ways to provide powerful simulations of the space experience on Earth.
11. Along those lines, I am currently working on developing the *Overview Experience Workshop* with colleagues Charlie Smith and Neil Mahoney, along with several other supporters of the idea.

CHAPTER 22

TO PLAN FOR A CENTURY
ISU's VISION OF EDUCATION IN SPACE

MICHAEL SIMPSON, PH.D.
PRESIDENT, THE INTERNATIONAL SPACE UNIVERSITY

From the very beginning of its Founding Conference in 1987, the International Space University (ISU) has lived with the vision that one day it would be able to educate students in space. The founding vision saw three steps in the development of the University: first, a postgraduate summer program (which continues today as the Space Studies Program); second, an offering of space related Masters Programs with a permanent campus (which was inaugurated in 1995 and which operates out of facilities in Strasbourg, France); and an extraterrestrial facility, initially in Earth orbit (which remains a dream, yet appears more attainable as each year passes).

In a promotional film that he prepared for ISU in 1987, the University's first Chancellor, Sir Arthur C. Clarke, made no secret of the University's orbital aspirations. Early in the presentation he notes, *"Whoever attends ISU on Earth or in its orbital facilities in the future will require the highest aspirations of any students in the world."* Entitled, *To Plan for a Century*, the full video is visible in several places on the Internet including at this address at the Space.com site:
http://www.space.com/common/media/video/player.php?videoRef=080319-Clarke.

Sir Arthur's straightforward message was drawn from the Chinese parable that to plan for a day one plants a seed; to plan for a decade one plants a tree; while to plan for a Century, one educates the people.

In materials prepared to support ISU's 1987 Founding Conference, Peter Diamandis and Kenneth Sunshine wrote of their vision for the evolution of ISU declaring, *"In the Twenty-first Century when permanent manned presence in Earth orbit has been firmly established, it is hoped that the University will have permanent facilities in space."*[1]

We believe that what we accomplished between our founding and the end of the Twentieth Century advanced this vision. We also believe that the Twenty-first Century demands still more of us.

Of course dreaming of taking an educational mission into space is the easiest part of the enterprise. To fulfill the mandate given to many generations of ISU students that they must 'dream with rigor,' we need not only to solve the question of how we actualize the dream, but also why.

Of these two questions, the latter seems the most important to me.

One of the greatest benefits of education about space and space activity has been the expansion of perspective. Working against the vastness of the cosmos and at scales which dwarf anything we can experience from studying Earth alone, space studies have not only pushed forward our understanding of Earth's place in the universe, they have also enabled us to see and understand things close to home to which we had been too close to notice or too preoccupied to find. Certainly the insight into the greenhouse effect that we gained from robotic exploration of Venus and sharp analysis of the data thus gained is one tangible example. Another is our emerging understanding of Earth's fragility, gained from stunning images of our sapphire and aquamarine planet hovering in the blackness of its cosmic neighborhood.

Increasingly we also draw perspective from the slowly growing database of human presence in space, which yields insights into the capacity and limitations of the human body's ability to adapt to microgravity, increased radiation loads, and transition stresses. Up to this point, however, the largest volume of new knowledge exists only in databases but not in the experience of living human beings. With only a few hundred active astronauts who have had personal experience adapting to even a near-Earth space environment, we do not have a large pool of people to call upon, if as many authors in this volume suggest, there are emerging commercial opportunities to exploit in space.

Thus, the first answer to the question 'why' is that we need a cadre of very smart people with experience using their intellects, physical capacities, and problem solving abilities in space. This was the early vision

[1]   Diamandis, Peter H. and Kenneth H. Sunshine, "Creating an International Space University," briefing paper prepared in support of International Space University Founding Conference (1986), unpublished, ISU Archives, pp. 3-4.

of Robert Heinlein's 1948 book, Space Cadet,[2] which quite presciently illustrates simple challenges of adjusting to life in space juxtaposed with the full rigors of a demanding, multi-disciplinary curriculum. Yet this Heinlein-created curriculum was destined for a very special group of guardians, a co-opted caste of peacekeepers for the solar system, but not for the general education of spacefarers.

If orbital manufacturing, asteroid mining, space tourism, lunar habitation and other such visions have any chance of commercial success they, too, will soon need a very specially prepared group of people to attend to the on-site tasks needed to achieve success. Beyond this classic vision of a need for an experienced, private space cadre, a combination of cosmic merchant marine and space-proven technical representatives, if you will, there is an even more pressing need. It emerges from the natural consequences of any or all of these early commercial visions for activity beyond earth being truly successful.

The implication of success is that human settlement will follow. It has always happened that way in the past, and there is no reason to believe that it will be otherwise this time. In the face of that expected reality we need a lot more than just ship drivers and equipment experts. We will need space-proven expertise in every field essential to the infrastructure of a human community. Hence, we will need education in space because after years of sending the occasional human to orbit, we are on the threshold of sending human society to space. Groups of humans can go anywhere without educational institutions, but human society exists only where there is also education.

At ISU we see this as rooted in our mission. After a few direct statements about the impact we seek to have on Earth, our mission statement concludes by linking those objectives to our calling to help humankind advance beyond its home planet:

"...[ISU Programs] encourage the innovative development of space for peaceful purposes: to improve life on Earth and advance humanity into space." The full mission statement, along with the founding credo expressing similar sentiments, can be viewed at http://www.isunet.edu/.

Thus the first answer to why there should be educational facilities in space is derived from the great likelihood that a significant piece of humanity's future will unfold there. The farther out our species goes from its planet of incubation, the greater will be the need for education not only to prepare the voyage, but to interpret it and adjust to it.

There is a second reason as well.

For the next several hundred years at least, most humans will live on Earth. As they continue to advance in their ability to identify, solve, and,

---

[2] Heinlein, Robert, *Space Cadet*, New York, Orb Books, 2006, 224 pp., ©1948.

yes, even create problems, their future will be greatly aided by the perspective of research and insight acquired off planet. We know from several generations of astronauts that even in low Earth orbit, our home planet looks different, and that the orbital environment in which our spacefarers live teaches us through challenges not present on its surface. Whether through the overview effect or through the opportunity to perform experiments in microgravity or hard vacuum, space opens the possibility of new perspectives and points of view. By bringing people of different nationalities, disciplines, and cultures into densely packed communities of spacefarers, spaceborne facilities open the way to better understand teamwork, synergy, and community itself. More than most earthly conditions, it may duplicate the intense interdependence that seems to have played such a critical role in the evolution of our species.

Beyond our atmosphere, the slightly more than 500 people who have had the privilege to fly in space have been able to see things differently, solve medical mysteries, explore alternative materials, and inquire into scientific principles and applications under a very different set of limits than those present on Earth. The result has occasionally been scientific breakthroughs, but even as importantly it has led to the reformulation of questions and rethinking of paradigms. This is the kind of result sought by every teacher who has ever worked to lead bright students into the world of critical thought. It is a result I expect to see achieved through education in orbit before the 21st Century is finished.

•••

DR. MICHAEL K. SIMPSON

Dr. Michael K. Simpson became President of the International Space University in May 2004. His academic career extends over 32 years and four continents. He has also been president of Utica College and the American University of Paris with a combined total of twenty years of experience as an academic chief executive officer. He has lectured in political science, international relations, business management, international law, leadership, and economics at Universities in the United States of America, France, China, the United Kingdom, and Australia.

Dr. Simpson received his Bachelors Degree Magna Cum Laude from Fordham University in 1970 where he was elected to Phi Beta Kappa. He has also been elected to academic honor societies in the fields of political science and business management. After graduating from Fordham University, Dr. Simpson accepted a commission as an officer in the U.S. Navy where he served as an Oceanographic Watch Officer, Communications Officer, Leadership and Management Instructor, Repair Officer, and Political Military Action Officer. In 1993 he retired from the Naval Reserve with the rank of Commander. He holds numerous commendations including the Defense Meritorious Service Medal.

Dr. Simpson completed his Ph.D. at The Fletcher School of Law and Diplomacy of Tufts University, holds the Master of Business Administration from Syracuse University; and two Master of Arts degrees from The Fletcher School. He has also completed two prestigious one year courses in Europe: the French advanced defense institute (Institut des Hautes Études de Défense Nationale) and the General Course of the London School of Economics.

He is a board member of the Space Week International Association, a member of the Board of Governors of the National Space Society in the United States and an observer representative to the UN Committee on the Peaceful Uses of Outer Space. In 2005 he served as a participant in the workshop on *Humanity and Space the Next Thousand Years* hosted by the Foundation for the Future and from 2006-2008, he served as a panel member of the Association of Space Explorers workshop on mitigation policy for threats from near earth objects and currently serves on the commercial Spaceflight Safety Committee of the IAF. He is a co-founder of the International Institute for Space Commerce and a founding trustee of Singularity University. He is a corresponding fellow of the International Academy of Astronautics.

Seeing universities as nodes in an interconnected lattice of educational opportunities, Dr. Simpson has been responsible for concluding partnership agreements with Universities in Australia. Asia, North America, the Middle East, and Europe and has brought ISU into the Space Education Consortium in the United States as the only international partner in that body.

During his tenure as President of the International Space University, the school's already widely respected curriculum has been enhanced to include more material on satellite operations, management challenges of space projects, personal spaceflight, entrepreneurship, space policy, and prospects for commercial activity in space. An ISU Executive MBA enrolled its first students in June 2009.

The International Space University is headquartered in Illkirch-Graffenstaden in the urban community of Strasbourg, France. It offers three Masters Degrees, including the recently inaugurated Executive MBA. Each year from June through August it offers a prestigious, 9-week long session known as the Space Studies Program (SSP) that prepares high potential participants for rapid advancement in the space sector. The school also offers a number of short professional development courses tailored to the needs of space agencies and businesses.

He is also the author of Chapter 5 of this volume, *Spin-Out and Spin-In in the Newest Space Age.*

CHAPTER 23

FROM SPACE BOOTS TO CYBER SUITS
MERGING NEUROPROSTHETIC DEVICES AND VIRTUAL REALITY ON MARS

DAWN L. STRONGIN, PH.D.
ASSOCIATE PROFESSOR, CALIFORNIA STATE UNIVERSITY AT STANISLAUS
AND
DIANDRA HILTON
CALIFORNIA STATE UNIVERSITY AT STANISLAUS

SERENADING THE STARS

> *"The reasonable man adapts himself to the world;*
> *the unreasonable one persists in trying to adapt the world to himself.*
> *Therefore, all progress depends on the unreasonable man."*
> George Bernard Shaw

Invention has freed the brain from its bodily constraints, leaving the imagination unencumbered to envision paths that lead to obtaining even our wildest dreams. Like a shark, the brain never stops swimming in thought (Leher, 2010), and as it seeks new discoveries, the brain's architectural landscape becomes reshaped. Recent innovative tools capitalize on the brain's adaptive malleability, blurring the separation between nervous and cyber systems and in effect creating a symbiotic relationship. It is this interconnection that will enable humans to thrive on other worlds.

The human brain reached its current size more than 250,000 years ago, yet it was less than 40,000 years ago that human innovation began its leap from *"stone to silicon"* (Husick, 2008), excelling beyond even our Neanderthal cousins whose cranial sizes exceeded our own. While the precise mechanisms that facilitated this profound change are still unfolding, it is clear that the brain's characteristic malleability was a contributing factor, which ultimately may help us survive on our inhospitable neighboring planet.

Compared to the physical attributes of our nonhuman brethren, we are dawdling, hairless, gravity-bound creatures. Yet it is our shared and uniquely human characteristic – the libido sciendi, or the 'lust for knowledge' – that enables us to overcome our limited physical capacities and frontiers. Driven by curiosity, creativity, and dreams, the highly adaptive human brain nourishes the ingenuity needed to thrive in environments exceeding our corporeal limitations. From molecules to Mars, we not only imagine unseen worlds, we invent the tools so that we may experience them. For in the words of John Updike, *"Dreams come true. Without that possibility, nature would not incite us to have them."*

Archeologists unearthing artifacts and stone tools suggest that Neanderthals and early humans intelligently and creatively developed techniques for survival. However, from the time when the Aurignacians began to replace Neanderthals in Asia, Europe, and North Africa 40,000 years ago, early consciousness shifted from survival's immediacy to realms beyond Earth's atmospheric edge. The earliest evidence found so far of this shift is engraved on a sliver of woolly mammoth bone depicting Orion's outstretched arms and legs, the most visible cluster of stars in the night sky (Rappengluek, 2006). Humans have continued to close the distance between Earth and Cosmos by maintaining a steady gaze on naked-eye celestial bodies – from Cro-Magnon's planetary maps on the walls of Lascaux caves, and the astronomical alignments of Stonehenge and Egyptian pyramids, to the current Mars Exploration Rovers, so appropriately named Spirit and Opportunity.

Our glowing red planetary neighbor has especially dominated the human imagination for millennia. Early Romans worshipped Mars as the god of fertility, but paradoxically, its bloody appearance was later associated with the god of war, and offerings of human sacrifice prior to combat were hoped to ensure success (Barbree, Wright, & Caidin, 1997).

But until recently, humans could do no more than dream of life on other planets. Now, tool development has advanced to the extent that we may not only travel to these worlds, but by integrating them with our active nervous systems, we can thrive under the most difficult conditions.

PHYSIOLOGICAL CHALLENGES OF THE MARTIAN VOYAGE

*"Every great advance in science has issued from
a new audacity of the imagination."*
John Dewey

Today, many of the international community's intellectual, financial, and creative resources are focused on establishing Mars as the first space settlement. Although we now have the technological capacity to push against Earth's gravitational force with enough velocity to escape into the vacuum of space, our bodies are severely stressed as they endure the long trip without gravity.

Travel to and from Mars is dependent on the orbital coordination of Earth and Mars. While both planets revolve in the same direction around the Sun, the elliptical trajectory of Mars is a little more 'stretched out' than Earth, doubling the length of its orbital circumference. The paths of Earth and Mars converge only once every 25 months, creating a small window of opportunity to return home (Stern, 2004). Martian explorers will need to time their launches perfectly so that the spacecraft reaches Mars when the planets are along aligned paths to keep transit down to seven months. After landing on Mars, Martian explorers will have to remain on the planet for 11 months before the window reopens for the optimum seven month trek home. This prolonged duration of weightlessness while journeying to the planet (in space) and Mars' relative microgravity upon arrival (1/3 Earth's gravity) will permanently weaken the bodies of the space faring travelers.

Healthy human development relies on the only Earthly constant – the downward pull of gravity. Weight-bearing postural muscles in the legs, hips, feet and shoulders, use gravitational resistance to facilitate bipedal navigation, which requires the rhythmic oscillation of opposable actions (LaMothe, 2010). To move, our bodies must have something to push against, and before we can jump, we must bend. Resistance helps to guide and strengthen the clarity of our movements, but our postural muscles are rendered useless over time without gravity (Williams, Kuipers, Mukai, & Thirsk, 2009).

Although rigorous exercise in space will prevent excessive loss of muscle mass, the bones that cling to these muscles require additional gravitational resistance to maintain their strength. Like most cells in the human body, bone cells go through a cycle of regeneration, resorption (or degradation), and formation of new cells, and bone mass regeneration is activated in response to weight-bearing signals. Hormones and growth factors stimulate osteoblasts to produce the collagen that forms a new bone matrix. But in weightless conditions, resorption occurs faster than the formation of a new bone matrix, resulting in net bone loss.

A four-year study found that space farers on the International Space Station lost as much lower body bone mass in one month as an elderly woman loses in an entire year (Roy, 2007). Hence, traveling to Mars for seven months in this weightless condition would presumably reduce bone mass by one-third. Although bone mass can be replaced within one year after return to Earth's gravity, the bone structure and density in the weight-bearing bones cannot recover, leaving the bones more massive than before, yet permanently more prone to fracture even though bone structure in the non-weight bearing upper body remains intact during prolonged weightless conditions (Roy, 2007).

Bone density will be further compromised by radiation exposure in space and on Mars. Earth's magnetosphere (which Mars lacks) shields it from the torrential million miles per hour solar winds. As space farers leave Earth's protection, they become vulnerable to the bombardment of bone-stripping, cancer-inducing radiation.

Further, landing on the lonely planet will be less welcoming than the chasm of space for the space traveler. Beginning when Mars is closest to the Sun in the southern hemisphere, highly oxidized dust storms with surface wind speeds ranging from 67 to 111 miles per hour rage for months, leaving behind rusty global skies (Kahn, Martin, Zurek, & Lee, 1992). Polar temperatures average -80° F and frequently dip below -195° F in the extreme atmospheric conditions of 95% carbon dioxide and only .13% oxygen. The weakened and brittle Martian explorer will be reliant on protection, and yet will be unable to physically support the spacesuits designed for navigation on Martian terrain.

While grounded on Earth, space farers' boots and suits weigh approximately 255 lbs, and are virtually weightless once in space. The gravitational pull on Mars is 1/3 the pull on Earth, which will reduce the suit to a mere 85 lbs. However, the frail Earthling will crumple under the burden of even this weight.

If these travelers were to remain orbiting in the vacuum of space, the resultant physiological changes would be less bothersome, as gravity's pull would not challenge their weakened bodies. In fact, astronauts have reported that in weightless conditions, their legs 'just get in the way.'

We can therefore conceive that generations of weightless humans may evolve along the path of the whale. Ambulocetus, the genus of the whale ancestor, were dog-sized land animals that evolved into buoyant ocean creatures to compensate for their growing brains and bodies. Their forelimbs maintained their mammalian bones in the arms and hands, but their weight-bearing hindlimbs became useless and inarticulated. Small 'floating' vestigial reminders of life on land are all that remains (Gatesy & O'Leary, 2001). However, while humans could possibly float perpetually in space, this does not address the inherent challenge of Mars colonization, so we must assume that it will be necessary to compensate for humanity's physiological limitations.

The brain is a tremendously adaptable system, and it readily adjusts to many environmental demands despite the body's limitations. Neuroprosthetic devices and virtual reality technology are two exciting tools that will make space exploration possible. These tools involve directing movement of remote devices through thought alone and operate by harvesting the brain's natural energy resources. But to understand the technology behind these neurologically controlled devices, one must first understand brain functions.

THE RESILIENT BRILLIANT BRAIN

> *"It's the mind that makes the body."*
> Sojourner Truth

Just as each new generation of astronomers seems to discover that the universe is much vaster than previously imagined, technological advances continue to reveal layers of brain complexity, like a set of never ending nested Russian dolls. The most resilient and adaptable human attribute is the brain, which constantly strives to optimize function and efficiency by fine-tuning its internal communication in the context of environmental input. Unlike plastic that stretches and returns to its original shape, our brains respond to the environment like malleable thermoplastic; they change and continue to change. Neuronal networks are modified to accommodate environmental changes, and it is this capacity for modification, or neuroplasticity, that offers our greatest potential for Martian survival.

Although encased in bone, the power of the human brain is uncontainable. This tofu-textured three-pound ball consumes an enormous 20% of its body's fuel to sustain itself and manipulate its environment to suit its needs and wishes. Atop a brainstem stalk and subcortical bulb (a phylogenetically old bit of brain), rests a highly wrinkled mass called the neocortex. Ironed flat, the neocortex is the size of an open newspaper three nickels thick, and contains more neurons (i.e., nerve cells) itself than the stars in our Milky Way Galaxy. Never quiescent, the brain hungers constantly for input. Even as early as 28 weeks before birth, the brain dreams and creates increasingly more elaborate connections. In fact, the number of connections among neurons (i.e., synapses) in the human brain is truly astronomical – far exceeding the number of stars in our known universe.

Adaptive change predominately takes place within and among neurons. Repeated and persistent stimulation strengthens synaptic connections among neurons to form integrated functional systems, and to promote increasingly more efficient cortical processing. An example of neuronal networks changing to accommodate environmental input was provided by a series of experiments on the Space Life Sciences Mission flown on the Shuttle in 1991. These experiments were designed to identify what specific nervous system changes permit space farers to adjust to the feelings of nausea and disorientation associated with 'space sickness.'

In terrestrial gravity, the brain receives information about balance and orientation from the vestibular apparatus in the inner ear. Continuous reference signals are also gathered from our eyes, muscles, tendons, joints, and tactile receptors for accurate information concerning body position. Removing gravity creates conflicting signals, causing feelings of nausea and disorientation. However, within three to four days, astronauts become less nauseated and are able to adapt to the zero gravity atmosphere.

Ross (1996) found that rats residing in zero gravity for a prolonged period of time developed much denser and more elaborate neuronal connections at approximately the same rate that the rats adjusted to weightlessness. This finding suggests that new neuronal connections (i.e., synaptogenesis) are the nervous system's method of adapting to shifting environmental conditions.

NEUROPROSTHETIC DEVICES

> *"Great ideas originate in the muscles."*
> Thomas Edison

How can we take advantage of the brain's adaptive resilience? Despite the daunting physiological challenges of the Mars voyage, advanced technological devices capitalizing on this capacity of the brain will permit humans to pioneer Mars. Neuroprosthetic devices and virtual reality, two astonishing advancements that play on the brain's neuroplasticity, will facilitate survival on Mars.

Neuroprosthetics depend on electronic devices that sense the complex neuronal signals and movement intentions within the brain. These signals have been recorded by deeply penetrating brain tissue with needle-like electrodes, but the sharp electrodes may create tissue damage and inflammatory responses, and the inflexibility of the electrodes cannot accommodate the occasional shifting of the brain in its skull which can lead to further damage.

In response, Brian Litt, M.D. and his colleagues recently developed a silk-based microelectrode array that molds to the brain like shrink-wrap. As the silk dissolves, the attached metal electrodes, no larger than the thickness of five human hairs, hug the intricate contours of the brain, capturing a more robust set of signals that can control refined prosthetic movements. John Rogers, Ph.D. suggests that it may be possible to further reduce invasiveness by compressing the silk-based implants and delivering them into the brain through a catheter.

Advances like these lead us forward to more complete integration of the body and prosthetics, outside of body devices. Such integration also requires changes inside. The brain and body are unequivocally connected, and any changes occurring in one can affect the other. Both thinking and moving provide the brain with stimulation that changes neural circuitry. Movement is etched into the brain with practice, like a carving on a tree, creating bodily skills that require little effort to enact. This kinesthetic intelligence allows us to use our bodies in skilled ways by continuously integrating patterns and sensations.

Simply thinking about movement activates neuronal circuits involved in physically creating these etchings, and visualizing movement improves motor performance because skill and coordination originate in the brain. While there is an obvious difference between thinking and acting, from the brain's perspective the two are essentially the same.

It was through a demonstration by Pasqual-Leone that the brain's ability to change shape merely by activating the imagination (mental practice) was revealed. He split musical novices into two groups, physical players and mental players, and introduced them to the fingering and sound of a piano piece in five sessions. Scans of the participants' brains after the fifth session revealed the same pattern of neuronal changes in the motor regions of both groups. Remarkably, when the mental practitioners were asked to physically practice for one two-hour session, their musical performance was equal to the group who physically practiced for five sessions. These findings clearly demonstrate the capacity of the human brain to change its structure simply through imagination.

Technological advances have capitalized on the findings that physical and imagined experiences activate nearly identical neuronal patterns. Perhaps reminiscent of the malevolent machines that harvested electrical currents from active human brains in the film series *The Matrix*, researchers have found a way to intercept and translate the electrical language of the brain into movements that control remote robots. Given the loss of structural integrity in the weight-bearing postural muscles and bones from reduced gravitational signals, these neuroprosthetic devices eventually could enable space farers and Martian dwellers to compensate for the debilitating effects of muted gravity by controlling remote robots with the power of thought.

Miguel Nicolelis, codirector of the Center for Neuroimaging at Duke University, developed an organic robotic neural interface between the brain of a macaque monkey named Aurora and a prosthetic arm. Eventually, as Aurora imagined herself walking, the sensory-motor signals from her cortex were captured and used to control a bipedal robot 10,000 miles away, and in real time, demonstrating that the actions of a robot can be directed by merely interpreting the thoughts of the brain as expressed through its own electrical activity. Visual feedback has been used to close the loop between the user and the machine, but because vision is processed more slowly in the brain, Nicolelis is devising a sensory feedback loop that Aurora (and those who follow) can use to optimize control over devices.

The mechanism behind neuroprosthetic devices requires a reorganization of the body schema. Of all our sensory modalities, the most persistent and yet least conscious is proprioception, or our body sense. Blending vision, touch, balance, and weight, proprioception allows us to *"feel our bodies as proper to us, as our property, as our own"* (Sacks, 1987, p.30). From this fluctuating mosaic of brain activity, our sense of an embodied self emerges (Ramachandran & Rogers-Ramachandran, 2010). Constant low-priority signals from the body create an enduring impression of where the body ends and the world begins, establishing a sense of self-awareness and body schema. As the brain activates body movement, feedback loops return somatic sensations to the brain for a visceral sense of body position. For example, sensory feedback allows us to adjust our grasp of that piping hot cup of coffee, and we can offset tactile silence (e.g., from a sleeping arm) with visual input (but the odds the coffee will not burn our laps are slim).

Our brain's capacity to expand its body schema allows us to manipulate tools, reflected in larger brain region activation. By extending our self, we can sense food texture with fork prongs instead of fingers, and skillfully manipulate keys, cars, and electric guitars.

This body schema even endures after quick amputation. Persistent sensations from missing limbs enable amputees to more effectively use prosthetic devices, compared to those who do not experience these phantom limbs. When long-term interactions with a prosthesis occurs, the brain devotes cortical space to it, and learns to interpret its tactile feedback, allowing individuals with phantom limbs to feel the prosthetic as an extension of the body schema, as part of themselves. Neuroprosthetic devices capture the electrical activity of extended body signals to manipulate robotic limbs, as seen in the macaque monkey.

"If an arm can survive physical annihilation, why not an entire person?" Ramachandran's intriguing question has practical implications. With less gravity to counteract the decline of their wasted muscles and delicate bones, travelers will necessarily encase themselves in full-body mobile neuroprosthetic devices to navigate the Martian frontier. Using these technologies, pioneers will be able to climb over rocks and through unlit caves, and to brave the dust winds to explore and discover the uncharted landscape of the planet, all the while remaining under full protection.

To achieve optimal manipulation of neuroprosthetics, the brain requires a way to 'hear back' from the device. Researchers are working on embedding 'bionic neurons,' or sensors, to achieve mutual communication between the device and the nervous system. These sensors will be designed to amplify the existing neuronal signals to the prosthetic limbs, which in turn will send a flurry of signals back to the brain. The wearer could then monitor the degree of pitch, force, thrust, and orientation of the prosthetic for smoother mobility. Researchers are also working to design bionic neurons that return signals from other sensory modalities as well, including sound, smell, and taste, to brain regions that can interpret them. For example, cochlear implants stimulate once-nonexistent auditory signals to endow hearing in the deaf.

And of course the full-body exoskeleton does not have to abide by the normal range of human capabilities. With practice, the brain could actually control a Martian neuroprosthetic device with many 360° radial leg extensions and panoramic visual fields to navigate the rocky, slippery, windy terrain.

Already a cathedral of complexity, synaptic connections within the brains of Martian adventurers will increase in complexity through the use of such tools. It will be particularly fascinating to note how brain architecture changes to accommodate the new body schema, but it must also be made clear that as their physical bodies become more debilitated in reduced gravity, they will become more reliant on these technologies, with all of the attendant risks.

VIRTUAL REALITY AND THE MARTIAN DOPPELGÄNGER

"I am a brain, my dear Watson,
and the rest of me is a mere appendage."
Sherlock Holmes

The long, confining trip to Mars will be psychologically and physiologically challenging. Today, cosmonauts prepare for the journey to Mars by utilizing virtual reality to simulate the roundtrip flight and the exploration on the planet in 'real time.' Their hope is to uncover key factors that mitigate the psychological challenges inherent in the arduous journey. It appears that virtual reality technology may ameliorate many of the physiological challenges as well.

Virtual reality systems apply a high-end user-computer interface that immerses users in a realistically interactive environment. Goggles covering each eye project slightly different images to produce perceptions of three-dimensional space, while a computer tracks the motion of the head. An interface device covering the body tracks position and motion, combined with continuously updated images as the head swivels and tilts, giving the viewer a sense of living in a vividly lucid dreamscape.

Researchers are working toward integrating neuroprosthetic and virtual reality technologies to control doppelgängers, or mechanistic alter egos, from afar. Users with doppelgängers will have the capability to explore and to work without leaving their Martian settlements, or their spacecrafts, and thus avoid risking harm from radiation and injury.

Remotely controlled technology exists in its embryonic form today. Individuals unable to move or talk can now mentally control a cursor to type their thoughts. This technology is also used to train autistic children to establish neuronal connections that are characteristically underactive for social communication. By sustaining specific brain oscillations, they learn to move cars and planes on the computer screen through thought (Pineda, et al., 2008). The gaming industry has enhanced virtual reality to such an extent that individuals have a first person interactive experience.

The greatest challenge of this technology is adequately deceiving the brain's perception of self, so as to leave its host body and 'merge' with its remote doppelgänger. To date, virtual reality researchers have induced sensations of disembodiment into doppelgängers for moments at a time. When a user is filmed from behind in a simulated room, a 3D decoder inserts the image into virtual reality goggles. The user then sees his/her image several yards in front. When the backs of the virtual and real selves are stroked synchronously, the brain confuses where the signal is coming from. There is often a sense of awkwardness, followed by a sense of being pulled toward the doppelgänger. Some users have felt that they became their doppelgängers for a moment, until the real body's gravitational and visceral signals brought them back to their more conventional orientation.

Space farers who do not receive gravitational signals aboard a spacecraft may make these leaps into their phantom selves more readily. They will not be bombarded with proprioceptive feedback from their own bodies, allowing them to immerse more fully into their doppelgängers. And perhaps a sustained illusion of becoming a living doppelgänger can occur if the doppelgänger's 'experiences' can signal visceral sensations in the user simultaneously.

As more people remotely control their doppelgängers, they will rub shoulders with other doppelgängers while collaborating to build the Martian settlement infrastructure. As social creatures, people certainly will enjoy controlling their doppelgängers during playful interactions with each other as well, perhaps creating sub-societies. However the forms these doppelgängers take may change the quality of these social interactions. We tend to connect more deeply with animate and inanimate beings that can be anthropomorphized. Therefore, non-anthropomorphized doppelgängers may have strictly utilitarian value, and those that represent human qualities may be cherished for the ease in which they enable people to connect with the doppelgängers and each other.

Until doppelgängers can achieve perfectly realistic human features, they must remain less realistic than current technology can produce. Roboticist Masahiro Mori found that humans are receptive to lifelike robots, up to a specific point. A virtual face that is 90% lifelike is great. A 95% lifelike face is the best. However once the realism reaches 96% lifelike, people become disturbed, a threshold known as the 'Uncanny Valley' (Steckinfinger & Ghazanfar, 2009).

The sophisticated computer animators who created the Shrek movies inadvertently stumbled into this Uncanny Valley with the first version of their Princess Fiona, as her nearly perfect face actually frightened an audience of children (York, 2010). Missing or distorted facial expressions, so subtle that in most cases they are perceived only unconsciously, create discomfort in others. Seemingly false smiles and dead eyes trigger a sense of caution when the intricacy of musculature and reflected light are absent. The reason the Uncanny Valley exists is due to the silence of specific cells called mirror neurons. Normally, when people communicate with us, our mirror neurons become active so that we may mimic these facial expressions unconsciously. As we move, the brain interprets our own facial expressions as emotional experiences inducing an empathetic bond. Thus, mirror neurons dissolve the barrier between self and others.

Because computer animators and roboticsts do not have the technology to make exquisitely realistic facial expressions, we cannot fully empathize with their creations. The Uncanny Valley can be avoided by resisting the desire to make perfect human doubles. Placing function well above form, the design of the Martian doppelgänger even can transcend human shape.

The brain can certainly accommodate wild distortions into the body schema, a benefit for better control of unusual Martian doppelgängers. Cyber pioneer Jaron Lanier devised one of the earliest nonhuman doppelgängers in the early 1980s. While he wore virtual reality goggles, a computer tracked the movements of his real body as he looked down at a virtual lobster body making jerky mimetic responses. The motor combinations used in his real body to flex his lobster joints were too complex and subtle to master at first, but practice and intuition eventually led him to incorporate this strange new body into his sense of self. Like those using prosthetic devices, Lanier unconsciously learned to manipulate the extra legs and claws as his own. However, without tactile stimuli to close the sensorimotor feedback loop, the illusion was intermittent.

One way of sustaining tactile illusions is to create sensations that are spaced and timed at exacting intervals such that a sensation in the gap between the two original points will occur. For example, Lanier learned to wriggle a short tentacle growing from his doppelgänger's navel. Well-timed buzzers fooled his brain into feeling this tentacle from tip to base. He noted that, *"When you get the visual and tactile experiences going together, it becomes just astonishingly convincing. When you combine somatic illusions with visual feedback like that, you just get to this whole new level. It's like your [body schema] is maximally stretched at that point."* As scientific machinery is designed to perfect the timing of this illusion, tricking the brain to embody Martian doppelgängers will become quite natural.

The physiological struggles that await Martian voyagers are formidable. However, as we have seen here, merging the brain's ability to extend its sense of self through neuroprosthetic devices and remote doppelgängers will make life in the extreme Martian environment possible. The neurotechnology available today, combined with the radical improvements envisaged for the future, may enable the space explorer to capitalize on the most adaptable human attribute to inhabit and control otherworldly bodies.

Academic researchers and intrepid entrepreneurs are already working on these technologies. The application of these tools and methods to space travel and the colonization and development of worlds beyond Earth seems only a matter of time. Their use in space will improve their efficacy on Earth, just as the countless technologies of Mercury, Gemini, Apollo, the Space Shuttle, and the ISS have done. Science, technology, commerce, and the human imagination remain inextricably linked. With each new tool that stretches the mind, we realize there are no dreams too large, no innovations unimaginable, and no frontiers beyond our reach.

"Only with the freedom to dream, to create, to risk,
Man has been able to climb out of the cave and reach for the stars."
Igor Sikorsky, aviation pioneer

•••

DAWN L. STRONGIN, PH.D.

Dawn L. Strongin, Ph.D. is an Associate Professor at CSU Stanislaus, specializing in cognitive neuroscience. She earned her Ph.D. at the University of Northern Colorado in Neuropsychology, Applied Statistics and Research Methods, and minored in Educational Psychology. Dr. Strongin's areas of research include: detecting preclinical neuropsychological symptoms in Alzheimer's disease patients, neurotoxic effects of organophosphates and solvents, and psychometric development. Courses she teaches include Physiological Psychology, Cognitive Processes, Perception, Introduction to Neuroscience, and Psychopharmacology. When not researching, teaching, and traveling, she is dreaming...of life on distant rocks.

DIANDRA HILTON

Diandra Hilton is completing her Master's degree in the Department of Psychology at California State University, Stanislaus. Currently she is researching the neuropsychological underpinnings of preclinical Alzheimer's disease. Outside of her immediate studies, Ms. Hilton's research interests lie in discerning the molecular exquisiteness of neurons, brain mapping, and the construction and perception of the self

REFERENCES

1. Barbree, J., Caidin, M., & Wright, S. (1997). *Destination mars: In art, myth, and science*. Penguin Studio Books

2. Gatesy, J. & O'Leary, M. (2001). "Deciphering whale origins with molecules and fossils." *Trends in Ecology & Evolution*, 16 (10), 562-570.

3. Husick, L. (2008). "From stone to silicon: A brief survey of innovation." Foreign Policy Research Institute. Retrieved from: http://www.fpri.org/

4. Kim, D-H et al. "Dissolvable Films of Silk Fibroin for Ultrathin Conformal Bio-Integrated Electronics." Nature Materials, published online April 18, 2010.

5. Kahn, R. A., Martin, T. Z., Zurek, & R. W. Zurek, & Lee, S. W. (1992). "The martian dust cycle" (pp. 1017-1053). In Kieffer, H. H., Jakwosky, B. M., Snyder, C. & Mathews, M. (1992). *Mars* (2nd ed.). University of Arizona Press.

6. Lehrer, J. (2010). "The frontal cortex: Why we dream." Retreived from: http://scienceblogs.com/cortex/2010/03/why_we_dream.php

7. LaMothe, K. (2009, February). "Come to your senses." *Psychology Today.* Retreived from http://www.psychologytoday.com

8. Nicolelis, M. A., & Chaplin, J. K. (2002). "Controlling robots with the mind," *Scientific American Mind,* 16-22. Scientific American, Inc.

9. Pineda, J. A., Brang, D., Hecht, E., Edwards, L., Carey, S., Bacon, M., Futagaki, C., Suk, D., Tom, J., Birnbaum, C., & Rork, A. (2008). "Positive behavioral and electrophysiological changes following neurofeedback training in children with autism." *Research in Autism Spectrum Disorders,* (2) 557-581.

10. Rappenglück, M. A., (2006). "The Planet Earth: Carved and drawn prehistoric maps of the cosmos." In A. Curtis (Ed.), *Space Today Online: Covering Space from Earth to the Edge of the Universe.* Retrieved from: http://www.spacetoday.org/SolSys/Earth/OldStarCharts.html

11. Ramachandran, V. S., & Rogers- Ramachandran, D. (2010). "Hey, is that me over there?" *Scientific American Mind,* 18-20.

12. Ross, M. D. (1996). "Gravity sensor plasticity in the space environment." NASA-Ames Research Center. Retrieved from: http://astrobiology.arc.nasa.gov/workshops/1996/astrobiology/speakers/ros s/ross_abstract.html

13. Roy, S. (2007). How long does it take to rebuild bone lost during space flight? Retrieved from http://www.nasa.gov/mission_pages/station/science/subregional_bone.html

14. Sacks, O. (1987). *The Man Who Mistook His Wife For A Hat And Other Clinical Tales* (4th Ed.). New York, NY: Harper & Row.

15. Steckenfinger, S. A., & Ghazanfar, A. A. (2009). "Monkey visual behavior falls into the uncanny valley." PNAS, 16(43), 18362-18366. doi:10.1073pnas.09010063106

16. Stern, D. (2004). "Flight to mars: How long? Along what path?" In D. Stern (Ed.), *From Stargazers to Starships.* Retrieved from: http://www-istp.gsfc.nasa.gov/stargaze/Smars1.htm

17. Williams, D., Kuipers, A., Mukai, C., & Thrisk, R. (2009). "Acclimation during space flight: effects on human physiology." Canadian medical Association, 180 (13), 1317-1323. doi:10.1503/cmaj.090628

18. York, J. (2010, March). "Hollywood Eyes Uncanny Valley in Animation." [Transcript] National Public Radio. Retrieved from: http://www.npr.org/templates/story/story.php?storyId=124371580

CHAPTER 24

CONCLUSION
SPACE COMMERCE, 2020 – 2100

LANGDON MORRIS
INNOVATIONLABS LLC
AND
KENNETH J. COX, PH.D.
ATWG FOUNDER

> *"It is impossible for the man who takes a survey of what is already known, not to see what an immensity in every branch of science remains to be discovered."*
> Thomas Jefferson, 1799[1]

The journey through the twenty-three preceding chapters has taken us across the spectrum of space science and its application in space technology and to living and working in space, as we understand them today, in 2010. It has been a mere 211 years since Jefferson wrote his prophetic words, and while the storehouse of our knowledge has advanced immeasurably since then, and humanity has since constructed a globalized, industrialized civilization of unprecedented power and scope, it is equally

---

[1] Jefferson wrote this in a private letter in 1799. It was first published in the journal *Scripta Mathematica* in 1932.

obvious that even today there remains a great deal that we have yet to discover. Among the unknowns of interest to us in this book is how we will ultimately live and work in space.

But while we do not know the 'how,' we remain convinced that indeed we will.

In these pages we have heard from engineers, scientists, managers, educators, investors, customers, manufacturers, soldiers, attorneys, and citizens, all of whom are convinced that the extension of our human community into space is inevitable and that done well and correctly, it will prove to be of great benefit to all humans.

Some of these authors are veterans of many decades in the space endeavor, while others are at the beginning their careers. But no matter how long they have been part of this effort, their voices are clear and their message is unanimous: space is an important part of humanity's future, not only because of the vast commercial opportunities that we will find and create there, but also because of what the exploration and settlement of space means for the human psyche, as well as for its significance to the survival prospects of our species.

THE TRANSITION DECADE

We mentioned in the Introduction that the period from 2010 to 2020 has all of the appearances of a transition decade. During these years we will see a shift, an inexorable realignment away from a space movement that has been led by just two driving forces, governments and satellite communication providers. To accompany them we will soon see many dynamic industries filled with numerous participating organizations from across the spectrum of economic activity, and across a huge range of national origins, means, motivations, and methods.

Already the space economy is very large. The Space Foundation estimates that in the US alone, 260,000 people worked in space industries in 2008, and they earned more than $23B in wages (an average of $90,000 each).[2] In the European Union, there are about 30,000 workers in space-related industries. And as the space industry grows, employment will grow with it.

As with all things in this life, there are no guarantees. But the evidence is certainly available to those who wish to look for it, and it seems to us that this book has presented considerable evidence in support of this conclusion as well.

---

[2]   The Space Foundation. *The Space Report, 2010*, John M. Diamond, Editor.
        This report is an invaluable resource for anyone interested in the details of the
        space economy. www.SpaceFoundation.org

As witnesses to the birth of a movement, we also observe the large and growing roster of companies that are doing (or intend to do) business in space. There are probably a lot of them that you have not heard of, but perhaps one day soon you will.

And perhaps one day there will be a stock index that tracks space commerce, just as there are indices for high tech, industry, transportation, utilities, and for global regions, etc. Actually, that day has already begun. The Space Foundation Index[3] tracks 30 public companies that have significant (but not necessarily exclusive) operations that are space-related:

The indexed companies are organized into four categories:

- Manufacturers and system integrators (11 companies)
- Ground Segment and Satellite Component Manufacturers (10 companies)
- Consumer/Retail Services (4 companies)
- Enterprise/Government Services (11 companies)

(Six of the companies participate in more than one category, which is why there are a total of 36.)

Perhaps one day NanoRacks, or ManSat, or Virgin Galactic, or Lunar Transportation Systems will also be listed on this index, or on one of the other competing indices that are likely to emerge as the significance of space commerce increases as a proportion of the global and by then transglobal economy. And when research firms like Forrester regularly publish reports on the space economy, and investors take note just as they now follow the auto, oil, or retail industries, then the forecasts will have become the realities.

What it will be like when all these companies are working, thriving, in space? How frequent will the launches be? How many people will live and work in space? How large will the space economy be? How important will it be to the global economy?

If we plot the growth of space commerce on a graph, by dollars, what we see looks a lot like Figure 1.

In Chapter 1, Will Pomerantz showed us that revenues from Moon-related projects alone could be in the $1 trillion range by 2020, but even without this level of growth we have merely to extend the existing revenue growth curve on its current trajectory to anticipate what might happen. We see that space commerce grows from its current $200B towards and well beyond $1 trillion, or more. The exact shape of the curve is impossible to predict, but the general trend of the curve is quite evident, and barring a dreaded and massive economic collapse, there are many reasons to expect the curve to fulfill these expectations, for the needs and opportunities are certainly great.

---

[3]   http://www.spacefoundation.org/spaceindex/

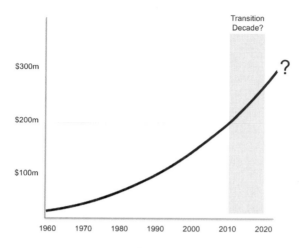

Figure 1
Annual commercial revenues of about $200M, 50 years into the space age.

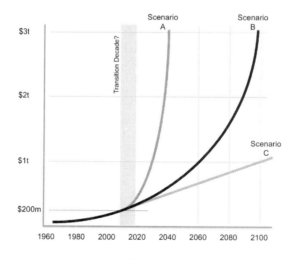

Figure 2
Will the growth of space commerce achieve annual revenues of
Scenario A, B, or C?

And when we look at the emerging structure of space commerce in detail, we see companies, both established ones and start-ups, competing in nine major industries, working along side governments and global consortia to create wealth and solve problems. Each of these industries is an enormous contributor to terrestrial commerce today, and each could also be enormous in space.

BEYOND 2020: INDUSTRIES IN SPACE

With the help of Amaresh Kollipara, Managing Partner of Earth2Orbit, LLC, we compiled the following overview of nine space-related industries that we expect to achieve significant scale in the coming decades.

TELECOMM

To date, the bulk of the money earned in space has been from telecommunications. Commercial satellite revenues were about $90B in 2009. Satellites surround the Earth because despite their cost and complexity, they're still cheaper than the alternatives, and in addition they do things that cannot be done on Earth alone. At present there are about 900 functioning satellites in orbit, and about 400 of them perform telecommunications functions.

TRANSPORT

The business of transport is about getting the satellites, as well as equipment, supplies, robots, and people into orbit. There are many commercial space transport companies, both in the public and private sectors, and this is also a thriving business today. For example, SpaceX currently shows a launch manifest of 27 flights between 2010 and 2015 for a variety of paying customers. As space commerce expands, the transport sector will expand along with it. In fact, the transport sector will have to evolve ahead of most of the other industries, because inexpensive and reliable transport to space is the enabling factor on which the others depend.

TOURISM & ENTERTAINMENT

As we read in Chapter 7, space tourism is now emerging as a potentially significant economic force. But if you don't want to wait in line for your chance to ride on Virgin Galactic, perhaps you'd be interested in another space tourism venture, Zero-G (http://www.gozerog.com/), a commercial aircraft that flies aerobatic maneuvers in the atmosphere so that passengers experience weightlessness. As market demand increases, there will be others. And if you liked your suborbital ride on Virgin, for maximum thrills we can't wait until someone opens the first zero-g amusement park!

EDUCATION

As we discovered in Chapters 20 and 21, as more people become engaged in commercial activities in space, education will naturally move there as well, so that students have meaningful experiences of living and working in space before they are called upon to locate there.

EARTH SCIENCE

One of the earliest benefits we received from the space program was the ability to observe the Earth in new ways. Today, Earth scientists utilize satellite images and measurements to monitor and understand the weather and the climate, to track storms, tsunamis and glaciers, while farmers use satellite images to manage the planting and fertilizing of crops, and natural scientists to monitor forests and fisheries.

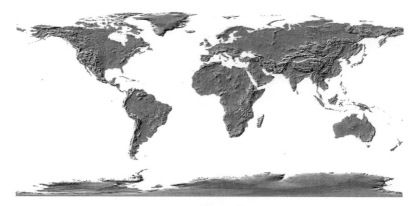

Figure 3
Earth Science from Space: The Global Land One-kilometer Base
Elevation (GLOBE), Digital Elevation Model, Version 1.0.
Made by Japan's Advanced Spaceborne Thermal Emission and Reflection
Radiometer (ASTER), an instrument aboard NASA's Terra satellite. ASTER
took 1.3 million images from space to create the most complete topographic
map of the Earth. *Credit: NASA/METI/NOAA.*
http://www.ngdc.noaa.gov/mgg/topo/globe.html

ENERGY

As we read in Chapters 11 and 15, it is possible that energy from the Sun can be used to power civilization on Earth. The impact of this industry, working at large scale, would be transformative to Earth's economy. The solar system contains other natural resources that may also power our planet, including abundant Helium-3 on the moon.

And it may not be so far in the future. Solaren Corporation recently announced a commercial supply contract, through which it is obligated to provide 200MW of power to Pacific Gas and Electric Company, the Northern California electric utility, beginning in 2016.

MINING

There are many minerals and compounds throughout the solar system that offer value in the human economic system, among them, of course, water.

MANUFACTURING

Scientific research and perhaps manufacturing in 'microgravity' at Low Earth Orbit may have significant impact on the pharmaceutical industry, as some drugs can apparently be formulated in space that are impossible to create on Earth.

SPACE SCIENCE

Beyond the interference of Earth's atmosphere it is possible to study the solar system, the galaxy and indeed the entire cosmos in ways that are simply impossible on Earth.

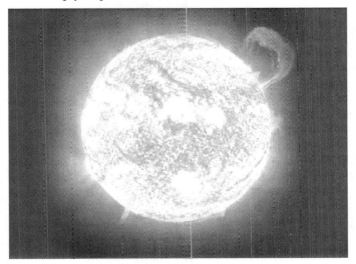

Figure 4
Space Science from Space: Extreme Ultraviolet Imaging Telescope (EIT) image of a huge, handle-shaped prominence taken on Sept. 14,1999 taken in the 304 angstrom wavelength. Courtesy of SOHO/Extreme Ultraviolet Imaging Telescope (EIT) consortium. SOHO is a joint project of ESA and NASA.

There is a tenth major space industry, and it is one of the largest. It is space militarization. The worlds nations spend billions each year to spy on each other from orbit, and to manage and communicate with their Earth-based military forces, including aircraft, unmanned aircraft, and naval fleets. These expenditures will continue to grow, as new technologies create new possibilities for offensive and defensive efforts. But as we have seen, the military also has a supportive role to play in space, providing security and emergency response in an inherently high risk environment.

What other industries will emerge? The history of business on Earth shows that as needs emerge, as new technologies are developed and put to use, as social and economic patterns change, then new ways of doing business are created in response. If space indeed becomes a thriving commercial setting, then we can be sure that new, unanticipated needs and opportunities will arise, and entrepreneurs and established companies will step forth.

Many of these needs may have to do with addressing the problems of life on Earth, from the basics of food, water, and energy, to climate and weather issues. And perhaps we will even find ways to address tumultuous issues such as politics and ideology in space more effectively than on Earth. This is, indeed, the promise that Frank White has so aptly labeled "The Overview Effect."

NASA AND AMERICA'S NATIONAL INTEREST

As these industries develop, those familiar with the space industry's history will naturally wonder about the organization that has to its credit a great many of the milestone accomplishments of the Space Age, and which has pioneered much of what we do in space today.

As we write these words, we are sadly aware that NASA is an agency dealing with difficult challenges and organizational change. The agency is filled with uncertainty about its mission, suffused with organizational conflict, and it remains at the mercy of a dysfunctional, annualized funding cycle in a political system that treats it as a pawn in ideological conflict, and an ongoing saga of Congressional job-brokering.

Part of the difficulty is a matter of circumstance, but a great deal is the result of the agency's own doing. Because, as we well know, what NASA has lacked these many decades since the end of the Apollo program is a mission worth of its magnificent Apollo heritage.

The emergence of space commerce as powerful, global phenomenon, offers NASA the opportunity to play exactly the right role, one in which its many strengths and massive store of accumulated knowledge can make a profound difference in accelerating the emergence of these new industries. This role we might define as catalyst, advisor, or facilitator.

But the agency is clearly not destined to be 'the doer' with respect to space commerce, nor should it be. This facilitation role has been widely recognized, and now its up to NASA to embrace the role with enthusiasm and skill.

There are already agencies of the US Government that are also seeking to fill important facilitation roles. For example, there is an "Office of Space Commercialization" that is a joint activity of the Department of

Commerce and NOAA (http://www.space.commerce.gov/). Similarly, the FAA also has an Office of Space Commercialization.

NASA faces an additional challenge in the coming years, and that is the aging of its workforce. A significant percentage of NASA employees are approaching retirement age, and the loss of their accumulated expertise could be quite detrimental to its capacity to deliver the results that it promises.

A corollary of this is the difficulty that space industries have in recruiting young talent. The worldwide demand for talent in science, engineering, and management is increasing each year, and with so many options available to them across a wide range of the economy, inducing a sufficient number of future leaders to join the space endeavor becomes a constant challenge, just as assuring that school-age students attain sufficient mastery of the STEM (science, technology, engineering, and mathematics) disciplines is certainly critical to the long term viability of every industrialized nation.

Therefore, it's clear that it will not just be the US Government that will catalyze this emerging industry. Many nations are making significant investments in space, and while their underlying motivations may vary considerably, their prospects of future success should not be underestimated.

It is entirely possible that China or India may take the leadership role in the development of space commerce through their ongoing space programs, and while this would be likely to cause severe heartache for many Americans, much as the Soviet launch of Sputnik provoked a wave of self-doubt across the nation, in the end it could well provide a significant acceleration to humanity's progress in space.

But if we see the commercialization of space become a matter of nationalist pride and sectarian interests, then the enormous potential it has for all of humanity will be severely compromised.

Is it realistic to hope that we can see the development of space as a human endeavor, and not a national endeavor? Perhaps it is naïve or idealistic to think so. But we have not yet given up on this dream. (And in support of this ideal, we anticipate that the next ATWG book will focus on international cooperation for the development of space.)

So which nations should benefit from the space endeavor? All of them, certainly. For who can claim to own a spot in orbit, or an acre of lunar soil? 19 nations plus the 18 nations of the European Union all have space agencies, through which they collectively spend around $44B each year on civil space activities (plus billions more on military space, and billions more on top of that on their space spy agencies).

Just one example of a national space program outside of the US is the effort in the UK, which in 2010 brought all of its commercial space activities into a single agency, and notes on its new web site, that *"The*

UK's thriving space sector contributes £6.5B a year to the UK economy, and supports 68,000 jobs. "

Country	Agency	Budget (USD)
United States	NASA (National Aeronautics and Space Administration)	$17,600 million[45]
ESA [show]	ESA (European Space Agency)	$5,350 million [46]
France	CNES (French Space Agency)	$2,590 million [47]
Russia	RKA (Russian Federal Space Agency)	$2,400 million
Japan	JAXA (Japan Aerospace Exploration Agency)	$2,100 million
Germany	DLR (German Aerospace Center)	$1,821 million
Italy	ASI (Italian Space Agency)	$1,550 million
China	CNSA (China National Space Administration)	$1,300 million[48]
India	ISRO (Indian Space Research Organization)	$1,268 million[49]
United Kingdom	UKSA (UK Space Agency)	$414 million
Iran	ISA (Iranian Space Agency)	$400 million
Canada	CSA (Canadian Space Agency)	$373.5 million
Brazil	AEB (Brazilian Space Agency)	$343 million
Ukraine	NSAU (National Space Agency of Ukraine)	$250 million
Belgium	BISA (Belgian Institute for Space Aeronomy)	$230 million
Spain	INTA (Instituto Nacional de Técnica Aeroespacial)	$175 million
Netherlands	SRON (Netherlands Institute for Space Research)	$160 million
South Korea	KARI (Korea Aerospace Research Institute)	$150 million
Switzerland	SSO (Swiss Space Office)	$110 million
Sweden	SNSB (Swedish National Space Board)	$100 million
World	All space agencies (Total of listed budgets)	$44,400 million ($44.4 Billion)

Figure 5
National / Multinational Space Agencies and their 2010 Budgets.
Note that the figures are confidential for some countries, so determining the 'real' number is a matter of guesswork. Consequently, the figures can differ considerably depending on who's counting. On an order-of-magnitude basis, the figures in this table are consistent with other estimates.
Bolivia, Mexico, South Africa, Vietnam, and Sri Lanka have all announced and/or approved plans to initiate their own space agencies.
Source: http://en.wikipedia.org/wiki/List_of_space_agencies

CHALLENGES

Even though we're spending billions, there remain, of course, countless challenges, and among them we have selected a few to highlight.

IT'S NOT LIKE THE MOVIES...

There is a widespread perception, one that has been promoted through science fiction and popular movies and TV shows such as *Star Wars*, *Star Trek*, and many others, which suggests that living in space is a lot like living on Earth, and by extension, making money in space is like making money on Earth as well.

However, at our current level of knowledge and technology, this is simply not the case.

Living and working in space is fundamentally different in every way. The demands that weightlessness places on our bodies are fundamental, and cannot be underestimated. Likewise, the need to bring the entire life-supporting living environment along with you wherever you go is complex to say the least, and the life support-related risks are immeasurably greater than on Earth.

The constraints that the need for 'life support' imposes on space inhabitants will profoundly influence the nature of space commerce for decades if not throughout the entire 21st century, even as our knowledge and technical means continue to improve.

DEGREES OF SEPARATION

The farther from Earth humans venture, the more limits and constraints the voyagers experience. It becomes progressively more difficult to manage life support for the voyagers when they are progressively farther away from the reliable source of supply. And similarly, the farther they go, the greater their vulnerability to unplanned events, and the worse the likely negative consequences would be.

Facing up to the difference between the popular imagery and imagination, and the actual difficulties of providing uninterrupted life support, suggests that a development strategy based on learning from initiatives in Low Earth Orbit before moving further outward from Earth would be wise. Hence, the learnings from the ISS and other LEO efforts will be invaluable in subsequent journeys and outposts further beyond. We can anticipate that we will progress in stages.

A consequence of the increasing risk is the increasing attractiveness of robotics. On Earth today, it is estimated, there are nearly 8 million robots in use across a wide range of activities, including millions in manufacturing, but also performing in services, from office and medical deliveries to surveillance, milking cows, and vacuuming floors. Robotics is a rapidly expanding industry, and with continuing progress in computer chip miniaturization and declining computer chip prices, the future of robotics promises progressively greater capabilities. At some point before 2020, it is reasonable to expect robotic intelligence to progress to the point that robots could do what astronauts were once required to do. This will change the nature of space exploration and development in a fundamental way.

WEIGHTLESSNESS AND CHILDBIRTH

To highlight just a couple the life support and lifestyle challenges, let us look to the previous book in this series, *Living in Space*, in which coauthors Dawn Strongin and E.K. Reese examined many of the anatomical and physiological issues related to life in weightlessness in their chapter entitled, *Earthlings on Mars: The Physiological Psychology of Cultural Change*.

They point out that,

> *"Weightless and low gravity conditions also affect our bones. Although rigorous exercise in space will prevent the excessive loss of muscle mass, sustaining bone density requires additional gravitational resistance. Like most cells in the human body, bone cells go through a cycle of regeneration, resorption (or degradation), and formation of new cells, and bone mass regeneration is activated in response to weight-bearing signals. Hormones and growth factors stimulate osteoblasts to produce the collagen that forms a new bone matrix; but in weightless conditions, resorption occurs faster than the formation of a new bone matrix, resulting in bone loss. A four-year study found that spacefarers on the International Space Station lost as much lower body bone mass in one month as an elderly woman loses in an entire year" (Roy, 2007)[4]. Traveling to Mars for six months in this weightless condition would presumably reduce bone mass by one-third. Although bone mass can be replaced within one year after return to Earth's gravity, the bone structure and density in the weight-bearing bones cannot recover, leaving the bones more massive and yet more prone to fracture. However, bone structure in the non-weight bearing upper body remains intact during prolonged weightless conditions (Roy, 2007).*

> *"Bone density will be further compromised by radiation exposure in space and on Mars. Earth's magnetosphere (which Mars lacks) shields it from the torrential million miles per hour solar winds. As spacefarers leave Earth's protection, they become vulnerable to the bombardment of bone-stripping, cancer-inducing radiation. This*

---

[4] Roy, S. (2007). "How long does it take to rebuild bone lost during space flight?" Retrieved March 26, 2007, from http://www.nasa.gov/mission_pages/station/science/subregional_bone.html

combination of factors will most likely evoke new and unforeseen adaptive behaviors."[5]

Astronauts have also noted many other physiological, neurological, and psychological phenomena, including fluctuating metabolisms, sleep problems, changes to the functioning of memory, as well motion sickness and sensory conflicts in weightlessness.

Until we learn to overcome these issues (and many others), through adaptive practices and/or genetic engineering, the prospects for long term space habitation are not so great. This will, in turn, have a fundamental influence on the emergence and development of space commerce, on who goes, and how long they stay. It will also provide additional impetus for the development and use of highly capable robots.

FAMILIES IN SPACE

From the Asian migrations across the frozen Bering Straits thousands of years ago to the Puritans crossing the Atlantic on the Mayflower hundreds of years ago, to the covered wagons of the 18th century plains during the westward expansion in the US, or the waves of migration occurring around the world today, migrants generally prefer to bring their families with them, or to start new families when they arrive. In space, though, things will be different.

One reason, as Strongin and Reese point out, is that giving birth in space is at present simply not an option.

"Weight-bearing bone loss and muscle atrophy of the extended low-gravity condition may make sexual intercourse and human childbearing, as we currently know them, impossible. When considering brittle bones, creative Martian sexual practices would need to replace 'dangerous' Earthly coitus. Certainly, the Sensation Seeking settlers would put imagination and technology to good use.

"Unless pregnant women lived in zero gravity chambers or large bodies of water, the compromised pelvic bone integrity would make carrying a child to term difficult, even with Mars' lower gravity. Natural childbirth would be prohibitive. Test-tube babies might therefore become a necessity, creating completely novel cultural associations concerning parenthood. The ramifications are far-reaching, including changes in gender roles, as women would no

---

[5] Strongin, D., and EK Reese, "Earthlings on Mars: The Physiological Psychology of Cultural Change," in *Living in Space: Cultural and Social Dynamics, Opportunities, and Challenges in Permanent Space Habitats.* Sherry Bell, Ph.D. and Langdon Morris, Editors, ATWG, 2009.

longer be the bearers of children, and unplanned pregnancies would be nonexistent."[6]

Because of these constraints, space commerce will simply not unfold as it has on Earth. Our present understanding of space science and its impact on human physiology tells us that the very nature of living in space will continue to be a constraint on the nature of commerce for the foreseeable future.

SPACE JUNK

In addition to the many functioning communications and observation satellites that are currently in orbit around the Earth, there is also a great deal of space junk. *"The United States now tracks more than 10,000 pieces of debris four inches wide or larger, but tens of millions of smaller fragments are also whizzing through space at speeds that can exceed 17,000 miles per hour,"* says Mark Matney of NASA's Orbital Debris Program. *"At such speeds, a collision with even an apple-size object could shatter a spacecraft into hundreds of pieces."*[7]

NASA notes, *"Most 'space junk' is moving very fast. It can reach speeds of 4.3 to 5 miles per second. Five miles per second is 18,000 miles per hour. That speed is almost seven times faster than a bullet. And if a spacecraft is moving toward the debris, the total speed at which they collide can be even faster. The average impact speed of a piece of orbital debris running into another object is 22,370 miles per hour. To keep astronauts safe, scientists use radar to keep track of all the debris in orbit. They classify it by its size. About 13,000 known objects are bigger than 10 centimeters in diameter. Scientists believe that there are more than 100,000 pieces of orbital debris between 1 cm and 10 cm. And tens of millions of pieces are smaller than 1 cm. All pieces of debris larger than 10 cm are carefully tracked using radar and telescopes."*[8]

The existing inventory of space junk presents a significant but manageable problem in and of itself, but if there were to occur a serious accident or a military conflict in space, then it is possible that the resulting profusion of new junk would render vast stretches of orbital 'territory' unusable for commerce due the very high risk of future orbital junk collisions.

---

[6]   Strongin, D., and EK Reese, "Earthlings on Mars: The Physiological Psychology of Cultural Change," in *Living in Space: Cultural and Social Dynamics, Opportunities, and Challenges in Permanent Space Habitats.* Sherry Bell, Ph.D. and Langdon Morris, Editors, ATWG, 2009..

[7]   http://discovermagazine.com/2006/nov/map-space-junk

[8]   http://www.nasa.gov/audience/forstudents/5-8/features/what-is-orbital-debris-58.html

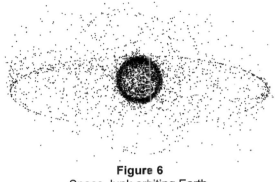

Figure 6
Space Junk orbiting Earth.
Image courtesy of NASA

There are many reasons to resist the militarization of space, and this is just another one, for even a small conflict could render a tremendously valuable commons resource quite useless for everyone.

Figure 7
A crack about 1 millimeter wide in a space shuttle window.
This was the result of a collision with a space trash particle about one tenth of a millimeter wide. Image courtesy of NASA

A GLOBAL LEGAL FRAMEWORK

Space junk is not just a problem for American spacecraft, nor just for Russian, nor Chinese, nor Indian, nor ESA, nor indeed for any single nation's endeavors in orbit. It is a problem for all. And the need to manage it in the interest of all space endeavors brings forth the need to create a broad, global framework that defines agreements. In other words, we need a global framework of space law that is accepted and adhered to by all spacefaring countries and companies, without exception. And this will also require a mechanism for enforcement, lest the Somali pirates simply relocate to orbit to prey, unmolested, on shipping there. Captain Brent Ziarnick's Space Guard becomes elevated to a practical requirement, not just a matter of speculation. (See Chapter 20)

SOUND BUSINESS JUDGMENT

There are many other challenges, to be sure, but the last one we will mention here is simply the need for sound business judgment. To explain the problem, let us examine the cautionary tale of Motorola's Iridium. Most space entrepreneurs are already familiar with this story, but it is worth repeating here even if you remember what happened.

> *"The decision by top executives of Motorola to launch the Iridium satellite telephone business was driven largely by an intuitive 'vision' of customers being able to use a single portable phone to place calls from anywhere in the world, despite the extensive data that Motorola itself generated showing that this would be an economically unsound business. The phone would have to cost $3000, the service would have to cost $3 per minute, and communication would have been impossible indoors or in cities with skyscrapers. The product was ideal for the desert nomad with a few thousand dollars burning a hole in is pocket, but impractical for everyone else. Iridium failed within a year of launch [nine months to be precise], and ultimately lost almost $5B."[9]*

If you happen to do a web search for 'iridium' today, you will find a company that appears to be thriving. The reason is that the original Iridium company was bought from bankruptcy for about $25M (or about $1/200^{th}$ of the original investment). Having obtained its capital infrastructure at .5% of its cost, Iridium can now afford to operate a satellite telephone network at rates that are reasonable. And since they own all the hardware, it's electronically secure. Consequently, a major customer seems to be the US military. A competing company sued when it was revealed that Iridium received a large government contract outside of the normal competitive bidding process, but the lawsuit was stopped, by the government, due to concerns about confidential military information being exposed at trial.

The story is a microcosm of terrestrial commerce – high technology, risk, failure, a second try, a big contract, competition, and litigation... But unlike business on Earth, the core of the story is 66 satellites that cover the entire globe, from equator to poles. It might make a good movie. And it certainly constitutes a good warning that space entrepreneurs must heed, the need to balance their visions with hard line business judgment.

---

[9]   Chabris, Christopher and Daniel Simons. *The Invisible Gorilla.* Crown Books, 2010. P 232.

The Race: Evolution vs. Culture

We have considered many of the practical issues, as well as organizational concerns and global, governmental topics as well. Now let us step back and look at a broader pattern of human history.

We are referring here to the contrast between human evolution and human culture, and the significance of this contrast for today and tomorrow.

If we compare them, we see some differences and some similarities:

Evolution works on a time scale of generations, through reproduction, while culture operates at a time scale of minutes, days, and years.

Evolution's impacts are felt first by individuals, and then on populations, while cultural mutations are created by individuals, but then almost immediately broadcast across large populations, where they are experienced by and exert their influence on individuals and groups.

The mechanism of evolution is genes, while the mechanism of culture is ideas. But both genes and ideas impact on individuals first and then on populations second. In fact both are only meaningful when they do scale up from the individual to the population. A genetic mutation that dies out in an individual has no meaning to evolution, while an idea that dies out in one individual has no meaning to culture.

While natural evolution still depends on genetic mutation/adaptation across generations, the cycle of cultural evolution has been compressed. Whereas it once occurred on a scale of centuries (during Medieval times, many people were born, lived their entire lives, and died within a few miles of their homes) it then shortened to decades (once the printing press was invented, things began to speed up), and now because of the Internet, mobile phones, and TV, culture seems to advance minute by minute, and as a result we now have acute problems related to our short attention span and the trivialization of … everything.

There is one aspect, however, in which the action of genes and evolution is identical with the action of ideas and populations. This is the in the subject area we will call 'survival strategies.' It is the strategy of the gene to reproduce itself abundantly as part of the larger strategy of evolution to encourage rampant experimentation. These twin strategies, abundance and rampant experimentation, working at different scales, are the driving forces of evolution itself, and thus of adaptive change.

Similarly, it is the strategy of culture to broadcast ideas abundantly, from which experiments and attitudes emerge, and to evolve according only to which ideas take hold.

The reason that this is worth discussing at all, and why it is relevant to space commerce, is two-fold.

First, the strategy of abundant (or excessive) consumption is how nature conducts the process of natural evolution; one tree makes and broadcasts millions of seeds; one ant lays millions of eggs. Currently human life on Earth is also largely geared toward abundance of consumption: one middle or upper class family consuming Earth's resources disproportionately.

But this trend is coming to a staggering end as we reach and then pass 7 billion humans, most of whom aspire to the middle class lifestyle. There simply isn't enough Earth to go around, enough for everyone to have a life of material abundance such as the wealthy or even middle class now experience.

In fact, if everyone on Earth today were to have the approximate lifestyle of American middle class, it has been suggested that we would require the natural resources of three or four Earths. But we have only a single one.

Therefore, we know that the strategy of abundance as evidenced by evolution is not a workable survival strategy for 7 billion people living on Earth. Instead, will the force of culture enable us to learn fast enough to avoid an environmental apocalypse of our making? So this is what we mean by 'the race:' human survival and well being seems to be a race between evolution's innate preference for abundance and a learned, cultural adoption of widespread self-restraint.

Second, the space enthusiast notes that the solar system has many additional resources; we have 'merely' to gain access to them. Again, it is through the force of culture that we may do so, culture in the form of space travel and large scale space commerce. By sheer necessity, then, are confronted with this intriguing dichotomy in the coming decades, and these are our strategic options:

1. We will learn to consume differently and consequently to live differently.

2. Or we will import resources from off-Earth to augment what is available here. This is the space enthusiast's dream.

3. Or we will export people to off-Earth. This option has some appealing aspects if we are talking about enthusiastic migration, a human diaspora across the solar system. But there is also a very dark side reminiscent of the history's worst human rights abuses; this issue must be thought through with great care.

4. Or, as is more likely, we will apply some combination of these three.

Space commerce, if it happens at any significant scale whatsoever, will play a role in all these scenarios.

Consequently, we see that 'culture,' as manifested in space technology and space commerce, will have an accelerating impact on the process of evolution, because space exploration, habitation, and commerce are essentially cultural phenomena that will also, secondarily (in our classically short-term view) have fundamental consequences for human evolution itself.

For the physiological reasons noted above (and additional reasons also nicely explored by Strongin and Reese in *Living in Space*, and by Strongin and Hilton in this volume, and as Frank White also points out in *Living in Space*), human inhabitants in space and on other worlds may rapidly evolve into new species due the sever environmental pressures in which they will reside.

It was not our purpose in this book to make a major theme out of this concept of evolution vs. culture, but we do think it is worth mentioning. And while we cannot know much for certain, it does make for fascinating conjecture.

WHAT'S NEEDED

A review of key points from throughout the preceding chapters brings forth these pivotal ideas about what's needed for the robust commercial space industries to become established.

RELIABLE, INEXPENSIVE HEAVY LIFT LAUNCH

The fundamental factor that will enable space commerce is clearly reliable, low-cost launch services. Entrepreneurs are appropriately targeting their new systems to reduce costs by a factor of between 10 or 100 below current costs, and if they succeed the impact will be immediate and enormous.

A NEW NASA ROLE

As we mentioned above and as many authors in this volume noted as well, it is essential that NASA adopts the role of enthusiastic supporter of the private sector entrepreneurs and corporations, both in the US, in other nations as well, and in multi-nation consortia. We have seen that NASA has many of the necessary legal and organizational mechanisms at its disposal, such as Space Act Agreements, to play this role, and play it well.

It is an oft-repeated management cliché that there comes a time when one must lead, follow, or get out of the way. NASA has been the leader for a long time, but now it's time for others to share the leadership role. This won't necessarily be easy to accept, but it is necessary for the private sector to have NASA's support to realize potentials that NASA itself can never achieve, and in fact that NASA, as a government agency, should not pursue.

Without doubt, NASA's accumulated expertise is of the utmost value. But that extraordinary capability must be brought to bear in a different way with respect to the commercial space sector, through many novel organizational forms including public-private partnerships and other joint operating models.

GLOBAL PARTICIPATION

The $44B of annual space expenditure by the world's governments, if invested in a cohesive and strategic manner, is just possibly enough to catalyze the emergence of a vast wave of economic growth and development that would benefit all peoples of all nations. No one country, even America, should see itself as the first among equals. The development of space is a global issue of importance to all humans, and a global consortium must guide it.

LEGAL, MANAGERIAL AND ORGANIZATIONAL INNOVATION

The successful development of space will depend as much on how well the process is organized, as it will on the technological solutions to a bottomless list of technical challenges. In fact, it's likely that the technical solutions will emerge most readily in an environment where the organizations are fluid and flexible, and where sound innovation methods are widely applied. Consequently, it is quite realistic to note that a whole range of legal, managerial, and organizational innovations will be required for the space sector to achieve its potential.

HONEST BROKERS

The notion of an honest broker has come up repeatedly in recent years in discussions about the complex issues, questions, and choices surrounding space development. Choices will have to be made, difficult choices on which a lot is at stake for companies (and the people who compose them) and for governments (and their citizens). To date, most voices in the space industry have spoken from a particular vantage point, as advocates of specific objectives and ideas.

Because of the extraordinary degree of technical sophistication involved, in combination with the exceptional levels of business risk and human danger, it will be necessary for organizations to emerge that can play the role of trusted, honest broker.

These organizations will help decision makers to understand and assess risks, to evaluate technological options, to monitor the performance of organizations, and to help improve the efficacy of the entire space endeavor.

THE EMERGING ATWG VIEWPOINT

In the words of our ATWG colleagues Charlie Smith and George Robinson, *"A robust commercial space sector has the potential to generate new technologies, products, markets, and human well being in this decade and beyond."* It is to this prospect, and to the commitment of the development of space for peaceful purposes to the benefit of all humans, that the ATWG is dedicated.

If the decade from 2010 to 2020 is to be the transition period, and if the years following 2020 do indeed see the rapid spread of space commerce (and its attendant space habitats) throughout the Solar System, then what sort of off-world civilization might we see by 2100? We could speculate, of course, but in truth it is clear that our efforts would be no better than science fiction.

It is characteristic of humanity that we can readily see a step, or perhaps two steps from where we presently are, but beyond that we can only speculate. We must therefore consider each step carefully, and advance according to principles in which we feel confident.

The development of space commerce is just such a process. We cannot see precisely what it will become, but we are convinced that it will happen, and indeed we have found in the chapters of this book that it is happening already. So as we pursue its development, we must remember and apply the important guiding principles of business, and equally important the guiding principles of human values.

In space we may find solutions to some of the great problems confronting our civilization. We may learn to tap the energy resources of the sun to ease need to extract and burn still more fossil fuels from the depths of the Earth. We may find new science and new technologies to help us live better, and care better for one another and for our home planet. We may create alternative habitats in which some of us may over time evolve into new species with quite different relationships to gravity, oxygen, and transportation than do our Earth-bound ancestors.

A thriving space commerce and all of the attendant factors which enable it to come into being will make it possible for these things to happen. It is for these reasons, and for the sheer challenge and adventure, that we go to space. In this endeavor, profit and altruism are not opposite poles, estranged from one another, but rather they offer the potential to unite in the development space by and for the benefit of entrepreneurs, investors, explorers, citizens, and humans, and for Earth. This is the profound promise of space commerce.

•••

LANGDON MORRIS

Langdon Morris is a partner of InnovationLabs (www.innovationlabs.com), one of the world's leading innovation consultancies. He is recognized globally as a leader in the field of innovation, and his recent clients include organizations such as NASA, GE, Gemalto, Total Oil, the Federal Reserve Bank of the US, Johnson & Johnson, Tata Group, France Telecom, Stanford University, Cap Gemini, Wipro, L'Oréal, Accor Hotels, and many others.

He is a member of the leadership team of ATWG, and also Senior Practice Scholar of the Ackoff Center at the University of Pennsylvania where he is researching complex social and business systems. He is a Senior Fellow of the Economic Opportunities Program of the Aspen Institute, a member of the Editorial Committee of the International Journal of Innovation Science, and a member of the Scientific Committee of Business Digest, Paris.

He has taught MBA courses in strategy at the Ecole Nationale des Ponts et Chaussées in Paris and Universidad de Belgrano in Buenos Aires.

He is the author or co-author of numerous white papers and four highly acclaimed business books, with editions in Japanese, Chinese, Korean, and French. He was a contributor to and co-editor of the previous books in this series, *Beyond Earth: The Future of Humans in Space* and *Living in Space*. He is highly sought after as a speaker and workshop leader, and participates frequently at conferences and workshops worldwide.

KENNETH J. COX, PH.D.

Dr. Kenneth J. Cox earned his bachelor's degree in 1953 and his master's degree in 1956 in electrical engineering from the University of Texas/Austin, and his PhD at Rice University in 1966.

In 1963 he joined NASA to develop the flight control system for the Little Joe II Booster Vehicle. Later, Dr. Cox became the Technical Manager for the Apollo Digital Control Systems, which included the Lunar Module, the Command Module and the Command/Service Module, the first spacecraft to fly with a digital flight control system.

Ken is coeditor of this volume, and coauthor of Chapter 1 and Chapter 16, *A Space Commercialization Model: Ocean Ports and Intermodal Transportation*. He has been the leader of ATWG since it was established in 1990.

INDEX

O

P

R

S

SPACE
COMMERCE

THE INSIDE STORY BY THE PEOPLE WHO ARE MAKING IT HAPPEN

AN AEROSPACE TECHNOLOGY WORKING GROUP BOOK

IN PARTNERSHIP WITH

THE INTERNATIONAL SPACE UNIVERSITY

AND

THE INTERNATIONAL INSTITUTE OF SPACE COMMERCE